CONTENTS

Introduction   1

**PSYCHOANALYSIS AS A PRODUCT OF HYSTERIA:
THE DISCOURSE OF THE MASTER**   5

1.   *Freud's encounter with hysteria: desire*   7
        Bread-and butter job versus research
        Displacement and desire
        Historical note

2.   *From trauma to fantasy: the Real as impossible*   21
        The divided subject and the
        Unconscious structured as a language
        The Real as traumatic
        The father as prehistoric Other

3.   *The theory of repression: the Imaginary as defence*   33
        Manifest content: repression and
        resistance
        Latent content: The Woman

4.   *Dora: the lack in the Symbolic*   55
        Freud and knowledge
        The lack in the Symbolic

5.   *Psychoanalysis as a consequence of hysteria: the
     discourse of the master*   67

THE POST-FREUDIANS AND THE DISCOURSE OF THE UNIVERSITY   75

6.   *The great confusion*   77
         In search of hysteria
         Questioning the questioners
         Hysteria within the sexual relationship

7.   *Lacan and the discourse of the hysteric*   95
         The theory of the four discourses
         The Hysteric between master and analyst
         The discourse of the university

THE FORGOTTEN FREUD: THE SHIFT TOWARDS THE DISCOURSE OF THE UNIVERSITY   121

8.   *Freud's second theory of hysteria*   123
         Re-evaluation of the first theory: the hydraulic model
         Hinge between the first and second theories:
         Erinnern, Wiederholen und Durcharbeiten
         The second theory: jouissance

9.   *Consequences of Freud's second theory: primary phenomena*   149
         From repression to primary repression
         From fantasy to fundamental fantasy
         From Oedipal father to primal father

10.   *The rock of castration*   205
         The black continent
         Oedipus revisited
         Moses and the reintroduction of the father
         The rock in the black continent

Conclusion: from Freud's hysteric to Lacan's The Woman   241

Notes   249
Bibliography   271
Index   281

DOES THE WOMAN EXIST?

FROM FREUD'S HYSTERIC
TO LACAN'S FEMININE

LIBRARY

·1246 ?`` `4 EXT. 3301

` or

UNI`
C

PAUL VERHAEGHE

translated by Marc du Ry

REBUS PRESS

Originally published in Dutch as
Tussen Hysterie en Vrouw
by Acco Leuven/Amersfort 1987
2nd Edition © 1996 Acco (Academische Coöperatief c.v.),
Tienestraat 134-136, 3000 Leuven (Belgium)

English translation copyright © 1997 Marc du Ry

Rebus Press LImited,
76 Haverstock Hill,
London NW3 2BE

ISBN 1 900877 05 8

INTRODUCTION

"The discourse of the hysterical subject taught him (Freud) this other thing, which really comes down to this: that the signifier exists. In gathering up the effect of this signifier in the discourse of the hysterical subject, he succeeded in giving it that necessary quarter turn which changed it into analytic discourse".

(Jacques Lacan, XX, 41).

One hundred years ago, Freud began a dialogue with hysterical patients. What was initially meant as a bread-and-butter job, a step away from the beloved laboratory and so a step away from the possibility of discovery, became a theory that would turn knowledge about man on its head - and therewith all knowledge as such. The effect of this, which Freud considered the third narcissistic blow to mankind, is far from fully known.

One effect would seem to be the disappearance of hysteria, a disappearance coinciding with the worldwide acceptance of psychoanalysis. Conversion symptoms have become rarer and rarer, the great hysterical attack 'à la Salpêtrière' is today a curiosity to be nurtured. According to several historians, this disappearance is the result of the prophylactic influence of psychoanalysis. The worldwide dissemination of the insights produced by its theory has changed society to such an extent that hysteria has become superfluous and thus obsolete.

But, even a minimum acquaintance with Lacan's theory of the four discourses is sufficient to give the lie to this naive optimism as it shows the ubiquity of hysteria as an invariable structure. It seems that we are dealing with two different interpretations of history.

Our interpretation is based on a Lacanian reading of Freud's work: as a result of this the latter acquires a certain historical dimension. Lacan's theory is that the history of psychoanalysis can only be deciphered insofar as it is itself inscribed in the history of the Unconscious. There is quite some distance between a study aspiring to survey the history of the Unconscious from a cumulative point of view, and one that considers history and the Unconscious as two sides of the same coin.

The conclusion of our study can be expressed in one argument: the theory developed by Freud over four decades follows the same twists and turns as a single treatment of a hysterical patient. The time scale, the historical dimension of a treatment, is the same as the one governing the development of Freud's theory.

This historical scope can be described in terms of a certain relationship between three different registers. Hysteria and psychoanalysis both start from a discrepancy between the Real and the Symbolic, a mismatch which calls upon the Imaginary for help. The effect of all this is that the Real disappears under the Imaginary stronghold of the neurosis, while the Symbolic lags behind in two crucial respects: the function of the father and the problem of becoming a woman.

Freud encountered the greatest difficulties in his conceptualisation precisely on those two points; the points where hysteria falters. The whole of his work can be viewed as a repeated attempt to formulate an answer to the riddle of how a woman becomes a woman, and the role of the father in this process. Each time he thought he had found an answer, the hysterical patient rose up to demonstrate its insufficiency. His various solutions were always typifications of a specific social bond and can hence be perfectly well understood in terms of the four discourses. In addition, one can verify that a coherent and closed conceptual framework is completely inadequate for clinical practice. Freud opted for clinical practice with the result that his final theory escapes the fallacy of a coherent and paranoid mousetrap system.

The road he followed throughout this time inevitably brought him back to his starting point: the traumatic Real as the basis for hysteria. Nevertheless, the journey raised his vision to a completely new level. Freud followed the hysteric's imaginarisations (imaginary elaborations) to their ultimate consequences in his theory - one of them is the idea of penis envy - because this was the only way of going beyond the impasse of hysteria. The fact that this going beyond was not heard, except by Lacan, is just another illustration of the historical dimension of the Unconscious: it never stops disappearing.

We conclude with this going beyond. Beyond the hysterical impasse Freud shows the way to another conceptualisation. The feared or challenged castration of the Imaginary changes into the constitutive division of the Subject, in and through the Symbolic, thereby founding the lack which opens up the opportunities for creation. And therein lies the difference between the hysterical perpetuum mobile and The Woman, between analysis as an Exhaustive Theory and analysis as a discourse, an analytic discourse.

Since Socrates, we have known that truth is found in dialogue, and only in dialogue. Since Freud, we have had a special form of dialogue through which the truth of the subject can be revealed. Lacan demonstrated that this subject and his truth occupy a constitutive position in every science, so that every science has to find its starting point there if it wants to yield something of the truth.

This implies that science, too, has to find its origin in dialogue, something which can never be expressed with the kind of monologue a bibliography constitutes.

This book is the result of a dialogue that we have conducted over several years with Julien Quackelbeen. For this, any word of thanks is insufficient. To the extent that our work is on a level with those dialogues, it will be the best expression of my gratitude.

This English translation would not have been possible without the efforts of Marc du Ry, Kirsty Hall and Oliver Rathbone, who have become friends in the process. Last but not least, my gratitutde goes to Rik Loose, one of those few friends for life, who introduced me "accidentally" into the English-speaking psychoanalytic world.

Paul Verhaeghe
E-Mail: Paul.Verhaeghe@rug.ac.be

PSYCHOANALYSIS AS A PRODUCT OF HYSTERIA: THE DISCOURSE OF THE MASTER

"The discourse of the hysterical subject taught him [Freud] this other thing, which really comes down to this: that the signifier exists (...)".

CHAPTER 1.

FREUD'S ENCOUNTER WITH HYSTERIA: DESIRE

Bread-and-butter job versus research

Neurologist without a job

A neurologist certainly: between 1877 and 1893 Freud published no less than twenty-seven papers on neurology, providing each one with an exceptionally exhaustive bibliography.[1] Certain small discoveries - starting with a new staining method for neuronal cells in order to make them visible and ending with research into the mysterious genital organ of the eel - bear witness to his interests (making visible the great riddle of sexuality), but were not sufficient to give a Jew in a Viennese University laboratory the job security he needed. Having missed the boat in the cocaine business, the only thing left from which he could make a living was the setting up of a medical practice. Benevolent elder colleagues referred patients to him - for them it was a unique chance to rid themselves of hysterical, meaning bothersome, clients.

Freud worked with the same thoroughness in his new occupation. He read everything that he could lay his hands on. He tried every new method. Yet he just didn't understand a single thing. His painstakingly gathered and repeatedly tested neurological and anatomical knowledge was being undermined by those who were supposed to give him confirmation of it: the patients. They are simulating, his wiser and older colleagues suggested. They are suggestible. Or degenerates, tainted hereditarily. Perhaps they have a dynamic lesion, that is, a lesion which has to be there but which we just cannot find. Freud was reminded of the joke about the cauldron and concluded that, when logic does not succeed, one has to start anew. He began to write down his observations, and by 1898, he had collected over two hundred case studies. The neurologist had entered new territory.

At first there were some isolated discoveries, mostly negative. He came to the sobering conclusion for example - against the ideas of Charcot - that the word hysteria denotes in the main a compilation of negative characteristics as well as prejudices.[2] Its chief use lies in its differential diagnosis from *real* neurological diseases, a direction which would be developed subsequently by Babinski. At best, it is a *nosography*, a mere summary of symptoms.[3]

Besides these negative discoveries, he also stumbled upon some loose ends. One example was the 'preference' for symptoms in the realm of feeling: to feel nothing, anaesthesia, or to feel too much, hyperaesthesia, both accompanied by the bewildering observation that the laws of neurology did not apply to them. Another example was the existence of a latency period between the motive and the outbreak of a symptom,[4] and another that suggestion as a method beyond criticism brought another element with it: the patient's auto-suggestion, to which the therapists' suggestion had to be attuned if it was to be effective.[5] Moreover, hysteria may well be the result of a pathogenic idea, but getting rid of this idea did not suffice as a therapy since it did not cure hysteria itself.[6] And, with respect to the treatment, different as all the methods undoubtedly were, time and again Freud discovered one central factor to be decisive: the 'person' of the therapist himself, together with the patient's belief in him.[7]

Behind these wide-ranging remarks one can already see the outline of Freud's major innovation, major because it will result in the birth of psychoanalysis: he abandoned the visual field and began to listen.

This innovation, which was going to have such a pervasive influence on our century, is remarkable for at least two reasons. First of all, Freud could not have learned it from his teachers, because they either limited their work to anatomic pathology or considered hysterics as mere degenerate imposters. Furthermore - and this is the second reason for wonder - hysteria made its appearance above all in the visual field, something Freud would note several times in his *Studies on Hysteria*. Charcot considered himself to be 'un visuel', and that is precisely why he was such a privileged partner for the hysteric. His main hobbies were drawing and painting, and the development of photography was immediately put into effect in his clinic: no less than four editions of the *Iconographies de la Salpêtrière* were edited between 1876 and 1888.[8]

Leaving the medical clinic with its accent on visual observation was not without consequences, of which the most important, in this respect, was the fact that the hysteric lost visual control of the other. The gaze of the observer, which traditionally incarnated her desire, was refused to her. Freud obliged her to speak, thus bringing out *her* desire and *her* division.

First results of the listening process

Others had already observed that there was a traumatic aetiology to hysteria. Nevertheless, Freud would be the first to listen to this trauma and to interpret it as having an effect on the psyche and hence on the soma. That is why he borrowed concepts from contemporary psychology and philosophy, a psychophysics which considered psychological functioning as a mechanical-energetic flow of representations (ideas).

His paper entitled *A Case of Successful Treatment by Hypnotism* (1892-93) was the first attempt at a dynamic explanation. The course of the illness was understood as follows: there is an 'antithetical' idea which the patient wants to remove from her consciousness, that is, separate from her normal associations. Once this idea becomes unconscious it produces an innervation effect on the body. Freud adds that it is very likely that those two steps are in reality only one.[9] The question of the pathogenic idea's origin was addressed in his footnotes to his translation of Charcot, footnotes the French master was not very pleased with. The pathogenic idea is a *memory*, going back either to one trauma or to a cumulative series of little traumas, or even to memories that have subsequently received the status of trauma. In view of these different possibilities, the very idea of trauma had to be reconsidered. It concerns an '*Erregungszuwachs*', Freud said, an increase in tension that cannot be adequately abreacted by the neuronal system.[10]

Nevertheless, the mechanism of symptom formation remained mysterious, especially in the light of neurological knowledge. In 1893, Freud wanted to dot the 'i's' and cross the 't's' in the paper with which he bade goodbye to the medical approach to the neuroses: *Quelques considérations pour une étude comparative des paralysies motrices, organiques et hystériques* (Some considerations for a comparative study of motor, organic and hysterical paralyses). Written as a result of prompting by Charcot and originally published in French, it was at the same time Freud's farewell to the Charcotean approach. In this paper, one finds a comparison between hysterical and organic paralyses, proving that a hysterical paralysis does not comply with established neurological laws.

Based on this comparison, Freud formulated a decisive conclusion - one that would have sounded presumptuous if it had been uttered by a psychologist, but which was all the more convincing in coming from an experienced neurologist - in matters of hysterical paralysis, neurology and anatomy do not explain anything at all. The so-called explanation of the 'dynamic' or 'functional' lesion is only a deus-ex-machina, and Freud brushed it aside with some keen arguments. He returned to his observations in order to discover the nature of the determining idea in hysterical paralysis. Following Janet, he discov-

ered and confirmed that it is the popular representation[11] of the body
and its parts that is central in hysteria, especially a visual representation. He left Janet and his observational conclusions behind when he
attempted his first dynamic explanation, which was, itself, actually a
continuation of his previous attempt in his paper on *A Case of Successful
Treatment by Hypnotism*. In that paper, he had already put forward the
idea that the disappearance of the antithetical representation from conscious associations on the one hand, and the somatic process of innervation of the same representation on the other hand, could very well be
two sides of the same coin. His new explanation ran as follows: the ego
consists of an associative chain in which the body has a central position. These representations are associatively linked and each representation contains an 'Affektbetrag', a quantum of affect. For the sake of
psychic health, it is necessary that this energetic investment is abreacted, either by way of motor actions, and/or by psychic associative
activity. In the case of hysteria, he came to the conclusion that the pathogenic representation can no longer enter into the conscious associative activity of the conscious Ego, and *that the paralysis is caused precisely
by this associative exclusion.* Why is this so? Because this exclusion
entails the impossibility of abreacting the quantum of affect linked to
that particular representation - of the arm, for example.

This was Freud's first explanation of a hysterical conversion symptom. It makes clear what his next points of interest were going to be:
why is the pathogenic representation not available for conscious associative activity in the Ego, and what is the operative link between this
associative exclusion and the conversion symptom? The first point
would find an explanation. The second one - how does conversion
come about - would remain a mystery for Freud.

'Abwehr' theory and the Q-hypothesis
In 1893 Freud urged Breuer to publish their *Preliminary
Communication*, the paper that is widely recognized as the birth of the
trauma theory. According to Freud and Breuer, a hysteric was someone
who had been the victim of one or even several traumas, the repressed
representations of which remain pathogenically active due to the fact
that they have not been abreacted. Our focus is on the hows and whys
of this absence. Freud first repeated the thesis of his previous paper
concerning the necessity of abreaction and then questioned once again
why this abreaction seemed impossible in hysteria.[12] The paradoxical
conclusion was that these representations are alive and kicking on the

one hand, and on the other hand that the patient does not have any conscious access to them! Several explanations are possible (the nature of the trauma, the psychological condition of the patient at the very moment of the trauma), but they all boil down to one central hypothesis: the existence of a *splitting* in psychic functioning, a dissociation between two states, in which one group of ideas is unavailable to the other. In addition, one group exerts a defensive pressure against the other. Therapy of hysteria would therefore consist of recombining these two groups associatively, thus enabling the possibility of abreaction. Freud added that this theory only explained the mechanism of symptom formation while remaining silent about the inner causes or aetiology of hysteria itself. Hysteria kept slipping out of reach.

He repeated the same findings in his next two papers, together with his pessimism concerning aetiology. In 1894, the emphasis shifted from 'Abreaktion', abreaction, to 'Abwehr', defence, particularly in his paper on *The Neuro-Psychoses of Defence*. Freud was convinced he had found the solution; he was so enthusiastic about it that he generalised his hypothesis to include almost the whole field of psychopathology. Hence the subtitle of the paper: *An attempt at a psychological theory of acquired hysteria, of many phobias and obsessions and of certain hallucinatory psychoses.* The cause of the 'Spaltung', splitting, is a conflict between the Ego and an incompatible group of representations referring to sexuality. The Ego's solution is to weaken this group by taking away its quantum of affect, with the result that the group disappears from conscious associative activity. Owing to this process, a free-floating amount of energy, an *Erregungssumme*, becomes available and has to be invested elsewhere. This investment can be very different, depending upon the kind of 'neuropsychosis of defence'. In the case of hysteria, this investment results in conversion: the amount of energy is used in a symptom written on the body, thus becoming a mnemic symbol of the repressed representation. In the mean time, this symptom becomes the centre of the second psychic group.

This part of early Freudian theory was very important because it made explicit a formulation that had already been applied implicitly, and it also particularised this assumption in relation to hysteria. We will start with the relationship of this formulation to hysteria. The general extension of the idea of defence to the whole of psychopathology implied that this mechanism could no longer be used as a tell-tale sign of hysteria. Thus, the particularity of hysteria no longer lay in defence but had to be found in conversion: hysteria equalled conversion. From this point on, up to the discovery of anxiety hysteria or phobia, this was going to be the typical characterisation of hysteria. And what is this conversion? It is an investment of energy, i.e. a process that invests the quantum of affect belonging to the group of ego-incompatible representations, either in the sensory or in the motor sphere. In a natural situation, instead of being invested, it would have been abreacted, either through associative or through motor activity.

This part of the theory presupposed an assumption that had already been applied, but which became explicit here as the Q-hypothesis: "I refer to the concept that in mental functions something is to be distinguished - a quota of affect or sum of excitation - which possesses all the characteristics of a quantity (though we have no means of measuring it), which is capable of increase, diminution, displacement and abreaction, and which is spread over the memory-traces of ideas somewhat as an electric charge is spread over the surface of a body."[13]

This hypothesis formed the basis of the abreaction theory, commonly known as the cathartic theory. Again it presupposed another basic assumption concerning the pleasure principle and the principle of constancy. Freud had mentioned it twice, but the proper elaboration would only take place in 1920 in *Beyond the Pleasure Principle*. Elaboration, we might add, which would profoundly alter it.

This Q-hypothesis would remain a part of Freudian theory in a way which insisted upon being enigmatic. It was essential with respect to conceptual coherence, it was operational in clinical practice, but nevertheless, it remained enigmatic. This Q showed itself to be harmful if it was fixed or coagulated, and had no possibility of being abreacted and thus reduced. The possibilities of abreaction cover two areas, the combination of which looks rather strange: the locomotor and the associative.

In his subsequent paper on anxiety neurosis, we find it applied to conversion. His starting point concerns the question about the relationship between the psychological and the somatic in matters of sexuality. The normal process is described as follows: above a certain threshold a somatic sexual impulse produces a stimulus in the psyche which has to be abreacted. Freud distinguished three possible pathological outcomes. 1) 'Inadequate abreaction', mostly masturbation, resulting in neurasthenia. Here the relation between the somatic-sexual aspect and the psychosexual desire (libido) is normal, but the abreaction is wrong. 2) 'Psychical insufficiency' which results in the somatic impulses, however strong, failing to result in their psychical working-over.

Compelled to stay within the somatic they become the cause of anxiety neurosis. 3) 'Defence with substitution'. Hysteria belongs to this category. Here too, we find a summation of somatic tension, together with a psychical failure to process this tension. The result is that the energy is sent back to the somatic region where it provokes conversion as a substitute. Nevertheless, there is an important difference from the second form mentioned above; in this case the somatic impulse has been psychically processed, but because of a psychical conflict the impulse is sent back to its point of origin, the body.[14]

Hence, we can deduce that the mysterious Q can appear in at least two forms: a purely somatic one, and - through its processing - a psychical variant: the libido. The Real of the body is processed and elaborated through the Imaginary and the Symbolic. Hysterical conversion is the result of a defence/repression through which the psychically processed quantum returns to, and inscribes itself on, the body.

Freud's next step was the discovery that the original defence also explains the patient's resistance when asked to remember the repressed representation: "One gets the impression of a struggling demon, afraid of the daylight because he knows that that would be the end of him".[15]

The discoveries from this period no longer seemed so heterogeneous. The pieces of the puzzle had begun to fall into place and form a picture.

1. Psychopathology - hysteria included - is caused by an excessive defence (excessive, that is, compared to the normal form of defence) against psychosexual representations, each one provided with a quantum of affect.

2. With hysteria, this initially somatic quantum of affect is psychically worked into a psychosexual group of representations; this group will be warded off by the Ego and sent back to the somatic region, resulting in conversion. This conversion functions as a mnemic symbol, thereby setting hysteria apart from all other neuroses. The possible displacement of Q is true for all neuropsychoses of defence.

3. In this way two different groups of representations come into being: one that is repressed, and one that represses. Moreover, resistance functions as a border between the two.

Freud's explanation contains one recurring element that demands further explanation: the quantum of affect. The examination of this factor will lead us to the conclusion that it is linked to Freud's method of listening and is therefore part and parcel of a theory of language.

Displacement and desire

Affect, energy, investment, cathexis, summation of impulses?

The fact that the Q-hypothesis appeared with so many labels was a sign that there was already some difficulty inherent in it. In the history of its usage, by Freud and others after him, we can distinguish three different meanings.

The first use brings us the idea of a quantity of somatic, *material* energy, based on the pseudo-neurology of the *Project* and the contemporary discovery of neuronal chains.[16] Alongside Freud's use, the term was part of the discourse on energy between 1850-90, rightly described by Jacques Claes as omnipresent and jubilant. Freud had only to pluck the term from this discourse.[17]

Nevertheless, right from the start we find Freud using it in a different way. From its somatic origin, energy becomes elaborated into psychical tension, linked to psychosexual representations. This is the nucleus of the idea of libido, a mysterious, *immaterial* quantity of energy. Considered from this point of view, Freud would be in line with the likes of Robinet (the active principle), Herder (the organic powers), Lamarck (the power of life), Stahl (vitalism), even Schopenhauer (blind striving will). The only difference lies in the fact that Freud explicitly links this mysterious source of power with psychosexuality. When all is said and done, this use remains more mysterious than useful. At least, that is the conclusion of Russelman, who made a thorough study of Freud's use of the idea, (commonly known as the 'dynamic model'), as well as its application both before and after him. His study also shows that it is still used to this day, an example being the idea that modern homo faber has a need for giving vent to his emotions, letting off steam, etc.[18]

This contemporary conception brings us to a third usage, in which the emphasis has shifted from 'quota of affect' to 'affect', from which it is only a small step to speak of 'emotions'. Doubtless one could find in Freud some indications pointing in this direction. He wrote in the *Studies*, for instance, about freeing the 'hemmed-in affect', which is an idea that is even used today as a justification for so-called scream-therapies. Nevertheless, if one wants to hold on to this rather restricted point of view, one will neglect several other passages in Freud in which he makes a differentiation between emotions and underlying energy processes. The clearest formulation can be found in *The Unconscious* where he notes that "affects and emotions correspond to processes of abreaction, the final manifestations of which are perceived as feelings".[19] As an answer to that, one could venture the opinion that there is a difference between unconscious affects and conscious emotions, and that the aim of therapy is to abreact these unconscious, possibly dammed-up, affects into conscious emotions. But even this is refuted by Freud: in the same passage, he adds that there are no unconscious affects in the sense of unconscious emotions.

So, every single one of these uses is impractical. They either level Freud's ideas uncritically with older ones, or they dilute it to affective-emotional twaddle. In either case, the most important aspect of Freud's discovery gets lost: that the quantum of energy can be *displaced*.

Displacement

What was the core of Freud's discoveries in this early period? That every neurotic symptom expresses something for which it is not the right, the normal form of expression. There is, he said, 'eine falsche Verknüpfung', a false connection, a neurotic knot.[20] tc "What was the core of Freud's discoveries in this early period? That every neurotic symptom expresses something for which it is not the right, the normal form of expression. There is, he said, 'eine falsche Verknüpfung', a false connection, a neurotic knot.[20]"

In other words: this 'something' is *displaced* into a form of expression which does not belong to it. With this point Freud had discovered the most important mechanism of the Unconscious and of the primary process: displacement. Most important because, according to Lacan, it is not only the basis, but also the necessary precondition for that other mechanism of the primary process, condensation.[21]

Something is displaced. Freud calls it 'energy', 'quota of affect', 'summation of stimuli'. Indeed, at that time, the metaphor of energy was ready to hand. But he elaborated it and made it specific. His clinical descriptions reveal time and again that this 'something' amounts to a *Wunsch*, to *desire*. Even more: it concerns a *psychosexual* desire about which the patients do not want to know anything at all and against which they erect a resistance.

As far as we are concerned, this discovery was the real starting-point of psychoanalysis. From that point on, hysteria was no longer determined by some mysterious trauma, but by an inarticulable desire that kept on being displaced. On 27 October 1897, Freud generalised this point and made it the most fundamental characteristic of hysteria: "Longing is the main character-trait of hysteria, just as a current anaesthesia (even though only potential) is its main symptom."[22] Desire and anaesthesia. Lacan was going to formulate it in his well known: "The desire of the hysterical subject is to have an unsatisfied desire".

A desire that cannot be articulated by the subject and keeps on being displaced. This was the basic idea behind three important Freudian studies: *The Interpretation of Dreams*, the dream as the fulfilment of a forbidden desire; *The Psychopathology of Everyday Life*: bungled actions as successful realisations of a repressed desire; *Jokes and their Relationship to the Unconscious*: jokes as a safety valve for the same forbidden desire.

Lacanian theory permits a further elaboration. Displacement is nothing but *metonymy*. What has to be displaced is *desire insofar as it is meaningful*. Neuroses keep on demonstrating that this process is full of tension, hence Freud's use of the energy metaphor. There is of course no shortage of emotions in this process, but this is no excuse for reducing psychotherapy to an emotional circus. In his *L'envers de la psychanalyse* Lacan reduced the relation between emotion and desire to its right proportions. There is only one affect for the human being, namely the effect of division in and through language.[23] Desire actually finds its origin in and through this division, precisely because this division results in the irrevocable loss that he called object *a*; thus, the relationship between affect, language and desire is given from the very start.

According to Lacan, each speaking being - 'le parlêtre' - is by definition divided and therefore hysterical with it. This gives us the problem of a conceptual differentiation between normal and pathological hysteria.[24] Leaving this aside, we can conclude that the relationship between language and hysteria is present in Freud's theory from the very beginning. The linguistic structure is obvious with hysteria: a signification refused by the Ego is displaced through several signifiers, becomes fixated, and inscribed on the body. In one way or another, a cure will have to work with words, and Freud, already in 1890, reflected on their magical power "as an essential instrument in psychical treatment".[25]

Historical remark

It is not our aim to study hysteria throughout its age-old history. Others have already done so, most recently Libbrecht for hysterical psychosis and Micale for male hysteria.[26] We only want to put a single point forward for discussion because it is a point of controversy.

This point concerns the relationship between Freud's cultural background and the creation of psychoanalysis. There are several hypotheses about this relationship. Freud was a child of his time. Freud was the product of a broader development, as well as of romantic philosophy and academic psychology, each one trying in its own way to study the Unconscious. Freud discovered the laws of the Unconscious through his self-analysis.

We do not want to discuss the relative merits of each of these hypotheses. Without doubt, several aspects of Freud's scientific education can be uncovered in his psychoanalytic theory. At several points, the theory is a reflection of the spirit of the times, as well as of Freud's Jewish background. Nevertheless, there are other aspects that cannot be simply explained by reference to these factors, chief amongst which is the plain fact that, as well as being preoccupied with signifiers, he *listened* to his patients.

The fact remains that the majority of Freud's first patients were hysterical. In this respect, his scientific education would not have been very useful, to say the least. Our thesis is that Freud, in spite of his extensive formal education and in spite of his training with Charcot, went on to elaborate a theory of hysteria that went counter to all contemporary theories and methods. In order to explain our thesis, we will make a rough distinction between two periods in the history of hysteria, each one with a particular conception.

The first period, usually called pre-scientific, is one in which a mixture of religion, magic and science obstructed the progress of science itself. The second period is that of the Enlightenment in which the idea of 'real' science found its golden moment.

When applied to the study of hysteria, we find the rather amusing theories about the migration of the uterus. Already in 2000 B.C., this theory was written down in a papyrus named *Kahun* after the place where it was discovered. It describes the uterus as an independent living organism. If not sufficiently irrigated, it becomes lighter and can start wandering around through the body, resulting in hysteria. Besides a number of very pragmatic tricks to get the uterus back to its proper place, the priest-doctors recommended marriage as a guarantee for the necessary 'irrigation' that would keep the thing in its proper place.

With some modifications, this theory prevailed for several centuries in the work of Hippocrates, Galenus and Paracelsus. The most explicit expression is to be found in Plato: "The womb is an animal which longs to bring forth children. When it remains barren for too long after puberty, it is distressed and sorely disturbed, and straying about in the body and cutting off the passages of the breath, it impedes respiration and provokes in the sufferer the most acute anguish and all manner of diseases besides."[27]

The Enlightenment arrived with Charles Lepois (Carolus Piso) and Willis. In the seventeenth century, both of them situated the cause of hysteria in the brain. The next step was taken by Sydenham, who considered 'excessive emotions' as one of the causes of hysteria. This spelled the end for magical theories. The scientist-doctor became an objective observer whose piercing gaze became more and more accurate thanks to his continually improving range of instruments. Charcot proudly called himself 'un visuel'. Famous for his autopsies - looking *inside* the body - of all kinds of neurological diseases, he approached hysteria with the same gaze, thereby transforming this former object of opprobrium into one of serious science. The young Freud was full of admiration for his method and the resulting discoveries; he returned to Vienna a confirmed devotee of Charcot.

Oddly enough, in the year preceding his death, Charcot threw the whole of his medico-organic and hence objective theory overboard in an apparently casual fashion, preferring what he called 'the mental factor'.[28] Two of his followers divided his theory between them. Babinski, the private detective of neurology, developed a rigorous scheme of observation in order to expose the hysteric as an imposter, a fake patient without any real neurological disorder. Janet, on the other hand, developed the psychological aspect.[29]

And Freud? Freud was the one who listened. But, he not only listened, he also heard; he heard the metaphorical significance of what he came to call hysterical conversion symptoms. In his paper on hysterical paralysis, he noted that the cause did not reside in the body. The structure became ever clearer to him: something is displaced from 'downstairs' to 'upstairs'; and that something was not acceptable 'upstairs', which is why it was sent back 'downstairs'. This structure was recast in several different formulations. At this early stage it was understood in terms of an endogenous energy investing a group of psychosexual representations, which could either lead to a normal abreaction, or be sent back to the place of origin, the body.[30] Later on, this theory of 'sending back' evolved into a proper concept: instead of 'suppressing' (*unterdrucken*), it became 'repressing'. The theory of repression was born.

Something rises up, is refused access and gets itself inscribed, together with the refusal, elsewhere on the body; displacement and conversion, said Freud. The uterus is not irrigated, dries up and starts wandering around in the body, thereby causing hysterical symptoms, dixit Kahun.

Displacement, migration: with his early theory, Freud was closer to his predecessors four thousand years before than to his contemporaries. His predecessors had one big advantage: the uterus as independent organ is pre-eminently feminine. They had forged a signifier for The Woman, as an equivalent to the phallus, even if it remained within the register of the imaginary. It was precisely the lack of such a signifier that forced Freud to develop his theory over and over again.

CHAPTER 2.

FROM TRAUMA TO FANTASY:
THE REAL AS IMPOSSIBLE

The divided subject and the Unconscious structured as a language

Studies on Hysteria was the starting-point of psychotherapy in general and of psychoanalysis in particular. From that moment on, neurotic patients were listened to and the theory left the medical field.

It was a honeymoon period. Freud distinguished three forms of hysteria: hypnoid hysteria, retention hysteria and hysteria of defence.[1] In each of those three the same nucleus can be found: a particular psychical experience cannot be followed by an adequate abreaction.[2] With hypnoid hysteria, abreaction fails due to the particular condition - a hypnoid one - in which the experience took place. With retention hysteria, there are special external circumstances, mostly social ones, obliging the patient to renounce abreaction. Thirdly, with the hysteria of defence, the cause is to be found in an internal conflict; the ego represses certain painful contents, thereby making abreaction impossible.

Freud came to lay more and more emphasis on this third form to the point where the hysteria of defence became synonymous with hysteria as such. This might seem a small step, just a discussion about frequency of occurrence, but this was far from being the case. Rather, it is at this point that we have to place a major conceptual shift made by Freud, for it implies the idea of division, a *spaltung* of the psyche. This was going to be Lacan's first rediscovery: the divided subject, $, a concept with which psychoanalysis distances itself irrevocably from every form of psychology.[3]

It is in the hysteria of defence that the idea of 'incompatible' representations comes into its own. The ego considers a certain group of representations as being incompatible with itself and rejects them. The consequence of this conflict is that the affect belonging to this group can no longer be abreacted, resulting in the working-over of a second psychical group, the source of eventual pathology.

This second group contains representations that are 'bewusstsein-sunfähige', literally: incapable of becoming conscious. They form the core of the pathological complex and consequently the aim of the treatment. Freud considered them to be the pathological remnants of a psychical trauma which the subject preferred to forget and therefore repressed. Once excluded from the normal chains of associations, they exert a pathological influence, rather in the manner of '*Fremdkörper*', which are bacteria foreign to one's own body that cause infections the body needs to defend itself against.[4]

Two points in this description demand some clarification: 'exclusion' and 'foreign body'. Exclusion from the normal chains of associations - that is, repression - is caused by the incompatibility between that representation and the dominant group of representations in the Ego.[5] Nevertheless, they cannot be that 'foreign' since Freud was obliged to advance a more subtle distinction further on in his paper. Indeed, the repressed representations may have disappeared from ordinary conscious associations but they still have to have some link with the symptoms that they determine. Freud thought of two possible solutions.

His first answer concerned what he called '*falsche Verknüpfung*', false connection. The affect of an unconscious representation is falsely connected to a conscious representation.[6] What he would later call 'transference' was already included in this category.[7] The process is to be understood as a rationalisation: the patient does not know the relationship between the symptom and its unconscious determination and produces a plausible explanation. Freud gives the example of a patient who stuck both of his thumbs into his mouth following a post-hypnotic suggestion, and then excused himself by saying that he had injured his tongue. This is very clear in the case of hysteria: the division between conscious and unconscious representational complexes is not a rigid and clearcut one; rather there exists a *compulsion to associate* between the ideas of the conscious group on the one hand and the accompanying feelings of the unconscious group on the other.[8]

The second solution is much more important and appears in Freud's discussion of the three layers of psychical material in cases of hysteria.[9] These three layers are grouped around a pathogenic traumatic nucleus. The first layer contains a purely chronological ordering of the material, perfectly illustrated by Anna O. who could recall, under hypnosis, all of the events leading up to her symptom in their exact, but reversed, order. The second layer is a concentric stratification of the pathogenic material around the pathogenic nucleus, in which the degree of resistance increases in proportion to the proximity to the nucleus. The third layer is the most important one: "(...) an arrangement according to thought-content, the linkage made along logical lines which reach as far as the nucleus (...)".[10]

This last layer is a dynamic one, crossing through the other two and producing the logical connections; it is a complex system of connections with nodal points, in which the multiple determination of symptoms becomes apparent.

In other words, the Unconscious is *ordered* ; the representations are linked to each other in a precise manner. At this point, we can recognize a second major Lacanian rediscovery: *"L'inconscient est structuré comme un langage"*, the Unconscious is structured like a language. The first layer is the diachronic one; the second gives the synchrony of all signifiers; but the most difficult point in his theory is the third layer which is, for Freud, the signified: desire as refused by the patient.

As we have already said, these three layers surround a nucleus. Freud used different metaphors for this nucleus throughout his work: *Kern unseres Wesen*, core of our being, *Nabel*, navel, *Urzene*, primal scene, *Mycelium*. Its most essential characteristic is that there are no words for it, neither for Freud nor for his patients. In spite of Freud's urging, they were never able to verbalise it. It is obvious that this is the Lacanian Real, that register which cannot be put into words.

Employing the hypno-cathartic method, Freud assumed that once he had managed to call up the absent representational complex, thereby enabling its concomitant affect to be freed and abreacted, then these previously absent representations would enter into the chain of normal associations. Freud called this 'associational correction'.

A striking feature that keeps on returning in the individual case studies is the opposition between pathogenic representation on the one hand and the verbalisation of it on the other. The repressed elements often emerged in the form of images, even very lively *visual* images: "Many other hysterical patients have reported to us that they have memories of this kind in vivid visual pictures and that this applied especially to their pathogenic memories".[11] So frequently in fact, that Freud came to the conclusion that hysterical patients were visually very gifted: "hysterical patients, who are as a rule of a visual type..."[12] From this followed his therapeutic command: "Well, what have you seen or what has occurred to you?"[13] The goal of the treatment became the erasing of these images by putting them into words. In the case studies, expressions such as *absprechen, aussprechen*, to talk away, are quite frequent. This was the 'talking cure', applied to the hysterical patient who preferred to appeal to the desire of the Other in his gaze. The cure essentially consisted of the putting into words of these visual images. In the actual description of therapeutic effectiveness, this verbalisation was linked to the idea of releasing the 'strangulated affect'.

At this point theory and practice seemed complete. Each overdetermined symptom was the point of application through which the path to the pathogenic memories could be traced back. One could then abreact and the symptom would disappear.

One small problem remained, however: the hysteric kept on producing traumatic memories. Every time Freud had dug up two of them, four others would spring up... With Emmy von N, Freud noted that the symptoms had not yet completely disappeared because the catharsis had released only two major traumas. There were quite a few secondary ones left, and he got the impression that new ones were being produced as he went along. In his paper on the aetiology of hysteria he discussed two fictional examples of hysterical symptoms with a traumatic basis. He preferred the fictional ones because the discussion of a real clinical case would take too much space and time, precisely because of the very complicated network that lies between the symptoms and the traumatic basis. He compared the inter-relating chain of associations to a complex family tree in which some members even had the audacity to intermarry...[14]

Conclusion: the pathological strangulation of an affect was not so much liquidated by a therapeutic catharsis as endlessly *displaced*. The idea of catharsis or abreaction was not totally sound.

The Real as traumatic

From "abreagieren" to "agieren"

The subsequent history is so well known that we will restrict ourselves to rendering the outlines. Freud started with the assumption that hysteria has its origin in an infantile trauma. The gist of this trauma is a scene of sexual seduction which, at the time, the child could not have understood as being sexual. It was an idea Ferenczi worked on twenty years later. Freud spoke of a 'presexual sexual fright'.[15] The memory is retained without understanding and the traumatic effect makes its appearance only after the onset of puberty, triggered by a second incident which recalls the first one.[16] This is the hysterical 'proton pseudos ust', a 'false statement following on a false assumption'. The fact that the first scene has been forgotten hinders adequate abreaction, and this in turn results in a *nachträgliche*, a 'deferred' psychopathology.[17]

Real and not understood as sexual, those are the two main characteristics of this original scene. Freud had to modify both of them, thus abandoning the cathartic theory. In the famous letter 52 to Fliess, he had already formulated his discovery that a hysterical attack - which he had up till then conceived of as a form of pathological abreaction - was not so much an abreaction as an action, *agieren* instead of *abreagieren*. And, as an action, it shows the original characteristic of every action, that is: "a means of reproducing pleasure".

Insight into infantile sexuality was beginning to dawn. A necessary consequence of that insight was a revision of the trauma theory: the first trauma was not innocent after all, but it contained an element of pleasure for the victim. Ten years later, Abraham published a paper with the meaningful title, *The Experiencing of Sexual Traumas as a Form of Sexual Activity*. This paper's salient point is the fact that the original scene had already contained an element of conflict for the patient; hence Abraham's conclusion that the characteristic silence of the victims changed them into accomplices. It was precisely this characteristic that enabled him to make a differentiation between those children who were already hysterical and normal ones. His conclusion was that in hysteria representations are both incompatible and pleasurable right from the beginning.

The theory of abreaction and catharsis quietly disappeared. The failure of hysterical defence was not due to a failure of the process of discharging the memory of an external trauma. Hysterical defence fails because it has to make a compromise between a desire and the repression of this desire. This can very easily be verified in clinical practice: all the incompatible representations of the patients in the *Studies* contained a sexual desire which could not be assumed by the patient; conflict was unavoidable.

Trauma versus fantasy

The sequel to this well known part of psychoanalytic history is - if possible - even better known. Where Freud originally considered the seduction of the child by its 'uncle' - as a matter of fact, it was always the father - as causal trauma, he eventually discovered the seduction *fantasy*. The famous letter 69 to Fliess was meant to draw a definite line under the trauma theory.[19]

Freud, and especially after those him, followed this with endless discussion about the impact of a trauma, whether real or imagined, against the background of the ever present question of whether hys-

terics are victims or imposters. Freud himself quoted the studies by
Brouardel concerning indecent assaults on innocent children which
were obviously not uncommon. More recently, Armstrong did a study
on incest, while Masson judged it necessary to rake up the old quarrel
with what he believed to be new evidence.

This infantile "yes it is, no it isn't", loses sight of the most important point in the discussion, *the relationship between fantasy as a source of
meaning and the Lacanian Real as that which resists the Symbolic*; a relationship that is all important in hysteria. This aspect got lost in the ensuing
controversy about the trauma theory, and it is only through Lacanian
theory that it has come back into focus. For the sake of fairness, we
have to add that Freud also struggled with it. It is a part of his theory
that never appears with the same decisiveness in his official papers as
it does in his correspondence with Fliess. That is why it will pay us to
take a look at this correspondence.

In letter 59, we find our first hint. Freud wrote that the hysteric's
solution lay in a particular source of unconscious productions which
he had neglected until then: fantasy. Almost casually he added that
these fantasies "regularly, as it seems to me, go back to things heard by
children at an early age and only understood later".[20] The first two
important determinants were already included in this passage: on the
one hand, the Real; on the other the 'having understood', the working
over, either in the Imaginary or in the Symbolic.

Freud elaborated this new discovery throughout his correspondence between 1897 and 1899. In letter 61 we find a first real development.[21] In hysteria, everything goes back to the reproduction of 'real'
(sic) scenes which are hidden behind fantasies. These latter construct a
deferred understanding of these scenes. In the same paragraph, Freud
introduced a second novelty: hysterical repression does not bear on
memories, but on excitations coming precisely from those primary
scenes. Fantasies function as a defence against these scenes.[22] As a
defence, they consist of several editions spread over time, and
arranged in order of increasing resistance, the primary scene evoking
the most resistance.[23] The official elaboration of these ideas can be
found in a passage in the *Studies* concerning the threefold structure of
hysterical material.

Letter 66 - a highlight in Freud's self-analysis - sounds a different
note. The neurotic defends himself not only with, but also against, falsified memories and fantasies. Freud discovered more and more of
these falsifications, to the point where he was obliged to abandon the

trauma theory in letter 69. The way in which he discarded this theory adds another piece to the puzzle; indeed, the question concerning the reality of the primary scenes disappeared with the conclusion "that there are no indications of reality in the unconscious, so that one cannot distinguish between the truth and a fiction cathected with affect."[24]The next step in this sequence was the first mention of the Oedipus complex as "a universal event of early childhood".[25]

The development of the theory went further and further. In letter 75, we find an elaboration of the idea of repression, as well as a first glimpse of the idea of libidinal development based on the erogenous zones: oral, anal, and genital. Infantile experiences and/or fantasies go back to those three zones, of which the first two show a very particular characteristic: "that a quota of libido is not able, as is ordinarily the case, to force its way through to action or to translation into psychical terms".[26] Something that has not been psychically elaborated stays within the realm of the Real, and from there exerts a pathological traumatic force. This tallies with a previous discovery which we consider to be highly important. In his Draft K, Freud had already described the onset of hysteria as follows: "This first stage of hysteria may be described as 'fright hysteria'; its primary symptom is the *manifestation of fright* accompanied by a gap in the psyche."[27] In Draft E, two years earlier, he had already given an elaborate description of this process, while trying to explain the way anxiety arises. There too, the lack of psychical working-over was considered as the causal factor, this time resulting in anxiety.[28] Hence, both hysteria and anxiety neurosis are '*Stauungsneurosen*', 'neuroses of damming up': that which cannot be psychically processed accumulates and becomes pathogenic. This happens primarily in the 'prehistoric' time, i.e. between the first and the third year of life.[29]

These ideas permit us to anticipate a discovery that Freud still had to make, that of phobia as anxiety hysteria. Indeed, the theory already outlined, rudimentary as it may be, demonstrates that the primary form of hysteria is always anxiety hysteria. The further defensive working-over of it can lead either to anxiety hysteria with a secondary object, that is a phobia, or to conversion hysteria. The eventual absence of anxiety with the latter may obscure the fact that conversion, just like phobia, is nothing but a secondary working-over of a primary anxiety.

There followed a period in which the subject of hysteria stayed in the background. Freud was working on the study of the dream, but this did not prevent him from developing an earlier discovery in a way which proved useful for his later papers: *switch-words* or puns. In letter 80 he mentioned a sublime linguistic analysis made by the patient himself; an anxiety attack while trying to catch a *Käfer*, a beetle, is retraced by way of several magnificent switch-words to *Que faire?*, what shall I do? - the man, who'd had a French governess, recalled the indecisiveness of his mother concerning her marriage...[30] In letter 94, we find the first linguistic analysis of the forgetting of a proper name (Julius Mosen). This was but a finger exercise for the analysis of the Signorelli case which followed two letters later.[31]

From this analysis, Freud learnt that the connections between fantasies and the 'experiences' from childhood are made by what he called switch-words or word connections. His many examples permit us to say quite clearly that what thay concern each and every time is the signifier; as described by de Saussure, this is an acoustic image that is independent of the concept. It is the signifier which connects the subject to his childhood days. Connecting to what in this childhood ? A few years earlier, Freud would have answered with the idea of trauma. Now, his laconic answer was: "Nothing, but the germ of sexual impulse was there".[32]

The year 1899 was ushered in by letter 101. Freud had come a long way. The idea of a trauma that really happened as the cause of hysteria - the seduction by the father - had disappeared. Instead he had discovered the erotic impulses of childhood. Obviously, these impulses develop themselves along the lines of the erotogenic zones. The moment they emerge, they are strange, even 'alien', to the psyche. It is only much later on that they are psychically elaborated. This happens in the first place through fantasies. These psychical constructions work with switch-words and are arranged defensively with respect to the original impulse, following a hierarchical order. The actual nucleus is defensively cathected in such a way that it can never be put into words. Freud noted that the same holds for dream analysis: the navel of a dream, which goes back to the same prehistory, remains inaccessible, the 'core of our being' can never appear in the (pre-)conscious.[33]

From a Lacanian point of view, this can be understood as the relationship between the Real and the other two orders. Freud's core, navel, primal scene or mycelium, i.e. the dynamic drive element, is the impossible Real that lies beyond the Imaginary and the Symbolic, resisting every attempt to give it representation. Lacan's definition of trauma is consistent with these Freudian ideas: "the opacity of the trauma (...) its resistance to signification"[34] and "the pathogenic nucleus as what is being sought, but which repels discourse - what discourse shuns".[35] The Real is apparently traumatic *in itself* and yields a primal anxiety as a basic affect. The psychical working-over of it within the Imaginary and the Symbolic aims at building up a defence against this traumatic Real.

Another question presents itself here: how does it come about that the psyche - the Imaginary and the Symbolic - has so much trouble elaborating this kernel of Real? How does this defensive working-over succeed in the Imaginary and/or in the Symbolic? The answer will necessitate the development of the theory of repression. Before going into that, we want to highlight another point. In Freud's early theory on hysteria, the father had a central role. What had happened to this idea during the conceptual development sketched here?

The father as prehistoric Other

If, in this new theory, the origin of hysteria could be sought in infantile wishes and their working out, then the role of the father would seem to be minimal in comparison with the previous theory. However, the letter in which Freud put aside the idea of father-as-seducer was precisely the same letter in which he reintroduced the father in a new way. After the passage already quoted concerning the lack of any indication of reality in the Unconscious, he noted: "Thus, the possibility remained open that sexual fantasy invariably seizes upon the theme of the parents."[36] The elaboration in his next letters shows that, of both parents, it is again the father who takes the central role, albeit within the framework of fantasy.

The new import of the father, outside of the trauma theory, can easily be reconstructed. In letter 52, the most important letter of the series, Freud had already discovered that every hysterical symptom is an appeal to the other. The exact words in which he expressed this idea emphasised one of the most important characteristics of the Lacanian Other: "Attacks of giddiness and fits of weeping - all these are aimed at *another person* - but above all at the prehistoric, unforgettable other person whom no one coming after can equal".[37] In letter 57 he discovered that the high standards of love required by the hysteric, which inevitably result in dissatisfaction, go back to the idealised image of the father, impossible to match for any man.[38] Unless, of course, this man can be identified with this same father, in which case a flood of jouissance results. Freud soberly described a patient in one such situation, who experienced four to six orgasms with every act of coitus: "The old man, clearly owes this effect to a possible identification with the immensely powerful father of her childhood, thus liberating the libido attached to her fantasies. Instructive!"[39] Freud concluded by predicting that she would be frigid once she married a young man.

"The immensely powerful father of her childhood": from traumatising pervert to idealised image as lover - that is the considerable shift in Freud's theory concerning the role of the father. Let us note in passing that a third father figure can be seen here: the real one in the lives of the patients. In sharp contrast to the two previous figures, we are here confronted time and again with fathers who are ill, even dying; one has but to read the *Studies* for examples. But at the time, the only thing Freud picked up from this recurring characteristic, was the supposition that a daughter's protracted nursing of her father will render her vulnerable to the development of hysteria.[40]

What is the relationship between this and that other development in the theory, in which the erotic impulses of the child eventually emerge as the traumatic Real? This relationship was actually being prepared sporadically in the wings when Freud was talking about identification. In letter 125 things finally became clear. Erotic impulses develop in two layers, an auto-erotic one and a hetero-erotic one. Auto-erotism has no psychosexual aim and strives only for local experiences of satisfaction. Hysteria, on the other hand, "is hetero-erotic: its main goal is identification with the loved person".[41]

Hetero-erotic impulses, fantasies and identification: the father as beloved person has to be situated in this sequence. In order to explain the development of true hysteria in the Freudian sense, one important element is still lacking. "The construction of symptoms by means of identification is linked to fantasies, that is, *to their repression in the Unconscious.*"[42]

CHAPTER 3.

THE THEORY OF REPRESSION:
THE IMAGINARY AS DEFENCE

Manifest content: repression and resistance

Double Trauma

"Repression, cornerstone of the analytic edifice", Freud wrote in his account of the history of the analytic movement.[1] This metaphor evokes the idea of solidity, of incorruptibility. Indeed, nobody after him has questioned it as a concept. Nevertheless, the concept underwent two radical changes, often lost again later on, in the Freudian theory itself. Alienated *homo psychologicus,* as we know him today, uses it for better or for worse: "Yes, I will probably have repressed that", thereby unwittingly adhering to Freud's very first theory in which repression is described as a voluntary act. One consciously wants to rid oneself of an embarrassing memory which goes back to a relatively recent, unpleasant, even traumatic event. As a process this fits perfectly with normal defence; there is only a difference of degree between normal and pathological repression. In the early period of the theory, this could be applied as a mechanism to every form of 'neuro-psychosis of defence'. The specific differentiation between the different forms has to be looked for in what happens to the energy of the repressed material after repression has taken place .

Differences of intensity are not very satisfying as a basis for a differential clinic. Why would a hysteric impose a repression on her unpleasant memories that was so excessive that it caused a psychical splitting, *'Spaltung',* while this is not the case with a normal person? The only explanation Freud could produce at that point was not very convincing: the hysterical patient was supposed to have a certain 'disposition' which would account for the excessive nature of the process of repression.[2]

Freud himself was not very happy with this explanation à la Charcot. His first paper of 1896 was explicitly addressed to Charcot and his school and presented a novel idea: a specific aetiology for every neurosis.[3] The theory of repression had not yet been elaborated, but it received a completely new foundation. The recent memory can only produce a traumatic result if it goes back to an even earlier trauma. The emotional reaction to this first trauma only comes into

effect through the second one. In his following paper he linked this discovery to repression, thereby raising it to the status of a key pathological mechanism. "In the place of this undefined hysterical disposition
we can now put, wholly or in part, the posthumous effects of a sexual
trauma in childhood. 'Repression' of the memory of a distressing sexual experience which occurs in maturer years is only possible for those
in whom that experience can activate the memory-trace of a trauma in
childhood".[4] The defence against a recent and unbearable representation becomes a repression because this recent representation carries the
weight of a much older infantile sexual trauma. This is the condition
for every repression.

The theory seemed complete and Freud merely refined it in the next
two papers.[5] His ideas up to this point can be summarised as follows.
A hysterical patient has experienced a sexual trauma during her childhood in the position of passive victim. At the moment of its occurrence
there was no reaction because the child could not understand the
meaning of the event. The memory is retained as neutral, without any
signal of unpleasure, and is re-activated during a second, later scene at
the time of puberty. It is only with this second scene that the unpleasurable sensations belonging to the primal scene are released. The
whole complex is then repressed, resulting in conversion symptoms,
which function as mnemic symbols that are over-determined.

Freud was satisfied; he had turned round his previous pessimism
regarding therapeutic success and insight into the hysterical structure.
He looked back on the hypno-cathartic method, from the years with
Breuer, and called it a mere treatment of symptoms. With his new
insights he believed he could promise the "genuine cure of hysteria".[6]

Freud went on to apply it to two phenomena: the forgetting of
proper names and screen-memories.[7] Both papers touch on hysteria in
a number of ways. In the first one we find the famous analysis of
"Signorelli". Freud had forgotten the name of the painter of the Orvieto
frescoes. His analysis of the substitute names that occurred to him
demonstrates the triple structure already present in *The Studies*: the
diachronic and synchronic level of signifiers, and the signified linked
to the nucleus as the most repressed element. A second analogy with
The Studies is the inversely proportional relationship between visual
image and word. As long as Freud could not remember the name
Signorelli he saw his portrait with unusual clarity. Once he remembered the name the image disappeared.[8] Freud stated that this small
case study could be considered as a model for the construction of a

psychoneurotic symptom: a recent, and less important impression is taken over by a repressed content and is thereby also repressed. The motive for the repression is the unpleasure associated with the repressed material. Hence, said Freud, the resistance that we meet with in our patients when we try to make the material conscious: "Half the secret of hysterical amnesia is uncovered when we say that hysterical people do not know what they do not *want* to know; and psychoanalytic treatment, which endeavours to fill up such gaps of memory in the course of its work, leads us to the discovery that the bringing back of those lost memories is opposed by a certain resistance which has to be counterbalanced by work proportionate to its magnitude".[9] The analysis of resistance was born. In the second paper the same resistance was held responsible for the mechanism of screen-memories: something innocent which is retained with visual clarity in one's memory acts as a screen to obscure something that is not innocent at all.[10]

Repressed wishes and erogenous zones

This theory was raised to another level through a dialectical movement once Freud had complemented the idea of trauma with that of fantasy and infantile sexuality. We deliberately write, 'complement', because, in our opinion, Freud never abandoned the trauma theory.[11] It is obvious that from his point of view, something insistently traumatic lies at the basis of hysteria.

From this point on, any conceptual difficulties can be studied by means of two main questions: *why* is there repression, and *what* is there to be repressed?

The *why* of repression was more or less clear in the trauma theory: the unpleasurable character of the first trauma was expressed by the second one, resulting in an automatic repression of both, automatic due to the influence of the pleasure principle. We say, 'more or less clear' because there were already some difficulties within the framework of this first theory. The core of the problem lies in what Freud called a psychological riddle, namely: how should we understand the unpleasure of the first trauma when the first scene's traumatic and unpleasurable nature only becomes apparent as such when released by the the second trauma? Then again, the second scene's traumatic and unpleasurable nature is determined as such by this mysterious primary unpleasure, so any explanation would ground the concept in its totality. At first Freud tried to explain this first unpleasure in the child by invoking the affects of shame, disgust and morality, but he rejected this explanation before the end of the text. There must, he wrote, be an independent source of unpleasure in the field of sexuality itself.[12] But this gave rise to a second problem: if the original experience itself was unpleasurable, why wasn't it repressed at the time? Freud could not produce any answer to these questions. Once he had discovered infantile sexuality, the argument became superfluous and even irrelevant: the child experiences pleasure from his form of sexuality. The very basis of the first theory of repression thereby falls away: without unpleasure there can be no repression.

The discovery of infantile sexuality was the starting point for a different theory of repression. During its development a child makes use of several non-genital zones such as the mouth and anus in order to get satisfaction. Freud remembered what Charcot had told him about the hysterogenous zones, and the relationship between the two suddenly fell into place. Hysteria now became the negative of perversion, going back to infantile erogenous zones which should have been abandoned in the course of normal development. The pleasurable activity procured by these zones is accompanied by fantasies. This gives us the answer to the second question - *what* is repressed? Precisely these fantasies.

The second theory of repression can now be summarised as follows: a child develops by itself a desire for pleasure and it gets satisfaction through certain non-genital erogenous zones; this satisfaction is accompanied by fantasies. Once the genital stage is reached the previous complex has to be repressed. In later periods of life this complex can be reactivated thus necessitating a new defence; the eventual failure of this defence will give rise to a pathological breakthrough.

Analysis of resistance

This theory is still widely accepted today, albeit with the necessary variations and controversies. One persistent point of controversy concerns the genital or oral character of hysteria. One group maintains that hysteria is a regression and/or fixation to the primary erogenous zone, thereby forcing an exclusively oral interpretation of these fantasies. One author pleads obstinately - of course - for the anal zone. Another group considers hysteria as the 'genital' neurosis par excellence, in view of the fact that hysteria genitalises/phallicises everything. The same discussion returns in a different guise with the question of whether hysteria is an Oedipal (genital) or a pre-Oedipal psychopathology.[13] Another point of discussion, which is still current today, considers the relative share of fantasy and reality with respect to the trauma.[14] The only constant in this medley can be put as follows: in order to provoke hysteria at least two conflicts are necessary within the sphere of sexuality, one occurring during childhood (before the onset of puberty) and the other at a later age. It is their conflictual nature which then explains the repression, an idea harking back to the 'incompatible representations' in *The Studies*.

To put it differently: the only constant is repression itself. The attentive reader will have noticed that we have returned to our starting point: why does repression take place? Why would a child repress a fantasy which procures pleasure? Where does the conflict originate which obliges a child to repress a satisfying fantasmatic activity, and, subsequently, as a young woman, to repeat this in a second conflict?

The theory given above cannot answer such pertinent questions. As is often the case, the theory just starts functioning as established knowledge so that the problem is no longer even noticed. One concentrates on the pragmatic side: repression implies a repressive agency, and hence, a resistance. This resistance has to be destroyed if one wants to reach the repressed material.

The result of this argument is very obvious: one ends up very quickly with one of the many degradations of psychoanalysis, in this case the analysis of resistances. Freud took the same road; the analysis of Dora will show us how. He did not leave matters there, however, and the same analysis will show us why.

The theory of repression and hysteria, as we have outlined it until now, still lacks something else besides the problem of primary motive: what is its relation to Freud's previous discoveries? The father as figure of identification within the fantasy, primary anxiety as a basis, the inadequate psychical working-over of infantile scenes and/or wishes? All these seem to have disappeared from the manifest content. The time is therefore right to consider the latent content. As in every analysis, this latent content comes as a complete surprise. One can approach the same material with a diffeent reading and emphasis and end up with a completely different story.

Latent content: The Woman

The reading of the theory of repression presented hitherto is a conventional one. As such, it is still used today within the *International Psycho-analytic Association* as established knowledge, albeit with a few

modifications regarding primary repression and with a shift of emphasis in the direction of the analysis of resistance.

As a constituted knowledge it is to a great extent subjected to a
process of wear and tear. One does not need to be very shrewd to pinpoint its lacunae. In an analogy with the interpretation of dreams, we
have called this theory the manifest content. Freud teaches us that
omission is the main mechanism of censorship operating between
manifest and latent content. What has been omitted from the original
theory? We have already given the rough outlines of the parts that
have disappeared: the Real as traumatic nucleus, the father as a
seducer and/or figure of identification in the fantasy, hysteria as a hetero-erotic neurosis with respect to erogenous development. The beauty
of it is that the neglected contents return in an insistent manner.
Indeed, every single one of the actual points of discussion about hysteria can be traced back to them, and in that respect they constitute nothing less than the return of the repressed. Thus, the question of whether
the trauma is real or fantasmatic can only be answered if one studies
the Real from a different point of view. The same applies to the controversy about whether hysteria is oral-pre-Oedipal or genital-Oedipal. In
order to answer the latter we have to turn to Freud's first ideas on
erogenous development and on repression.

The Woman as traumatic Real - primary defence
At the end of 1895 Freud wrote to Fliess: "Hysteria necessarily presupposes a primary experience of unpleasure - that is, of a passive
nature. The natural sexual passivity of women explains their being
more inclined to hysteria". [15]

Hysteria and passivity. Although Freud never abandoned this idea,
he continued to struggle with it. In the same text, he added that hysteria in the male too goes back to a scene which is experienced passively.
Even in cases of obsessional neurosis he found that behind the active
chidhood scene laden with pleasure, there was a passive scene preceding it. Every obsessional neurosis has a hysterical basis. In other words,
every psychoneurosis starts with an unpleasurable passivity which has
to be fended off by means of a defence.

Passivity and femininity: "the natural sexual passivity of women".
This sentence started one of the most well known controversies in psychoanalysis and, in spite of all his attempts to give a more balanced
view, Freud never suceeded in putting an end to it. The problem that

he tried to tackle is not even clear to everybody: how to express the difference between men and women from a psychological point of view? Ernest Jones brushed this question aside by means of a simplistic reference to the Bible: "He created them Man and Woman"; he just didn't see what the problem was. As a matter of fact, the formulation given above is not exact.[16] Freud's difficulty was not the differentiation between man and woman, it was in defining womanhood.[17] The only solution which kept on coming back but with which he was never fully satisfied was his first answer: from a psychological point of view, femininity can only be represented through another idea taking its place: the much challenged idea of passivity.[18]

Hysteria, passivity, femininity. On 25th May, 1897, Freud wrote: "It is to be suspected that what is essentially repressed is always what is feminine".[19] This conclusion, surprising as it may be, is completely consistent with the previous ideas: every neurosis starts as a passive traumatic scene which is experienced as unpleasurable; passivity means femininity; hence, the core of the repressed is femininity. There does not seem to be a place for the woman in the psychical economy.

At this point we have to make an important link with Freud's previous discoveries during his 'trauma' period. At that time he had discovered that there was something, a nucleus, navel or mycelium, which could not be psychically elaborated and which gave rise to anxiety as the only possible reaction. We have already described this as the Lacanian Real, situated beyond the signifier. Freud now discovered that this something was always of a passive, unpleasurable and traumatic nature. Passive and therefore feminine. To be more accurate: passivity became a substitute signifier for femininity because even Freud could not find the right words for it.

In other words, the traumatic Real, for which there is no signifier in the Symbolic, is femininity. *Freud had discovered the lack in the Symbolic system: there is no signifier for The Woman.* Half a century later, Lacan wrote this down as $Ⱥ$, meaning that the totality of signifiers is never complete, that the Other has a lack.

This traumatic Real is repressed, fended off. It is a process which takes on a special form. Indeed, the traumatic and Real nucleus cannot be repressed in itself for the very simple reason that there isn't anything to repress, as there are no signifiers, '*Vorstellungen*', for it. When Freud used the word 'Repression' in this respect, he was aiming at a very special instance: "Repression does not take place by means of the construction of an excessively strong antithetic idea but by the intensification of a boundary idea".[20] Instead of the Real, we find a *boundary signifier*, a signifier S for the lack A : $S(A)$. Later on, a secondary defence is directed against the working-over of this signifier in fantasies, and this secondary defence is repression proper, which is always a *Nachdrängen*, literally an 'after(re-) pression'.

We will concentrate on this primary defence for the time being. A fuller exposition can be found in two letters to Fliess, letter 46 and letter 52. It runs as follows: psychic material is ordered and written down in a specific script which varies according to the period of life. At the boundary of each consecutive period, there is a transcription or translation of the psychic material into the language of the next period. In letter 46, Freud stated that the traumatic nucleus is 'not transcribed', meaning 'not transcribed in word-presentations', '*Wortvorstellungen*'. Hence, a typical consequence for hysteria: "that the arousal of an Ia sexual scene leads, not to psychical consequences, but to conversion".[21]

Letter 52 takes up this idea of transcription in a more general manner.The psychic mechanism develops by way of '*Aufeinanderschichtung*', i.e. a process involving layer upon layer, during which the material already acquired is transcribed/translated into a new form of expression from time to time. The translation into the language of a following period takes place at the boundary of the consecutive periods of life. An exception is made for some of this material, which is not translated. "A failure of translation - this is what is known clinically as 'repression'."[22]

This Freudian argument allows us to take another step. The conversion from what is not psychical to the psychical is followed by a development within this psychical working-over. In his discussion of this elaboration Freud took up once again his three-layered structure from *The Studies*. The trauma at the basis of hysteria, the passive unpleasurable 'scene', i.e. femininity, is to be situated *outside* or beyond all forms of psychical working-over. The first step of this latter is the erection of a boundary representation, after which further defensive workingover can take place. In our opinion, this primary defence by means of a boundary signifier can easily be subsumed under what Freud later conceptualised as primary repression, something which appears first of all to be a primary fixation. Something stays fixated, set outside the realm of the psyche. The only possible reaction to it is a working-over by way of boundary material which substitutes for it and which can afterwards become an appropriate target for repression as such. primary repression can thus be understood as the leaving behind of The Woman in the Real.

Imaginarisation of a lack

Primary defence aims to cover up a hole, to fill in a gap. This defence, primary repression, is realised first of all by the erection of a boundary structure, a representation situated on the edge of a lack. This representation becomes "the first symbol of the repressed material"[23] and is covered over by a first substitute signifier, S($\not{A}$); 'first', because the development doesn't stop there. This boundary representation, intended as defence, will be developed into ever more complex psychical constructions which all have the same function: *psychical working-over of the traumatic Real.* Freud discovered these constructions a little later: "...The point that escaped me in the solution of hysteria lies in the discovery of a new source from which a new element of unconscious productions arises. What I have in mind are hysterical phantasies...".[24]

The importance of the fantasy in hysteria is well known. Every hysteric has his/her '*Privattheater*', just as Anna O did. There is less agreement when one turns to its function. The discussion gets lost in the controversy about what has really happened and what is fantasmatically constructed afterwards, the underlying question being the difference between 'real' patients and malingerers. This discussion can also be retraced in Freud's work, but there is much more to it. In his first papers, he had no doubt that fantasy had to be situated between primary defence - primary repression - and a subsequent defence, repression proper. Its function was also very clear. Freud noted time and again that fantasies, as typical neurotic constructions, elaborate *an understanding a posteriori of what was originally not understood,* that is, they furnish a further working-over of the boundary representation at the boundary structure of the traumatic Real.[25] The hysteric appeals to the Imaginary in order to deal with the Real. To be more specific: to work out that aspect of the Real where the Symbolic lacks a definite signifier. That is why she becomes the champion of interpretation: every hysterical symptom is an over-determined mnemic symbol, Freud said. Every hysterical symptom is an Imaginary interpretation of the Real as well as a superstructure on top of it.

Expressed in terms of the Lacanian registers this implies that hysteria begins at the junction between the Real and the Symbolic. The Real does not completely enter into the Symbolic and the Symbolic shows a lack in relation to this Real: R > S. Its defensive working-over in hysterical structure takes place through the Imaginary which predominates over the Real: I > R. At the same time, the complete structure of the three registers demonstrates that the Imaginary is subjected to the Symbolic: S > I > R.[26] Therefore, a solution in terms of the Imaginary is doomed to failure. This Imaginary has to produce an answer to the lack in the Symbolic; as this Imaginary is itself determined by this Symbolic, the same lack will reappear in it. Freud had already said so and we shall see how this happens further on.

The thesis that the hysteric tries to deal with the traumatic Real in the Imaginary allows a conceptual clarification of a number of clinical phenomena.

A first characteristic, often commented upon, concerns the preference of hysterics for visual representation. One could understand this preference in terms of a negative alternation between word and image. The more the visual character of a memory or fantasy dominates, the more the words seem to be lacking: Freud sees the picture with unusual clarity, but the proper name, Signorelli, is lacking. This phenomenon can be conceptualised in terms of the preponderance of the Imaginary with hysterics. Lacan states that this register begins at i(a), the body image. Freud had already highlighted the prevalence of popular *visual* representations of the body in cases of hysterical paralysis. The preponderance of visual material in the Imaginary seems an established fact.

Secondly, we could shed some light on the always mysterious conversion symptoms as well as hysterical hallucinations. From within the Imaginary there are two possible avenues. One leads to the Symbolic: when it has the upper hand over the Imaginary the visual aspect has to disappear. This tallies with clinical experience: once the word is found, the image disappears. The second road leads to the Real, where the preponderance of the Imaginary gives rise to *realisations*, i.e. effects in the Real. This can already be read in full in Freud: "that the arousal of a Ia sexual scene leads, not to psychical consequences, but to conversion". The same argument accounts for hysterical hallucinations, placed by Freud alongside conversion, at the same structural level: the hysterical hallucination is a sensory conversion.[27] The hysteric tries to produce a solution to Ⱥ in the Imaginary, and this results in the overtaking of the functional soma by the imaginarised body. The precursors of psychiatry had an implicit understanding of this process, but they too stayed in the realm of the Imaginary with their solution and with their hysterical patient. Indeed, at the time of Hippocrates these theories had already promoted the uterus to the position of specific signifier of femininity, albeit with a pathological connotation. The so-called migration of the uterus can be understood as the inscription of this looked-for signifier of femininity on other places in the body. Their therapy was meant to nail down this signifier in its proper place.

A third, hitherto mysterious clinical phenomenon can now also be placed within the greater theoretical framework. The hysterical patient is said to sexualize or eroticize 'everything'. This is a direct consequence of the imperative to deal with the traumatic Real in the Imaginary. Every hysterical symptom is a stab at answering the question: what is a woman? The lack of a symbolic answer results in an ever increasing series of Imaginary as-if answers. We are now in a better position to determine this hysterical pansexualism in a more specific way, and (in the meantime) to explain why it cannot but fail as an answer to $\cancel{A}$. To do this, we have to keep in mind the relationship between the Symbolic and the Imaginary. Lacan's elaborations of primary and secondary narcissism demonstrate that the Symbolic determines the Imaginary: $I(\cancel{A}) \rightarrow i(a)$. As a system, the Symbolic is based on the phallus and contains no signifier for the woman. The determination of the Imaginary by the Symbolic implies that the Imaginary is also based on the phallus:

$$
\begin{array}{ccc}
\text{Symbolic} & \longrightarrow & \text{Imaginary} \\
\text{I(A)} & & \text{i(a)} \\
\\
\Phi & & -\phi
\end{array}
$$

hysterical pansexualism is a pan-*phallicism*: the hysteric phallicizes everything, and that is the reason why the solution in the Imaginary for $\cancel{A}$ automatically fails. The discussion about whether hysteria is genital-phallic or pregenital-oral receives a definite answer. In hysteria the genital stage is dominant because this is where the lack is felt. It is precisely this gap which hysteria tries to bridge. Because the woman lacks a phallus, she phallicizes everything. This 'everything' comprises the pregenital realm as well, and that explains why the oral aspect can be so all-embracing. It is, however, an orality which was phallicized a posteriori. The best example of this remains the case study of Dora. But as early as letter 52 to Fliess, Freud had already made an explicit link to the development of the erogenous zones, and had not restricted the translation into a new registration to 'indications of perception', 'conceptual memories' and 'word-presentations' only. Thus the oral and anal phases can be rewritten in a 'genital' way, that is, in a phallic way. He confirmed this in 1906 for hysteria, when he wrote that: "a number of erotogenic zones attain the significance of genitals".[28]

A fourth clinical point concerns the relative ineffectiveness of interpretations. As long as the analyst uses his analytic knowledge in order to produce interpretations, the hysterical structure will not shift one inch, in spite of the fact that the patient often confirms the interpretations and even extrapolates from them. How can this be explained? Since a hysterical phantasmatic system is itself one massive interpretation of the relationship between the Symbolic and the Real, though from an imaginary point of view, any attempt on the part of the analyst to complement the hysterical 'understanding of what was originally not understood' with his own understanding will produce interpretations that can only achieve a confirmation of a frozen imaginary. Only a symbolic interpretation which aims at the function of the fantasy as a defensive working-over of, and potential solution to, $S(\not{A})$, can result in a transition to the Symbolic and produce a therapeutic analytic effect.[29]

Last but not least, there is a fifth clinical phenomenon which can be theorised by means of the idea of the fantasy as a defensive interpretation of the Real. Freud had already observed in *The Studies* that hysterical patients can have a compulsion to associate, resulting in the unconscious complex overflowing into the contents of consciousness in an almost obsessional manner.[30] In the same vein we can understand another one of his conclusions, namely that it is impossible to reach the end point of a chain of associations, the 'real' trauma beyond them. The hysteric neither can nor wants to reach that ultimate point. Instead, she wants to produce an answer to the original lack with her imaginary productions. No wonder that at first Freud considered these fantasies as obstacles on the way to the nucleus, as defensive roadblocks.[31] Once he had given up the theory of traumatic seduction, he situated infantile-sexual impulses in this nucleus. This opened up a new perspective for the development of the defensive imaginary: the erogenous zones.

Masculinity as a form of defensive imaginary - the second repression

When Freud was elaborating his stratification of the psyche in terms of the forms of expression of the material in letter 52, he put forward another idea almost incidentally: that the development of the psyche follows the development of erogenous zones. The impulses originating from these erogenous zones are elaborated *a posteriori* in fantasies.[32]

At this point in the development of his thought, Freud did not say much about the development of these fantasies. They go back to erogenous zones which are left behind, especially the mouth and anus. During childhood, these areas of the body are used to obtain pleasure.[33] Fantasies have to be situated in a series going from auto- to hetero- erotic. Hysteria belongs to the last category, with the result that its imaginary productions are always directed to the other (cf. above, n.31). The parental figures are very important in this respect, especially the father who functions as a standard for every love relationship.[34] We also learn that identification with the beloved person is a key factor in hysteria. In this respect, fantasies can even take the form of genuine family romances. The identification that takes place within this framework has to be linked to symptom-formation. This brings us to another new point: fantasies, insofar as they work over a primary defence and extend a boundary representation, can themselves become a target of subsequent repressions.[35]

All these pieces of the puzzle are very important, because they permit us to place a new Freudian discovery in a coherent framework: without them, this discovery would remain incomprehensible. These pieces can be put together as follows. Hysteria starts from the traumatic Real and can be understood as an attempt to elaborate it psychically by way of the Imaginary. This elaboration by the Imaginary begins at a boundary representation and is continued with fantasies. The allo-erotic fantasies of the hysteric are directed to the other, and especially to the father. This is accompanied by a typical characteristic, namely an identification with the beloved person, i.e. the father. To put it more precisely: *the end point of the defensive elaboration by the Imaginariy is an identification with a man.* For the hysteric, the ultimate answer to the lack of a signifier for the woman lies in an identification with the man-father.

This implies that in the end the hysteric is confronted with a second series of incompatible representations - with a second conflict. Both of them can now be accurately phrased: *the psychosexual conflict at the basis of every hysteria concerns sexual identity.* First of all, there was an opposition between the Real and the Symbolic, because there was no specific signifier in the Symbolic with which the woman could identify herself from the Real. On the contrary, there was only a lacuna causing anxiety. The solution, the imaginary working-over, ended in a second conflict: being a woman, the hysteric identified herself with a man. The defence against the first conflict consisted in a primary defence or primary repression; with the second conflict, the defence became repression proper.

This new Freudian discovery - that the hysteric operates an excessive repression of her masculine sexuality - can also be considered as the coherent result of a long development. The first notion of it can be found in letter 75 to Fliess, where this idea is linked to erogenous development and to fantasy. The imaginary working-over of the first psychosexual conflict ends in masculine sexual activity in which the clitoris becomes an equivalent of the penis. This has to change at puberty. "But the main distinction between the sexes emerges at the time of puberty, when girls are seized by a *non* neurotic *sexual* repugnance and males by libido. For at that period a further sexual zone is (wholly or in part) extinguished in females which persists in males. I am thinking of the male genital zone, the region of the clitoris, in which during childhood sexual sensitivity is shown to be concentrated in girls as well as boys".[36] In this respect, it is worthwhile remarking that Freud is speaking of the process of *normal* development: "a *non* neurotic *sexual* repugnance" (his italics).

Although the pathological process received no further elaboration in his correspondence, there was some mention of it on two other occasions.[37] The first one concerned the analysis of Dora, of which he said that the main part was played by "the opposition between the male and the female tendency". The second went somewhat further. Freud stated that repression, which remained his main problem, only becomes possible through the interaction of two sexual currents. And this brings us to a new idea which afterwards, with the post-Freudians, went on to function as received knowledge: bisexuality.

Mono-sexuality: "Il n'y a pas de rapport sexuel"

As a neurologist, Freud had searched for the mysterious gender difference of eels. As an analyst, he was confronted with an analogous problem. During the first stages of their development, both male and female children take their distance from what cannot be expressed in signifiers: the passive-feminine. This led Freud to a surprising conclusion: "The auto-erotic activity of the erotogenic zones is, however, the same in both sexes, and owing to this uniformity there is no possibility of a distinction between the two sexes such as arises after puberty".[38] Every human being starts with one gender only; childhood is marked by mono-sexuality. To put it differently: there is only one signifier for both sexes and this signifier is the phallus.

This has enormous consequences. If there is only one signifier in the Symbolic for sexual difference then the implication is that sexuality within the Symbolic is fundamentally *without any rapport*. It is in this conceptual framework that one of Lacan's provocative statements has to be understood: "Il n'y a pas de rapport sexuel", there is no sexual rapport, for want of two different terms that could be related to each other. This much-contested Lacanian proposition is in this respect totally in line with Freud and can be read as part of Lacan's return to Freud.

Nevertheless, during this period Freud often talked about bisexuality as the determining factor in every neurosis. In letter 113 to Fliess he wrote that every sexual act had to be considered as a process between four individuals.[39] It is well known that the idea originated with Fliess, who afterwards made a fuss about priority in this respect. How can this idea be reconciled with that of mono-sexuality? This is much easier than it appears to be. Right from the start, Freud and Fliess had very different views on what bisexuality might be. In letter 71 Freud wrote that he had not yet tried to apply Fliess' hypothesis concerning bisexuality. He remarked that this hypothesis was completely in opposition to his own ideas.[40] The subsequent correspondence makes clear that Fliess' theory is nothing other than the classic idea of complementarity in a new guise: every human being has a dominating gender and a repressed complement. Every man latently contains a woman, and vice versa: every woman latently contains a man. Fliess replaced the concept of bisexuality with that of bilaterality, thereby stressing the aspect of complementarity. It is at this point that Freud definitively broke away from Fliess.[41] He kept on using the word, but in such a way that there was never any mention of complementarity.[42] For him, the problem still remained the same: how does a feminine identity come into being, based on a development in which there is only room for masculinity?

Oddly enough, in the post-Freudian period it was Fliess' conception which became prevalent, though it was ascribed to Freud. In the post-Freudian literature, the idea of latent homosexuality as a basis for neurosis was still understood in terms of androgyny. A neurotic is someone who has not repressed his feminine side, or her masculine side, enough. One could also say: his anima or her animus. A hysterical woman is nothing but a failed man, a virago; a hysterical man is not a real man, but a feminized one. Freud's idea about the fundamental problematic of female identity as such had disappeared.[43]

Mono-sexuality until puberty, followed by a *"non* neurotic *sexual repugnance"* (see note 35), was supposed to make the masculine-phallic current of the girl disappear. Does this imply that a definite symbolic gender differentiation sets in *after* puberty? Freud never produced a straight answer to this question. Instead, he always referred to clinical experience: "The fact that women change their leading erotogenic zone in this way, together with the wave of repression at puberty, with which, as it were, they put aside their childish masculinity, are the chief determinants in making them more prone to neurosis and especially to hysteria."[44]

So it seems self-evident that a woman is almost predestined to become neurotic. As if this wasn't explicit enough in itself, Freud added immediately afterwards that it was bound up with the essence of being a woman.

This was repeated almost verbatim in the 1908 paper on infantile sexual theories.[45] In another paper dating from the same period he discovered that hysterical symptoms are often determined by a double fantasy: a masculine, active one and a feminine, passive one, resulting in a clash between the two.[46] It is the same conflict that recurs at the time of puberty. Freud's very last paper dealing explicitly with hysteria ends with the following sentence: "In a whole number of cases the hysterical neurosis merely represents an excessive accentuation of the typical wave of repression which, by doing away with her masculine sexuality, allows the woman to emerge".[47] This last sentence is very interesting. It teaches us two things. Firstly, according to Freud, the normal development of womanhood goes through the repression of masculine sexuality. Secondly, hysterical patients do not so much fail in this process as go through it in a way which is excessive. In comparison with an ordinary female child who wants to become 'a' woman, the hysteric wants to be the woman. And that is where things go wrong.

Repression revisited: a vicious circle for the woman

It is time to recapitulate and to evaluate. According to Freud, hysteria starts with a primary experience which the psyche cannot deal with. The attempt at a defensive working-over begins with boundary signifiers and continues with fantasies. This primary experience can be understood as the traumatic Real, as seen in relation to the lack in the Symbolic, A̸. This starting-point is nothing but primary repression, which is essentially a primary fixation: the woman has to stay behind in the Real. Passivity seems to be the only substitute signifier offered by the working-over by the imaginary, $S(\cancel{A})$. The resulting fantasies become a target for later repression. They become replaced by their 'active', or masculine counterparts. At puberty, this gives rise to a second conflict, resulting in a second repression: the masculine part has to disappear so that The Woman can arise.

This conceptualisation brings a solution to a number of previous problems but also raises new questions. The difficulties concerning unpleasure as a motive for repression have disappeared. This problem was presented as follows: where does the unpleasure necessary for repression come from if the whole of it is based on an infantile sexuality which procures pleasure? The answer was that this infantile sexuality develops towards two opposite poles. The pleasurable fantasies which accompany infantile masturbation are active and therefore directed against a dreaded passivity. This can be extended to children's games: the child repeats actively what it had to undergo passively at the hands of its parents. The unpleasurable passivity is the primary motive for repression, the first conflict. In 1905 Freud brought us a dawning insight into its development when he stated in his *Three Essays* that sexual activity is a development of the earliest nursing relations between mother and child. The child takes its first independent steps when it starts to suck at objects outside the mother, when it makes the transition from being suckled passively to an active sucking.[48] Freud took twenty years before giving this discovery its full implementation. The second wave of repression at puberty is caused by a second group of incompatible representations: the masculine-active pleasure felt during childhood has to be abandoned for a feminine-passive form. Freud considered this latter as being unpleasurable even though he himself was already having serious doubts about his understanding of the balance between pleasure and unpleasure.[49] Indeed, if his previous understanding was correct, it would imply that there could be no pleasure for a woman after puberty, unless of a masculine, active kind, one she had to repress. This major problem remained unsolved.

One would not be wrong in concluding that the problem had shifted to another point in the meantime: why did passivity have to be so unpleasurable? For Freud, this was a simple matter of fact, and his problem lay more in the problematic analogy between femininity and passivity. Remarkably enough, the same fact reappears in a totally different context. When Veyne gave a seminar at the famous *Collège de France* in 1977-78 on the subject of sexuality and the family in ancient Rome, one of his conclusions concerned the same topic. Indeed, in the late Roman empire almost everything was permitted; both homo- and heterosexual acts. Even the taboo on incest was almost non-existent, considered no worse than farting in merry company. Only one thing was rejected as scandalous: passivity. One had to be active. Whilst this is a confirmation of Freud's clinical experience, it doesn't explain anything: why is passivity so unpleasurable, why does it have to be dealt with defensively to such an extent? It is quite clear that only a different conception of pleasure and unpleasure can shed light on this problem. Lacan's introduction of the concept of 'jouissance' proves illuminating in this respect.

Once again, this concept makes explicit an implicit Freudian idea. Freud discussed the transition of being suckled passively to active sucking as a very important step in the development of the child's sexuality. It meant acquiring a desire of its own. At the end of his career, he would pay more and more attention to the pre-Oedipal mother-child relationship in the aetiology of hysteria. Based on Lacan, we can recognize in this "la jouissance de l'Autre", the jouissance of the first big Other, the mother, which implies the reduction of the child to a mere object *a* of the desire of this Other. It has no existence of its own. *It is being enjoyed* by the Other.

It is at this very point that we recognise passivity as a primary experience of unpleasure against which every neurosis tries to guard itself. This is Freud's Oedipus complex, understood by Lacan as the most important structuring process in the becoming human of a speaking being. For Lacan, this process of taking one's distance takes place through a double mechanism: alienation and separation. It provides the child with a signifier of its own through the intervention of the symbolic function of the father, the 'Name-of-the-Father'. Thereby, it becomes a divided subject, freed from the previous impasse, with a desire of its own. It is precisely this process which does not run smoothly for women, owing to a structural difficulty: there is no proper signifier for femininity, she can only turn to the phallus. Hence, Freud's close ties between hysteria, femininity and passivity. The relationship to masochism could also be mentioned in this context.

Freud's new theory of repression thus gives a solution to a previous difficulty. The opposite is also true: a previous solution now becomes very doubtful. In the beginning, Freud was at pains to make a differentiation between normal and pathological repression. He had to resort to a mysterious disposition in order to explain the pathological one. This unsatisfactory solution became superfluous after the discovery of a traumatic infantile experience the memory of which, working retroactively, resulted in a subsequent pathogenic repression. With the discovery of infantile sexuality and the generalisation of 'polymorphous perversity', this argument became invalid, and Freud was obliged to return to his starting-point: repression is a universal and normal process that takes place in an excessive way with hysteria, thereby causing the pathology. The difference between normality and pathology becomes once again a matter of degree, even of constitution. This is one of the stumbling blocks in the *Three Essays*, so much so that Freud had to conclude with the notion of a generalised hysteria: "After all, Moebius could rightly say that we are all to some extent hysterics".[50] The nosological differentiation can no longer be made within the theory itself except in terms of intensity.

We can note an interesting shift in the theory: the problem of hysteria changes into the problem of womanhood. Everyone is polymorphously perverse as a child, everyone goes through the motions of repression before reaching the genital end point. However, this disposition to polymorphous perversity in infancy remains almost unchanged in "an average uncultivated woman".[5] In our terms: owing to the lack of a proper signifier, she can choose whatever path is available. Moreover, as a woman, she has to go through a special repressive process at puberty in order to become a woman. Hysterical repression is only an extremely intense form of this process (see note 45): hence, the essential relationship between woman and hysteria (see note 42) and hence the fact that repression occurs more often in women.[52] Freud had discovered a new area. It would take more than two decades before he entered 'the dark continent'. This postponement was not accidental but had - as we shall see - a clear reason which can be described in the structural terms of discourse theory.

To end this chapter, it is worthwhile asking the following question: what is actually repressed in hysteria? The classical post-Freudian answer is rather confusing. Insofar as the question is asked, the answer talks about pregenital, partial drives, which determine symptoms through the return of the repressed. The general preference was for oral drives, although this gave rise to the problem of a genitalized orality. There then followed the discussion about genital-pregenital, etc. Freud arranged things more clearly. The originally repressed element is the *feminine* one, to be more specific: passive feminine fantasies. The defensive imaginarisation is masculine active and develops alongside the erogenous zones and the accompanying fantasies. The last one of the series, the clitoridal one, has to be repressed at puberty. Freud considered this as a repression of the *masculine* element which is necessary for the transition to the vaginal-feminine: in other words, to install the reign of the genital zone. This repression is superfluous for the man, who has to stick to his last erogenous zone, the phallic one, which gives rise to a completely different problem.[53]

It seems evident that the series stops right here. In that sense, hysteria would be the result of a failure of that last repression, thus explaining why a number of hysterics take on the appearance of she-men. However, for Freud, there is yet a third content that has to be repressed: *the genital in itself.* "In that neurosis, repression affects the actual genital zones most of all and these transmit their susceptibility to stimulation to other erotogenic zones (normally neglected in adult life), which then behave exactly like genitals".[54] In the light of the theory this statement is at first sight very surprising indeed. On the other hand, anyone with clinical experience will have no difficulty in recognizing this phenomenon: most hysterical neuroses are triggered during or after a sexual-genital confrontation. Freud noted that psychoneuroses usually break out "as a result of the demands of normal sexual life".[55]

We seem to be entering a completely new domain which doesn't fit the totality of the picture so far. How can this repression of the genital be connected to the previous conceptualisations? Freud did not enter into this. As far as we are concerned, we think that the solution is rather simple. With this last repression, focusing on the genital, we have simply returned to the starting-point of the process of repression: the lack of a signifier for womanhood. Here, it is very important to understand that the development runs along the lines of a vicious circle. A woman starts at $S(\cancel{A})$, with primary repression; through the ensuing development discussed earlier she leaves passivity behind and elaborates the erogenous zones in an active-masculine way. The last erogenous zone, the phallic-clitoridal one, has to be repressed together with the accompanying active fantasies and to be exchanged for the passive-vaginal one. In other words: woman is once again confronted with $S(\cancel{A})$, and the first repression repeats itself, together with a renewed working-over of the previous erogenous zones "which then behave exactly like genitals". 'Genitals' has to be understood in the phallic sense, because this is the only gender with a proper signifier. Thus the pregenital is phallicized, the circle closed, and the flywheel keeps on turning.

During this study of repression, we have crossed, together with Freud, the turning of the century. In 1905 he caused a scandal with his *Three Essays*. As if this wasn't enough, he published a paper which had been languishing for five years in his drawer: *Fragment of an Analysis of a Case of Hysteria*, his first major case study. Written in 1900 and slightly retouched, it gives us a picture of Freud's clinical practice around 1905. How does the theory work?

CHAPTER 4.

DORA: THE LACK IN THE SYMBOLIC

Freud and knowledge

Normalisation of hysterical desire

On the second page of *Fragment of an Analysis of a Case of Hysteria* we learn that "hysterical symptoms are the expression of their most secret and repressed wishes". With Dora, we again find one of those elements which Freud had discovered right from the start: desire. Originally, it had been Freud's intention to entitle this case study *Dreams and Hysteria*. The dream as expression of what he called indestructible unconscious desire, hysteria as a variation on this theme: every hysterical symptom contains a double wish-fulfilment. Both are techniques of circumventing repression. But Freud changed his title to *Fragment of an Analysis of a Case of Hysteria*. By accident, or not? We shall see.[1]

Bruchstück, fragment, not complete. This was not only due to the fact that the patient left after three months of analysis, but also because Freud chose to present us only with a summary report of the results, not with the technical means that led to them. If he had done this, the paper would have been far too exhaustive. The reason for this is essentially the same as in *The Studies*: there is a substantial amount of material between the overdetermined, manifest symptoms and the latent, underlying desires - "the long thread of connections which spun itself out between a symptom of the illness and a pathogenic idea". A *Verneinung* makes it clear that Freud was tired of all that circumstantial material: "I need no longer apologize for the length". He even quoted Goethe's *Faust*: "Nicht Kunst und Wissenschaft allein, Geduld will bei dem Werke sein!" (Not Art and Science serve alone; Patience must in the work be shown). The same patience that was exhausted by his patients, as he admitted in his paper on Dostoyevsky.[2]

Conciseness is a characteristic feature of a master. Dream-analyses are exhaustive, far too exhaustive for Freud. He immediately warned against giving them too prominent a place with hysterical patients.[3] Moreover, in 1911, he thought it necessary to publish an explicitly didactic paper in which he cautioned his pupils not to dwell too long on dreams within a therapeutic framework. Hysterical patients tell too many dreams, they bring complete notebooks full of them to the analysis. The analyst, said Freud, can't keep up with it and the analysis itself deteriorates. Dream-reporting becomes a resistance of the patient who has discovered "that the method is unable to master what is presented in this manner".[4]

After all, the change of title isn't accidental at all. Freud set off once more on an agonizing road. His original, endless quest for the actual trauma, the real nucleus, repeated itself in the quest for unconscious desire.[5] On meeting the same story all over again and never finding a definite answer, he finally had to conclude that desire *in itself* was the essence of hysteria, independent of any content whatsoever: "Longing is the main character-trait of hysteria, just as a current anaesthesia (even though only potential) is its main symptom".[6]

One has to admit to the difficulty of it. Every time he managed to put a finger on the sore spot another trauma emerged, a new desire. With Dora he enforced a shortcut: she desired Mr. K, who had taken the place of her father, and that was that. That she didn't want to admit to this desire was precisely the proof that she *was* hysterical. Anyone who reacts with disgust at a sexual situation which is arousing in an ordinary manner *is* hysterical. Moreover, a normal girl ought to be able to handle such a situation by herself, without making a fuss.[7]

Obviously, Freud had taken a new position: that of the master.

The master figure

The meanderings of hysterical desire, always shifting, seem endless. Freud didn't go into the necessity of these shifts - the defensive imaginarisation of the basic lack - but was determined to put an end to them right from the start. The way in which he implemented his decision was devoid of any hesitation or doubt. Freud the seeker whom we met in *The Studies* and in the correspondence with Fliess, had been transformed into the Freud-who-knew.

Not surprisingly he began the case study with a bungled action which made his change of position crystal clear. What pseudonym should he choose for his patient? The name of 'Dora' compulsively insinuated itself.[8] And who was Dora? The servant girl of Freud's sister, who wasn't even allowed to keep her own name - Rosa - because that was the name of her mistress. The parts were clearly allotted from the start: handmaiden versus master. Being a hysteric Dora was very quick to see through the game. In the end, she settled her account with Freud - he was given a fortnight's notice, the period normally applicable to servants...[9] The roles were reversed.

Before this point, Freud appeared on the scene as a master. It is important to stress that this mastery did not concern the content of his interpretations, at least in the first instance. The mastery showed itself in another respect, more particularly in the style of his interpretations. Freud explained, taught, proved... He was the one who knew, he just had to convince his patients of the truth. The accent was put on the combat against resistances and the motives for illness. All means were justified; for example, he reveals that the contradictions in the patients' account were evidence "which I did not fail to use against her". The case study became one big demonstration. One example among many is Freud's explanation of the jewel case. It is a splendid didactic and dialectical exposé, with such close reasoning that Dora couldn't get a word in edgeways. All that was left her was to reject the whole thing. Years later, Freud warned against this form of analysis, one which explains and demonstrates; the patient has to find the unconscious contents by him/herself. Psychoanalysis cannot be reduced to a therapy of 'insight' or a pedantic and didactic means of instruction.[10]

The knowledge of the master: Oedipus Rex

Knowledge is a recurrent theme throughout the case study, and more particularly, knowledge about sex. This is remarkable, not only because of its frequency, but also because Freud commented upon it quite regularly without ever being able to account for it from his theoretical point of view. Thus we learn that Dora was suspicious of all members of the medical corpus; only the family doctor was exempt. The reason for this exception was soon discovered by Freud: the family doctor was the only one whom she was quite sure wouldn't be able to discover her secrets, to steal her knowledge.[11] Moreover, she had a special preference for knowledge and learning. She liked to attend 'conferences for ladies' and she dedicated herself to serious studies. She preferred not to marry, precisely because this might prove a stumbling-block on the road to learning.

Moreover, this knowledge wasn't neutral. As the case study continued, it became more and more clear that this knowledge concerned sexuality. Dora asked for advice on it from one of her governesses as well as from Mme K. This latter had given her the book by Mantegazza *Physiologie de l'Amour* - quite a scabrous text for that period. She wasted no time consulting medical encyclopaedias by herself. Curiously enough, Dora always tried to hide her sources of information from Freud. He had to play Sherlock Holmes in order to discover the role of the governess, of Mme K and of the encyclopaedias.[12]

All these things were written down by Freud, but he just didn't make use of them. Indeed, for him, the whole situation was crystal-clear. Dora was in love with Mr.K, but didn't want to admit it, not even to herself. She appealed to her father in order to save her endangered 'jewel case'. Nevertheless, all her symptoms proved her infatuation: she was aphonic in Mr. K's absence when he could only be reached by letter; she was the accomplice of Mme K and her father, the two lovers, as long as this relationship suited her; she was furious with Mr.K the moment he wanted only sex and not a proper relationship.

Freud's insight into this burlesque situation was backed up by an earlier hypothesis, transformed here into an observation and receiving the status of established knowledge. At the beginning of the case study, he mentioned 'the normal sexual attraction' between father and daughter on the one hand and mother and son on the other. Further on in the text the Oedipus theory was applied at length, while referring to a passage in *The Interpretation of Dreams*.[13] Dora was behaving as a jealous spouse by putting herself both in her mother's place and in that of Mme K. She was in love with her father. Freud called this a typical situation, becoming pathological only with those whose constitution is responsible for an extreme form of it. The supposition was that for a long time Dora had kept her love for her father on ice, so that it reappeared only reactively. As a hysteric, she couldn't deal with an ordinary sexually exciting situation involving Mr.K. The infantile love for the father served as an escape route to an infantile paradise.[14]

All this was nothing but a neurotic variant of Oedipus Rex. Freud had made a first draft of his Oedipus theory in *The Interpretation of Dreams*. Infantile sexual desire can be neatly divided: the first affectionate stirrings of the girl are aimed at the father, while the boy concentrates on the mother. Hence, the feelings of rivalry, and even the death wishes directed to the parent of the same sex. Freud talked about a 'natural trait', which is a very strange idea if we consider that it was Freud who would demonstrate in his *Three Essays* that there is scarcely anything 'natural' in the choice of an object... Three decades later, he radically revised his Oedipal theory, but at the time of Dora he was still convinced of this distribution of roles, which has since become classical.

The lack in the Symbolic

Imaginary duel: analysis of resistance

Earlier on we observed that it is not so much the content of Freud's interpretations which are open to criticism as their style. Incidentally, these critical reflections only become possible thanks to Freud himself, as we will see later on. We have already qualified this style as exegetical and aiming at conviction; the style of the master. This description is not sufficient as an argument since it does not fit into a structural context, so we have to go further.

The road travelled by Freud until then can be described as a working-over of the Real on the way to the imaginary. He had discovered the defensive imaginarisation of the traumatic Real with his patients, focused on what he called psychosexual desire. From 1900 onwards, he began to recognise the Oedipal structure in it, albeit with a certain flaw in his argument: *the Oedipal situation, which is a symbolic structuring, was initially understood by Freud as an Imaginary or dual elaboration.* Dora illustrates this very well. It is remarkable how the mother has disappeared from this case study; apart from mentioning her 'housewife psychosis', there is no trace of her in the case study. It means that the rest of the story lacks one of the three essential pillars and is reduced to an Imaginary trial of strength between two. Dora is in love with her father. In the transference Freud receives the position of the father, and even the position of Mr K at one point. Dora - her father; Dora - Mr. K.; Dora - Freud. One cannot get a relation which is more dual and the impasse is obvious. Hence, the only solution becomes an analysis of resistance, of which transference is thought to be only one particular form.

Analysis of resistance is a necessary preliminary stage before one can start with the analysis of the material. This is the traditional division which Lacan equates with the division between analysis of the Ego and the analysis of discourse. In his first seminar, he focuses on a case study by Anna Freud taking Ego psychology as his target. This critique can be transposed without any difficulty to the Freud who analysed Dora. Anna Freud floods her patient with interpretations relating her symptoms to her mother - with the analyst in the position of the mother in the transference, needless to say. Dora received interpretations which explained her symptoms by connecting them to an undeclared love for Mr. K., the substitute for her father, whose place was taken by Freud in the transference. In other words, each time we find two Egos in opposition to one another, then battle can commence. These interpretations are called dual by Lacan; they are wrong, if only on account of the mere fact that they imply a knowledge on the part of the analyst which he does not possess. Lacan's further comment makes it obvious that he has serious doubts about these classical Oedipal interpretations. He does not question the importance of the Oedipal in itself, his doubts concern the way it is used. Its application should focus on the unveiling of the Oedipus complex as a symbolic constellation "où se décide l'assomption du sexe", where the taking on of a sexual position is decided.[15] And this goes against any form of preconceived knowledge, against the position of the master retaining such knowledge.

Lacan recognised the first encounter with the master in the mirror stage, where the child meets the other as an alienating totality. The confrontation with this total master results in the depressive position, from which the child flees through an identification with the master, that is, the specular 'Urbild' or primary image which is a basis for the ulterior Ego-ideal.[16] The beauty of the case is that the same solution is applied in Ego psychology, which is just another confrontation with a master: identification with the analyst. The fact that this succeeds often enough and is not without therapeutic results, does not suffice to call it analysis. Dora refused this identification with the master in the only way that was left to her: she refused almost everything coming from Freud.

This specular relation repeated itself in what Lacan called the Imaginary stage of the Oedipus complex. Briefly put this is: 'either me or you'. This dual-imaginary aspect does not permit any alternative and contains the aggression of the mirror stage. It is only the symbolic structuring of the Oedipus complex which allows a possible escape from this deadly dual impasse.[17] The necessary precondition lies with the function of the real father and symbolic castration, but those were still a long way away for Freud. He hadn't yet discovered the function of the phallus, nor the symbolic import of the Oedipus complex. He would first have to give up his recently acquired position of master and go back to the position of pupil, taught by the hysteric.

Freud against Freud

These critical reflections on Freud are inspired by Freud himself. It is well known that he preferred the publication of what he himself considered to be failed, problematic case studies. The idea was that they are the only ones that can teach us anything as they oblige us to question our theory. At the end of Dora we find enough material and arguments to prepare the ground for the above critique. Freud was preparing himself for another dialectical step in the elaboration of his theory, this time on another level.

It is in this respect that he critically discussed his mistakes in the handling of the transference. During this discussion he introduced a certain nuance, the impact of which has not been fully noticed to this day: he confessed his ever-growing conviction that his main error consisted in not having observed that Dora cherished a 'gynaecophilic' love for Mme K.[18]

Gynaecophilic? How does this fit his contemporary conception of the Oedipus complex? Especially when he had to come to the bewildering conclusion that Dora was jealous of *her father* with respect to his relationship with Mme K. This doesn't fit the classical schema: 'father for the daughter, mother for the son'.[19] If that were the case, Dora should have been jealous of *Mme K* as the one who had taken away her father. Freud observed that it was in fact the other way round. Moreover, this situation was in itself already a repetition of an analogous one with a governess.

At first he tried to explain this by invoking an underlying homosexual current, something which was consistent with a neurotic predisposition. During the process of formulating his explanation, he introduced a remarkable nuance: "These masculine, or rather, *gynaecophilic* currents of feeling are to be regarded as typical of the unconscious erotic life of hysterical girls".[20] The concept of bisexuality had already been considered insufficient earlier on, and homosexuality didn't suffice either. It had to be 'gynaecophilic' love for the woman. Freud was on the brink of discovering the hysterical reaction to the lack of a proper signifier for The Woman. To the question "What is a woman?", the hysteric tries to find an answer in a third party, another woman. A *third*, because there is a man in between as a relay. In this case: Dora - father - Mme K. and: Dora - Mr K.- Mme K.

Mme K., with her 'beautiful white body', incarnated the hysterical question arising from the lacking signifier (cf. note 20). This was Dora's Oedipus complex as symbolic constellation through which she tried to reach her sexual identity. She looked for an answer to the question "What is a woman" in the mistress of her father. An identification with her father, in the position of Mme K.'s lover, is a standard hysterical answer. Let us stress the fact that here it is the father who is supposed to know.

Freud had observed all these things but he had been too late. His position as the one who knew did not give him a chance to see that the hysteric seeks knowledge as such. It is a search which makes her reject every normalising piece of knowledge. The reason for this refusal of established knowledge is not yet clear. What is clear is her refusal of the master and his knowledge. When Dora visited Freud, after the interruption of her analysis, she told him about a new symptom: a facial neuralgia. Freud saw through it: "When did it occur for the first time?" "A fortnight ago". Again the ubiquitous fortnight. Freud smiled and pointed to the fact that just a fortnight ago she had read something about him in the newspaper. A fortnight ago Freud was nominated as a professor at the University...

Refusal of the master, refusal of his knowledge. The hysteric has more in store. When Freud was enthusiastically analysing the second dream and inundating Dora with his knowledge, her only answer was: "Why, has anything so very remarkable come out?".[21] It is not *that* which the hysteric wants to know.

A lack in the Symbolic

In the case of Dora Freud began once more with the idea of a psychical trauma as a basis for hysteria, and again it became an endlessly deferred search.[22] In our previous chapter, we conceptualised the primary trauma as the lack of a signifier in the Symbolic for the female sex. Its working-over by way of a boundary signifier and fantasies gives rise to a defensive imaginarisation of this lack in the Symbolic. In this respect, all hysterical symptoms are nothing but an attempt to arrive at a sexual identity. The fundamental character of this lack means that each answer is insufficient, which gives rise to an endless series of answers.

With Dora, Freud diametrically opposed this 'interminable' aspect by fixing an end point. Dora longed for Mr K. who was a father substitute: all the rest was resistance. Nevertheless, this short-sighted vision did not alter the fact that the case study remains a marvellous illustration of the hysterical working-over in the Imaginary of the lack in the Symbolic.

The first dream concerned her mother's jewel case, for which the father did not want to sacrifice his children. Freud noted that the concomitant associations were hesitant and rather meagre,[23] and he remarked that this jewel case belonged to the most repressed material of the dream. His observation was right; they were the most intensely repressed, in the sense of a primal repression, that is, a staying behind in the Real, or in other words: $\cancel{A}$. The jewel case was Dora's attempt to formulate an Imaginary answer by way of a boundary signifier: S($\cancel{A}$); moreover, it was situated at a very particular point in the relationship between the parents. Freud did not go into this important association: that the father refused the jewel case of the mother and chose his children. At this point, it can already be seen that, at least for Dora, the core of the dream concerned *the question* of the female sexual position within the Oedipal constellation, while Freud put the emphasis on this element *as an answer*. So it wasn't a great surprise when Dora reacted with a refusal. Freud's answers continued to display a massive conviction: the *Frauenzimmer* (literally feminine room; figuratively: woman) that he lifted out of the associations could be 'opened' or 'closed' with a well-known 'key'.[24] Moreover, in German, the word '*Frauenzimmer*' has a definite pejorative ring. The same conviction returned with another signifier - the purse - so that he could conclude that a number of dream-elements (box, purse, jewel-case) stood for the female genitals.[25]

The defensively-intended imaginarisation became even more obvious with the second dream, which can be read integrally as an imaginarisation of the lack in the Symbolic; moreover, this was explicitly linked in the dream itself to the father as a *dead* father. This last aspect is not to be neglected.

The very first association was already meaningful: "Where is the 'Schachtel'?". *Schachtel* means 'box', but in German it again has a derogatory connotation: a woman! The question was addressed to the mother and associated with another dream-element: "She asked a good hundred times...". Here too, Freud neglected the question mark, and put all the emphasis on the answer. The box *was* a woman. The same was true of another question: "Where is the key?". The key *was* the penis. Freud called the continuation of the dream 'symbolic sexual geography'. The bridging words *Bahnhof* (railway station) and *Friedhof* (cemetery) led to *Vorhof* (mount of Venus); the *Nymphen* were the labia minora and the *dichter Wald* (dense forest) related to the pubic hair. The totality became a *Weibsbilde* (literally: image of a woman), again a derogatory expression for a woman...[26]

In our opinion, Dora's symptomatic productions can be understood as a drawn-out search for a signifier which simply wasn't there. In the last dream, even the medical encyclopaedia appeared as a work of reference, though only after the death of the father. The dead father and knowledge: we will meet this combination again later on. What we have already described for the dreams also holds good for the symptoms. Freud considered a hysterical symptom as the sexual activity of the patient.[27] To put it differently: every hysterical symptom is a realised fantasy.[28] These fantasies always treat of the same subject: what does a man want from a woman, how is she defined within the sexual relationship? The lack of a fundamental signifier results in the normal genital relationship being abandoned, repressed, because it is impossible.[29] Dora had to fall back on a pregenital relationship. In her fantasy, the 'rapport sexuel' took the form of an oral relationship.[30] The associated fantasies in turn determined the oral symptoms: tussis nervosa, aphonia, nausea, globus hystericus.

Dora was continuously looking for what a woman was or could be. The answers kept on shifting and were never really satisfying. She was certain of only one thing: what a woman was *not*, or was not allowed to be. Precisely at this point the derogatory connotations of femininity emerged: *Frauenzimmer, Schachtel, Weibsbild*. Her refusal of Freud's answers fitted in with another refusal: a woman was not allowed to be reduced to a mere object of masculine desire. This was very obvious in the case-study. At the exact moment when she recognized this reduction, she stopped the game in which, until then, she had played the role of a willing accomplice. When Mr K. uttered the famous: "Ich habe nichts an meiner Frau", ("You know I get nothing out of my wife"), the hysterical mise-en-scène fell to pieces.[31] Indeed, if Mme K. meant nothing to Mr K., how could it be possible for her, Dora, to mean anything to him, since she was precisely looking for her sexual identity with Mme K.? At the moment of Mr K.'s statement, she was reduced to a mere object of masculine desire. Her reaction was a slap in the face for Mr K., both literally and in the figurative sense. Moreover, she had already gone through the same experience much earlier on with a governess for whom she was only important as an entrée to her father (cf. note 31).

This behaviour of the hysteric is well known, it is part and parcel of the opprobrium which surrounds her. They are called *allumeuses*, inciting every man with their vamp-like behaviour, in order to enjoy their ensuing refusal all the better. The familiarity of this behaviour is no explanation in itself. The conceptualisation which we gave above, allows us to explain it in structural terms. When Dora was placed outside the chain which linked her to Mme K., off the path which led to a possible sexual identity, it implied her reduction to a mere object, to a passive object of the desire of the Other. This reduction threw her once more outside the Symbolic and closed the circle: as an object she was again confronted with the lack in the Other, that is, the exact point which she wished to avoid...

Moreover, for Dora the effect of this was painfully redoubled because of her last name. In his discussion of the second dream, Freud cursed the deontology which obliged him to be discreet; indeed, the disclosure of the name would show its equivocation and confirm the dream analysis. Since the paper by Rogow, we know the real name of Dora: Ida Bauer.[32] *Bauer* means farmer, but the word has an equivocal meaning which is not without importance in this respect. Indeed, *Bauer* also means bird cage. Ida, the bird cage. Ida, nothing more than a bird in a cage...

CHAPTER 5.

PSYCHOANALYSIS AS A CONSEQUENCE OF HYSTERIA: THE DISCOURSE OF THE MASTER

Reversal of positions

The case of Dora opened a new dimension in the field of hysteria, an opening which was also immediately closed in a movement typical of the Unconscious.

Freud was confronted with two things: the attitude of the hysteric with respect to the master and with respect to knowledge. He now had a ready answer for both of them: transference and resistance. The two concepts were narrowly associated at this time. Transference is merely a special form of resistance and analysis of transference is used to convince the patient and to break down the resistance once and for all. Hence, it is the knowledge of the therapist which is the determinant. Hysteria can be reduced to 'a not wanting to know'.

This implies nothing less than an actual reversal of positions. Originally, Freud was the one who was taught, who always took the position of the pupil. His attitude to Brücke, Meynert, Fleischl, Charcot and Breuer bore witness to this. The correspondence with Fliess can be typified as a relationship between a pupil who tries to satisfy his master by providing him with ever fresh material. The same testimony, though at another level, can be found in his first discoveries. His first conceptualisations derived from his hysterical patients because he let himself be taught by them. He had to give up hypnosis owing to constant failure - he did not incarnate the master in a convincing way. He was taught not to focus on symptoms by Emmy von N. In the end, there was not much left apart from passive listening. In our previous chapters, we have demonstrated how fruitful this listening method was. Freud's theories from this period had not seen their equal before him, and would afterwards be corrected only by himself. Hysteria, as an affliction of the womb, can with good reason be called the womb of psychoanalysis.

This changed around 1900. We have seen that Freud changed course 180° with Dora. What was the reason for this radical change? Serge André has pointed to a first important factor: it is the period in which Freud was emancipating himself from Fliess. His self-analysis allowed him to take his distance from a central figure of transference, one who was supposed to know. This last aspect should not be underestimated. As a probable paranoiac, Fliess incarnated absolute knowledge, and to this only two reactions are possible: either a radical refusal or a submissive adoration. This latter is typically hysterical, and it is the one Freud chose for five years. The turning point came with the death of his father, the first master. From that point onwards, his transference to Fliess changed: Freud started questioning his knowledge and instead put his own discoveries forward more and more. The master began to fail for him. Normally, the classical hysterical solution is the replacement of a failing master with a new one. Nevertheless, Israël has demonstrated that there is another possibility, less frequent and less well known: the hysteric can himself replace the failing master and assume his position. Israël does not apply this idea to Freud, but in our opinion this is exactly the case. Freud solved his 'little hysteria' in an elegant manner.

To crown it all, he received his first official recognition: "Public acclaim was immense. Congratulations and flowers were pouring in, as though the role of sexuality had suddenly been officially recognized by His Majesty, the significance of the dream certified by the Council of Ministers, and the necessity of a psychoanalytic therapy of hysteria carried by a two-thirds majority in Parliament." After four years of candidature, Freud was nominated as *Professor Extraordinarius*. We are not so naive as to assert that this nomination turned him into a master. It is rather the other way round: precisely because Freud had exchanged the hysterical position for that of the master, he could allow the necessary steps to be taken for his nomination, as mentioned in the same letter to Fliess.

Together with Julien Quackelbeen, we can recognize in this nomination a second important factor in accounting for Freud's change of position, one explicitly linked to hysteria. Freud's candidature had been buried for four years in the bottom drawer of an anti-Semitic ministry. He wrote to Fliess that he was tired of the "Martyrium" and that he was now resolute. For advice, he turned to Exner who told him to use personal influences. These took the shape of Frau Gomperz, a former patient of Freud, but her intervention with the minister risked failure. At the last moment, things changed for the best: "Then another force was applied. One of my patients, Marie Ferstel (...) heard of the matter and began to agitate on her own. She did not rest until she had made the minister's acquaintance at a party, ingratiated herself with him, and secured his promise through a mutual friend that he would give a professorship to her doctor, who had cured her."

Frau Gomperz, who was a former patient, a second patient and a mutual friend, also supported his nomination. Not only did hysteria procure Freud with a theory, it even helped him to obtain his professorial dignity. Freud had let himself be turned into a master by the hysteric; not only that but he himself believed it, at least for a certain period. Once this had been achieved, everything could be made ready for the second act: the hysteric would put the home-made master to the test. How strong was he, or in the words of Julien Quackelbeen, how much weakness could he tolerate?

The discourse of the master and the theory

This radical reversal is not without important effects for the theory. The very last paper by Freud which explicitly deals with hysteria dates from 1909. Does this imply that Freud had solved the riddle of hysteria? Far from it! During the course of his work, the emphasis shifted: the problem of hysteria had become the riddle of femininity. This did not happen overnight: the first paper on femininity came out only in 1925.

In between, Freud was successfully elaborating the position of the master. This had two effects. On the plus side was the international breakthrough which saw his theory propagated throughout Europe. But on the down side, the development of the theory itself came to a standstill. A master does not get taught, he teaches himself. It is the period of the didactic exposés. From 1904 to 1917, Freud published more than twenty of them. A separate discussion of those papers is scarcely necessary: with the exception of a few of them, they are all interchangeable. Each time, we find the same characteristics. Each one of them is a clear and self-contained unit in which psychoanalysis is presented as an established knowledge, with scarcely a hint of difficulties or incompleteness. Much later, Kuhn would state in his work on *The Structure of Scientific Revolutions* that the teaching of a science should never be guilty of using advanced literature. For if it is really advanced, it will question certain aspects of the established theory, thereby confusing the pupils. Freud felt this danger intuitively; if he stumbled upon a difficulty in these papers, he would always refer the solution to the future, while calling the papers themselves 'preliminary'.

Another constant was the periodical emission of historical overviews. In 1914, he wrote his *Geschichte* on the history of *Die Sache*, the psychoanalytic movement. The main preoccupation of this paper was to separate dissidents from the mainstream. Many of these smaller papers start with a historical introduction: from hypnosis through hypno-cathartic method to psychoanalysis proper. This is also typical: once one is convinced of having reached a satisfying result, one starts to produce historical overviews. Looking more closely at this 'satisfying result' we see that its core was always resistance and analysis of this resistance, even up to re-education! In this period, Freud became a real master in discerning and emasculating the resistances and antagonisms of his public, even before they themselves knew of them. Anyone reading only a couple of these papers has to admire what we will call Freud's 'didactic analyses of resistances'. Each and every time, he himself formulated the critique of his public - much better than they could have done themselves - and each time he took the edge off the argument.

In addition, Freud worked deliberately and explicitly with the aim of gaining acceptance and of protecting his work. The polemical presentation he held in 1895 for the *Wiener medizinisches Doktorenkollegium* was swept away in 1904 and replaced by an unctuous plea, in which he stated that his theory was "generally known and understood" by the contemporary public. Further on in the paper, we learn that he only wanted to present the reader with an account of the technique, as this is still too often confused with other techniques, and that a specific training was necessary in any case. This aspect of transmission remained a constant preoccupation. He wrote a number of *Ratschläge zur Technik der Psychoanalyse* (Recommendations on the Technique of Psychoanalysis) and in 1910 he warned against what he called 'wild' psychoanalysis.

Another aspect is a group of papers which he used for the 'propagation of his theory'. A typical example is art. Initially, Freud used works of art - especially literary ones - in order to find a confirmation of his theory; then, it was exactly the other way round: he submitted works of art to his method. The field of application kept on expanding: from religion to law, and from enlightenment and education to philosophy and linguistics. In 1913, he presented a summary of all these possibilities in *Scientia*, a semi-popular scientific periodical.

On the brink of World War One Freud was almost sixty years old. His health was bad. The generalised 'Weltuntergang-' (End of the world-) fantasies in declining Austria after the first defeats were not very stimulating either. Fliess' previous calculations about his day of death popped up again; Freud was convinced that his days were numbered. Directly related to the idea of his death, he conceived the idea of writing one exhaustive synthesis of his entire theory. It had to be a compilation, consisting of twelve parts, an all-embracing summary. He frantically started writing on 15th March 1915, and the whole thing was finished by the end of August. Of the twelve essays thus produced, seven were destroyed by Freud himself. The five remaining ones are known under the name of *Metapsychological writings*, and they are anything but a summary of the previous theory, on the contrary.

Instead of a failed summary, we get another synthesis: the famous *Introductory Lectures on Psychoanalysis*. Freud announced in advance that the four semesters from 1915 to 1917 were to be the last ones he would teach at the university. The book turned out to be a real bestseller: during his lifetime it was translated into sixteen different languages, even in Chinese! It is still one of the most sold and most read of Freud's books. Remarkably enough, he himself judged the book rather unimportant; in his introduction to it, his tone is rather deprecating, *because the book is only a summary and does not bring anything new*.

Freud destroyed more than half of his 'summary', and the other half wasn't a summary at all. Freud was deprecating about the ever popular *Introductory Lectures*. What was going on? Nothing other than that Freud was abandoning the position of the master, and was starting to discover again. A whole new theory was waiting, one which would alter the previous one to its very core. Once again, hysteria played a central role, but this time in another guise: she appeared on the stage as a woman.

The pupils and the master

Unfortunately, by then the cow was sold and the milk had been drunk. Psychoanalysis spread in the form of a textbook psychology. The extremely simple, not to say levelling *Five Lectures on Psychoanalysis* conquered the world. The same was true for the *Introductory Lectures*, even if they were rather less simple. It was in English that they conquered the world, and this was not without certain consequences. Quite a number of selective compilations of Freud's didactic/technical writings from the above mentioned series also appeared in print in several languages. Their didactic qualities caused them to enter virtually every human sciences department. This was obviously not enough, because in 1924, Harvard University asked Ernest Jones to make a summary of Freud's work, preferably reduced to one ninth and with a clear introduction! Freud's reaction was pre-monitory: "Fundamentally the whole idea is very repellent to me, typically American. One can be sure that when such a 'source book' exists no American will ever touch the original writings. But perhaps he will not do so anyhow, and will go on getting his information from the muddy popular sources." From this point on, we are confronted with a very peculiar cultural phenomenon. Psychology, under which psychoanalysis is classified, has to be comprehensible to the man in the street. If a layman reads a book about chemistry, electronics or whatever, and doesn't understand one bit of it, he considers this to be normal. But if the book is about psychology, then everybody thinks it's a downright scandal.

In his *Discours de la méthode*, Descartes produced a poetically accurate description of the pupil: "They are just like the tendrils of an ivy, never reaching higher than their supporting tree; indeed, often they start their way downwards again, long before they have reached the top ....". To which we should add that in Freud's case, the tree was only half-grown when the ivy started on its way down.

Post-Freudianism is what I should like to call *Vorlesungspsychoanalyse*, the psychoanalysis of Introductory Lectures. The theory it refers to is limited to the last phase of Freud's first period. Of course certain words from his later period were used - especially the handy Ich-Es-Über-Ich machinery - but the theory as such was not changed. In its totality, it became more and more of a caricature, a hybrid creature which survived itself by means of arguments from authority: "Freud has said that...". The dialectic between treatment and theory was completely lost, the treatment became more and more a confrontation between two Egos. The analyst was the one who knew, and, being the latest specialist in town, he would apply it wherever he could. It was the period of the Great Understanding. They understood everything and discovered nothing. There was - besides Freud - only one exception: Theodor Reik with his paper *Der Mut nicht zu verstehen* ("The courage not to understand"), as a lonely precursor of the later Lacanian *Gardez-vous de comprendre*, beware of understanding. This initial furor interpretandi - in the thirties, everything elongated is a phallus, and everything round and open is a vagina - made room slowly but surely for a safe silence. Safe, because untouchable. After the Second World War, the emptiness in European analytic circles caused by the exodus was very quickly filled. Together with the Marshall plan, popcorn and Coca-cola, Ego psychology appeared. Freudian psychoanalysis - and this is unfortunately not a pleonasm - had disappeared.

And what about hysteria? What had happened to the pathology that had nourished psychoanalysis?

THE POST-FREUDIANS AND THE DISCOURSE OF THE UNIVERSITY

Passio hysterica unum nomen est, varia
tamen et innumera accidentia sub se
comprehendit (Galenus).

CHAPTER 6.

THE GREAT CONFUSION

In search of hysteria

From the 1920s onwards both psychoanalytic and psychiatric publications which were analytically inspired multiplied with dazzling
speed. Unfortunately, this increase was not a guarantee of quality. One
is confronted in them with the old question that Freud started with:
how can hysteria actually be defined?[1] The answers from this point on
were formulated in a strange dialect, a combination of psychoanalytic,
psychiatric and neurological language. Banished from their original
context, these concepts lost their accuracy and often deteriorated into
meaningless stereotypes. If one reads the bulk of these papers, one cannot but wonder at the very divergent and often contradictory descriptions and statements. There is no symptom which cannot be produced
at one time or another during the hysteric's illness, to the exasperation
of those who want to catch the essence or the core of hysteria in one
description.

This frustration produced two reactions. Either, there was the idea
that the contemporary studies didn't go far enough and that the final,
exhaustive definition would come later. Or - and at a given time this
was very fashionable - the concept was thrown overboard and people
loudly proclaimed that hysteria just didn't exist.

Both reactions, although seemingly contradictory, were fundamentally related. Both of them situated the 'error' in the *object* of study. In
the first case, that object was a difficult one, in the sense of being complex and heterogeneous. In the second case, one went a step further by
proclaiming that hysteria did not exist as a separate entity, precisely
because of that heterogeneity.

The *method* itself did not receive any attention at all. The ideal of
Linnaeus was taken for granted, without ever questioning whether the
object of description could be reached. The constant failure of this
attempt became a stimulus either to an intensification of research or to
negative value judgements. Freud, on the contrary, came to the conclusion that the purely descriptive method could very well be a failure
in itself. He had seen Charcot at work with his attempts at classifica-
tion: real hysteria had already been divided into several types ("les
types"), and then there were those mitigated forms ("les formes

frustes") which did not possess all the typical features. Freud compared Charcot's nosography not only with Cuvier's systematic nomination of fauna and flora, but also with Adam, who received from God Almighty the instruction to name all creatures great and small in Paradise! As early as 1893, he noted: "But the exclusively nosographical approach adopted at the School of the Salpêtrière was not suitable for a purely psychological subject".[2]

Almost a hundred years later, this idea has still not sunk in. In this respect, the studies show a distressing heterogeneity which we could set out as follows.

1. Researchers wanting to catch hysteria *in itself.*

This had already been true of Charcot. The failure of this approach usually entails the conclusion that hysteria does not exist. Exemplary for this first group is Slater. With three major successive studies, he not only came to the conclusion that hysteria didn't exist but also that, from a medical point of view, so-called hysterical symptoms testified to the good health of the patient as they confirmed the absence of afflictions which were organically determined! He felt that the methodological purity of his design ought to be a convincing guarantee for his final conclusion: "The diagnosis of 'hysteria' is a disguise for ignorance and a fertile source of clinical error. It is in fact not only a delusion but also a snare".[3] This methodological purity consisted in the search for a genetic background by studying twins, followed up by studies into the persistence of potential organic bases. All this was carried through by purposely ignoring psychical symptoms: the cause had to be found in the organic realm.

A comparable study by Whitlock concluded that the organic factor - dysfunction of the brain - was central, after having very carefully selected his population in such a way that this conclusion became inevitable: "Although a proportion of cases to be described showed features of the so-called 'hysterical' or 'histrionic' personality, no cases whose sole disturbance was in the realm of personality have been included".[4] His result - purely descriptive and very unsatisfactory - led again to the above mentioned conclusion.

Still within this first group, but diametrically opposed to its first representatives, we find those researchers who effectively did discover *hysteria.* Thus Gachnochi and Pratt looked at hysteria within the walls of the psychiatric clinic, and they found a more or less consistent clinical picture, after very carefully excluding all patients with a physical-traumatic aetiology - just as Whitlock did, albeit the other way around.[5] Perley and Guze occupied themselves with a follow-up study inspired by Slater. Their diagnostic criteria are as severe as they are arbitrary: they require the presence of at least twenty-five symptoms distributed over at least nine out of ten preconceived categories. The conclusion of their study is exactly the opposite of the one by Slater: not only does hysteria exist, it is also a consistent and constant syndrome which can be understood in terms of clinical diagnostic descriptions. Unfortunately, they had to take into account some types who seemed to be hysterical but who were, according to their criteria, not *really* hysterical.[6] We are back with Charcot and his *formes frustes*. Lewis also conducted a follow-up study concerning the constancy of the diagnosis, and he also concluded - against Slater - that there was a constant, on condition that hysteria was considered in terms of 'reaction'. A pleasant feature of his paper is that, having taken a historical distance in his introduction, he demonstrated that both contradictory conceptions - hysteria as *the* neurosis versus hysteria as non-existent - alternate in the history of psychiatry. In this respect, he quotes fifteen authoritative authors for the period 1874 - 1966.[7]

2. Studies which divide hysteria descriptively into smaller entities.

Where the first group often gives an impression of caricature because of its extreme position, the second group is more balanced. The fact that they do not begin by excluding the diversity of the research population results in diverging descriptions of hysteria. Hence there is a division into smaller, clinically observable entities, which are supposed to be uniform and constant. The net result is a decrease in the number of diagnoses of hysteria: indeed, one is now supposed to have more subtle criteria at one's disposal, instead of the old cruder labels.[8] A typical example is the DSM-III approach in which hysteria is distributed over many categories: conversion, dissociation, personality and psychosis. Only perversion is missing.[9]

Unfortunately, the authors do not agree with each other about the definitive division... Chodoff and Lyons talk about a 'conversion reaction', 'hysterical personality' and 'hysterical personality with conversion reactions'.[10] Trillat concludes simply that hysteria is diverse, without bothering to detail this diversity.[11] Lazare, Klerman and Armor propose three different groups of personality traits, based on an exhaustive study of the literature. When they apply a factor analysis, the result is a mixture of the 'oral' and the 'hysterical' personality types.[12] Zetzel sees four groups, starting with the 'true, good hysteric'(!) and ending, not with the truly bad one, but with the 'pseudo-

Oedipal and pseudo-genital hysteric'.[13] Kernberg[14] pleads for the differentiation between a 'hysterical character' versus 'an infantile personality', Easser and Lesser[15] for 'true hysteria' versus 'hysteroid', while Sugarman[16] sticks to 'hysterical personality' versus 'infantile personality'. More recently, the concept of 'hysterical psychosis' is taken up again by Maleval, but this author has to be situated in the next group.[17]

The procedure of this second group also results in the disappearance of hysteria, this time by distributing it over smaller groups. The title of Satow's paper is proverbial: "Where has all the hysteria gone?". Moreover, she regrets that Freud based his diagnosis solely on descriptive criteria (!), and she is very happy that contemporary analysts got rid of that and base their diagnoses on the "level of object relations, ego-functioning and anxiety"!

3. The structural-dynamic approach.

In opposition to the two previous ones, this group did hear Freud's message - that it was necessary to change the nosographic method. Following in the footsteps of Freud and Lacan, we propose a structural-dynamic approach to get a grip on clinical diversity.

Questioning the researchers

Our critical review shows the necessity of paying more attention to the method. One of the most fundamental mistakes in a descriptive approach is that it either neglects the position and the influence of the observer, or considers it as irrelevant. The same is true of those methods in the anatomico-pathological line of thought which are pseudo-explanatory, such as: "This psychological syndrome can be explained by a stasis of the libidinal organisation during the oral stage". We refer the reader to the critique formulated by Clavreul.[18] It is typical of such an approach that one can take the position of the Know-all but that one can't do anything at all with this knowledge in the clinic. Just like Adam-Charcot, one has only given names.

The great Know-All is an expression which already shows something of the subjectivity involved. This was basically Freud's aim when he used the concepts of Unconscious, Oedipus and (counter-)transference. Lacan follows suit when he recognises the position of the subject and his desire at the heart of any science.[19] Was it not Hegel who wrote that science is the making human of the world? This conception transforms the position of the questioner into the position of the one who has to be questioned. But the experience of the psychoanalytic hall of mirrors is more difficult and much more threatening than the experience of the nosographic hall of horrors.

Let us now return to our starting-point, the post-Freudian papers on hysteria. The conclusion is threefold.

1. There is no agreement concerning the so-called essence of hysteria. Contradictory statements abound.

2. A very striking phenomenon is that the authors, in spite of their position as objective observers, almost always fall back on moral value judgements. And far from being uniform, these judgements are as diverse as the descriptions of symptoms! Going from the very positive, the intelligent and attractive hysteric - today called a *jarvis*, as the epithet *hysterical* sounds too negative - to the very negative and disgusting hysteric. All shades and combinations in between are possible. Sometimes it is almost impossible not to get the impression of reading a plea for or against somebody, addressed to an Imaginary judge from whom one expects the final verdict... We could illustrate this abundantly with various quotations, but this would usurp quite a lot of space. Therefore, we refer the reader to the above-mentioned diversity in the second group, one which could be reduced almost every time to an opposition between 'good, real, adult' versus 'bad, fake, infantile'. However, we do not want to withhold one particular quotation. Based on an exhaustive study of the relevant literature, Chodoff and Lyons concluded with the following group of traits as a common denominator of the hysterical personality:

1. Egoism, vanity, Egocentrism, self-centred, self-indulgent.

2. Exhibitionism, dramatisation, lying, exaggeration, play acting, histrionic behaviour, mendacity, pseudologia phantastica, dramatic self-display, centre of attention, simulation.

3. Unbridled display of affects, labile affectivity, irrational emotional outbursts, emotional capriciousness, deficient emotional control, profusion of affects, volatile and labile emotions, excitability, inconsistency of reactions.

4. Emotional shallowness, fraudulent and shallow affects, go through the motions of feeling.

5. Lasciviousness, sexualisation of all non-sexual relations, obvious sexual behavior, coquetry, provocative.

6. Sexual frigidity, intense fear of sexuality, failure of sex impulse to develop towards natural goal, sexually immature, sexual apprehensiveness.[20]

This objective result of modern science brings to mind an older list, one made up without any research at all; in 1450, Antoninus of Florence drew up the *Alphabet of female vices*:

a. Avidum animal (greedy animal)
b. Bestiale baratrum (beastly abyss)
c. Concupiscentia carnis (concupiscence of the flesh)
d. Dolorosum duellum (painful duality)
e. Aestuans aestus (passionate passion)
f. Falsa fides (fake faithfulness)
g. Garrulum guttur (garrulous tongue)
h. Herrinys armata (armed fury)
i. Invidiosus ignis (flaming envy)
k. Kalumniarum chaos (source of gossip)
l. Lepida lues (seductive plague)
m. Monstruosum mendacium (monstrous lie)
n. Naufragii nutrix (cause of shipwreck)
o. Opifex odii (instigator of hate)
p. Prima peccatrix (first sinner)
q. Quietis quassatio (firebrand)
r. Ruina regnorum (ruin of reigns)
s. Silva superbiae (forest of haughtiness)
t. Truculenta tyrannis (gruesome tyranny)
v. Vanitas vanitatum (vanity of vanities)
x. Xantia Xersis (ruthless fanaticism)
y. Ymago idolorum (image of idols)
z. Zelus zelotypus (jealous envy)

This is the alphabet used by Jacop Sprenger and Heinrich Institoris in 1539 in their *Malleus Maleficarum*, better known as the witch's hammer.[21] Chodoff and Lyons have strange predecessors...

3. A third point is a historical one. It is remarkable that, throughout history, hysteria has always manifested itself in relation to persons holding a high office. The shifts in this respect were convincingly mapped by Clavreul and Wajeman.[22] On the whole, this function was initially taken by the physician-priest (Aesculapios). Later on, it was taken solely by the physician (Hippocrates). In Western Europe, it was the father confessor, and even the father/priest as member of the Inquisition. During the period of classicism, the accent shifted to the medical man. Much later on, it became the physician-psychiatrist, embodied in the concept of neuro-psychiatry. Nowadays, it is the psychiatrist-psychotherapist, under whose banner the analyst can also be

found - such is the diluting effect of post-Freudianism that the idea of 'eclecticism' furnishes a welcome lifebuoy. Of course, this evolution is not an exclusive one: Lourdes still has its magnetic power and, according to the estimates by Israël and Shoenberg, half of all hysterics are still treated by G.P.s.[23]

Let us take a closer look at these three points, in reverse order, focusing on the position and impact of the researchers.

The third one of the series has a certain consequence: as the above-mentioned high office changed, so did the way one looked at hysteria. This has been commented on by several authors.[24] Summarising with Shoenberg, we can state that the specific relationship between hysteric and therapist determines the specific perception of hysteria. A physician will try to formulate a diagnosis in terms of physio- or neuropathology - cf. Slater and Whitlock. He will define the disease in this way and he will attune his treatment to that definition. A psychotherapist interprets the anamnesis in terms of psychogenesis, if necessary in terms of a 'good' and a 'bad' self - cf. Gachnochi and Pratt. The medieval exorcist tried to exorcise the bad spirit: the soul is possessed, but underneath there remains the normal person.

We could even go further than that: the relation between therapist (whether priest, physician or psychotherapist) and patient does not only determine the way in which one looks at the ailment, it even determines the form it takes. One look at the evolution of the phenomenon makes this clear. First of all, from a historical point of view, where have all the saints and all the possessed gone? Once in a while an isolated occurrence is reported, but the good old epidemics of sacred possession are gone. Where has the dramatic 'grande hystérie' of Charcot gone? Where are the famous vapours that overwhelmed the previous century? And - closer to us - contemporary analysts are beginning to worry about the fact that they don't see as many conversion symptoms as they used to. Secondly, on a smaller scale: Shoenberg has demonstrated with two case studies that the nature of the symptoms (medical, psychical) can alter according to whether the therapist takes a medical or psychotherapeutic attitude.[25] Moreover, this can also be perfectly well applied to Dora. Twenty years after her analysis with Freud, she consulted F. Deutsch in America; during her first visit, she complained about loss of hearing, dizziness, an indifferent husband who was probably unfaithful, an ungrateful son, and on top of everything else, sleeplessness. At the second consultation, all these complaints had disappeared. Dora had discovered that Deutsch was one of Freud's intimates, and on the spot, her symptoms changed into analytic ones: she complained about her unhappy childhood, the lack of love, her mother's obsessions that caused her identical constipation, her vaginal secretions and premenstrual pains. Deutsch concluded that Dora was one of the most repulsive hysterics he had ever seen.[26]

We seem to have shifted inconspicuously to our second point: the moral value judgement. We are not the first ones to suppose that hysteria seems to have evolved together with culture. The evidence is that hysteria produces symptoms which are in tune with the cultural and familial context. This brings us to the idea of the bad, hypocritical hysteric simulating symptoms in a theatrical, dramatic way. In medieval times, she was either referred to the stake, or she received the holy nimbus; nowadays, she is just pointed at. It becomes all the more interesting if we ask at whose behest the hysteric produces her symptoms. It takes a minimum of two in order to stage a hysteria, says Israël.[27] Each demand brings forth the offer of a supply, and there is no reason why this thesis should be restricted to economics. Charcot demonstrated 'his' hysterics to an attentive public. Under hypnosis, he evoked all the stages of the great hysterical attack, in the precise way he had described them. Moreover, on the wall, there hung a beautiful lithograph on which one could see... Charcot with his patient during a demonstration. Blanche Wittmann, his favoured patient - who, being an out-patient, was not hospitalised - had imprinted on her *carte de visite*: "Première patiente du professeur Charcot". Who was demonstrating whom in this case?[28]

"But the hysteric is very susceptible to suggestion! We all know that." This is supposed to be the ultimate explanation for the diversity of hysterical symptoms. In one way or another, at different times in history, different therapists are supposed to have suggested to 'their' patients different patterns of symptoms. The exorcists would just have elicited demoniacal powers in their credulous women, just like Charcot was able to elicit whatever symptom of paralysis he chose. The contemporary disappearance of a symptomatology once so diverse would then simply be proof of the rather meagre powers of imagination of our therapists. In this respect, the hysteric is not the hypocritical creature who makes believe but, on the contrary, the suggestible, credulous and weak creature without any personality of her own - certainly not a real patient.

But if the whole thing can be reduced to a matter of hypnosis, then why can't the therapist simply suggest to them that they be sane? And where do the flood of theories come from, at the basis of which one invariably finds hysteria? This last point is a very interesting one. There is no phenomenon which has given rise to so many different theories as hysteria. Of course, we are tempted to think with amused condescension of those ancient theories about migration of the womb, vapours and so on. But if we have a look at contemporary theories, we find a no less widely divergent range of theories, suppositions and therapeutic approaches. Let it be noted in passing that, at the end of his career, Charcot made a conceptual turn usually passed over in silence and which, in fact, obliterated all his previous ideas; that it was Anna O. who called Breuer's procedure a 'talking cure'; that the division between a 'good' and a 'bad' self came from the same Anna O; that Justine, Janet's patient, hallucinated situations in which she asked him for advice, gave herself the answer and thereby corrected his previous real suggestions; last but not least, that it was Emmy von N. who introduced free association for Freud. Who is the suggestible one?[29]

In the meantime, we have arrived back at our first point: hysteria is not only a source of a wide range of varying theories, it is also the main cause of their failure, precisely because of its ungraspability. Theories and therapies come and go, but the hysteric still stands (by) her man... Michel Foucault demonstrated that at the end of classicism, the entire conceptualisation concerning 'la folie et la déraison' was completely undermined by what would later be termed 'les maladies nerveuses', i.e. hysteria and hypochondria.[30] He also mentions that this provided a new impetus for moral value judgements.

Taking a closer look we discover yet another remarkable fact: not only are there many different theories, there is also a remarkable discrepancy between a more or less coherently elaborated theory on the one hand, and, on the other hand, the concomitant praxis. Wajeman calls this the gap between 'le médecin comme savant' and 'le médecin comme guérisseur', the scientist versus the healer. Whatever the scope of the theory may be, the treatment results, in most cases, in a code of conduct that holds as much - if not more - for the therapist as for the patient. Let us take two examples. In the midst of the previous century, R.B. Carter had elaborated a theory of hysteria in which the later Freudian theory, focused on the repression of sexual contents, was already present in essence. Still, at the core of his therapeutic chapter one finds only the 'moral treatment', with an exhaustive description of the way in which the physician has to behave. Here is a quotation: "The practitioner will be called upon to place unwavering trust in his own professional opinion and to act upon his faith: to express himself with such determination as to show the hopelessness of a contest with him..." [31] The rest of the chapter focuses on the unmasking of the patient, on the process of convincing her that one sees through her, even on the idea of blackmailing her by threatening to tell her family about the unmasking. A second example can be found in Wajeman, who focuses on Gilles de la Tourette. He also conducts a lengthy discussion into the qualities the physician must display in order to acquire 'une autorité morale' with the patients: "All efforts of the physician (...) should be aimed at convincing the patient of one's competence in these matters" (see note 22). The moral authority achieved thereby has to result in the identification of the patient with the good example set by the doctor: identification with the ideal.

These two examples are pre-Freudian ones. The third example is nothing other than post-Freudian Ego psychology itself. The discrepancy between theory and practice is just as obvious here, albeit with one important exception. The physician of the nineteenth century kept theory and practice clearly apart. In matters of 'treatment' he did not hesitate to take draconian measures if necessary. In order to stop a hysterical epidemic in a nunnery, Boerhaave gathered all the patients, had a number of iron instruments heated up till they were red-hot before their eyes, and issued the laconic statement that "the first one to have an attack would have the posterior part of the spine cauterized". Everybody was cured on the spot.[32] In the Twentieth century, the branding irons are superfluous: the theory itself has taken its place. The therapist does not use his theoretical framework as an instrument, but as an argument of authority to which the patient has to adapt himself in order to reach social conformity. The therapeutic aim is what we have already described above, albeit under another name: identification with the Ego of the analyst. This can also be seen with Freud during a certain period: his therapeutic effectiveness was at its greatest during his uncertain and questing years, and at its least effective once he was promoted to the position of great Knower. We can add to this that therapeutic strength is precisely situated in the continuous questioning of one's own method, one's own theory, of oneself. The clinico-therapeutic effectiveness of Reik's *Der Mut nicht zu verstehen*, of Lacan's *Gardez-vous de comprendre* is thereby illustrated, but not yet explained. It would seem that there is a fundamental relation between hysteria and knowledge.

What, then, is the basis of therapeutic success or failure if we restrict ourselves to this 'traitement moral', to these codes of conduct? It is the therapist who incarnates an authority concerning knowledge, an incarnation of which he himself has to be convinced first of all, and of which, secondly, he has to convince his hysterical patient: "Ce n'est que par la soumission de l'hystérique que le médecin peut prendre la mesure de sa puissance".[33] It is this conviction which determines the success or failure of the therapy, and so, of the theory. The diversity of theories already makes us guess to whom 'the hopelessness of a contest' applies...

Hysteria within the sexual relationship

In these last pages of our study, a certain fact has slowly but surely emerged, one often remarked upon but seldom discussed. Hysteria shows itself pre-eminently in the field of tension between man and woman. The essential link between hysteria and a socially important high office held by a *man*, the moral value judgements, the militant, even warlike, nature of the treatment (it used to be called thus, but since the spread of democracy, such terms belong to an oldspeak and are forbidden), the fact that transference was not only discovered with this neurosis but even promoted to the dignity of a therapeutic instrument, all these things point in the same direction. We had a first tell-tale sign of it when we met Lacan's expression "There is no sexual rapport". We hope to illustrate this further.

For centuries, men and women have been playing a game with each other. Hysteria is one variation of it, with the rule that neither side is allowed to recognise either the implied subjectivity or the associated pleasure. It does not concern subjectivity in the sense of what can be experienced through introspection, but as a trans-individual given and as a part of the Unconscious. The expression "The Unconscious as discourse of the Other" has to be taken literally. It evolves in an individual through an intersubjective history, in which the Oedipal square is the central feature, precisely because it is there that sexual identity will be determined. That is why the core has to be looked for in the original family, in the family romance. A play, or more correctly, a shadow play, is staged between a number of players, but also over their heads. We could call it 'the failing master', or 'the disappointed spouse'.

At this point cultural critics could mount the rostrum and voice the following remark: "Why do you restrict this to the family? It is culture, society, that is at fault. That is where a woman is repressed, within the

confines of a phallocratic male society. The family is just an exponent
of that. It is all very clear: hysteria was at its peak precisely during the
extremely repressive Victorian period." Let us not be too hasty. It is
true that at the end of the previous century, women had almost no
opportunities for intellectual and sexual education. Indeed, the ladies
of the higher bourgeoisie suffered from what Emmy von N. very aptly
called 'l'affreuse mélancholie du bien-être'. Spoiled, pampered and
kept ignorant by their husbands, they could permit themselves their
hysterical attacks. Moreover, the doctor's consulting room was an out-
let for their frustrated developmental possibilities. The fact that it was
precisely the physician who was their main confidant was not without
an effect on the nature of their symptoms: paralyses, anaesthesias,
paresthesias etc. And what about Charcot's patients in the Salpêtrière?
Women and men from the lower social strata, about whom anything
could be said, except that they suffered from this 'affreuse mélancholie
du bien-être'? The last remaining argument is of course sexual and
intellectual repression. One could argue that this last one is especially
outdated, that nowadays within Western society there is no reason for
complaint in this respect. Is there? Which therapist hasn't already
heard the following complaint: "If only I had *not* studied, if only I had
stayed ignorant and illiterate, then I would never have had all these
problems!". Time for Rousseau to come on stage, hand in hand with 'le
bon sauvage'.

Rich or poor, working or idle, intellectually developed or not, none
of it matters very much. And repressive phallocracy, the hobbyhorse
of the feminists? Opinions differ greatly on this score. One group holds
that, owing to the so-called sexual revolution, this repression has
almost disappeared. They think they find an argument for this in the
fact that contemporary hysterical symptoms are rather viewed as the
expression of repressed aggression. In their opinion, it is the aggressive
drive which is too repressed. Would it be necessary, then, to have an
aggressive revolution as well? Without pursuing this line of thought
any further, we only wish to remark that for Freud, each manifestation
of a drive is always mixed, due to the fundamental *Triebmischung*: a
fusion between aggressive (i.e. death) and erotic (i.e. life) drives.
Others, among them Israël, have serious doubts about a revolution
whose aim is to obliterate the difference between man and woman.[34]
In this, they recognise the very negation of difference itself, while it is
especially this difference which is literally and figuratively fruitful.

It seems that cultural explanations don't explain much. Let us return to the clinic. The hysteric comes to a man who is supposed to know: a priest, physician, psy-specialist. In short: a master. The ensuing relationship is one which focuses on the authority of knowledge; the content of it is less important than its power of persuasion. The ancient Egyptians had understood this very thoroughly: in order to get the wandering womb back to its right position, they melted a perfumed waxen statue of an ibis under the vagina. They did not simply count on the operational effect of the pleasant odours; the ibis bird was the symbol of Thot, one of their major gods. And who was this Thot? The *masculine* god of *wisdom*, inventor of script and guardian of the holy books of learning. The medieval hysteric had to be content with much less subtle therapeutic practices: "that a carrot-shaped root of lovage, cooked and smeared with axle grease, be tied under the navel".[35]

Our contemporary therapists can't fall back on the same degree of authority as their predecessors. The patient presents her symptoms, her complaint. A physician understands them in terms of signs, referring to something, not to somebody, to the person. He looks for this illness, but does not find anything definite: 'functional disturbances without any obvious organic basis'. Exit this master, and in comes the next. A psy-specialist interprets the symptoms as consequences of an infantile trauma, an oral fixation etc. The symptoms are still signs which refer to something else and, depending on the theory, this something can be almost anything. But the therapy fails yet again, in spite of the theory. And if it succeeds it is often enough in spite of the theory, as if it were a miracle and without any theoretical predictability. One doesn't get any further than naming or labelling. We already mentioned Adam as the first namer. Wasn't he also the one who received the apple?

The knowledge at stake is an 'objective' knowledge. The subject is excluded beforehand, in a silent complicity between therapist and patient. The theory has to focus on objectively observable phenomena which refer to this knowledge: a syndrome, organically or psychologically determined as traumatic. That the 'subject' of the patient could be involved is already difficult to imagine, but the therapist! The therapist can't possibly have any lack whatsoever, his moral code of conduct takes care of that. Yet the fact that he should not display any lack under any circumstances - doesn't this in itself prove that there is a lack? This is the core of hysteria: *the Other, lack and the resulting desire.*

This allows us to lift the first veil from the sexual relationship as it appears in hysteria. Sexual relationships have to be understood here as the relationship between the two sexes. The hysteric is in search of a certain kind of man, in relation to whom she can define herself as a woman. The man seems to fail in his assigned role every time he dares to assume the position of master. The consequence of his impotence is that the hysteric also fails to signify herself as a woman. The signifiers which she has received from the specialist do not suffice to give her a sexual identity so that a relationship becomes all the more impossible.

Of course, our current and ubiquitous 'psychologising' has a ready-made explanation. As a child, the hysteric would have had a weak father. This continuous trauma explains the never ending search for strong men. Once she has gained this 'insight' as a patient during her therapy, her search will end and she will be 'cured'. The wishful thinking of a scientific fairytale...

It is not so simple. When Easser and Lesser were studying the fathers of hysterical patients, they came to a paradoxical conclusion (see note 15). In their opinion it is inexplicable: they found two groups of fathers who were more than completely different, they were diametrically opposed. On the one hand, the first group were weak, subjugated, often alcoholic fathers, not without a spark of seductive energy, but on the whole, throw-away fathers nonetheless. On the other hand, the second group were active, dominating, controlling and seductive fathers. However studiously Easser and Lesser may have tried to apply Freud's first theory of seduction, the second group just didn't fit in with this theory.

The Other, the lack and the resulting desire constitute the nucleus of hysteria. The lack should not be looked for in reality, but in relation to the Real. The Symbolic does not furnish a signifier for The Woman. The hysteric tries to signify her sexual identity in relation to the Other: "jenen prähistorischen unvergesslichen *Anderen*, den kein späterer mehr erreicht", the prehistoric, unforgettable Other, "who is never equalled by any one coming after".[36]

This last subtle nuance was lost on most of the post-Freudians. The call of the hysteric for a masterful master was heard all the more, so much so that whole hordes of therapists tried their luck in assuming this position. Lack of insight concerning the theory was in the worst cases replaced by an Indian dress, a heavy beard and a deep bass voice; in the best cases by a monotonous reference to the primary master: "Freud said". Analytic discourse was not even replaced by that of the master, but by the more impoverished discourse of the university. We will develop this later on.

In the meantime, the primary master was eventually supplemented by a second one. After Lacan's death, official psychoanalysis suddenly seemed to have discovered his importance. This is in itself a beautiful illustration of the theory that we have already confirmed with Freud: only the dead master is supposed to know. Indeed, it is not very difficult nowadays to find papers in IPA journals in which Lacan is profusely quoted. Alas, most of these quotations remind me of the Christmas turkey, reheated on the 2nd January, drenched in the sauce of New Year's Eve. In other words: the same tragic fate that befell Freud's work is in store for Lacan's. Jacques-Alain Miller observed in 1980 that a lot of people don't understand that Lacan's oeuvre is a complex, dynamic entity from which it is impossible to scrounge the best bits without arriving at grotesque conclusions.[37]

This does not keep the hysteric from consulting the analyst. In her search for a signifier signifying The Woman, it is no surprise that she knocks at the door of the supposed specialist in sexual matters. The vulgarization of analytic knowledge is such that her first complaint is often "Doctor, I have an Oedipal problem...".

During the Middle Ages, imbued as they were with religious ideas, the hysteric was the one who announced the Reformation. A couple of centuries later, she made the scientifically schooled physician look foolish and thereby inaugurated neuropathology. Charcot and Babinsky shared the same fate, and a similar changing of the guard is promised for psychoanalysis.

Another half a century later, we have to ask ourselves the question of whether psychoanalysis is a similarly ephemeral phenomenon: like these previous incarnations of the discourse of the master, the umpteenth hunting trophy on the wall of the hysteric, or - just the other way around - the umpteenth tombstone in her mausoleum. The degradation of psychoanalytic theory and practice described in this chapter only confirms this. A bad omen in this respect is that, within this approach, hysteria tends to 'disappear'. In the transition from religion to medicine, the possessed disappeared. In the Golden Age of neuropathology, the great hysterical attack was omnipresent, its paradigm being provided by epilepsy. This was obliterated in a very short time and replaced by more 'psychological' symptoms when the star of psychoanalysis was rising. Ilsa Veith confirms this and other shifts - except for the last one - in her study of the history of hysteria. In two hundred and seventy pages she tells us a spellbinding and very well-documented story, permitting us to conclude that knowledge about hysteria is to a large extent lost. However, her conclusion puts a damper on the quality of her work, transforming it into an auto-illustration of this loss of knowledge: in her epilogue, taking only a page and a half, she tells us that hysteria has almost disappeared these days (1965), thanks to the prophylactic influence of psychoanalytic insights which have become generally acquired cultural knowledge... In the 1984 edition of *The International Journal of Psychoanalysis* we can read: "Today we face the question of the existence or non-existence of hysteria".[38]

Hysteria is supposed to be disappearing. One look at history, inspired by Foucault, rather suggests the opposite conclusion; hysteria is not disappearing, it only changes its appearance and, if need be, its partner.

First of all, as far as the change in appearance is concerned, the hysteric is always one step ahead of the master in the development of his knowledge. While he is looking for conversion symptoms and frigidity, he is presented with something new, unexpected and thus unknown: the *borderline*, and, more broadly, *personality disorders*. We are back with naming in the style of Adam, one which barely suffices to cover up the lack of understanding. This lack even works retroactively: Anna O was not a hysteric, not at all, she fell victim to a severe psychosis.[39] The rest of the patients in *The Studies* are at least cases of 'borderline' pathology. According to Miller, this hybrid nosological concept is nothing but the most recent manifestation of hysteria. And even in this case, the relief of the guard is already announced. Not without humour, J. Quackelbeen speaks of 'Lacanian hysteria' as the latest form, referring to a patient of his who enlarged the Lacanian difference between pleasure and jouissance with five further subtle distinctions.[40] As a consequence of a cultural-medical shift, the epileptic paradigm was replaced by the schizophrenic one. This was not without disastrous effects for the patients (psychiatrisation and pharmacologisation) resulting in the anti-psychiatric movement of the sixties. Eventually, this became the main impetus for the development of new forms of psychotherapy.

The effect of all this was a change in partner. As Ego psychology transformed itself more and more into an ego-trip, the hysteric turned to more alternative masters. Indeed, the alternative nature of Freud's discoveries had already been hidden for a long time behind the diplomas, neatly framed and displayed in waiting-rooms. Israël explains the popularity of sects, cults, initiations and other marginal 'para-'practices as follows: the fact that they are situated on the boundaries of established science means that the hysteric hopes to find there an answer to her question insofar as it was rejected by that established science. Being part of and an accomplice to that establishment, the analyst disappears from her field of interest.

The kind of psychoanalysis hitherto considered is restricted to Freud's first period. We have deliberately opted for this restriction, because in the post-Freudian period, *official* psychoanalysis is nothing but a mitigated version of this first period. It is this version that can be considered as ephemeral. There is more to it, however; in 1914 there was a turning-point whose importance is still hardly understood. With this turn, Freud inaugurated the discourse of the analyst. In order to put this into focus, we have to go into the structural differentiation between the four Lacanian discourses.

CHAPTER 7

LACAN AND THE DISCOURSE OF THE HYSTERIC

The theory of the four discourses

With respect to hysteria, the post-Freudians were only able to offer a confusing mass of data. The only sensible thing to do at the time was to bring some order into this chaos. By taking our distance and considering things from a historical point of view, we were able to conclude that hysteria was fated to disappear for this particular form of psychoanalysis. The reverse, however, is equally true: that this particular form of psychoanalysis is disappearing from the hysteric's field of interest.

Exit all post-, para- and anafreudians. As a post-post-Freudian, Lacan became the first Freudian. An exposition of a key part of his teaching will allow us to take three steps: first of all, to confirm a previous conclusion, namely, that Freud's position at the end of his first period can be understood as that of a master; secondly, to demonstrate the usefulness of the university discourse as a concept with which to group most post-Freudians together, insofar as they constantly refer to the master, (and probably, in the next decennia, all post-Lacanians too); thirdly, to introduce Freud's later theory in which analytic discourse plays a central role.

The reader will probably be wondering why we discard chronology. Why fit the post-Freudians and Lacan between Freud I and Freud II? There are a number of reasons for doing this. We have already mentioned the first one: although most references to hysteria after Freud were limited to his early theories, they were embellished with concepts and remarks from his later period. As a result, the post-Freudians can easily be understood with reference to Freud I, and even to the pre-Freudians. Another reason is our conviction that the best way to understand Freud II is by means of the pathways opened up by Lacan. Indeed, Lacan has made explicit a number of concepts implicit in Freud without which his second theory would remain incomprehensible. The two most important concepts with respect to hysteria are 'jouissance' and 'pleasure', where the latter is in opposition to the former. The most important reason of all concerns the crucial post-Freudian confusion in relation to hysteria. We have already noted that from 1920 onwards, the question "What is hysteria?" was not so much answered as brushed aside. Lacan's theory of the four discourses will provide us with a structural solution which is consonant with Freud's later ideas. As these ideas are precisely the ones that have been forgotten, we will become acquainted with a relatively unknown Freud. The whole of our attention will focus on this Freud in our last section.

Towards a new diagnostic: the discourse

During the late sixties and the early seventies, the intellectual talk of the town was of structuralism and the structuralists, and Foucault, Lacan and Barthes were its stars. The fact that each of these three denied being a structuralist was considered irrelevant, and merely added a bit of Parisian spice and frivolity to the discussion.

As far as Lacan is concerned, it is rather difficult to answer the question whether he was or was not a structuralist. Of course, everything depends on the definition one adheres to. Nevertheless, one thing is very clear: Freud was not a structuralist and if Lacan was the only post-Freudian to lift psychoanalytic theory to another and higher level, then this "Aufhebung", this raising up in Hegel's sense, has everything to do with Lacanian structuralism and formalism. The rest of the post-Freudians stayed beneath Freud, descending to the level of the pre-Freudians as often as not.

It is obvious that Freud was fundamentally innovative and operated on his own to effect a shift towards a new paradigm in the study of mankind. He was so fundamentally innovative that it seems almost impossible to go any further. This immediately raises a question concerning the gains of Lacanian theory.

In order to appreciate the gain, we have to return to the fundamental difficulty of the psychological study of man. Within a classical scientific approach, one starts with observation and description, and then takes the step towards categorisation and generalisation. This was the approach of pre-Freudian and post-Freudian psychology and psychiatry, and in both cases it proved to be a failure. Taking the step from the observation of an individual to a generalised category proved to be a very frustrating business. Everyone who has been trained in psychodiagnostics, which is the first step in this kind of scientific approach, knows exactly what this frustration is about. By means of observation and interview, the clinician takes a sample of a number of characteristics of an individual patient, which then have to match with the characteristics dictated by a psychiatric handbook. They have to match, but of course they never do. The solution of the classical approach is always a variant on the same theme, involving a differentiation between primary and secondary characteristics; the primary and the secondary characteristics of schizophrenia for example. The latest solution to the same problem is illustrated by the DSM-IIIR, where one is left with an element of choice: a patient is called borderline if he shows at least five symptoms out of a list of eight, etc.

What is interesting about this failure is that its core is the tension between clinical reality and conceptualisation, which always returns in one form or another. Lacan has summarised this tension in one of his paradoxical statements: "Psychanalyse, c'est la science du particulier", that is: "Psychoanalysis is the science of the particular". One of Freud's innovations was his solution to this problem. Instead of constructing his own categorical system in which every patient had to find his proper place, and then trying to convince the world that his system, and only his, was the useful one, he opted for a completely different approach. Every patient was listened to, and every case study resulted in a category into which one and only one patient fitted. In his *Studies on Hysteria* he had already remarked that hysteria did not exist as a separate category, and that clinical reality always revealed mixtures of different kinds of neuroses whose pure form is only found in textbook psychology. The paradoxical result of this Freudian approach, which privileged the individual, even the individual symptoms of one individual patient, was that Freud was the only person who succeeded in making a general theory of the human psyche. His method is anything but secret. In order to make the step from individual clinical reality to a general conceptualisation, Freud made use of a ready-made theory, or almost ready-made. Indeed, the core of Freudian theory is based on classical myths and stories, the tragedy of Oedipus and the story of Narcissus being the most famous examples. If one looks in the last volume of the Standard Edition, one finds ten pages filled with references to works of art and literature. Freud went even further with his solution by inventing a myth when he could not find a suitable one: the primal father in *Totem and Taboo*.

This Freudian approach resulted in a major breakthrough and a new paradigm. Nevertheless, there were a couple of serious disadvantages. This method was only useful so long as the story is kept sufficiently vague. The moment one studies the myth in its particularity, it becomes part of that science of the particular. Oedipus himself had his own version of the Oedipus complex... A second and even more important disadvantage concerns the content of these myths, specifically the possibility that this content might come to be psychologised and given substantial reality. That is what happened to Jungian and post-Jungian theory. Without going any further into this, one Lacanian quotation suffices to point out the pitfalls. "Authentifier l'Imaginaire, c'est remplir l'antéchambre de la folie", "If you authenticate the Imaginary, you fill the waiting-room of madness".

It is in this light that we have to consider Lacanian theory as a major breakthrough. Whereas Freud made the step from the individual patient to the underlying myths, Lacan made the step from these myths to the formal structures that govern them. The most important Lacanian structure in this respect is the theory of the four discourses.

The advantages of these formal structures are obvious. First of all, there is an enormous gain in the level of abstraction. Just as in algebra, almost anything can be represented by those 'petites lettres', the small letters, the a, the S and the A, and the relationships between them. It is precisely this level of abstraction that enables one to fit each individual subject into the main frame. Secondly, because these formal structures are totally stripped of flesh and bones, they diminish the possibility of psychologising. If one makes the comparison between the Freudian primal father and the Lacanian S_1, the difference is very clear: with the first one, everybody sees before them an ageing silverback gorilla, running riot among his females. It is very difficult to imagine this ape when writing S_1... and it is precisely this that opens up the possibility of other interpretations of this very important function.

This brings us to the third advantage: these structures allow us to steer clinical practice in a very efficient way. Indeed, it makes an enormous difference whether one uses the discourse of the master or that of the hysteric within a given situation; the respective formulas allow one to predict what the effect of a particular choice will be.

There is of course one disadvantage with this system. Compared to the Freudian myths and age-old stories, the Lacanian algebraic structures are seen as boring. There is no flesh on them, they concern the bare bones and are therefore utterly lacking in the attractions of the Imaginary order so prevalent in those stories. That is the price one has to pay.

The diagnostic criteria based on this way of thinking are completely new. The most fundamental differences from classical psycho-diagnostics can be summarised as follows. Firstly, it is a linguistic structure which furnishes the starting-point. Secondly, the other receives a very prominent place in the diagnosis. Thirdly, the core of the system concerns jouissance, albeit in a very strange way - each discourse is a specific method of avoiding jouissance, of erecting a protection against it and of keeping desire intact. In the end, every discourse delivers an answer to a question that occupied Lacan's mind from the start: who is speaking? What is the position of a subject within speech?

Qua theory, the discourses represent the pinnacle of Lacan's thinking about psychical identity. They also mark a break with the neo-Freudians as well as with Freud himself. Until then, the psyche was thought of as a substantial essence that was buried deep 'somewhere' - the inner self of a personality - and the unconscious was the reservoir of all wishes constituting the basement of this inner self. For Lacan, this basement, indeed the whole house, is empty. Everything takes place on the street. identity is always outside with the Other or, more precisely, in the particular relation to this Other. That is the meaning of (in)famous statements such as "The Unconscious is the discourse of the Other" or "Man's desire is the desire of the Other". This vision is so new that it has hardly penetrated, even within Lacanian circles. The temptation to think "I am a God in my deepest thoughts" is probably too great. The theory of discourse is a formalisation of this new vision.

Discourse and communication: positions and disjunctions

Discourse naturally evokes the idea of communication, which has been at the centre of attention for the last twenty-five years in many different fields, from human relations through electronics to genetics. There is one unifying aim which characterises these different aspects of so-called communication theories: they want to bring communication to a standard of perfection which eliminates any kind of 'noise', so that the message can flow freely between sender and receiver. The basic myth governing these theories is the ideal of perfect communication without any hitches whatsoever.

This idea has nothing to do with the original concept of discourse, as it was coined by Michel Foucault in December 1970, during his inaugural speech at the Collège de France. For him, there was a very special relationship between power and discourse. The impact of a given discourse makes itself felt by imposing its signifiers on another discourse. For example, during the Gulf war, bombing was described as being "surgical measures carried out with surgical precision", and these metaphors were expressions of the power of medical discourse, insofar as they were used outside their proper field of application. In this respect, the analysis of a discourse is a very useful instrument of historical research on the evolution of power, which is precisely what Foucault wished to do.

Lacanian discourse theory has nothing to do with either of these two. His theory is even in radical opposition to communication theory as such, because it starts from the assumption that communication is always a failure, and, moreover, *that it has to be a failure*, and that is the reason why we go on talking. If we could understand each other we would all remain silent, and the perfect, dreamt-of *communio* would take place within an appropriate silence and with hands in front of closed eyes. Luckily people don't understand each other, so they have to speak to one another. The discourses draw a number of lines along which this impossibility of communication can take place. This is where the difference with Foucault's theory shows itself. In his theory of discourse, Michel Foucault works with the concrete material of the signifier, which puts the accent on the *content* of a discourse. Lacan, on the contrary, works beyond the content and accentuates the formal relationships that each discourse establishes in the very act of speaking: "...as a necessary structure of something that largely exceeds always more or less casual speech. (...) it consists of fundamental relations that literally would have no existence without language". This implies that Lacanian discourse theory has to be understood in the first place as a *formal* system, independent of any spoken word as such. A discourse exists before any concrete word is spoken and, to go further, a discourse determines the concrete speech act. This effect of determination is the reflection of a basic Lacanian assumption, namely that each discourse incarnates a fundamental relationship, resulting in a particular *social bond*. As there are four discourses, there will be four different social bonds.

It is important to understand that each discourse is empty to start with. They are nothing but empty vessels with a particular form which will determine the content that one puts into them, and then they can contain almost anything. The moment one reduces a given discourse to one interpretation, the whole theory implodes and one returns to the science of the particular. As a vessel, each discourse has four different compartments into which one can put things. The compartments are called *positions* and the things are the *terms*.

There are four different positions, standing in a fixed relationship to each other. The first position is obvious: each discourse starts with somebody talking, called by Lacan the *agent*. If one talks, one is talking to somebody, and that is the second position, called the *other*. Those two positions are of course nothing else but the conscious expression of each speech act, and in that sense they are at the core of every theory of communication:

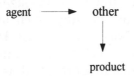

Within this minimal relationship between speaker and receiver, between agent and other, a certain effect is aimed at. The result of the discourse can be made visible in this effect, and that leads to the next position, called the *product*.

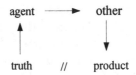

Up to this point, we are still within classical communication theory. It is only the fourth position which introduces the psychoanalytic point of view. In fact, it is not the fourth, but the very first position, namely the position of *truth*. Indeed, Freud demonstrated that, while man is speaking he is driven by a truth, even if it remains unknown to himself. It is this position of the truth which functions as the motor and as the starting-point of each discourse.

agent   ⟶   other

↑   ↓

truth   //   product

The position of truth is the Aristotelian Prime Mover, affecting the whole structure of a discourse. Its first consequence is that the agent is only apparently the agent. The ego does not speak, it is spoken. Observation of the process of free association leads to this conclusion, but even ordinary speaking yields the same result. Indeed, when I speak I do not know what I am going to say, unless I have learned it by heart or I am reading my speech from a paper. In all other cases, I do not speak so much as I am spoken, and this speech is driven by a desire with or without my conscious agreement. This is a matter of simple observation, but it wounds man's narcissism deeply; which is why Freud called it the third great narcissistic humiliation of mankind. He expressed it very pithily: "dass das Ich kein Herr sei in seinem eigenen Hause", "The ego is not master in its own house". The Lacanian equivalent of this Freudian formula runs as follows: "Le signifiant, c'est ce qui représente le sujet pour un autre signifiant". In this turning of the scales - since it is not the subject but the signifier which leads in the definition, - Lacan defines the subject as a passive effect of the signifying chain, certainly not the master of it. The agent of discourse is only a fake agent, "un semblant", a make-believe entity. The real driving force lies underneath, in the position of the truth.

A second consequence of the introduction of this driving force is that the communicative sequence of a discourse is disrupted. One might almost be tempted to expect a logical sequence following which the agent translates the truth into a message, which is then directed to the other and resulting in a product which, in a feedback movement, is returned to the sender. This is not the case. In Lacanian theory, there is no such thing as a truth which can be completely put into words, on the contrary, the exact nature of the truth is such that one can hardly put it into words at all. There are always some elements in the Real which can never be verbalised. Lacan calls this characteristic "le mi-dire de la vérité", the half-speaking of the truth. Again, this is essentially a Freudian idea: complete verbalisation of the truth is impossible because primary repression keeps the original object definitively beyond the realm of language, which means at the same time *Beyond the Pleasure Principle*. The result of this is an endless compulsion to repeat, a never-ending attempt to verbalise the non-verbal. Another consequence, of course, is the endless insistence of this "mi-dire de la vérité", which was beautifully expressed by Kierkegaard: "Repetition is a beloved wife of whom one never tires." Hence, every discourse is an open-ended structure, in which the open-endedness functions as a causal element: because of the structural lack, the discourses keep on turning.

As well as these four positions, the formal structure of a discourse consists of two *disjunctions*, which express the disruption of the line of communication. These disjunctions are the most important and the most difficult part of the whole theory. On the upper level of the discourse, we have the disjunction of *impossibility*; on the lower level, we are confronted with the disjunction of *impotence*. The two are interrelated.

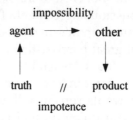

Disjunction of impossibility: the agent, who is only a make believe agent, is driven by a desire which constitutes his truth; as this truth cannot be completely verbalised, the agent cannot completely transmit his desire to the other; hence a perfect communication via words is logically impossible. This is the Lacanian explanation for well known difficulties of communication. However, this disjunction of impossibility goes further. What Lacan is expressing here is nothing less than the famous "Il n'y a pas de rapport sexuel", the non-existence of sexual rapport. This statement, already a very dense summary of a whole theory, is here even more condensed in the disjunction of the upper part of the discourse. The bridge between agent and other is always a bridge too far, with the important result that the agent remains stuck with an impossible desire. This is important because it forms the basis for the particular social bond which characterises each discourse. So each of the four discourses will unite a group of subjects by means of the particular impossibility of a particular desire.

Following this, on the lower level, there is the disjunction of impotence. This impotence concerns the link between the product and truth. As as result of the discourse of the other, the product has nothing to do with the truth of the agent. If it were possible for the agent to verbalise his truth completely for the other, this other would respond with an appropriate product; since this precondition is never fulfilled, no product can match what lies in the position of truth.

To depict these two disjunctions in a simple way, it is best to start from the opposite point of view where these disjunctions are abolished, as in *"Le dimanche de la vie"*, the "Sunday of Life", and where the dreamt-of perfect communication and sexual relationship would be possible. In that case, the truth would find complete expression in the desire of the agent for the other, thus realising the perfect relationship between them, whose product would be the definitive satisfaction that embraces the truth. This Hollywood scenario would be conditional upon everything taking place outside the realm of the signifier, otherwise it would be structurally impossible. Once one speaks, the verbalisation of the truth of the matter becomes impossible, resulting in the impossibility of realising one's desire in the place of the other ("my place or your place?"), and thus in the impotence of the convergence between product and truth.

These two disjunctions are the most difficult and the most impenetrable part of the theory of discourse. They condense a major Freudian discovery, namely the constant failure of the pleasure principle and the consequences of that failure. It is a failure which finds its expression in the disjunction of impotence, with the resulting impossibility. Man can never return to what Freud called *"die primäre Befriedigungserlebnis"*, the primary experience of satisfaction, he is *unable (impotent) to* operate this return because of the primary *"Spaltung"*, the division of the subject in language. Nevertheless, he keeps on trying, and in the process he gets stuck, that is, he experiences *impossibility*. Every biography can be read as a story about this impossibility. Now, instead of lamenting the human condition, it is much more important to understand the crucial thing about this impossibility, namely that it is only an upper layer of an underlying impotence, and *that the structure in its totality is a protective one.* If we were able to return to this primary experience of *jouissance*, the perfect symbiotic relationship would be realised and this would imply the end of our existence as subjects. That is why the psychotic subject, who does not share in the structure of discourse, has to find a private solution to this ever present danger of disappearing into the great Other. A normally divided subject is protected against this danger. To put it bluntly: on the way towards the bliss of an all-embracing jouissance in which we would disappear, we get stuck at the point of orgasm which puts an end to it, at which point we can start all over again. Some people are so afraid that they don't even reach that point either, and stop at an earlier roadblock.

Terms and discourse

In this sense, the four discourses are four different ways for the subject to take a position in relation to the failure of the pleasure principle - the upper level, as well as four different ways of avoiding jouissance - the lower level. In that way, each of the four demonstrates a certain desire and its failure, resulting in a typical social bond. The typical character of each concrete discourse is determined by the position of the *terms*. Indeed, the four positions and the two disjunctions always remain the same throughout the different discourses; the difference is situated in the terms, more particularly in the rotation of the terms around the fixed positions.

The terms themselves are obvious, in that they find their origin in an earlier Lacanian theory of the Unconscious and the structure of language. There have to be at least two signifiers in order to have a minimal linguistic structure. This gives us two terms: S_1 and S_2. S_1, being the first signifier, has a special status, the Freudian 'boundary', the 'primary symptom', or the 'primary symbol' of the *Project*. It is the master-signifier which aims at obliterating the lack, posing as the guarantee for the process of covering up that lack. The best and shortest example is the signifier 'I' which gives us the illusion of having an identity in our own right. S2 is the name for the rest of the signifiers, the chain or network of signifiers. In that sense, it is also the name of 'le savoir', the knowledge which is contained in that chain.

The last two terms are both effects of the signifier. For Lacan, the presence of two signifiers is the necessary condition in order to have a subject: "a signifier is what represents a subject for another signifier". So the third term is the divided subject $. The last but not least of the terms, is the lost object, written as object *a*. The result of language acquisition is the loss of a primary condition called 'nature'. From the moment man speaks, he becomes a subject of language (a divided subject in fact) who tries to grasp an object which lies beyond language, or, more accurately, a condition beyond the separation between subject and object. This object represents the final term of desire itself; but as it lies beyond the realm of the signifier and thus beyond the pleasure principle, it is irrevocably lost. At the same time, it provides the motor which keeps man going for ever. For Lacan, it constitutes the basis of every form of human causality.

Indeed, the subject tries to recover his lost unity by accumulating signifiers combined into a network. This implies that the cause of the original loss is used as a means to cancel this loss. Obviously, this has to fail and it results in an endless repetition. Nevertheless, the accumulation of signifiers also produces a growing body of knowledge, and without a corresponding increase in jouissance for the subject. It is the Other, S2, that is enlarged. Lacan equated this knowledge with the jouissance of the Other: "le savoir, c'est la jouissance de l'Autre". Even this idea is a Freudian one. One of his first discoveries was that the Unconscious contains a knowledge which is unknown to the subject, and that this knowledge articulates a certain satisfaction beyond the subject: that is the conclusion of *The Interpretation of Dreams, Jokes and their Relationship to the Unconscious* and *Psychopathology of Everyday Life*. This linguistic learning device which is always expanding also enjoys itself. (cf. Joy-ce).

The relationship between knowledge, jouissance and subject is in certain respects a paradoxical one. knowledge restricts the jouissance of the subject. Again, it is the signifier which is responsible: the expansion of signifiers, S2, leads to a steadily increasing distance from jouissance and a confirmation of the loss of object *a* as 'plus-de-jouir'.

Repetition aims at this jouissance but can never reach it as it is always a repetition of signifiers, thereby confirming the original loss of object *a* and of the jouissance of the subject.

These four terms: S1 and S2, $ and *a*, have a sequential relation which is fixed. While the order remains the same, they can be permutated over the positions, giving four different forms of discourse. On the fifth rotation, one would be back at the starting point, because of the fixed order of the terms.

$$\frac{S_1}{\$} \xrightarrow{\quad\quad} \frac{S_2}{a}$$

Discourse of the Master

$$\frac{S_2}{S_1} \xrightarrow{\quad\quad} \frac{a}{\$}$$

Discourse of the University

$$\frac{a}{S_2} \xrightarrow{\quad\quad} \frac{\$}{S_1}$$

Discourse of the Analyst

$$\frac{\$}{a} \xrightarrow{\quad\quad} \frac{S_1}{S_2}$$

Discourse of the Hysteric

The hysteric between master and analyst

The Discourse of the master

In our first section, we learnt that the hysteric is always in search of an incarnation of the mythical master. As an incarnation, every actual master is doomed to fail. The structure of discourse will show us why. Moreover, the relationship between hysteria and knowledge will become much clearer once it receives its status in the discourse of the hysteric, and is seen in its relation to the discourse of the master.

This master discourse is understood by Lacan as logically prior. It founds the Symbolic Order as such, it gives the Oedipus complex a formal expression and it explains the constitution of the subject. It is the discourse in which both terms and positions seem to match. The agent is the master-signifier, pretending to be one and undivided. As Lacan puts it: it is this particular signifier which gives me the idea that I am (master of) myself: "maître/m'être à moi-même". The desire of this discourse is indeed being one and undivided, that is why the master-signifier tries to join S_2 in the place of the other:

$$S_1 \longrightarrow S_2$$

This desire is impossible: once there is a second signifier, the subject is necessarily divided between the two of them. That is why we find this divided subject in the position of truth: the hidden truth of the master is that even he is divided.

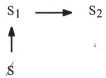

In Freudian terms: the father is also submitted to the process of castration, the primal father is only an Imaginary construct of the subject. The result of his impossible craving to be one and undivided through signifiers is a mere paradox: it results in an ever increasing production of object a, the lost object.

This object a, cause of desire, can never be brought into relation with the division of the subject. The effect is that the discourse of the master precludes the basic fantasy because of its very structure: $\$ \Diamond a$ is not possible, the master is *impotent* in assuming this relation. That is why he is structurally blind in this respect: $\$ \mathbin{/\mkern-5mu/} a$.

One of the most interesting things about this discourse is the relationship between master signifier in the place of agent and S_2 in the place of the other. This implies that knowledge is also situated in the position of the other, which means that the other has to sustain the master in his illusion that he is at one with this knowledge. The pupils make the master, or, in Hegel's terms: it is the slave who confirms, through his knowledge, the position of the master. Indeed, this upper part illustrates the fact that the master desires to be the Other, an incarnation of the knowledge desired by some other. It is at this very juncture that the hysterical subject awaits him.

It is also the point where the master's blindness is structurally determined. He is blind to his own truth, he cannot recognise this truth, because if he did he would fall from his position and cease to be master. The truth is that the master is also castrated. In Lacanian terms, he is divided by his introduction into language, just like any other speaking creature.

The master disavows his own castration by clinging to the master signifier. This signifier is the plug in the fundamental lack by means of which the master believes himself to be one, *m'être/maître à moi-même*. We have seen that the most characteristic example of this master signifier is the pronoun 'I', which has a particular status in linguistics. The I of the master is meant to be identical to itself, so that the gap and the difference between the I of enunciation and the I of what is enunciated is denied. For Lacan, this denial is the start of a new contemporary dictatorship: egocracy.

The failure of this is obvious to see in the upper part of the discourse. As an S_1, a subject identical to the unique master signifier, the master tries to reach S_2, which is the pathway to lost jouissance. He necessarily fails in this because if he really wants to take up the chain of S_2s, he has to give up his unique position as an S_1. Thus, the gap remains and jouissance stays out of reach.

This necessary failure of the position of master is very well illustrated in the relationship between Freud and Dora. Freud assumed the position of master by giving the impression that he knew everything there was to know about desire. He betrayed his position by a beautiful negation: "J'appelle un chat un chat", thereby proverbially illustrating the impossibility of naming the object of desire, even in French. At the very moment that he demonstrated his knowledge, $S_1 \rightarrow S_2$, he was also forced to show his own division and his own desire: Dora had to long for Mr K., who had to take the position of her father. His brilliant and persuasive argument was cut short by her sneering remark: "Why, has anything so very remarkable come out?". Freud's exasperation betrayed his loss of jouissance. His knowledge was lost in the act of speech, entropy was inevitable. This becomes even clearer in the discourse of the university which is a weaker form of that of the master.

The only way to uphold the position of master is to remain silent. To avoid signifiers saves one from being divided by them. In the end, the only successful master is a dead one, one who has entered eternal silence.

The discourse of the hysteric

When we rotate the terms by a quarter, we obtain the discourse of the hysteric. In the place of agent, we find the divided subject, implying that the desire of this discourse is desire itself, beyond any satisfaction. The social bond of this discourse is what Freud described as hysterical identification with a non-satisfied desire, and he theorised this type of identification in *Group Psychology and the Analysis of the Ego*. The classic example used by Lacan is the dream of the butcher's beautiful wife.

Hysteria as a social bond always emphasises the impossibility of desire. This discourse, which is the logical consequence of the discourse of the Oedipal master, is also the discourse of every ordinary neurotic. The moment one speaks, one loses the primary object and becomes divided between signifiers; the net result of that process is an identity which is always in flux plus a desire which insists and can never be satisfied or destroyed, as Freud discovered at the end of *The Interpretation of Dreams*.

$$\uparrow \quad \frac{\$}{a}$$

This desire, originating in a primary loss, has to express itself by way of a demand, directed to the other. In terms of discourse, one has to turn the other into a master-signifier in order to get an answer. In this way the hysterical subject always makes a master out of the other, an S_1 who has to produce an answer: $\$ \rightarrow S_1$

This peculiar relationship between hysteric and master was already evident in the post-Freudian publications on hysteria. Two conclusions were formulated: first of all, the so-called objectivity of scientists failed to cover up their inescapable subjectivity; secondly, the hysteric has a strange solidarity with the man as master. Time and again, she raises him up after having made him tumble. The best illustration is Janet's patient who corrected his suggestions while hallucinating.

During the May 1968 protests when hysterical students interrupted the very seminar in which he was preparing the theory of discourse,

Lacan gave them a very cold answer: "Ce à quoi vous aspirez comme révolutionnaires, c'est à un maître. Vous l'aurez", "As revolutionaries, you are looking for a master, and you will find one". It took them twenty years to understand... The questions put to the master are basically the same: "Tell me who I am, tell me what I want". Although this master can be found in different places - it could be a priest, a doctor, a scientist, an analyst, even a husband - there is always one common factor: the master is supposed to know, he is supposed to know and to produce the answer. That is why we find knowledge, S2, in the position of product. Typically, this answer always misses the point. S2 as general knowledge is *impotent* in producing a particular answer to the particular driving force of object *a* in the place of truth: *a* // S2. This inevitably results in a never ending battle between the hysterical subject and the particular master on duty. That is why revolutions always end with the introduction of a new master, as often as not more cruel and harsh than the previous one, and that is why every master sooner or later ends up with his head in a place where it is not supposed to be. Structurally, the discourse of the hysteric results in alienation for the hysterical subject and in castration for the master. The answer given by the master will always miss the point, because the true answer concerns object *a*, the object which is forever lost and cannot be put into words. The standard reaction to this failure is to produce even more signifiers but they only lead one further and further from the lost object in the position of truth. The inevitable result is a confrontation between the master on the one hand and the fundamental lack in the signifying chain on the other: it is impossible for the signifying chain to verbalise any final truth. This impossibility causes the failure of the master, and entails his symbolic castration. Meanwhile, the master, in the position of the other as S1, has produced an ever increasing body of S2, of knowledge. It is this very knowledge that the hysterical subject experiences as profoundly alienating: as an answer to her particular question she receives a general theory, a religion, a... Whether or not she complies with it, whether or not she identifies herself with it, is besides the point. In every case, the answer will be felt as alienating. knowledge as a product is *unable* to say anything important about object *a* in the place of truth: *a* // S2 .

Throughout history we find the following series:

a	S$_1$	S$_2$	*8*
?	Priest	religion	saint/witch
?	Scientist	science	believer/unbeliever
?	Analyst	psychoanalytic knowledge	good hysteric/ bad hysteric

The bonus in all this is the expanding body of knowledge. If one looks at the history of science, it is easy to arrive at the conclusion that it is essentially a *hystory*: science has always been an attempt to answer the existential questions, and the only result of that attempt is science itself... This is very clear in the human sciences, where even psychoanalysis is a product of hysteria. But the same thing can be said of every development of knowledge, even on a strictly individual level. A developing subject wants to know the answers to his own dividedness, that is why he keeps on reading, speaking and so forth. He will end with a considerable sum of knowledge, but that doesn't teach him very much about his own lost object in the place of truth.

The hysterical subject prompts the other to know. What she desires is knowledge as a means of jouissance. This is structurally impossible, and it transforms her from instigator of knowledge to source of failure, thereby demonstrating the fundamental lack. The hysteric not only sets up the man-master, but also unmasks him: his desire is also determined by object *a*, so even he is divided. At the same time, she also withdraws as his object of desire: it is not she who is desired by him, but object *a*.

This is how the hysteric exposes the paradox of the master as a desiring subject: his truth is that he is also castrated, divided and subject to the Law. The paradox is that in striving to attain jouissance, the only thing he can produce is a knowledge which always falls short and which automatically makes him fail as a master. Indeed, if he wants to display his knowledge he has to speak, but the moment he does, he reveals his division. The only way for a master to stay master is to keep away from the game of desire.

At this point, we have to make the transition from master to idealised father. The hysteric's real father is always a 'castrated' one. Both in *The Studies* and in the case of Dora, he appears as weak and ill. Often enough, his procreative potential is long past and he only functions on an honorary level: ex-procreator, as in ex-serviceman. It is here that the idealised father figure appears: as an ideal, he incarnates the possibility of creation in relation to the female, whilst he himself is 'out of service'.

This is the necessary condition if he wants to assume the position of the master: as an idealised father, he is an imaginary father, not subjected to primary loss, a complete father beyond castration. In Lacan's formulas of sexuation in *Encore,* this runs as follows: there is only one x not subject to castration: $\exists x \overline{\Phi x}$. Freud himself was already aware of the fact that only a dead father could take up such a function beyond castration. In *Totem and Taboo*, it is the murdered primal father who functions as inaugurator of the Law. Only he who does not desire is not submitted to castration, remains undivided and can occupy the position of master. It is interesting to note that anybody occupying the position of master during his lifetime is often credited with complete continence, even if it isn't actually prescribed. Wasn't it said that Freud was without sexual desire after his fortieth year? Another master, Ghandi, took a solemn vow of *brachmacharya*, (complete chastity), when he was thirty-six. Whether these are factual truths or not, is of no importance. For our thesis, it suffices that it was attributed to the master. In this respect it might be worthwhile to rethink the analytical rule concerning abstinence, and especially its interpretations.

The idealised father of the hysteric is the dead father; the one who, freed from all desire, is no longer subjected to the fundamental lack and can produce in his own name, S_1, a knowledge, S_2, concerning jouissance. Again, this is illustrated by Dora: in her second dream she is notified of the death of her father and that she is required to go to the cemetery for the funeral. What is her response? She goes to an empty flat where she feverishly starts thumbing an encyclopaedia, that is, the book in which she found her knowledge about sexuality. A dead father without desire produces knowledge.

The discourse of the analyst

Within the structural framework of the four discourses, the discourse of the analyst is the exact opposite of that of the master and is the last in the series of permutations or revolutions. This does not necessarily imply that it brings a solution to the latter; the etymological meaning of revolution is after all a return to the point of departure. The product of analytic discourse is the master signifier S_1, which means that it brings us back to the starting point, the discourse of the master. This is the danger inherent in the discourse of the analyst which is all too often realised. The general structure is as follows.

In the place of the agent we find object *a*, the cause of desire. It is this lost object which grounds the listening position of the analyst; it obliges the other to take his own divided being into account. That is why we find the divided subject in the position of the other: $a \rightarrow \$$

This relationship between agent and other is impossible because it turns the analyst into the cause of desire of the other, eliminating him as a subject and reducing him to the mere residue, the waste of the signifying chain. That is one of the reasons why Lacan stated that it is impossible to *be* an analyst. The only thing you can do is to function as such for somebody for a limited period of time. This impossible relationship from a to divided subject is the basis for the development of the transference, through which the subject will be able to circumscribe his object. This is one of the goals of an analysis. It is what Lacan has called "la traversée du fantasme", the crossing of the fundamental fantasy. Normally - that is, following the discourse of the master who sets the norm - this relationship is unconscious and partakes of the disjunction of impotence: $\$ \text{ // } a$. The discourse of the analyst, as the inverse of that of the master, brings this relationship to the forefront in an inverted form: $a \rightarrow \$$. From impotence it goes to impossibility, with the difference that it is an impossibility whose effects can be explored: "Ce qui ne cesse pas de ne pas s'écrire". The product of this discourse is the master signifier or, in Freudian terms, the Oedipal determinant particular to that subject. It is the function of the analyst to bring the subject to that point, albeit in a paradoxical way: the analytical position functions by means of a non-functioning of the analyst as subject, which reduces him to the position of object. That is why the end result of analytic discourse is radical difference: in the world of make-believe, "le monde du semblant" we are all narcissistically alike, but beyond this world we are all fundamentally different. Analytic discourse yields a singular subject, constructing and deconstructing itself throughout the process of analysis; the other party is nothing but a stepping stone. This reminds me of several folk tales and fairy tales in which the beloved, the object of desire, can no longer speak for one reason or another; in this situation the hero has to create a solution in which he is essentially confronted with his own being, a being which was unknown to him before.

The position of knowledge is remarkable in this discourse. One of the major twists in Freud's theory and practice concerned precisely this; the way an analyst makes use of his knowledge. This way, indicated by the discourse of the analyst, is paradoxical way; knowledge functions in the position of the truth, but - as the place of the agent is taken by object a - this knowledge cannot be brought into the analysis.

The analyst knows, oh yes, he does know, but he cannot do much with it as long as he takes up the position of analyst. That is why this knowledge can be termed a *Docta Ignorantia*, a "learned ignorance", as Nicholas of Cusa called it in the Fifteenth century. The analyst has wisely learned not to know, and in so doing he opens up a way for another to gain access to what determined his or her subjectivity.

The product of the discourse of the analyst is an S_1, a master signifier. The revelation of this signifier, which determines the vicissitudes of the analysand, is meant to annihilate its effects. It is strange, says Lacan, that the discourse most opposed to that of the master yields a product which is precisely the basis of the master discourse itself. Obviously, this has to take place in a completely different style: "Il doit se trouver à l'opposé de toute volonté au moins avouée de maîtrise", the analyst has to function at the opposite pole from any conscious desire for mastery. This is a structural expression of what is peculiar to the analytic position, even though it is all too often precisely on this point that the analyst fails...

In this way, the discourse of the hysteric can be situated between the discourse of the master and the discourse of the analyst.

$$\uparrow \frac{S_1 \longrightarrow S_2}{\cancel{S} \quad /\!/ \quad a} \downarrow \qquad \uparrow \frac{\cancel{S} \longrightarrow S_1}{a \quad /\!/ \quad S_2} \downarrow \qquad \uparrow \frac{a \longrightarrow \cancel{S}}{S_2 \quad /\!/ \quad S_1} \downarrow$$

$$\text{master} \qquad\qquad \text{hysteric} \qquad\qquad \text{analyst}$$

The barrier between $a /\!/ S_2$ in the discourse of the hysteric is lifted in analytic discourse and shifts instead to the incompatibility between the complete master, undivided and without desire, on the one hand, and knowledge as a means to jouissance on the other: $S_2 /\!/ S_1$. Analytic discourse demonstrates the impossibility of the discourse of the master providing a solution for hysteria. Indeed, the hysterical subject is on the lookout for a master ($\cancel{S} \rightarrow S^1$) who can produce knowledge of jouissance:

$$S_1 \longrightarrow S_2$$
$$\downarrow$$
$$a$$

The discourse of the analyst takes up this impossibility in the master discourse, $S_1 \rightarrow S_2$, and demonstrates the impotence of the master: $S_2 \mathbin{/\mkern-5mu/} S_1$.

The particularity of the discourse of the analyst resides not only in the avoidance of the classical hysterical solution - the introduction and removal of a master figure - but also in a structural working through of its necessary failure. The effectiveness of the discourse of the analyst is twofold. On the one hand, it forces the patient in the direction of the discourse of the hysteric: the answer to $a \rightarrow \$$ can only result in $\$ \rightarrow S_1$, which obliges the patient to subjectivise, to come to terms with the hidden truth of his symptom. Instead of offering his problems to someone else to solve, the patient is confronted with a permutation through which he has to see himself as the centre of the problem. In this way, it is possible for the analysand to come to the truth of his symptom, by exploring his fundamental fantasy. On the other hand, in the discourse of the analyst the impossibility at the heart of hysterical structure shows up very explicitly as the impossibility of setting up and simultaneously refusing the master. Between $S_2 \mathbin{/\mkern-5mu/} S_1$ in the discourse of the analyst there is a barrier on jouissance: one has to choose, the two together are impossible.

This is where one can experience the dialectical value of this formalisation of discourse: based on the reactions of the analysand to an interpretation, the analyst knows quite quickly which position is ascribed to him. If he is situated on the axis $S_1 \rightarrow S_2$, then he will be taken up in the hysterical series: $\$ \rightarrow S_1 \rightarrow S_2$. Only the analytical sequence is able to deliver the truth of the symptom: $a \rightarrow \$ \rightarrow S_1$. This is on condition that it does not topple over into the "envers", its other side: the discourse of the master. Insofar as this toppling does happen, it always ends up as a diluted form of the master discourse, namely, the discourse of the university.

The discourse of the university

For Lacan, the discourse of the university is a regression from that of the master. The discourse of the analyst, as its opposite, gives the other pole and the discourse of the university has to be situated between those two:

Master discourse:

$$\uparrow \; \frac{S_1}{\$} \; \xrightarrow{\quad} \; \frac{S_2}{a} \; \downarrow \qquad \mathbin{/\mkern-5mu/}$$

which, regressing a quarter turn, gives the discourse of the university:

$$\uparrow \frac{S_2}{S_1} \xrightarrow{} \frac{a}{\cancel{S}} \downarrow$$
$$//$$

Analytic discourse:

$$\uparrow \frac{a}{S_2} \xrightarrow{} \frac{\cancel{S}}{S_1} \downarrow$$
$$//$$

Regression of the discourse of the master also means regression of the master himself: S_1 disappears under the bar, knowledge takes the place of agent and its truth is guaranteed by an S_1. In the discourse of the university, the master functions as a formal guarantee for knowledge, thereby denying the ever-problematic division of the one who knows. In the end, this denial will be a failure.

It is this knowledge which takes up the position of agent in the discourse of the university. If we turn the terms in the discourse of the master back a quarter, we obtain the discourse of the university as a regression of the discourse of the master, and as the inverse of the discourse of the hysteric. The agent is a ready-made knowledge, whereas the other is reduced to mere object, cause of desire: $S_2 \rightarrow a$.

The history of psychoanalysis illustrates this aim of the discourse of the university: Freud is reduced to a mere guarantee of a closed and well-established knowledge. The problematic aspect of his work is put aside, only his name remains as the master signifier necessary for the guarantee: "Made in...". The unifying aspect of this S_1 already shows itself in the fact that post-Freudianism reduced Freud to a massive whole, a monolith without any internal dynamic. Certainly, the 'evolution' in his work was recognised, but only in the sense of a cumulative progression, which began before Freud ('dynamic' psychiatry), and resulted after him in the pinnacle known as Ego psychology:

$$\uparrow \frac{S_2}{S_1}$$

This is the social bond which results from a desire to reach this object through knowledge. This knowledge is presented as an organised and transparent unity which can be applied straight from the textbook. The hidden truth is that it can only function if one can guarantee it with a master-signifier.

Every field of knowledge functions by the grace of such a guarantee. In our field: "Lacan has said that...", "Freud has said that..." The primary example of this relationship between knowledge and master signifier is Descartes, who needed God to guarantee the correctness of his science.

In the position of the other, we find the lost object, the cause of desire. The relationship between this object and the signifying chain is structurally impossible: the object is precisely that element, *Das Ding*, which is beyond the signifier. As a result, the product of this discourse is a growing division of the subject: the more knowledge one uses to reach the object, the more one becomes divided between signifiers, and the further one moves away from home, that is, from the true cause of desire: $S_2 \rightarrow a$

The product of this discourse demonstrates its failure since the result is nothing but the divided subject $\$$. This is a consequence of the impossible relationship between $S_2 \rightarrow a$. Knowledge does not yield jouissance, only a subject divided by a knowledge expressed in signifiers. This subject, $\$$, can never be identified with an S_1 because it would require a state of non-division. Between truth and product, the disjunction of impotence insists: $S_1 /\!/ \$$.

Moreover, there is no relationship between the subject and the master-signifier in this discourse; the master is supposed to secrete signifiers without there being any relationship with his own subjectivity: $S_1 /\!/ \$$. This illusion is behind the 'objectivity' required in classical science.

This formalised exposition of the discourse of the university in relation to the discourses of the master and the analyst, permits us to chart the history of psychoanalysis after Freud. Lacan summed up post-Freudianism in terms of the discourse of the university, as a device for turning the development of the unconscious into a knowledge, a theory. The answer to that is the discourse of the hysteric, demonstrating where this knowledge fails. With Freud, all the emphasis was laid on the discovery, and especially on the way in which this discovery could be made. For Lacan, this can be summed up as the invention of analysis as a new social bond, as a new discourse which has to be understood in opposition to that of the master. This new social relationship is the transference as a means for discovery, for unlocking the unconscious. Indeed, this Lacanian thesis finds its best application in the field of hysteria. This was very convincingly demonstrated by André in an exposé whose title is in itself a summary of this thesis: *La psychanalyse, réponse à l'hystérie?*, (Psychoanalysis, an answer to hysteria?). Insofar as the hysteric is confronted with a cumulative psychoanalytic knowledge, where the analyst is the latest guru, she will repeat her time-honoured relation to the master. As she has much more experience at this game - in view of the structure of her discourse - this latest master will very quickly join the row of has-beens, of ex-servicemen. In this respect, we can now formulate an answer to the opening question of this chapter: "Where has all the hysteria gone?", by inverting the question. Hysteria did not disappear; it is rather this form of psychoanalysis which has become a past tense in the greater framework of a hysteria which never ceases to evolve. Moreover, at this point, a certain paradox appears: insofar as we are dealing with a discovery that is invalidated by making a theory of it, the best analysts are actually the hysterics themselves. If the analyst behind the couch produces one interpretation, the hysteric will add ten: she is perfectly at home in the interpretative system, since she started it herself with her defensive imaginarisation of the basic lack $S(\cancel{A})$. Multiplying interpretations, especially in the imaginary, does not make the structure itself yield an inch. The only solution for this 'master' behind the couch is either analysis of resistance or the choice of a prudent silence. As most hysterics do not have much trouble in returning the analysis of resistance back to the sender - eighteen-year-old Dora did not have much trouble with Freud - analysts evolved in the direction of what Julien Quackelbeen has aptly called 'ecouteurism', the silent analyst. This secured a kind of pseudo-analytical position, in the sense that it was a more or less harmless way of incarnating a master figure. The result, however, was that analyses became endless.

In opposition to this evolution, we see Lacan, with his "Return to Freud", rediscovering psychoanalytic practice. This practice determines a formal social bond within a given structure; its content is always different, albeit within the same structure. This is the discourse of the analyst, supported by an ethical imperative: to open the unconscious, which is always closing, at the point of cause and effect: $a \rightarrow \cancel{S}$. interpretation is not limited to an ever shifting desire; full attention must be paid to that around which desire circles in the fundamental fantasy: object a.

It is this shift in focus which Freud broached after 1914.

THE FORGOTTEN FREUD
THE SHIFT TO THE DISCOURSE OF THE ANALYST

(...)In gathering up the Effect of this signifier in the discourse of the hysterical subject, he succeeded in giving it that necessary quarter turn which changed it into analytical discourse". (Jacques Lacan, XX, 41).

In our first section we considered Freud's first attempts to formulate a theory, both from a formal point of view and with respect to its evolving content. The major shift we encountered with regard to content was the one from real trauma to desire within fantasy. The search for the original trauma was followed by the search for an always shifting desire. As the theory was developed, more and more stress was laid on the importance of this fantasmatic working out. As a consequence of this development, a former discovery was put aside - the essential failure of a psychical working over of the traumatic real. In Freud's theory, this traumatic real was equated with the feminine as passive. Through Lacan, we can read this as S($\cancel{A}$).

Contemporary with this shift in content, a formal shift occurred. Freud exchanged the position of surprised discoverer for that of a teaching master. The main effect on the study of hysteria was that from that point onwards he proffered knowledge, especially about desire. As a master-therapist, he bridled this mobile desire with an interpretation based on his first Oedipal knowledge: the boy for the mother, the girl for the father.

In our second section, we discussed the effects of this double development in Freud and his followers. The post-Freudian doctrine became a university discourse, anchored in the knowledge of the primal master. This knowledge was restricted to a confusing summary of Freud's work, the only constant factor being the so-called analysis of resistance; in its way of functioning, this could easily be likened to the pre-Freudian model of moral treatment.

Nevertheless, at the end of part I, we were confronted with a Freud throwing off the cloak of the master and setting out on a new path of discovery. The goal of this voyage was the black continent...

CHAPTER 8

FREUD'S SECOND THEORY OF HYSTERIA

Clinical practice yields a particular structure, in much the same way as the historical study of scientific publications has yielded particular structures. The theory of the four discourses enabled us to understand this in terms of the relationship between the hysterical discourse and the discourse of the master. Time and again, this relationship resulted in the rise and fall of a theory, that of knowledge. We saw how the hysteric gives the master a leg up, in order to pull his leg later on. This explained the evolution of the modes of appearance of hysteria throughout history, together with the accompanying theories. In Western Europe, religious discourse was followed by a medical one, which in turn had to surrender its place to a psychotherapeutic and psychoanalytic version.

At this point in our study, we have to raise the question whether Freud can be reduced to a temporary highlight in the series of those masters whose sole reason for existing depends on the benevolence of the hysteric. If this were to be the case, his theory would be as useful/useless as all the previous ones. At first sight, one can find several arguments to strengthen this idea. For example, Freud's attitude towards Dora is without any doubt that of a master, explaining to her how one ought to love. Haley's analysis of post-Freudian ego-psychology practice is indeed a caricature of the master-slave relationship.[1] Thus considered, psychoanalysis could be reduced to the age-old clash between master and hysteric.

Our thesis is diametrically opposed to this line of thought. We state that:

1) Freud elaborated two theories of hysteria, the second being a reworking of the first one by way of a dialectical *Aufhebung*;

2) post-Freudian publications, with a few exceptions, are based solely on Freud's first theory and thereby encounter the same difficulties and impasses; when they do invoke concepts of Freud's second theory, these are understood and applied in the light of the first theory, thereby giving birth to the so-called analysis of resistances, Ego psychology and the theory of object relations;

3) Freud never finished his second theory; it is Lacan who picked up Ariadne's thread.

Re-evaluation of the first theory: the hydraulic model

In his early period, Freud made one fundamental discovery after another. Just like his illustrious predecessors, he achieved remarkable results in his confrontation with hysteria. The accent has to be put on discovery: he didn't understand a thing about it and that is why he discovered. He did so more than his predecessors, sometimes endorsing them, sometimes contradicting, but always going further. For example, he endorsed Charcot's thesis that hysterical symptoms could be prompted psychologically by the equivalent of a trauma, but the latter's theory about hereditary factors was brushed aside.

Hysteria was a *psycho*neurosis for Freud. This means that sexuality in the psychological sense of the word, that which is highlighted in the idea of *Wunsch*, desire, is deeply implicated. A human being is first of all a desiring being, massively and endlessly desiring. His waking life does not suffice and the dream is called in to help to satisfy this insatiable desire. Even that is not enough, as one of the major conclusions of *The Interpretation of Dreams* shows.

Indeed, desiring is a precarious process. It is expressed in *Vorstellungen*, signifiers, which can be incompatible with the dominant group of representations in the Ego. If this is the case they are repressed. But they keep on returning, as "the return of the repressed". It is a return which is symptomatic and which insists beyond the conscious knowledge of the silently suffering patient in the very special form of conversion symptoms, "L'hysterique souffre de reminiscences". In a paper of 1894 Freud promoted them to the dignity of the defining characteristic of hysteria. The rest of the mechanism is true for every neurosis: repression of the representation charged with pleasure, then the return of the repressed. The hysterical return is a conversion: the repressed signifier is engraved on the body. By the time of *The Studies on Hysteria,* Freud had already discovered that this did not happen without pleasure: Elisabeth von R. became voluptuous during the medical examination, the game of doctors and nurses. Hence his conclusion that every symptom in general and conversion symptoms in particular are *inadequate* forms of pleasurable discharge, inadequate because of the inherent pathology.

Psychotherapy became necessary. In 1914 Freud noted that the aim of this therapy had remained the same for him over the previous twenty years.[2] Only the method had undergone some changes. That aim, he stated, was, from a descriptive point of view, the filling in of gaps in memory (these being the consequences of the repression); from a dynamic point of view, the aim could be described as the overcoming of the resistances of repression. These poor hysterical patients were nothing but victims of a dubious double moral standard: nothing sexual could be shown, let alone put into words. As a result, they had to repress the sexually charged representations of their desire, which then disappeared from consciousness and found pathological expression in symptoms. Freud resolutely took the opposite stance: "J'appelle un chat un chat", was his credo at the time of Dora. He was convinced of his ability to help these hysterics: once the repression had been removed in therapy, they would also be able to call a pussy by its proper name and to discharge their desire in an adequate way. The method Freud continued to use in the paper mentioned above was changing. Originally, that is at the time of the co-operation with Breuer, he had concentrated on the determining elements of the neurosis by means of hypnosis and the hypnocarthartic method, in order to achieve an abreaction or discharge through reproduction and rememoration. Later on, this was abandoned in favour of the new method of free association, which was used in a particular way in the beginning: allowing himself to be instructed by the material produced by free association, the therapist tries to guess and to interpret what the patient does not succeed in remembering. As this second method did not result in wholly satisfying therapeutic successes, he developed a further method, in which focusing on the 'forgotten' material was abandoned altogether. Nowadays, the accent has shifted to the study of what arises spontaneously on the psychical surface of the patient; this is dealt with therapeutically through the interpretation of resistance.

This was the nucleus of Freud's method until 1914. All the other analytical concepts from the previous period fit into this. Thus, the gradual discovery of infantile sexuality, together with the Oedipus complex and the mechanism of identification, were all used to explain the specific form taken by human desire, as well as the necessary decline of this Oedipal complex, repression. Another discovery, transference, was initially considered as sheer resistance, the umpteenth return of the repressed, even though this time with the figure of the analyst as the point of crystallisation. The bending of this element of resistance into a therapeutic device - a testament to Freud's clinical genius which cannot always be imitated - remained for a long time within the same conceptual framework, the same theory.

Theory. Freud had exchanged discovery for knowledge. A knowledge that he did not extract from the clinic, but was, on the contrary, imposed on this clinic. It was a knowledge that originated from elsewhere, a fore-knowledge or pre-knowledge, even pre-conception or prejudice. Initially, it gave orientation to his clinical observations, but it eventually became the cause of a derailment. The same Freud who, in 1893, radically brushed medical-neurological knowledge radically aside as an explanatory basis for hysterical paralysis, was now dazzled by an analogous, although different knowledge. It was analogous, but with the one major difference being that in Freud's case it was temporary; thirty years later, with the same radicality, he put aside the basic principles of his own theory and once again replaced them by discoveries.

What was this Freudian fore-knowledge and what were his preconceptions in this first theory? Which axioms was he handling and what were his dogmas? They were not earth-shaking, on the contrary, they belonged to that common sense which everybody knew to be true, to established knowledge.

Every human being, every living being for that matter, strives for pleasure, for satisfaction. Every living organism keeps as far away as possible from unpleasure. This was the first preconception derived from common sense which led to the installation of a first prejudice: *the pleasure principle*. Its modification by means of a reality principle does not alter this fact. On closer observation, this reality principle shows itself to be a thoughtful pleasure principle, not without common sense itself, that has learned that the pursuit of immediate pleasure is followed by an even larger share of unpleasure, commonly known as punishment. Through experience, it learns that some of the pudding is better than none of the pie. The pleasure principle, then, is the driving force of every living being.

Freud's second axiom treated of the way this pleasure principle functions. What is pleasure, what does the highest pleasure amount to? Inversely, what is unpleasure, what is to be avoided at all costs? Again, common sense produces a ready-made answer: unpleasure is nothing but tension, various increasing levels of increasingly unbearable tension. Obviously, pleasure has to be the relief from that tension, an abreaction resulting in its reduction, preferably to degree zero, but if this is not possible one could settle for a low and preferably constant level. Preferably constant because this is easier to handle. As the French say: "On n'oublie rien, mais on s'habitue à tout", one doesn't forget anything, but one gets used to everything.

The origin of these two axioms goes back to Freud's early papers. Thus, *the principle of constancy* found its first 'official' or published version in his talk for the Vienna Collegium of Physicians on 11th January,1893[3] where, though it hadn't yet received its name, it was elaborated through the invention of the idea of abreaction: every accumulation of tension has to be reduced to degree zero by way of abreaction. The same development can be found in *Die Abwehr-Neuropsychosen*, The Neuro-Psychoses of Defence (1894a), particularly in the two last sections. Odd as it may seem, it was Breuer who coined the term 'the principle of constancy' in his contribution to *The Studies*, whilst ascribing the discovery of it to Freud in the same passage.[4] Freud focused on it in his *Project for a Scientific Psychology*. In this famous manuscript, we find another term: *Tendenz zur Trägheit* or *Trägheitsprinzip*, i.e. principle of neuronal inertia, as well as another elaboration.[5] What he originally called the neurones (and later the 'psychical apparatus') aspired to a complete discharge up to degree zero; this turned out to be impossible because it was necessary to maintain a certain level of tension for the execution of the 'specific action'. Hence, the neuronal apparatus changed its aim and, while resisting any rise in tension, it strove for a level of tension which was as low and constant as possible.

A closer look at this Freudian manuscript reveals that the principle of constancy is an elaboration of an original 'zero principle' - cf. the later Nirvana principle - demanded by the necessities of life. It is interesting to see that the origin of this principle of constancy is neither new nor original: it formed part of established knowledge, particularly the psycho-physics of Theodor Fechner. This important figure in German academic psychology had already formulated his universal principle of stability in 1873 in a paper which is often quoted by Freud.[6]

The *pleasure principle* has a much shorter history but continued with a very productive life. It also stemmed from the established knowledge that was elaborated within the same psycho-physical domain by the same author, Fechner, who even coined the name: *Über das Lustprinzip des Handelns*, On the Pleasure Principle of Action.[7] Freud first of all called it the *un*pleasure principle, which is quite consistent with his conceptual elaboration. He referred to it thus in *The Interpretation of Dreams* and - analogously to Fechner - he described it as an automatic feedback system, something that today would probably be classified under instrumental or operant conditioning.[8] In the subsequent period up to 1914, Freud used it indiscriminately as a founding principle without any further explicit discussion. There is one exception; in the paper *Formulations on the Two Principles of Mental Functioning*, he related it to the reality principle, without ever touching on its fundamental character. But after 1914, he really investigated the principle and changed it in a radical way.

Up to then he was armed with this knowledge that led him to abandon the field of discovery more and more. A perfectly coherent theory had been set up. A human being strives for pleasure, the fulfilment of his desires, and avoids unpleasure. The working over of representations charged with desire entails a rise in tension which becomes unbearable because it produces unpleasure. Its abreaction drains away the excess, or surplus, of tension and thereby produces pleasure. With a 'normal' human being, this is rather easy to understand: when *he* desires his wife (rise in tension - unpleasure), he empties this excess of tension by means of the officially stamped tension-reduction-device, ejaculation. The male phallic orgasm is seen as a prototype of every form of pleasure. Needless to say, the same is true for a woman as well. It is only with neurotics that this fails. Due to their neurotic prehistory they have repressed the representations invested with desire, therefore the abreaction does not take place and the tension keeps on rising. Although, the representations may be 'forgotten', their effect does not fail to occur: unpleasure. Essentially, for Freud, these neurotic symptoms are an attempt to reach abreaction, that is, satisfaction by hook or by crook. The pathological element has to be situated in the fact that this ersatz satisfaction is inadequate because it does not follow the standard mechanism. Neurotics are *impotent* in getting satisfaction.

As a result, the treatment has to tread the opposite path, against that of repression, in order to neutralise it. Freud's successive methods (see above) always had the same aim: to free repressed representations, thereby enabling an adequate abreaction of the 'strangled affect' so that the hysterical patient might remember what she had previously striven to forget, the repressed. Once cured, she could again follow the straight path to satisfaction without any neurotic detours.

Considered in this way, the mechanism of the illness and its therapy can be seen as complementary though opposite processes (schema 1). The schema demonstrates the obviousness of one central feature: Freud's first theory was a perfectly closed system. It was precisely this feature which gave birth to a well-known appellation: the hydraulic model. From a structural point of view, it is the answer of the discourse of the master to that of the hysteric. As a result, Freud's first theory on hysteria is a theory that does not affect the hysteric. She receives it as a duck receives water on its back: it slides off.

There is one characteristic in the application of this schema which is very striking, especially in Freud's early period: the representation which was originally repressed is often a very banal one. Thus Anna O. could no longer drink from a glass because she once saw how a governess let her little doggy drink from a glass; thus Emmy von N. had awful hallucinations prompted by the reading of a certain article in a paper (an article which has never been traced). Things were even more complicated because the process did not limit itself to one representation. During the treatment one finds a whole series of them, revolving as if around a nucleus. In the last part of *The Studies*, this phenomenon gave rise to Freud's conviction about the mechanism of overdetermination. A couple of years later, in *The Interpretation of Dreams*, he spoke of the 'navel' of the dream, situated beyond any possibility of interpretation. It seems that a first moment is lacking, one which logically precedes. Hence the shaded, upper part in our schema. As a result, Freud had the frustrating experience in the treatment of continuing to find new representations beyond the one supposed to be the final one. Desire kept on moving through the chain of signifiers, the final term of the treatment kept on receding.

Freud's first theory prevented him from seeing this flywheel movement. Furthermore, the theory itself produced the necessary final term. In perfect conformity with this knowledge, he discovered very quickly - too quickly in fact - that Dora was actually in love with Mr. K., the Oedipal replacement of the father. Actually, she didn't yet know any of this herself because she had repressed the whole business. All the symptoms pointed in that direction: *globus hystericus* was a reaction to a repressed desire for coitus-fellatio following an embrace with Mr. K. (this Oedipal coating was beautifully endorsed, moreover, since her father - in whose place Mr. K. stepped onto the scene - was supposed to be *unvermögend*, impotent, and thus restricted to oral sex); mutism in Mr. K.'s absence, for why speak when the most important person is away? All this was obvious to everyone with one exception: Dora herself. And this is where Freud's calvary began: she did not believe him. Even worse: she mocked his interpretations and she dismissed him in the way one dismisses a servant. Freud would become wiser through experience - the reality principle - and dismiss the next Dora, that is, the female homosexual of 1920, before she had any chance to dismiss him. But the disappointment remained: hysterical patients escaped from his theory.

This makes the final outcome of this first theory a scandal: hysterical patients didn't want to know anything about Freud's cure. He was convinced that he could bring them the *Freude*, (the ability to have)

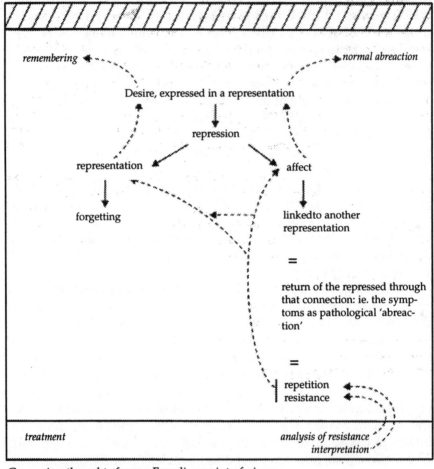

remembering   *normal abreaction*

Desire, expressed in a representation

repression

representation   affect

forgetting   linkedto another
                              representation

                              =

                              return of the repressed through
                              that connection: ie. the symp-
                              toms as pathological 'abreac-
                              tion'

                              =

                              repetition
                              resistance

treatment   *analysis of resistance*
                              interpretation

Governing thoughts from a Freudian point of view:
        Pleasure principle
        Principle of constancy
        repression
Lacanian interpretation
        phallic jouissance
        restriction of the desire to its expression in the signifier S1→$→S1
Schema 1: the hydraulic model

pleasure, but they refused. neurosis is a choice for impotence in relation to satisfaction. The same process can be demonstrated on a smaller
scale in a case study by Lucien Israël. A young hysterical woman suf-
fers from frigidity, and the analyst-novice tries as hard as he can to
make the analysis into a success, which is, from his point of view, to
enable her to enjoy orgasms. And - miracle of miracles! - the treatment
works: "Yesterday, I made love to my husband and I experienced an
orgasm". The analyst is in his seventh heaven, marvelling at his own
qualities as a therapist, until his patient wakes him from his rosy
dream: "My husband made me come, but now I definitely don't want
to make love to him anymore".[9]

They simply don't want to.

Hinge between first and second theory: Errinern, Wiederholen und Durcharbeiten (Remembering, Repeating and Working-Through)

At this point in his development, Freud demonstrated a very rare
quality: scientific honesty. Rather than sticking to his theory and con-
demning the hysteric as a cheat, or a fraud, or a comedian - as his predecessors had done and a number of his followers would do - he
started questioning his own theory. Initially, he managed to cope with
the therapeutic failures by referring to the concept of resistance: repression is maintained by the same force that was originally responsible for
repression itself, and which now functions as a resistance against the
idea becoming conscious, thereby obstructing the functioning of the
pleasure principle. Following this reasoning, the hysteric has to be per-
suaded to give up her resistance. To put it clearly: resistance itself has
to be interpreted, in order to make possible the interpretation of the
repressed material. Although this technique had a great future - the
analysis of resistances within Ego psychology - in the end it revealed
itself to be impossible; therapeutic failures piled up and analyses
became *unendlich*, interminable.

Freud's therapeutic enthusiasm also diminished. By 1914, four of
his five major case studies had been published; the optimistic idea of
the diffusion of psychoanalysis as a prophylactic measure against neurosis disappeared, together with the hysterical patients who were trying their luck with other masters.[10]

In 1914, the tide turned as a result of a relatively small paper:
Remembering, Repeating and Working-Through. Its importance was such
that it changed psychoanalysis radically, at least for those who were
willing to take it seriously.

Still with one foot in the previous theory, it summarised this theory in the first two concepts: remembering and repeating. As a result of the process of repression, the patient has forgotten a number of contents and is not able to remember them. Inevitably she has to repeat them in the form of the 'return of the repressed'. Freud's theory reached another level the moment he started questioning this so-called 'forgetting'. His questioning was so thorough that in the end, there was not much left of this idea once so important for psychoanalysis.

Forgetting 1. - It is remarkable, said Freud, that patients at the end of their analysis often proclaim that they knew beforehand everything they had been told during their analysis. It seems that forgetting is basically a not wanting to know, a dissociation. "Passion de l'ignorance", dixit Lacan.[11]

Forgetting 2. - At the point where the analysand has effectively forgotten something, Freud discovered that the gap that was left by the forgotten memory could always be filled by another mechanism: the screen memory. Just think of little boy Goethe chucking out his mother's crockery, and retaining this small fact of life as the sole memory of the period in which his baby-brother was born. What was he chucking out? As a signifier, this memory is referring to another, much more important content.[12]

Forgetting 3. - Freud said that, in the end, the whole idea of forgetting has to be relativised, because in the course of an analysis, the patient often discovers things he has never been conscious of, and could therefore never have 'forgotten'. These are the unconscious *fantasies*, which oblige the analyst to intervene with a new tool: *construction*. In passing, we want to remark that Freud was here taking the same road as in September 1897, when he wrote to Fliess that he had to abandon his trauma theory as an aetiology for hysteria. In that case too, the argument was that 'forgetting' could never be lifted, not even in the most favourable cases. There too, he had said that fantasy took the place of the (memory of) the real trauma. Freud was beginning to make a differentiation between a reality which was already linked with signifiers and a Real that stayed completely beyond this realm.

At this point the hinge turns towards the second theory. Remembering almost completely disappeared in this reworking of the idea of forgetting, and instead the duo of repetition and working-through appeared on the stage. The concept of repetition was the point of fracture. As a clinical phenomenon used in Freud's first period, it had almost served its purpose. At the time, Freud was convinced that it was the 'forgotten' part that returned in symptoms. But now that the idea of forgetting was itself undermined he had to find another origin for repetition, and was only partly successful in this paper. Freud later connected it to the idea of transference, thus reducing transference to mere repetition. However, at this point, he introduced a new note: instead of the previous 'Wiederholen' (repetition) he passed almost casually from 'Zwang *zur* Wiederholen' (compulsion to repeat) to 'Wiederholungs*zwang*' (repetition-compulsion). That is something completely different. And when we learn what this compulsion tends to repeat, we can see the degree of the changes involved in comparison with the previous idea of repetition: "he repeats everything that has already made its way from the sources of the repressed into his manifest personality - his inhibitions and unserviceable attitudes and his pathological character-traits".[13] Freud added as an afterthought : "and all his symptoms". This little addendum, however, was precisely the *only* element of repetition, in the form of the return of the repressed, that he posited in his first theory of repetition. It seems that in this paper of 1914, the idea is extended to include 'the manifest personality'. Repetition compulsion engages the whole being of the subject.

This in itself gave Freud yet another discovery. He reformulated the concept of transference neurosis by making it a therapeutic instrument. And here too we get a new note. We already knew that neurosis and resistance could walk hand in hand: the same power that originally caused repression, could afterwards exert a resistance against the idea becoming conscious. We said above that, due to the repetition compulsion, the material constituting the return of the repressed will be changed and extended; because of this we now find that the concept of resistance itself has to be changed and extended. Resistance can no longer be restricted to the symptom (as was the case in the first theory), it has to be extended to the 'manifest personality': *transference* resistance. At this point, it is quite obvious that most post-Freudian analysis, with its stress on the ego and the analysis of resistance, remains with Freud's first theory; indeed, with the second theory, it is impossible to install a working alliance with the 'healthy part of the ego', because this part just isn't there. All the later theories about a 'real', 'authentic' or 'good self' can be criticized from the same point of view. Lacan has made this clear in his theory of alienation: a subject always receives its identity from the Other, there is no original identity behind the screen. Indeed, there is no identity at all before or beyond this necessary alienation, only a naked being in the Real outside of any process of humanization.

This change from transference resistance on the level of symptoms, to transference neurosis on the level of 'personality', allowed Freud to chart another phenomenon he had not understood until then: the exacerbation of the symptoms, and even of the whole neurosis, under the influence of analysis. The concept of 'gain from illness' had long since been considered insufficient, and a couple of years later, he would introduce the idea of 'negative therapeutic reaction'. The extrapolation from 'transference resistance' to 'transference neurosis' had the result that merely pointing out a factor of resistance to the patient no longer sufficed to make it disappear. Something more was needed: *Durcharbeiten*, working through. In this paper, Freud did not give us much detail about this new idea. He declared it to be the most difficult part of the treatment, but one on which the success or the failure of the treatment depended. From a dynamic point of view, he compared this 'Durcharbeiten' with the "abreacting of the quotas of affect strangulated by repression".[14] In 1926 he would link it to the resistance of the Unconscious itself, that is, the resistance that results from repetition compulsion and which remains once one has conquered the resistances of the ego.[15]

This leads to the following conclusion: *Remembering, Repeating and Working-Through* indicates a major line of fracture in Freud's conceptualisation. Sadly, the paper is so easy to read that the fracture simply isn't noticed; Lacan was right about a certain style being 'too easily understood'.[16] If understanding comes too quickly, then it is only what was already known beforehand that is understood. Hence, we will end this section by listing these major shifts.

1. The very idea of 'forgetting' disappears, dragging 'remembering' along in its wake. Two of the most important ideas of the first theory become history. Lacan confirmed this shift when he changed the emphasis from 'infantile memories' to the fundamental fantasy constituted during the infantile period of the subject's history.

2. Two new concepts are introduced. First of all *unconscious fantasies*, concerning which Freud specified that they had never been conscious at all (thus differentiating them from preconscious or conscious daydreaming). A year later Freud gave them a new name: *primal fantasies*, thereby accentuating that they were to be understood and situated beyond any form of forgetting and remembering.[17] Along with this came a new therapeutic tool: *construction*. Though not yet mentioned by name in this paper, it was clearly present when Freud referred to the

case study of the Wolf Man.[18]

3. Moreover, a number of concepts underwent a radical change, though their implications were only worked out some years later. Repetition was changed into repetition compulsion. Resistance was extrapolated to *transference* resistance, and even to *transference neurosis*. Therewith a second new therapeutic tool became necessary: *Durcharbeiten*, working through, something which was literally unthinkable in the first theory. All these changes together could not but give rise to a new theory of the drives as well as a different conception of the Ego.

4. There was one thing which Freud did *not* tackle in this paper, yet it was going to prove the most important conceptual change of all: the revision of the two basic principles on which the whole of the first theory was built: the pleasure principle and the principle of constancy.

The second theory: jouissance

Phallic versus other jouissance

On the 10th January, 1915 Lou Andreas-Salomé wrote to Freud in response to his recently published *On Narcissism: an Introduction*. Among other things, the letter contained the following illuminating remark: "Isn't this then the major problem of sexuality, that it does not so much want to quench the thirst, but rather consists of the longing for the thirst itself? That the state of somatic relaxation and satisfaction reached is at the same time a disappointment, because it diminishes the tension, the thirst?".[19]

Again, it was the hysteric who showed Freud the way; she demonstrated the flaw in his argument and directed him towards a new solution. Sexuality is the *Durstsehnsucht*, the desire for thirst, the desire for desire itself, not its satisfaction. *Accumulation* of tension can be pleasurable, *discharge* of tension disappointing. The pleasure principle began to totter. It took Freud five years to put this simple remark into his theory, and it necessitated a revision of all his previous ideas.

It took him even longer just to begin working on it. A year after, he could still write in *Instincts and Their Vicissitudes* that the pleasure principle automatically regulated even the most intricate psychological processes, and that pleasure was equal to a reduction in tension, unpleasure to a rise in tension. But he added that the relationship between pleasure and unpleasure was more complex than that.[20] Four years later, in *The Uncanny*, he really changed his ideas: he posited a repetition compulsion which went beyond the pleasure principle, something which explained a number of strange phenomena at the end of the treatment.[21] And he referred the reader to a future paper in which he promised to develop these new ideas: *Beyond The Pleasure Principle*.

Indeed, this paper implied a complete U-turn. The introduction made it obvious that Freud was convinced that something was wrong with his basic principles, that something went beyond them. The trouble was that he just could not find out what that something was. The first two chapters gave expression to his conviction and the attendant search. After having given the most explicit formulation he had ever made of both the pleasure principle and the constancy principle, he started looking for elements that contradicted them; and he just couldn't find them: he examined their opposition to the reality principle, he looked at the way repression transforms previous pleasure into actual unpleasure, and at unpleasurable children's games - none of these provided him with an exception to the pleasure principle. On the contrary: they seemed to confirm it....[22]

The first main exception came along with the concept of repetition compulsion. As a therapist, Freud was forced to conclude that - in spite of his experience in uncovering resistance, in spite of his attempts to convince the patient to give up his resistances, even by using 'human influences', i.e. the place of the transference (sic) - the patient still succumbed to the power of the repetition compulsion.[23] Let us remark in passing that the concepts of transference and resistance were still used here in their 'old' meaning. Further on in Freud's paper, and in later developments, he changed them completely. In addition to this disenchanting fact, he made another major discovery: that resistance functioned in the service of the pleasure principle! This resistance emanated from the Ego, while the repressed material itself exerted no resistance whatsoever, on the contrary, it just wanted to become conscious (*Ibid.*). This no longer tallied with the first theory.

This repetition compulsion clearly involved unpleasurable material, in conflict with the pleasure principle. What is it that is repeated in a compulsive way? Freud called it *das Schicksal*, fate, and related it to the first devastating rejection by the first love partner, one of the parents: "Patients repeat all of these unwanted situations and painful emotions in the transference and revive them with the greatest ingenuity. They seek to bring about the interruption of the treatment while it is still incomplete; they contrive once more to feel themselves scorned, to oblige the physician to speak severely to them and treat them coldly; they discover appropriate objects for their jealousy..."[24]

The pleasure principle was badly shaken, the first exception had been found, the first spanner in the works. Freud's next discovery was all the more surprising; repetition compulsion did not contradict the pleasure principle, but was beyond it, 'jenseits'. Furthermore, repetition compulsion prepared the path for it. He followed this with the exposition of the traumatic neuroses, in which he made a differentiation between a trauma with and a trauma without anxious expectation. If expected, the trauma could be controlled - in Freudian terms, cathected, loaded with energy and therefore dischargeable later on. If it were not expected, then no cathexis would be ready, neither filled with signification nor linked to a signifier. From a Lacanian point of view, it resides in the Real. In that case, clinical practice shows us that the impact is much greater, much more traumatic. The ensuing repetition of the trauma is then nothing but an attempt to install the 'anxious expectation' initially missing. Why? Because the 'binding' thus installed makes the functioning of the pleasure principle possible. How? Once the tension is 'bound' to a representation, the unpleasurable tension accumulated can be abreacted. The pleasure principle can reign again.

Does this mean back to square one? If the only exception to the pleasure principle aims precisely to re-establish this principle, is it to be considered as an exception? At this point, halfway through his book, we are confronted with a turn that would be almost entirely unexpected were it not for Freud's conviction that something was wrong with the pleasure principle. He bypassed the question about the relationship between drive and repetition compulsion, and ended with the discovery of the opposition between the death drive versus a life drive, Thanatos and Eros. A drive always aims to the re-establish an original state of being. Freud considered this as an effect of inertia, which is supposedly inherent to organic life (for example, the 'neuronal inertia' in the *Project*). Ultimately, this original state is nothing but death, and it is at this point that the idea of Thanatos comes into its own. Diametrically opposed, we find the life drive, Eros, always directed towards fusion. In order to find the accompanying original state, Freud had to refer to Aristophanes' myth on the original unity of the two sexes, divided later on by the intervention of some divine instance. This is the transition from a non-divided species (an in-dividu) to a divided subject.

The consequences were far-reaching. Besides a completely new theory of the drives, it necessitated important changes in the theory of the Ego. It was the new theory of the drive that gave the pleasure principle the final deathblow. Indeed, of the new drives, it was Eros that subsumed within itself the 'life-enhancing' sexual drive. The Ego-drives were finished so far as self-preservation was concerned.[25] Moreover, in a later paper (1924c), Freud spoke about the deadly narcissistic dimension of the Ego. And how does this life-enhancing element of Eros work? Again, the example of coitus showed the way: its effect is not only the discharge of tension (the sole argument in the first theory); it also the addition of new quantities of excitation, in other words, coitus *increases* tension through these 'new vital differences'.[26] The pleasure principle panicked: all those new tensions had to be *abgelebt*, literally 'lived out', abreacted. So this was the price that had to be paid; more tension required more time to be lived out, with the result that life was extended.

In the mean time, the pleasure principle had received a new name: it was now called the *Nirvana principle*, a term proposed by Barbara Low and adopted by Freud. Thus, Freud had rediscovered one of his earliest hypotheses as well as an implicit solution for the associated problem. In the *Project* he had already postulated a zero hypothesis: the neurones aim for a zero level of tension (cathexis, investment). In reality, this was never the case, and it never became clear why it always failed. From that time on, Freud typically resorted to twin or double formulations in his papers: the pleasure principle strove for complete discharge but, when this failed, it had to be content with keeping the level of tension constant and preferably as low as possible. The pleasure principle and the principle of constancy complemented each other in this way. The ancient ambiguity was now solved: the pleasure principle rebaptised as the Nirvana principle strives for point zero, but is countered by another force that time and again succeeds in heightening the tension.

This brings us to a very strange, indeed frightening conclusion. The zero point of total discharge of tension, aimed at by the pleasure principle, is nothing but death - 'la petite mort'[27] foreshadows death proper. This implies that the pleasure principle operates in the service of Thanatos. At the opposite end of the spectrum we find Eros maintaining and enhancing tension in the service of life. At this cross-roads, Freud encountered serious trouble with his terminology about pleasure. Inevitably, he had to question his previous conceptions about pleasure and unpleasure in the light of his actual discovery that, following the 'pleasure' principle, the ultimate form of pleasure is nothing but death. With respect to this question, only raised implicitly in this paper, he looked for an answer by making a differentiation between the (un)pleasure of 'bound' and 'unbound' drive processes, respectively those of the secondary and those of the primary process. From his previous theory, we have already learnt that binding equals possibility of discharge and non-binding its impossibility. Freud now came to the paradoxical conclusion that unbound drive processes yielded most pleasure as well as most unpleasure; this is a paradox, because, following his first theory in which tension was equal to unpleasure, they should be solely *un*pleasureable, due to the fact that they were tension enhancing as well as impossible to discharge. No surprise, then, that Freud ended with a prophetic statement: "This might be the starting-point for fresh investigations".[28]

He never made the required development himself. In *The Economic Problem of Masochism*, he tried to introduce a further clarification, which only succeeded in bringer greater obscurity. He began by repeating the obvious: the pleasure principle automatically regulates psychical life to achieve less unpleasure and more pleasure; he even mentioned the new name, Nirvana principle. He then formulated the difficulty: there exists both a pleasurable tension and an unpleasurable release of tension; each one a contradiction in terms. At that point, he introduced a new definition of the different principles, new in comparison to *Beyond The Pleasure Principle*. The Nirvana principle was the expression of the death drive and strove for null tension, death. The pleasure principle was a modification of this Nirvana principle and functioned in the service of Eros, the life drive. Lastly, the reality principle expressed the influence of the outside world.[29]

It is obvious that what we have here - in spite of the unchanged terminology which promotes confusion - is a completely different pleasure principle; a pleasure principle which has even changed sides and now belongs to the life enhancing Eros, a pleasure principle which strives for a kind of pleasure other than the one aimed at by the pleasure-Nirvana principle.

Freud had discovered a second kind of pleasure, a pleasure that went beyond the common sense of the first theory, because it was a pleasure that could include pain. The pleasure principle in its original formulation contained an inherent failure. Freud was forced to emphasise the *striving for* pleasure, that is, desire, and not the final term, satisfaction. Though this final term might yield a certain form of pleasure - the relief of tension, *phallic pleasure* - there was nevertheless something else that went beyond this pleasure, the 'desire for the thirst', something that by definition is never finished because it strives for something beyond an end: it concerns *another enjoyment*. From a Lacanian point of view, this is where the double disjunction of discourse theory comes in: human impotence in getting satisfaction, the flaw inherent in the pleasure principle, is the basis for the impossibility of enjoyment: "Le plaisir marque la fin de la jouissance", pleasure marks the end/aim of enjoyment.

The divided subject and sexuation

In neurosis - and especially in hysteria, the neurosis par excellence - the repetition of failure stands out. Clinical practice shows us that this mostly takes place in so-called relationships. Freud explained this as an expression of a repetition compulsion: repetition insists in wanting to repeat an original or first failure with the aim of mastering it. Moreover, Freud's new drive theory presupposed two original states to which the organism wanted to return, each with its typical form of pleasure: Eros strives for fusion, its pleasure concerns the raising of tension; Thanatos strives for defusion, pleasure is situated at the level of zero tension, sleep, even death.

It seems as though we have entered the realm of philosophy. How can we understand these statements while working in the clinic of hysteria? Freud's description of repetition compulsion gives us a first well-known clinical fact: "(...)They contrive once more to feel themselves scorned, to oblige the physician to speak severely to them and treat them coldly;(...)". The repetition of the failure, the trauma, goes back to a first rejection by the first love partner in the first love relationship: parents versus children. A second point is that Freud, in order to describe this original ideal condition, had to refer to a myth, the one by Aristophanes in the *Symposium* which concerns the original fusion of the still undivided human being. Oddly enough, Freud did not realise that in so doing he was taking up a theme he treated twenty-five years earlier in his inimitable *Project*: the first mythical satisfaction in hallucinatory form, the most perfect satisfaction, the memory trace of which will function as a standard of comparison for all satisfactions to come and thereby condemn all of them as insufficient.[30] Strangely enough, a couple of years later Freud failed to link this to a 'new' discovery. The girl was supposed to make the transition to the Oedipal relationship with the father from the pre-Oedipal link to the mother, by means of the reproach, amongst others, of not having received enough (milk). In this discussion, Freud totally rejected the sociological argument (shorter period of breastfeeding due to cultural conditions) and favoured another idea: "It is as though our children had remained for ever unsated,..."[31] hysterical, unsatisfied, insatiable desire: in the same paper, Freud established an essential relationship between this pre-Oedipal mother-daughter relationship and hysteria. Moreover, the fact that Freud had left his first theory behind throws up an issue which is not unimportant: from 1925 onwards, he was able to study feminine and hysterical desire as something different, that is, different from a man's.[32] Before this, the Oedipal situation was always elucidated from the masculine point of view: the female version was 'the same, but reversed'.

The second theory thus makes possible a differentiation according to gender. But there is more: the second theory in itself treats of sexual difference. In order to explain Eros, Freud made use of Aristophanes' myth about the original complete human being, split by divine inter-ference. Divided into what ? Two *differentially sexed* creatures.

The importance of this central detail has been overlooked. Both the application of Aristophanes' myth and the whole business of Eros versus Thanatos are usually considered to be one of Freud's rare theoreti-cal lapses, to be forgiven in an older man. It does not have the ring of serious science. The need for acceptance on the international scientific scene was and is such that genuine psychoanalysis is often put aside.

We are convinced, however, that without this mythical reasoning it is very difficult to understand anything at all of hysteria. The myth used by Freud can be verified in clinical practice with every hysterical patient, both as a primary fantasy constructed *nachträglich* and, as a driving force, a leitmotiv that determines every production of the unconscious.

First of all a primary fantasy is constructed *a posteriori*. The infant is taken into language, thereby becoming a subject. As a subject, it can never completely coincide with the body of signifiers, that is, with the Other; there is a remainder, called object *a* by Lacan. Through this oper-ation, the subject becomes both divided and sexed: 'you are a son/daughter of...'. The hysterical subject is here confronted with an impossibility. Taken into language, it has to acquire a sexual identity through a symbolic identification with a signifier. For a woman, this signifier is lacking: S($\cancel{A}$). It is here that desire finds its origin, focusing on a retroactively constructed and therefore mythical condition dating from before the division, a condition in which an absolute subject is thought to have existed beyond any division whatsoever and thus beyond any problem of sexuation. We would like to call this *the hysterical unisex fantasy*; it is so obvious in clinical practice, be it in the particular importance bestowed on the other, or in hysterical fusion. The myth of 'empathy', of the perfect 'intersubjectivity' is hereby exposed as a hysterical fantasy.

Secondly, the driving force or leitmotiv. Hysterical symptoms are nothing but realised fantasies, attempts to produce an answer to S($\cancel{A}$); they always tend towards the myth of the absolute subject. The main characteristic of this absolute subject is that it promotes the idea that all subjects are alike; the idea that 'everybody is equal before the Law' is an instance of this unisex tendency. For someone familiar with the psychoanalytic clinic of hysteria, it comes as no surprise that in many cases this results in a form of social commitment. Anna O. became the first social worker and was commemorated decades later with a stamp bearing her effigy and an epithethon ornans saying: "Helfer der Menschheit" (Helper of Mankind).[33]

The hysteric longs for the unity of paradise lost. This longing should first of all be taken at face value. If one thinks that one can answer it, that one can supplement the lack of love by means of 'holding' - a therapy of support - one is in for a big surprise: the hysteric does not aim at the satisfaction of this desire, she just wants to maintain desire itself. Furthermore, the satisfaction of this desire is dangerous. Were this unity to be realised, the difference between the enjoyment of the Other and the other enjoyment would be lost, and the subject would be reduced to a mere passive object of the desire of the Other, from whence the last escape is hysterical psychosis.

Thus we have a divided subject $ looking for its sexual identity, failing to find one and therefore elaborating a fantasmatic return to the mythical wholeness that precedes every form of sexual differentiation. This is fuelled by Eros, aiming at fusion, at a pleasure that - in opposition to phallic abreaction - is tension enhancing and thus concerns another enjoyment.

Remarkably enough, this theory is confirmed by a number of post-Freudian papers, some of them very well-known. The famous paper by Balint on 'primary object love' teaches us that "The human child has the wish to continue living as a component part of the mother-child unit (a dual unit)".[34] The description of this desired fusion accentuates the non-differentiation of both component parts and mentions a characteristic which the author calls 'totally unexpected': the pleasure associated with this union is a very strange one that resembles *Vorlust*, foreplay - the pleasure that enhances tension. Six years after this paper, Winnicott discovered the transitional object as the first not-me possession. The child makes the transition from the illusory mother and child unity to a differentiated duality by appealing to an intermittent phenomenon. This transitional object may hark back to the mother's breast, Winnicott said, but it is potentially the mother's phallus which is represented by it.[35] The phallus of the mother is what in our reasoning fills up the lack in order to maintain a unity. When a child discovers the privation of the mother, it will fill up this gap precisely in order to avoid the rupture with the first great Other.

A further six years on, we find the most beautiful illustration by Peto, in a paper aspiring to discuss 'psychotic' episodes. This is rather misleading in our opinion, since all the 'borderline' patients presented belong, with one exception, to *The Studies on Hysteria*. Peto wants to discuss a certain transference phenomenon: "The phenomena consisted of recurrent states of deepest regression over periods of weeks or months. In these states the patient perceived himself and the analyst as being fused into a more or less amorphous mass of vague and undefinable character.(...) Soon this stage developed into a phase in which the two bodies became one mass of flesh".[36] Peto makes clear that these states concerned primal fantasies which were never conscious, for "these regressions always reached more archaic situations and phantasies in the transference than those that were actually remembered". They are appealing to a mythical prehistorical period in which a fusion with the mother was supposed to have existed. This fused condition shows no signs of classical pleasure or unpleasure; instead it evokes a kind of 'vague indefinable nothingness'. The author correctly leads this regression back to disturbances in the body image, but he does not succeed in formulating a further generalisation: each one of his patients has difficulties with his or her sexual identity, to which the regressively reached fused condition is the answer. Indeed, in this fusional condition, there is no sexual differentiation at all. This is very clear in his second case study, in which the patient learned to give herself over to these regressions: "She learned to slip into them whenever painful conflicts about anal or genital masturbation provoked an overwhelming feeling of guilt".

Body image implies mirror stage. Peto's patients stick to the Imaginary identification with the total image of the other. Total implies the lack of the lack, because it is filled by the object *a*; Imaginary implies the interchangeability of the elements, as they are dual-imaginary. The symbolic identification of Lacan's double mirror schema is not assumed, because that would introduce a lack through an identification with the signifiers of the Other.[37] No wonder that the author finds a kind of archaic thinking in these patients. This is what Gisela Pankow demonstrated with her work on the impact of the dynamic structuring of the body image in hysterical psychosis.

Consequences of Freud's second theory

These new findings imply a radical change of course for Freud. With respect to his theory, they inaugurate what we should like to call the period of the *Ur* phenomena: *Urverdrängung, Urphantasie, Urvater,* translated as 'primary': primary repression, primary fantasy, primal father. We understand this 'primary' to refer to a moment which logically precedes the constitution of the subject from a *nachträglich* (a posteriori) point of view. primary repression concerns the lack in the Symbolic corresponding to what was left behind in the Real. Primary fantasies are supposed to furnish an answer to that lack. The primal father then becomes the necessary element which has to be constructed in order to repair the lack in the Symbolic. In our next chapter, we will take a closer look at Freud's elaborations in this respect. As far as Lacan is concerned, it is at this point that we situate the introduction into language and the ensuing division of the subject $, as well as the irrevocable loss of unity and the movement of desire following from it.

This brings us back to the hysterical subject, though this time in the proper sense of the word, as the subject divided by language, $. Indeed, there is no other divided subject $ than the hysterical one, and the hysterical position is the necessary position of every speaking being. On the basis of that position, the hysteric $, aspires to the unity of a complete subject S. This implies a cross-roads with two directions: on the one hand we have the object, and on the other desire.

Desire finds its origin in the division of the subject, caused by language. $ expresses its desire in representations or signifiers, thereby changing it into a demand. This expression is never sufficient, hence the endless, insistent, repetitive character of the chain of signifiers which tries to give an expression to desire, $ → S1 → S2. Every ending is always a virtual one. The hysterical subject does not desire a ready-

made satisfaction as an answer to her longing. She refuses phallic pleasure and reserves herself for another enjoyment. Hence her necessary
dissatisfaction. The oft-mentioned 'lability' of the hysterical patient is
rooted in this, together with the triggering of a hallucinatory crisis at
the moment when she believes she has found unity, the perfect satisfaction.[38] Desire endlessly shifting through the chain of signifiers
results in a repetition of which the virtual finishing point is the
Lacanian Real, virtual because this Real lies beyond the scope of the
signifier. The meeting with this Real necessarily fails, and if it risks not
failing, the answer is hysterical psychosis and hysterical hallucination.
With this Lacanian conception of hallucination, we rediscover Freud's
original theory on the hallucinated satisfaction.[39]

Freud's first theory was focused solely upon the endless shifting of
desire, with its roots in the pleasure principle. That is why the treatment itself became a missed encounter. Only the discourse of the master could impose an end on the continuous displacement of desire.
With Freud II and Lacan, we can begin to look at the other side: the side
of the object and the fantasy: $ \$ \lozenge a $. Object a lies beyond the signifier, it
is the last term of desire which can never be expressed in signifiers. As
an object, it is situated between the big Other and $\$$, being the meet-
ing-point of what they lack respectively. The hysterical subject can only
meet the Other by way of a fantasy by which she veils object a in her
attempt to fill in the lack of a. This implies that the object becomes all
important as an answer to the lack in the Other, on the one hand as a
means of restoring the original unity, and on the other as an ultimate
proof that this is impossible. This explains the hysterical dependency
on the partner, also reflected in transference neurosis and transference
resistance.

It is obvious that this new theory radically changes the conception
of the treatment. The interpretation that focused on desire and its displacements $ \$ \rightarrow S_1 \rightarrow S_2 $, changed at the end of Freud's development
into two smaller pieces of technique, each with its own function. First
of all, *Deutung*, literally 'pointing', which focused on smaller sections
of free association and aimed at bringing 'indestructible' unconscious
desire to light. This was not sufficient. The aspect of indestructibility
remains, precisely because desire does not aim at satisfaction, at the
Eldorado of the genital drive, but, on the contrary, opts for the continuation of desire itself - like the dream of the butcher's beautiful wife.
The second technique aims to reveal the structure in which and
through which desire keeps on shifting. Freud's clinical experience

convinced him more and more that desire was indeed always shifting; it was something in relation to which every therapeutic ending could only be virtual. Freud's answer followed the same time span: *Durcharbeiten*, working through, was the countermeasure to the cause of the endless displacements, the repetition compulsion.

Lacan implemented the practical consequences of these changes and formulated the necessary conceptual extension. Desire keeps on moving because its starting point is an irreparable lack in the Other. The neurotic hears this lack in the Other as a Demand - that is, expressed in signifiers - and tries to furnish an answer with his fantasy. These fantasmatic productions stage the scene which plays out the scenario of desire time and again. The 'Deutungen' function as punctuations in the chain of free association of the analysand, x-raying the stratification of signifiers, and aiming at shifting desire. Their insistent character becomes clear when they appear in signifiers, that is, where desire is transformed into a Demand, and it is that insistence which has to be questioned time and again; this aspect is beautifully expressed in the figure of the 'interior eight', which makes this circularity visible.[40] It shows why the treatment must avoid interrupting displacements. The aim is to reveal the basic fantasmatic structure which has a specific object *a* as agent of analytic discourse. Freud's 'construction' and 'working-through' lead to Lacan's 'la passe' as a new solution for the problem of ending an analysis, 'la traversée du fantasme', the journey through one's fantasy paradoxically ending in the subject's dropping out of it. This is what he calls the *destitution subjective*, the destitution of the subject, mirrored on the Other side by the *désêtre de l'analyste* (literally, the dis-being of the analyst).[41]

This second Freudian theory can also be put into a schema(2).

In comparison to schema 1, it is quite clear that Freud's second theory is an open one. The discourse of the master has disappeared, there is room for hysteria once more. Freud has postulated a moment which is logically primary, a preceding period which is of capital importance for the constitution of the subject. He anticipated its elaboration in one of his most poetic papers: *The Theme of the Three Caskets* .[42]

This is a key paper, since it is the first to give a central place to the figure of the woman-mother. Her importance kept on growing in Freud's theory of hysteria. Every human being begins life as a satisfying unity with the mother, a unity which is lost and sought for later on in the figure of the partner. Freud specified later on that the same is true for the woman as it is for the hysteric: even her (masculine) partner can be contaminated by the mother-imago. He could serve as a means to reinstall the original fusion with the mother as first Other. This searched for fusion, the striving for love and satisfaction, shows a strange affinity with death and the non-verbal. It necessitates a defence, the necessity and endless displacement of desire,

This defence is nothing but the Oedipus complex, in which Freud

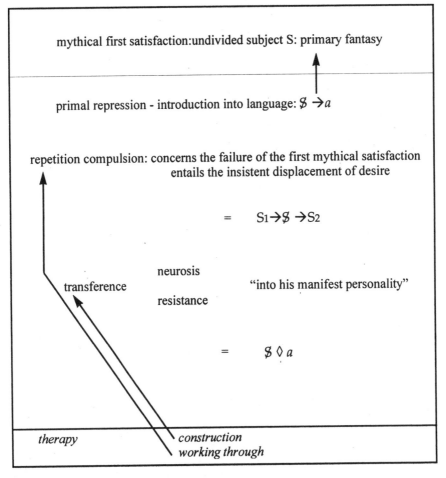

mythical first satisfaction:undivided subject S: primary fantasy

primal repression - introduction into language: $\emptyset \rightarrow a$

repetition compulsion: concerns the failure of the first mythical satisfaction
entails the insistent displacement of desire

$$= \quad S_1 \rightarrow \emptyset \rightarrow S_2$$

neurosis

transference

resistance

"into his manifest personality"

$$= \quad \emptyset \Diamond a$$

therapy

construction
working through

Basic concept: Freud   Eros-Thanatos
                        Primary fantasy - primal repression
                        Construction - working through
                Lacan   phallic jouissance and other jouissance
                        the divided subject $\emptyset$ and the loss of object ιa
                        expression in the signifier: - $S_1 \rightarrow \emptyset \rightarrow S_2$
                                                       - $\emptyset \Diamond a$

Schema 2.

postulated an Oedipal father who subjects the desire of the subject to the Law. In his early Oedipal theories, there was no room for the first central figure: the primal mother, the first Other. As a result, his theory was confronted with an impasse. Once again, it was the hysteric who showed him the way out of this deadlock.

CHAPTER 9

CONSEQUENCES OF FREUD'S SECOND THEORY: PRIMARY PHENOMENA

When he developed his first theory Freud had been a pupil at the school run by his hysterical patients. Repression was the central mechanism and the content of the repressed material concerned fantasies about the father which were woven around a kernel of reality. The failure of this theory in the very place where it should have received confirmation, in the treatment, urged Freud on to *Beyond the Pleasure Principle*. There is something beyond the pleasure principle, beyond his theory of the pleasure principle, something that is responsible for the resistance of transference, for transference neurosis, and for negative therapeutic reactions.

In this text, Freud discovered a form of pleasure which exceeded his pleasure principle, another enjoyment upon which the desire of the hysteric seemed to focus without ever expecting satisfaction. His first theory, based solely on the pleasure principle, no longer stood up. A complete revision was necessary and a new theory was going to take shape. 'New' is not the right word. Out of the treasure chamber of *The Project* and the letters to Fliess, he dug up and redefined a number of forgotten ideas.

One particularity of this new theory was that, in comparison to the first one, it became ever more 'primary'. The same concepts were reconsidered with respect to hysteria, but a new epithet was added: repression became primary repression, fantasy became fundamental fantasy and the father became a primary father. These three primary phenomena are usually considered independently of each other. In my opinion they are closely linked: all three of them are an effect of Freud's shift towards a new theory, and each of them has links to the other two. The thread running through all three of them is the process of psychic sexuation, with the emphasis on femininity. The question "What is a woman?" changed into "What does a woman want?". It is the same question the hysteric asks.

Primary repression, primary fantasy, primal father: three key concepts summarising Freud's new insights. But the series is incomplete and the omissions in it were to bring him once again to an impasse. Following the same line of thought, the series could be completed by the two terms, 'primary castration' and 'primal mother'. Freud took this step very hesitantly in his very last papers. The 'primal mother' received an implicit formulation in *Moses and Monotheism*, 'primary castration' was on the brink of being formulated in *Splitting of the Ego in the Process of Defence*. Death, as the primal mistress, prevented the finishing touch.

The first theory was re-elaborated, yet even the new edition had to be modified in turn. The changes show the same direction as the one which can be observed during the treatment of a single hysterical patient. It is a beautiful demonstration of the truism that each analysis consists in a rediscovery of the theory. In the beginning there was a certain relationship between the Symbolic and the Real which was both discovered and covered over by Freud. In order to cover up, he made use of the same register as his patients did: the Imaginary. Just as in hysteria, Freud built up this register in order to repair the lack in the Symbolic. This building up is fundamental and consists of the construction of ever more primary phenomena. Freud failed in this respect, and the hysterics failed together with him. Moreover, both of them stumbled in the same places: the father and the phallus. When Freud was forging his myth of the primal father, he was never able to transcend the character of reality: the myth had to refer to a concrete historical reality. The same was true for castration: the castration complex remained the real - real because biologically determined - stumbling block of every analysis. The step towards the symbolic function of the father, the Name-of-the-father as a signifier, towards the mother as first Other subject to the law of the Name-of-the-father, was never taken.

From repression to primary repression

Primary repression and the Real

Before the development of the second theory, hysterical repression functioned as an endless and circular process. Every repression carried its own failure with it, resulting in the return of the repressed, and necessitating in its turn a new repression. This endless displacement could only be chased by a treatment that would never succeed in catching up.

We have situated the reason for this circularity in the absence of a first logical moment. Freud brought in such a moment in three papers: his Schreber study, *Repression* and *The Unconscious*.[1] In these papers, he discerns three moments in the process of repression: primary repression which is the basic mechanism; the 'eigentliche Verdrängung' or 'Nachdrängung', that is, the one which comes afterwards (*nach*), a process made possible by the preceding primary repression; and lastly, the return of the repressed material in the form of symptoms.

Giving this primary repression a correct conceptualisation was a metapsychological nightmare for Freud. Laplanche and Pontalis rightly remark that this concept is first of all a postulate, based on what are assumed to be its effects.[2] Indeed, a representation can only be repressed if there are two powers at work: one that repels and one that attracts. The trouble lies with this latter: where does it come from? There has to be some kind of unconscious nucleus from which this attraction issues forth, a kernel originating in an unknown process. Freud assumed that this was the work of some primary repression which had caused this unconscious nucleus to come into being. Yet this primary repression, as 'primal mover', would necessitate a very special mechanism, since there can be no attracting nucleus at first. Indeed, this only comes into existence as an effect of primary repression itself. Thus, the only possible mechanism is the countercathexis.[3] If we follow our argument as developed in the first section, we can express this as follows: primary repression sets up a representation on the boundary of the lack in the Symbolic, the lack in which the Real makes its appearance. This implies that primary repression is not so much a repression as a *fixation*, a primary fixation in fact: something of the Real stays behind on a previous level, while the first development functions as a counter-representation ('Gegenvorstellung'), like a washer around the aperture.[4]

Unsurprisingly, Freud was not very happy with this limited mechanism. In 1926 he wrote: "Far too little is known as yet about the backgrounds and preliminary stages of repression". He continued by guarding against overestimating the role of the Super-ego, which originates in a later period. He concluded: "At any rate, the earliest outbreaks of anxiety, which are of a very intense kind, occur before the Super-ego has become differentiated. It is highly probable that the immediate precipitating causes of primary repressions are quantitative factors such as an excessive degree of excitation and the breaking through of the protective shield against stimuli".[5]

The further development of the concept - an urgent matter, according to Freud - did not take place; indeed, since Freud it has tended to disappear altogether. As proof, it is sufficient to look at *Grinstein*, the main psychoanalytic bibliography before the advent of the Internet; its

96,000 entries contain only four references to primary repression... The explanation for this paucity is very simple: the idea of primary repression just doesn't fit in the post-Freudian theory, which only goes back to Freud I.

Nevertheless, it is possible to make the necessary elaboration within Freudian theory itself. Let us take up our last quotation, in which Freud was talking about "the earliest outbreaks of anxiety and the breaking through of the protective shields by excessive excitations". Repression supposes a motive, unpleasure; analogously, we can reasonably assume that primary repression supposes a primary unpleasure, - "the earliest excessive outbreaks of anxiety". At this point, the reader will probably recognize something: thirty years earlier Freud had assumed that there was an experience of primary anxiety at the basis of hysteria, which emerged in a state of psychical insufficiency, a state in which the psychical apparatus failed to elaborate something. In other words, we are rejoining Freud's very first formulations concerning trauma.

Our reading of this theory in our first section permits us to formulate some conclusions. The trauma which could not be psychically processed, is the Lacanian Real. Originally, Freud thought that the only possible reaction left consisted in the investment of a *Grenzvorstellung* (boundary representation); in the present papers, he talks about a *Gegenvorstellung* (counter-representation). In our discussion of this investment and its further elaboration in fantasies, we concluded that these were nothing but a defensive working over in the Imaginary of the traumatic Real; in other words: an attempt at a psychical elaboration of something for which the words were originally lacking. This lack in the Symbolic is the Lacanian $\not A$, the signifier denoting this lack is $S(\not A)$. This signifier is what Freud used as a substitute signifier for a woman: passivity. In this respect, the counter-representation is a 'masculine' activity, it is Lacan's S_1 as one name for the phallic signifier. This latter also designates the primal father as a full father, what he called the 'l'au-moins-un', the one and only exception who escapes castration, that is, subjective division[6]. As such it fulfils the condition which makes the Symbolic as such possible, the S_2, the chain of signifiers together with its inherent lack.

Freud	Traumatic Real	→ passivity	←→ phallic activity	→ Oedipus fantasy
Lacan	$\not A$	$S(\not A)$	$\dfrac{S_1}{\not S}$ //	$\dfrac{S_2}{a}$

This schematic representation demonstrates two things: first of all, the coherence with other primary phenomena, still to be considered, such as primary fantasy and primal father; secondly, that from a Lacanian point of view, it is at this very point that the Unconscious starts to exist, together with the process of sexual identification, and that the condition for it is nothing but the discourse of the master. S1 founds the Symbolic, the chain of S2, which results in a divided subject $ and an object in the place of the lack in the Other. Moreover, this structure of the master discourse is the structure of the Freudian Oedipus complex as the necessary condition for the Symbolic. In our discussion of the primal father, we will return to this important point.

The thesis that the Unconscious finds its origin at this point, comes from Freud. The formalisation is Lacanian. Freud was working along developmental lines: the unconscious is not an a priori fact. It starts off at a definite point in the development of a human being - a mythical, certainly abstract moment that has to be understood as logically anterior to any subsequent 'Niederschrifte', the inscriptions which are so many psychical elaborations. The inevitable conclusion is *that the nucleus of the unconscious is the Real.* primary repression concerns S($\cancel{A}$), it is only with later repressions that other signifiers will be added to this first one. The structure of the Unconscious, then, is the one described by Freud in his *Studies*: an unreachable nucleus of the Real, enclosed by three layers ordered in a specific way. We have already discussed this when we demonstrated that this is the very point where one can say that the Unconscious is structured like a language. Now we can go a step further: the moment when the Unconscious becomes separated as a structure on its own, not taken up by the first system of inscriptions, is the moment of the introduction of language. Language and unconscious have the same origin, they presuppose each other in a reciprocal dependency. Hence, it is precisely at this point that the divided subject $ *comes into being,* that the *Splitting of the Ego in the Process of Defence* takes place.

This development led Freud into trouble with respect to the terminology of his first topology. 'Unconscious' was already no longer applicable in the original descriptive sense of the word, as not-conscious or 'forgotten'. As a topological concept, denoting a system, it blurred the boundaries of the pre-conscious. Thinking in terms of the dynamic-economic metaphor leads to even greater difficulties because of the still mysterious concept of psychical 'energy'. Freud chose a second topology in which 'unconscious' was not so much a system, but a mere adjective, a predicate. Alas, this did anything but solve the prob-lem; the Ich-Es-Über-Ich machinery was transformed into a personifi-cation. It became a bedtime story about a charioteer desperately trying to keep his horse under control whilst having lost his chariot two cor-ners earlier. In one of his earlier papers, Lacan proposed a more nuanced use of the term 'unconscious' through the application of another, more operational concept: the Imaginary.[7]

Primary repression and clinical practice

Primary repression as a postulate, as a process by which the Unconscious becomes a separate entity at a given moment: such for-mulations give rise to the suspicion that we are dealing with a concept which is first of all necessary for conceptual coherence rather than for clinical practice. This is not true: primary repression can be found in clinical practice. In view of the developmental background, the best illustrations are to be found in analysis with children. The fact that Little Hans was phobic, suffering from an anxiety hysteria, fits our pur-pose very well. When Freud was writing this case study, the concept of primary repression had not yet been formulated. Basing ourselves on his clinical descriptions and making use of Lacanian conceptualisation, we can pinpoint the place and function of primary repression without violating Freud's paper. The moment we do so, one major hiatus in Freud's theory on primary phenomena becomes clear: the role of the mother.

A child is born in a human, that is, a verbal world, in the field of the Other. As a future subject, it has to constitute itself in this field by its inherent doubling: the mother is the primary Other, the father is the second Other; together, they are responsible for the introduction into language, into the Symbolic.

With Hans, this introduction takes a very specific form. The ambi-guity of the utterances of the mother in combination with an all too indulgent father determine the onset of the phobia, described in the first chapter of the case study. Hans is obsessed by a search for the penis, he wants to see the penis of every living organism. The inter-ventions of the mother as first great Other, have a determining effect in this matter. She intervenes in three different ways, which in their reci-procal combination result in a very paradoxical situation. The first massive affirmation of the mother concerns her phallus: she pretends to have a 'Wiwimacher', a penis, too. This means there is only one gen-der. Secondly, she demonstrates her conviction that sexual matters are 'eine Schweinerei', filth, something that ought not to be done. At the same time, the threats of castration she utters remain without effect. Thirdly, Hans' amorous behaviour towards a number of little girls is a source of great pleasure for both parents, which is not concealed from the boy. Thus far, these paradoxes do not give him much trouble, he behaves, says Freud, as a real man, convinced as he is of phallic omnipresence.[8]

When he is three years and nine months old, this changes abruptly. For the first time, Hans produces a dream which is defensively elaborated; obviously, a first process of repression has taken place.[9] The next moment, the phobia breaks out. What has happened? What material has been repressed, and why did this repression take place?

To answer this question, we have to take another look at the discourse of the parents, especially the discourse of the mother. She taught Hans phallic omnipresence, without any mention of a lack. Everybody has a 'Wiwimacher', herself included. The threat of castration thus remains without effect and Hans goes on enjoying himself. This changes abruptly with the birth of Hannah: for the first time, Hans is confronted with a non-phallic living being, that is, from his point of view, with castration. His confidence is badly shaken, his world is shattered. If Hannah is castrated, maybe the same is true of his mother. Indeed, for all his attempts, he has never really seen her 'Wiwimacher'. Obviously, she must have lied to him, thus betraying the fact that she longs to have one. In other words: Hans is confronted with the basic lack and thereby torn from his basic security. The only solution is primary repression, which can be expressed here, as elsewhere in clinical practice, as follows: *Hans represses the want of the first Other*. Lacan demonstrates that the ensuing phobic development has a double function. On the one hand, Hans tries to answer the lack of the mother by filling it in himself; on the other hand the phobia aims at keeping the necessary distance between him and the threatening desire of the mother.[10] The mother cannot be permitted to desire him or the phallus, because this would imply an unbearable lack and a threat for the subject. She has the phallus. $S(\not{A})$ is avoided. The effect of all this is that Hans almost immediately enters 'le monde du semblant', the world of make-believe. Look, he says, how beautiful Hannah's Wiwimacher looks (see note 8). Presumably as beautiful as the one of his mother. His first recognition of sexual difference is as false as her hypocrisy.

Effect of primary repression : phallicisation of the world - le monde du semblant
    The example of Little Hans shows us that primary repression has to
be situated in the process of sexual differentiation. At the start of this
process, there is an opposition between what Freud called the 'active'
versus the 'passive' tendency. In our view, this becomes the opposition
between S_1, the phallic signifier and $S(\cancel{A})$, the absence of an equivalent
signifier for woman. At this point, we recognize the differentiation
made by Freud with repression proper: the attraction exerted by the
Unconscious on the material that has to be repressed is an effect of $S(\cancel{A})$
as a sucking vagina dentata, eventually as an astronomical black hole
absorbing all energy; the repulsion emanates from the phallic signifier
which refuses all non-compatible contents. These relationships can
very well be reversed: the phallic signifier attracts all compatible material, while $S(\cancel{A})$ precisely repels that kind of material.
    S_1 is the affirmative side, meaning: present, tangible. As a basic sig-
nifier denoting basic difference - sexual differentiation - it grounds difference in itself, and thereby too the whole system of signifiers.[11] This
is in perfect conformity with de Saussure's theory: a signifier only
exists in difference. The only trouble for de Saussure, being a linguist,
was the question about the origin of the very first difference. This problem is solved right here in the field of psychoanalysis, outside pure linguistics. In this way, we can understand why the human world is a
phallic world: a human world implies symbolic system, implies difference, implies phallic or non-phallic.
    This is not without major consequences. Freud had already
remarked that Little Hans, in his search for the phallus, made the same
mistake as colloquial speech, when he calls the tail of a monkey a
penis: indeed, 'Schwanz' means both tail and penis.[12] This almost
casual observation can be enlarged to gigantic proportions. S. André
and Julien Quackelbeen remark that the study of any erotic dictionary
inevitably leads to the following conclusion: that every word can be
used to denote something erotic, even the word 'nothing' can stand for
the female genitals.[13] We can endorse their remark with another observation: *namely that this process is not reversible.* The basic signifier can be
connoted by virtually all other signifiers, but the signifier 'penis' is
very much restricted in its connotation. Gorman came to this conclusion in a study conducted from a completely different point of view; he
concluded that all the so-called 'body words' permit an extremely wide
metaphorical use (with 'hand' as the classical example), with one
exception: the proper words for the genitals can only signify them-

selves.[14] The process of signification is a reversed pyramid, in which the fulcrum determines the whole of the upper structure, or, the other way around, in which the upper section crystallises downwards towards one and only one point:

$$\frac{A}{\text{phallus}}$$

This is the result of the metaphor of the Name-of-the-father. For once, Lacan is very clear: *"Die Bedeutung des Phallus* is in reality a pleonasm: in language, there is no other *Bedeutung* than the phallus".[15]

In clinical practice, this massive phallicisation can also be confirmed. Freud apologises for the monotony of psychoanalytic interpretations - ultimately, everything refers back to the phallus. The development of the body image illustrates this very well. We have already seen that all erotogenic zones become phallicised a posteriori - 'nachträglich'. In our previous discussion of this clinical phenomenon, it became obvious that the phallicisation of the oral and the anal is precisely an effect of the flight from $S(\cancel{A})$ by way of the 'compulsion to associate', that is, the determining effect of the phallic S_1 on S_2. In passing, we have to remark that this invalidates the accepted idea of a cumulative libidinal development of the erotogenic zones.[16] Clinical practice of hysteria provides massive confirmation of this phallic redundancy. No wonder that the characteristic double movement - away from $S(\cancel{A})$, attracted to S_1 - has been recognised by attentive practitioners. In 1957, Wisdom gave a conference on hysteria for the Dutch Psychoanalytical Society. The paper, which was published later, is more than simply interesting; in our opinion, it is one of the most thoughtful post-Freudian publications on hysteria. Wisdom's description of the symbolism used by hysteria brings, amongst others, two very interesting observations to our attention: that parts of the body are especially privileged as symbols; that these body parts always signify each time both the penis and castration at the same time. Usually this is explained by referring to a so-called 'phallic fixation', but in Wisdom's opinion, this doesn't explain anything at all, since it is only a diagnostic generalisation. Moreover, he also discovered a strange paradox: the penis itself can be a symbol for the phallus. His explanation: "The likelihood is that both phallic fixation and the anchoring of the symbol have essentially the same meaning and a common origin". Using this idea, he then formulated the phallus as the basic signifier constituting the Symbolic. There is more. After presenting a very captivating and thoughtful discussion of the Oedipus complex in hysteria, he returns to this phallic fixation with a clinically based assumption: that hysteria first of all 'opts' for this over-phallicisation *because of an anxiety about the vagina*.[17] This means that, having based his argument on a very careful listening practice, Wisdom took his distance from a levelled-out post-Freudian theory and came to the formulation of the same double conclusion as we did from our Lacanian point of view: the phallus is the basic signifier of the Symbolic order (S1) because of anxiety in relation to the lack of a feminine equivalent, S($\cancel{A}$).

In this respect, the feminist reproach - that psychoanalysis phallicises and patriarchalises everything - seems fair, but on one condition; as Juliet Mitchell says, in order to get rid of a painful reality, it hardly suffices to criticize its discoverer.[18] The tragedy of the Greek slave is presumably eternal: the messenger who brings bad news is put to death...

The feminist critique brings us to the central relationship between hysteria and phallus. In Lacan's opinion, this relationship is of central importance for psychoanalysis as it was formulated by Freud. He elaborates this in the final session of his seminar *D'un discours qui ne serait pas du semblant*. Insofar as the human symbolic universe is based on the basic phallic signifier, this implies that this world is a make-believe world, *le monde du semblant*. He considers the phallus as a 'semblant', not because it is lacking - every signifier is 'lacking'- but because it does not permit any 'parole', any word about sexual rapport. The hysteric demands this word, she is asking for an answer. It is at this point, in relation to hysteria, that Lacan situates the shift from phallus to father. The hysteric demands an answer from somebody placed by her in the position of phallus. From there on, she can choose between two options.

First of all, she can become the cheerleader for the father and thereby for the phallus. She avoids castration and installs in and through her fantasy the primal father as somebody who is and should be able to procure The Answer, as a master signifier without a lack. In our next section, the development of the hysterical fantasy will show us how the hysteric, through the setting up of this primal father, *reduces herself to that which fills up his lack*. Freud's theory of the Oedipus complex is nothing but the conceptualisation of this hysterical demand; moreover, with the conceptualisation of his first theory, he also avoided castration, that is, an unbearable lack, just as his patients did.

Secondly, she can opt for the complaint. The ever returning failure of fathers - even their words are not capable of inaugurating a decent sexual relationship - is then demonstrated by her. In this scenario, she will put the accent on a refusal: *she refuses to be the object of desire, she refuses to be reduced to that which fills up the lack of the other.* She refuses the reduction to object *a* and develops a love for which is sometimes extreme. Her leitmotiv is always the same: a plea for the equality of all people, which will become the core of a new hysterical fantasy.

From fantasy to fundamental fantasy

Right from the start, hysteria and fantasy are closely linked together. Often enough, hysterical fantasies provided the mirror in which scientific fantasists admired themselves. The history of this relationship could be the subject of a large study, in the line of Ellenberger and Micale. We will focus on the place and position of the fantasy in Freud's second theory of hysteria. Right from the start, hysteria and fantasy are closely linked together. Often enough, hysterical fantasies provided the mirror in which scientific fantasists admired themselves.

Freud's starting point was the traumatic Real as the primary basis for hysteria. We have already argued that he never left this thesis - contrary to common historical opinion - but augmented and re-elaborated it with a theory of the fantasy. The question about the role played by reality kept nagging him. In his second theory, he found an answer: the primary fantasy.

This second theory about the function of the fantasy enabled him to take into account a number of phenomena which did not tally with the first one. This is especially true in the case of knowledge: as a defensive imaginarisation, the fantasy always produces an answer to questions concerning the origin. When we treat of this point, we shall be able to establish a very important relationship with another Freudian discovery from that period: infantile theories of sexuality. Moreover, the question about the origin has to be related to the first primary phenomenon, primary repression.

'Always'. In the first theory, individual fantasies was considered to separate entities, but with the second theory it became clear that each fantasy should be studied as part of a series containing several variations on the same theme. Moreover, this imaginary series has a very clear function for the subject. Its goal is to regulate the relationship between the divided subject and the Symbolic Order, the Other, and this especially on one point, that of sexual differentiation. Thus, a fantasy can be considered as therapeutic, at the point where it aspires to bestow on the subject a sexual identity in the field of the Symbolic. This last point will oblige us to make an immediate connection with another Freudian primary phenomenon: the primal father.

Listened to in this way, fantasy reveals itself to be the central mechanism in the relation between subject and Other. Freud's discoveries in this area tended towards ever greater coherence, where only the basic concept: S($\not{A}$), was lacking.

Primary fantasy, knowledge, fantasmatic series, lack in the Other - through these four points appears what is sometimes called Lacan's 'invention': object *a*. Nowadays, a theory about fantasy is unthinkable without this concept. This object *a* will take a very specific place in Lacan's formula of a hysterical fantasy.

Primary scene, reality, primary fantasy

We have already described Freud's evolution from the trauma as reality to the idea of the Real. The function of the fantasy as a necessary filler, as an answer to the lack in the Other, has also been discussed. What we have to do now is to bring these elements of Freud's very first conceptualisations into relationship with his ulterior development. We have seen that during the development of his first theory, the Real was more and more put aside in favour of the Imaginary and the Symbolic. This loss is most obvious precisely at the point where Freud introduced the primary fantasy: the case study of the Wolf man.

This case study can be considered as Freud's last attempt to find a base in the Real for neurotic symptoms. Twenty years after the search for real seductions, Freud was looking with the same tenacity for a primal scene which had really been observed, even if only with dogs. Freud never accepted the Jungian thesis of a retroactive fantasising of the adult neurotic regardless of any real basis. There had to be a primal scene, the observation of which by the child triggered the neurosis a posteriori. We can recognise the same schema here as in traumatic seduction: an event that was not understood at the time it happened, then the interval of a period of time, and then a second event which works over the first one a posteriori and renders it pathogenic. The most remarkable thing about this polemic search is that Freud, at the moment when he had the answer at hand and was ready to vouch for the authenticity of a scene that really happened, at that very moment he brought us a new answer: the primary fantasy.[19]

The word itself is not new.[20] The best definition of it can be found in lecture XXIII, in which once again the relationship with reality is described. Primary fantasies are supposed to come into the place of a *missing* reality - the child who has never seen a primal scene will imagine one; therefore, these primal scenes appeal to a prehistoric, phylogenetic reality: seduction, primal scene and castration were once, in the childhood period of humanity, a reality that was all too real. As such, they belong to the phylogenetic heritage of every human child.[21] In Freud's opinion, their importance is very great: in a number of cases, individual reality is changed precisely under the influence of this phylogenetic heritage. Thus, the Wolf Man saw his father as the castrating authority, in accordance with the phylogenetic scheme and contrary to his own experience in which the threat of castration came exclusively from women.[22] It is quite clear that, in doing this, Freud subordinated an individual reality to a relationship operating structurally between the Real and the Symbolic.

At this point we have to recognise an implicit double movement in Freud which he never made explicit and which was lost after him. His primary search for the reality, for the hard facts in the individual history of a patient, is complemented and changed by a new concept, primary fantasy. This does not imply - and here we have to correct the post-Freudian prejudice - that Freud takes his leave of the idea of reality. In a second movement, he created a new relationship between primary fantasy on the one hand and a supra-individual prehistoric reality on the other hand. *Totem and Taboo* will furnish us with the most elaborate example.

Invoking a mysterious phylogenetic heritage as an explanation today would not be very convincing, and rightly so. This obliges us to think beyond the surface of this explanation and to look for Freud's elaborations in order to understand what he meant by them. Again it is the correspondence with Fliess that gives us an answer. In *Drafts L* and *M*, Freud discusses the architecture of hysteria. Using the term 'primal scenes' in the larger sense to mean something like primary events, he situates these scenes in a very definite relationship to fantasies; the goal of the hysterical patient is to 'arrive back' at the primal scenes and, in a number of cases, this is only achieved by a 'roundabout path via fantasies'. We have already seen this in our first part, when we assumed S(Å) as the primum movens from which the hysteric flees by way of fantasmatic elaboration. It is not the hysteric who wants to arrive back at these primal scenes but Freud himself... The way in which he describes these fantasies permits us to give an interpretation of this 'phylogenetic' perspective. These fantasies, he notes, are constructed from a combination of things which have been experienced, things which have been heard, past events (from the history of parents and ancestors), and things that have been seen by oneself.[23] To put it differently: the phylogenetic heritage is *the family story* into which the child is born, in which it already had a place before it was actually born, and in which it grows up.

With the introduction of primary fantasies, a new dimension arrives in the theory and in clinical practice. As a concept, it denotes an underlying and latent structure that was never conscious nor ever will be, and which is only knowable through its varying manifestations. As a structure, it does not so much appeal to individual experiences as, to be more precise, to determine and direct those experiences. As a consequence, the subject appears in a very definite way in the field of the Other. The therapeutic procedure is changed too: instead of interpreting the 'forgotten' or 'defensively deformed' contents, Freud put more and more emphasis on construction, the goal being to clarify the primary fantasy as an underlying structure that determines the subject down to his smallest neurotic symptoms.

This primary fantasy was elaborated gradually by Freud in the direction of what we like to call the *basic fantasy*. We prefer this name because it allows us to abandon the always precarious genetic-developmental paradigm. The clarification of this basic fantasy can very well be described as *the result* of analysis.[24]

This basic fantasy is also very basic in another respect. Earlier, we described the progradient direction, the constitutive relation between this basic element and all productions that are determined by it. Reversely, in the retrogradient direction, we can see that all basic fantasies always deal with the most basic problems. Freud never hesitated in this respect. There are three subjects: seduction, parental coitus and castration. All three concern the problem of origin. Castration has to ground sexual differentiation. Seduction assigns the father a very specific place in the origin of sexuality, that is, in the origin of desire. Parental coitus concerns the origin of the child itself. These three origins can be reduced to one central theme, the sexual relationship. To be more correct: these three fantasies procure three answers to the question about the sexual relationship formulated from three angles.

Basic fantasy, infantile theories on sexuality and knowledge

Knowledge is expressed in language, in signifiers. As it is symbolically expressed, human knowledge has a phallic foundation: the phallus as basic signifier grounds the human signifying system. What lies beyond the order of the phallus cannot be expressed symbolically. Hence, there is no knowledge about woman in the Symbolic, in the Other; there is no sexual relationship that can be symbolically expressed.

The lack of this knowledge confronts the child with insurmountable problems. What it finds in the Real cannot always be expressed in the Symbolic. It has to construct a solution of its own through the elaboration of basic fantasies in which a knowledge is constructed with signifiers in the Imaginary outside the realm of the Symbolic. This search for knowledge is continued, especially by the hysteric. The desire for knowledge has an urgent quality for her: she appeals to the Other in order to make him produce knowledge which is by definition unsatisfactory. She constructs an Other who desires to know. In our next section, this will provide us with the necessary link to the primal father.

In Freud's first theory there was not much room for this search for knowledge, but the moment he quit the master position and started discovering again, he could study the so-called epistemological drive in its own right. This shift in position can be illustrated very sharply by the many additions and complementary footnotes to the *Three Essays on the Theory of Sexuality* originally published in 1905. We are especially interested in those concerning the so-called infantile theories on sexuality, because we are convinced that these are the same thing as Freud's future primary fantasies. This line up demonstrates how Freud already laid the foundations for the link between basic fantasy, infantile *theory* of sexuality and knowledge. These additions will procure us with yet another confirmation. The section about infantile theories was added integrally in 1915, that is, precisely in the period in which we have situated the shift to the second theory in our previous chapter.

Another beautiful illustration of the transition can be found in Freud's attitude concerning sexual enlightenment. In 1907 he wrote enthusiastically on the subject: the adult should not withhold essential knowledge, on the contrary, he has to inform the children correctly, thereby making their incorrect, fantasmatic theories of birth superfluous. Thirty years later, he wrote that this prophylactic effect had been grossly overrated: enlightenment may furnish a conscious knowledge but it does not stop children from building up their fantasies.[25]

The many additions to the *The Three Essays* teach us two things. 1. The urge for knowledge originates at the same time as the first flourishing of sexuality. 2. This urge materialises in fantasies that are nothing but attempts at answering a number of typical infantile questions; these fantasies are the infantile theories on sexuality which will be taken up again at the time of puberty and which eventually will constitute the onset of later neurotic symptoms. Moreover, all of the pubertal fantasies evoked by Freud, are exclusively basic fantasies.[26]

What does the child want to know? Why is this knowledge doomed to fail? In 1915, Freud was still convinced that the central question for the child concerned the mystery of "Where do the little babies come from?",[27] although the case study of Little Hans should have taught him better. Indeed, infantile observation is first of all directed towards sexual difference, the way boys and girls differ; moreover, their question about birth and pregnancy concerns the role of the father. Precisely at the moment of writing his first and most important paper on woman, Freud changed this: it was not the origin of babies which was central; the focus of infantile research concerned the how's and why's of sexual differences. Moreover, in 1908 he had already observed that the first sexual theory establishes the universality of the phallus.[28]

To put it differently: the child starts with a monosexual phallic conviction in which there is no symbolic place for woman. The differentiation that can be found in the Real does not find its counterpart in the Symbolic. It is phallically interpreted through the primary fantasy about castration.

Once again, the differentiation between the Real, the Imaginary and the Symbolic demonstrates its usefulness. A number of discussions between Freud and some of his followers about whether a child 'knows' the vagina, whether there are vaginal sensations during childhood or not, can be brushed aside. Freud's refusal to acknowledge these data is an expression of his conviction about phallic primacy. From this point of view, the vagina stays terra incognita for the child. The differentiation between the three orders shows why this discussion could not be solved: they were talking about different things. Indeed, the child does not 'know' the vagina because, for lack of a signifier signifying femininity, the female gender remains in the Real.

The basic fantasy around castration can be considered the first infantile sexual theory, the first elaborated knowledge to bridge the gap. In the light of our previous arguments, this implies that this fantasy aims at producing an answer to S($\cancel{A}$). Its result - besides the effect of bridging the gap between the Real and the Symbolic - is the castration complex, of which penis envy is a hysterical variant.[29]

The child's second theory concerns birth and pregnancy, and especially the role of the father. In these theories, the pregenital takes the upper hand: babies are born orally, anally or even cloacally. Time and again, the child is at a loss when it tries to imagine what role the father plays in this situation. While even very small children have no trouble at all in detecting the role of the mother in procreation, the father's part seems incomprehensible. Conception is thought to take place by eating something, by kissing, even by urinating together... Insofar as the father is acknowledged as having a role, he is allotted the role of seducer.

At this point we can formulate a first conclusion. The two infantile sexual theories already discussed are nothing but the first developments of two basic fantasies. Each of them starts with a given mystery for which it tries to formulate an answer; this fails, and that is the reason why they never get any further and stick to these questions. Freud wrote: "There are, however, two elements that remain undiscovered by the sexual researches of children: the fertilizing role of semen and the existence of the female sexual orifice".[30] We recognize here the impossible relationship between the Real and the Symbolic on two well-defined points: the female gender and the role of the father.

The third infantile sexual theory furnishes us with the first elaboration of the basic fantasy concerning the coital primal scene. The many, mostly sadistic interpretations of children accentuate one thing: that sexual rapport is not evident for a child. They translate 'the mystery of marriage' into something pregenital: urinating together, defecating together, kissing... Pregenital, that is, not genital - for the child, there is only one sex, consequently, a relationship between two different sexes is unthinkable. Hence, the child will never acknowledge the link between coitus and conception. Later on, Freud added that these childhood ideas about sexual rapport are factors that will determine adult neurotic symptoms. Moreover, he didn't cherish any illusion about marriage. In 1908, he noted that "a girl must be very healthy if she is to be able to tolerate it" and "the cure for nervous illness arising from marriage would be marital unfaithfulness".[31]

The "Penis normalis, dosim repetatur" is no effective therapy for hysteria.[32] Conversely, sometimes a therapeutic effect is found in the fantasy as an attempt to answer to the basic lack.

Fantasmatic series and therapeutic effect

The function of the fantasy cannot be restricted to a mere attempt at escape from a frustrating world. It has to be considered in a larger context as a basic structure attempting to answer a basic lack, and is therefore structurally necessary. It starts with so-called 'infantile' sexual theories and continues with a hysterical fantasmatic series. We have deliberately chosen the word 'series', because the failure of the basic fantasy as an answer to the lack in the structure gives rise to a never ending series of fantasies in the hysteric. This failure does not have to be total: the imaginary series can result in a subject being able to constitute itself in the Other in a more or less satisfying way, i.e. that it finds a more or less satisfying identity.

This therapeutic effect of fantasmatic development is recognized by Lacan in Freud's case-study on the Wolf Man. At its height, the infantile neurosis of this patient has the same role and function of an analysis: the reintegration of the past in a law, in the field of the Symbolic: "What Freud shows us then is the following - it is in as much as the subjective drama is integrated into a myth which has an extended, almost universal, human value, that the subject brings himself into being."[33]

After Freud, this was explicitly applied in analyses with children. Melanie Klein, in putting the accent on children's fantasies and their elaboration in the treatment, aims at the introjection of the 'good object' and the expulsion of the 'bad object'. Bruno Bettelheim discovered that the predilection of children, some of them seriously ill, for particular fairy tales procured him an excellent therapeutic instrument. Gardner developed this into a mere technique, without any conceptual base: 'The mutual story telling technique'. In passing, let it be noted that Freud had already commented upon the relationship between infantile sexual theories, fairy tales and myths.[34]

Owing to the structural peculiarities of hysteria, its fantasy series of fantasies concentrates on the father, especially on the construction of a certain father. The basic fantasy about seduction aims at the establishment of the man-father in order to make a sexual relation possible. As an anxiety-hysteric, Little Hans builds a number of fantasies which focus more and more on that father figure needed by him to enable him to escape from the Oedipal deadlock. Lacan discusses this in his fourth seminar, where he compares the function of Hans' fantasies to the function of myths for a people, as described by Lévi-Strauss: each fantasy tries to solve a problem of origin - in the case of Hans, the role of the father (see note 10). The evolution of his attempts at a solution demonstrate the way in which he is solving his Oedipal situation.

The fantasies of Hans furnish us with one of the most beautiful examples of the infantile search for a father, but for now we will reserve its discussion for our next section, focusing on the primal father. Another very interesting, but less well-known example, is provided by Breuer's main patient in *The Studies on Hysteria*, Anna O., whose real name was Bertha Pappenheim; her life history is an excellent demonstration of the thesis that the development of a basic fantasy determines the way in which one lives one's life. The information about her life history comes from the book by Freeman. Among other things, she provides us with some of the contents of Bertha's 'Privattheater', dating both from the period of the treatment and afterwards. The evolution that can be discovered in these fantasies, combined with some other data, make it possible for us to interpret Bertha's attitude towards her father and the way this changed during her life.[35]

The first series is hysterical in an almost classical way. Bertha needed her father to signify her female sexual identity. The uncertainty in the father figure made the uncertainty in her female identity all the greater. Hence, she constructed her own father figure, with the result that she came to occupy his place herself: 'Elle fait l'homme'.[36] Her fantasies are a beautiful illustration of this situation, for example, the first fairy tale she told Breuer: "A poor little orphan is wandering around, looking for somebody that she could love. In an unknown house, she finds a father who is incurably ill and dying. His wife has no hope any more. The orphan refuses to accept the unacceptable and starts nursing him day and night. And - Oh wonder! - the man recovers and adopts the girl. Hence, she had found somebody to love."

The orphan girl is not looking for a home where she will be loved, on the contrary, she is looking for a father who can be loved by her. This remarkable content was realised by Bertha in different ways. For years, she herself had functioned as a nurse for her sick father. Years after the treatment with Breuer, she became the benefactor of... an orphanage. In order to procure the little ones some diversion, she told them fairy tales that she had invented herself and then edited them at her own expense: *In der Trödelbude* (in the second-hand shop). The basic frame, in which all fairy tales are placed, treats of the shopkeeper himself. It concerns a man living in the deepest misery because his wife has left him. The story ends happily the moment when his daughter, who was supposed to be lost, returns and brings him the tidings of the death of his wife, her mother. The daughter moves in with him, gives him back his lust for life, and everything turns out for the best.

This happy ending has a strange ring about it: the mother is dead, the daughter returns, and all is well. This was the period in which Bertha was very aggressive towards her mother. Once she had been promoted from benefactor to general manager of the orphanage, her housekeeping policy was on many a point exactly the opposite of her mother's style in her own home. The accent was put on education and study - search for knowledge - on repair work and on an extreme sense of justice - everybody is equal in front of the Law. Israël expresses the hysterical daughter's main reproach against the the the mother as, "You are not the woman that my father ought to have had". The woman-mother did not make the man-father, that is, she did not permit him to assume fully his symbolic function.[37] The daughter has to do it in her place. She makes The Man - and thus takes his place. In this respect, it is not surprising that Bertha signed her book with a double masculine pseudonym: Paul Berthold. The masculine first name is enhanced by the peculiarity of the patronymic: indeed, 'Berthold' is the masculine variant of her own first name, Bertha. It is under this name that she went public with her 'Privattheater'; in 1899, she published a play, enti-tled: *Frauenrecht*.

This play marks the entry into a second phase. The main theme of the first fantasmatic series concerned the construction of a father fig-ure, made necessary due to the lack of a consenting and corroborating mother. The second period brought a total reversal: the failure of the father was exposed and the mother was depicted as his victim. The central element between those two figures was the sexual relationship as that which can and has to be refused by women - this is precisely her *Frauenrecht*. The play illustrates this reversal in a dramatic way. The story is about a poor working woman, languishing in an attic room with her five year old little daughter. There is no father figure. The woman is denounced to the police by prostitutes for industrial action and agitation, and she is thrown into jail. Once released from jail, she is so ill that she is no longer able to sustain herself. The wife of a rich lawyer - rich because of his wife's fortune - asks her husband for a hundred marks to give to the poor mother. Initially the brute refuses, but eventually he consents to visit the poor woman's dwelling, together with his wife, in order to judge for himself. In the attic, he is exposed as the former lover of the poor woman, who was let down by him when she was pregnant. The scandalised spouse concludes that she will not leave him 'for the sake of the children', but that, from now on, she is going to refuse every sexual contact with him. "Il n'y a *plus* de rapport sexuel".

This second direction of the fantasmatic series is remarkable - but is only remarkable in the light of the first one. Currently, the central figure is the woman, to whom man owes everything, even his fortune.[38] The sexual relationship is depicted as a fraud, a make-believe one, and this is uniquely the man's fault. Women who are betraying The Woman are precisely those women who consent to this deceptive sexual relationship: prostitutes. "The" Woman can only refuse such a fraud.

Appropriately enough, this was the last production she signed with her masculine pseudonym; moreover, this pseudonym was already diminished, reduced from 'Paul Berthold' to a mere 'P.Berthold'. In 1900 she added her own name in brackets. Later on, the pseudonym disappeared completely and she signed only her real name.

In 1904 she established the 'Jüdischen Frauenbundes', with herself in the presidential seat. Her own local section in Frankfurt was aptly called: 'Feminine vigilance'. Bertha had assumed her female identity in such a way that it brought a complete reversal in comparison to the first phase.

In passing, let us remark that this second development enables us to situate Dora at the time of her analysis with Freud. In the first dream, she put a father figure on the scene who refused to sacrifice his children for his wife's jewel case. Our discussion of this dream in our first part, in combination with the evolution of Bertha's fantasies described above, demonstrate that at the time of the dream Dora was also trying to set up a primal father against the mother. When she entered the consulting room of Felix Deutsch twenty years later, she had chosen another position: the vindictive one. She complained about her father and depicted herself as a victim of men in general: her father, Mr.K., her husband, her son. At that time she had taken her mother's side, in opposition to the period of her analysis with Freud.

With Bertha, there is a third development in the fantasmatic series which demonstrates the therapeutic effect of the series at its best. Her mother died in 1905. Bertha took care of the funeral and arranged matters in such a way that she herself would be buried next to her, that is, neither with her father (whose grave is situated in Pressburg), nor with her sisters (Vienna). She opened a new establishment, which was not for orphans this time but for delinquent young women, most of them unmarried mothers. This shift from the father's side to the maternal signifier is typical of the second development. At that moment she started a new hobby which was equally typical: drawing up the genealogy of her *mother's* family. It is precisely with this search that the third phase takes off. During her investigations, she stumbled upon a forgotten fore-mother: Glückel von Hameln. In this figure she found an ideal identificatory model. Just like Bertha, Glückel had occupied herself with the Jewish problem, she had given shelter to the oppressed and persecuted, and all this as early as the seventeenth century. But unlike Bertha, she was married, and happily married for that matter. Just like her husband, she was in business, that is, business on her own. However, this did not prevent her from raising a dozen children. After the death of her husband, she wrote seven small volumes of stories "to chase away the painful memories that keep me painfully awake during many a night". Bertha was delighted: could there be sexual rapport after all? She embarked on a translation of the volumes, during which she discovered a parable that was going to become her leitmotiv from then on. "During a storm, a nest of young birds was at risk from flooding. Papa bird brought his little ones to safety, one by one. While flying above the teeming flood with the first of his young carefully held in his claws, he asked: 'Look at the amount of trouble I am going through in order to save you; will you do the same for me when I am old and weak?' - 'Off course I will', the first replied. At which the father promptly dumped him in the water, with the words 'One should not save a liar'. The same went for number two. When asking the question of the third and last one, he received the following answer: 'My beloved father, I cannot promise you that; but I do promise that I will save my own little ones'. Needless to say the papa bird saved this young one."

The father figure is saved because he does not have to be saved. The signifier which establishes the function has been passed on to the next generation.

Basic fantasy and S($\cancel{A}$): 'La femme n'existe pas' and 'Il n'y a pas d'Autre de l'Autre'

This survey shows that the basic fantasies try time and again to construct something at the point where the Symbolic fails, to signify something for which signifiers are originally lacking. For hysteria, these are The Father, The Woman, Sexual Rapport. The contents that have to be constructed are closely interrelated and belong to one main structure.

The father is established in such a manner that he should be able to produce the missing signifier for The Woman, thereby enabling the existence of Sexual Rapport. We have already demonstrated these links with Freud and shown its relation to a central Lacanian notion: S($\cancel{A}$). We want to proceed now with that combination, in order to give this difficult notion a better setting than is usually the case.

In 1971, Lacan reacted against a certain misconception: S($\cancel{A}$) was thought to be the equivalent of Φ, the symbolic phallus lacking in the Other. This misconception, cherished by a number of his pupils, obliged him to define more sharply what he understood by it. S($\cancel{A}$) is *not* the equivalent of Φ. It concerns something completely different; because it expresses the idea 'qu'il n'y a pas d'Autre de l'Autre', there is no Other of the Other and it thus implies that The Woman does not exist, 'La femme n'existe pas'[39]. In our opinion, this twofold aspect of S($\cancel{A}$)) brings us a formalisation of Freud's discovery, thereby demonstrating its coherence.

'La femme n'existe pas', hence: '~~Le~~ ' Femme', '~~The~~ ' Woman. This is the most well known interpretation of the lack of a signifier in the Symbolic. With children, we find its first defensive working over in the basic fantasy of castration; this elaboration always fails because it can only ground sexual differentiation on the presence or absence of just one signifier, the phallus. The hysteric's quest for a sexual identity of her own does not find a satisfying answer in this respect. If she wants to acquire a signifier specifically to signify the woman, the hysteric has to tackle the lack itself, the lack in the Other.

It is at this point that we meet Freud's second basic fantasy, the one about seduction, which has the father as cause and instigator of desire. The hysteric will imagine - and thus construct - a man-father as a total master, the one who knows about desire and enjoyment.[40] With this construction of a primal father, she tries to bridge the gap between the real father and the symbolic father figure. Once the master is set up, he has to deliver up the signifier for The Woman, thereby making a proper female identity possible. This is hysteria, *Between the belief in The Man and the cult of The Woman*, and it is the most typical manifestation of hysterical fantasy. This also fails, and it is at this point of failure that we meet the other side of S($\cancel{A}$): 'Il n'y a pas d'Autre de l'Autre'. The lack in the Other is irremediable, due to its structure.[41] The primal father is a drunken chimera which gives the hysteric a phallic hangover: if she wants to transform the man-father into a primal father, the only solution is to remove his incapability: to become the object that fills up his lack. We will see later on how Lacan formalised this idea in the formula of hysterical fantasy.

The coherence between the three basic fantasies becomes clear in the dreamt-of result, the 'Sunday of Life'. If there were a total Other, a primal father, then The Woman would acquire an identity of her own, thereby making sexual rapport possible between two differently sexualised subjects. Freud's last primal fantasy - parental coitus - has to be linked to the foregoing. The lack of sexual rapport in the Symbolic means that one has to imagine one. And in this imaginary construction, it is again the father who takes the central position. It may be true that the question of 'origin' adhering to this primary fantasy concerns procreation, the timeless 'Where do little babies come from?', but this should not lead us astray. For the child, the problem focuses again on the father and his role in the procreative process. The case study of Little Hans is very convincing in this respect. The difficulties encountered, the impossibility of finding a satisfying answer, result in the failure of the so-called infantile sexual theories. Clinical practice with hysteria makes clear what the aim and function is: the father has to be complete, the procreative function he is supposed to take care of, does not only concern the child, but also the child sexualised as female.

By applying a Lacanian concept we have explained the implicit coherence between fantasies, knowledge and sexual difference in Freud. S($\cancel{A}$) names the impossible; the impossibility of sexual rapport that never ceases not to write itself, 'qui ne cesse pas de ne pas s'écrire'. Fantasy is the structure in which this impossible writing never stops, and so has to be situated on the road of the Imaginary to the Symbolic.[42] The stumbling block on this road is object *a*.

Hysterical Fantasy and object a

In Freud's first theory, fantasy cannot be considered a central issue. At most, it occupies a special place in the series of symptoms. With the second theory, this changes in a drastic way: the introduction of the idea of a primary fantasy, together with that of construction and working-through, results in the fantasmatic structure itself becoming the therapeutic target of analytical practice. While in the first theory the interpretations were always chasing an ever receding desire, in the second theory the aim is the very framework in which desire runs around.

This second theory cannot be discussed without Lacan. His return to Freud is considered by us as being twofold. First of all, Lacan made the (re)discovery of Freud I, the Freud of the divided subject, of the

Unconscious structured as a language, in short: the Freud of the signifier. With Freud II, things become a bit more complicated; it was not a mere return any more, it was a further elaboration of a theory only halfway finished. Freud was struggling with the same problem as his hysterical patients: how to express, to put into words feminine psychological sexualisation, the becoming of a woman? Herein, he followed the hysterical solution because he also put the accent in his theory on the father figure who has to provide the answer to the question 'What is a woman?'. In his haste to reach the end, he skipped a certain step, the starting point. The lack in the Symbolic is the lack in the Other, and thus concerns the *desire* of the Other. The first Other is the mother, a figure who is completely absent from Freud's theory on hysteria until that period. The question 'What is a woman' has to be read first of all as 'What does a woman desire?'. In this respect, Lacan has enlarged psychoanalysis with a new concept: object *a* as the constitutive element of the fantasy.[43]

The importance of fantasy in Lacan's theory and consequent practice can only be demonstrated by the way in which he situates the fantasy in the becoming of a subject. Immediately linked to this, we find three fundamental human dimensions: enjoyment, anxiety and desire.[44]

The becoming of a subject is always a verbal becoming: the process of subjectivisation takes place through already existing signifiers. The mythical subject - described as mythical when it does not exist as yet - the mythical subject has to find its place in the field of the Other: 'How many times does S go into A?'. The first Other to supply signifiers is the mother, and this takes place at the level where primordial enjoyment has to be situated. This operation can be written down as an arithmetical division:

The result of this operation of division is determined by $\cancel{A}$, the lack in the Other. This results in the fact that the subject cannot enter completely into the Other, there is a remainder. This remainder can be called that which resists 'la significantisation', the part of enjoyment that cannot be reduced to the signifier. It is this remainder that is called object *a* by Lacan.[45] When the subject is confronted with this object *a*, there is always a moment of anxiety as a reaction to that part of the Real for which the signifier is lacking.[46] This lack appears clinically in the intervals between the signifiers of the Other.[47] We have met this already with the mother of Little Hans, who signified her desire, and thus her lack, to her little boy through her words, so that her son reacted with an anxiety hysteria. The operation of the subject can now be further elaborated:

$$
\begin{array}{ll}
S & \text{Enjoyment} \\
\not{A} & \text{Anxiety}
\end{array}
$$

In this operation, object *a* takes the position of the cause. It is here that we have to situate the division of the subject, together with the origin of desire. The cause of desire is structurally equivalent to the cause of the division of the subject: object *a*.[48] To what is desire directed? It wants to do away with anxiety by making *a* enter into the signifier, i.e. into the Other. Object *a* is in this respect the entry to the Other: "To desire for the Other is always to desire the object *a*", with anxiety functioning as a relay between enjoyment and desire. This relay also has a separating function: *a* refers to the central separation between desire and enjoyment.[49]

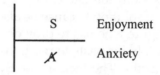

$$
\begin{array}{lll}
A & S & \text{Enjoyment} \\
a & \not{A} & \text{Anxiety} \\
\not{S} & & \text{Desire}
\end{array}
$$

At this point, we see fantasy as a support for, and a modelling of, desire. Fantasy creates a double bind between $ and Other. The desire of the subject is directed to the lack of the Other, in the first instance, the mother. This lack - object *a* - is situated outside the signifier, and is by definition unreachable for the divided subject as a speech-actor. Thus, first of all, the subject has to bring *a* into the realm of the signifier. The way in which this takes place provides us with a definition of neurosis in the fullest sense of the word: the divided subject translates the unspeakable desire of the Other into his Demand[50] and transforms this demand into the object of his desire: he has to procure an answer.[51] This is the first relationship between $ and *a*, alienation as an answer to the lack of the Other. In this alienation, the subject disappears - the 'fading' of the subject - under the signifiers of the Demand of the Other. Lacan considers this as a lethal process, subjectivisation stops, there is no desire of one's own: this is alienation.

$$\mathcal{S} \searrow \ \ a \qquad \text{alienation}$$

This fails because *a* cannot be reduced to the Demand of the Other. In the intervals between signifiers, the lack keeps on insisting, a lack which also concerns the subject as a speech-actor. The second operation between subject and object *a* is separation, in which the lack of the Other is answered by the lack of the subject. The necessary condition for this is the operation of the Name-of-the-father, symbolic castration, which permits the subject to lack - he does not have to fulfil the desire of the Other any longer but can develop a desire of his own.[52] This is separation.

$$\mathcal{S} \nearrow \ \ a \qquad \text{separation}$$

This double operation between subject and object *a* demonstrates that the fantasy establishes the lack in a circular process. The lack of the Other returns in the lack of the subject. Hence, the Lacanian thesis: "le désir de l'homme, c'est le désir de l'Autre".

Obviously, the conclusion of this relationship between subject and Other is that there is no rapport, except a fantasmatic one as an attempt at verbalisation of the essentially non-verbal. The beloved object *a* is nothing but object *a*: "This divided subject $\mathcal{S}$ only relates as a partner to the object *a* inscribed on the other side of the bar. It can never reach its sexual partner which is the Other, except by way of mediation which is also the cause of its desire. Therefore this is nothing other (...) than fantasy."[53] The impossibility of this relationship entails the continuous failure of the pleasure principle.

In the first part of our study, we described the function of hysterical fantasy as an elaboration of the lack in the Symbolic in relation to the Real, an elaboration which takes place in the Imaginary. The question now is, how can we understand our thesis in the light of the Lacanian theory on fantasy?

The function of the fantasy for hysteria can be demonstrated by developing the complete formula, which normally only appears in an abbreviated form: $\mathcal{S} \lozenge a$. The complete version shows us the aim - an Other without a lack - and the effect - a subject alienating itself from an object from which it will separate itself once again. Indeed, her 'belief' in a complete Other - in contrast to the paranoiac, who does not believe, but knows - results in the making of this Other. It is precisely this construction that takes place in and through the fantasy, in which the hysteric transforms herself into that object which is necessary in order for the Other to be complete.[54] As this lack is irrevocable for the Symbolic, this object has to be constructed in the Imaginary, and this results in the phallic version of object a:

$$\frac{a}{-\phi}$$

The completed version of the formula is then:

$$S \lozenge \frac{a}{-\phi} \lozenge A$$

The hysterical subject sets up the absolute Other by presenting herself as the filling up of his lack; thereby she disappears as a subject - *fading* of the subject - in this process of alienation and is reduced to a mere object. Her answer to the lack of the Other demonstrates her own imaginary castration in relation to the Other. The privation of the woman, symbolic castration as the lack of a signifier in the Other, is here reduced to a mere imaginary process in which the phallus can only materialise in a.

The aim was to establish the complete Other, the one and only, who is able to provide a specific signifier for a specific feminine sexual identity. In this way, the fantasy forms the bed for a possible sexual relationship. The necessary tail piece is the primal father.

From Oedipal father to primal father

Every study on hysteria stumbles sooner or later upon the queen of analysis, that is, the king, the father, the primal father. The dubious ring of this chess metaphor goes much further than a superficial play on words. In the noble game of chess, it is the position of the king which determines whether one is checkmated or not. Besides this all important point, he is rather unimportant in the course of the game, a point of inertia, mostly immobile and protected by the surrounding pieces, whose modalities are much more diverse - even the 'castle' moves more. Indeed, the proper queen of the honourable game of chess is of course the queen herself.

Before Freud discovered this queen he polished the king a bit more, an endless job which the hysteric was very glad to give him a hand with - every hysteric is a devotee of the father. In his early years, Freud had already staged the father in two different forms: the perverse father, causing hysteria in his daughters, and the idealised father, featuring as exemplary model in love and sexual relations. He thereby supplied the hysteric, within the framework of her fantasy, with an ideal, but alas, masculine, identificatory model. Feminine identity remained as inaccessible as before.

We have seen the main scaffolds of the theory fall away: the pleasure principle and principle of constancy lost their sense of security, the road to jouissance opened up. What securities were there left for Freud concerning the father figure, the point of checkmate or victory? At least the following: that he had to secure the security.

The Oedipal template as a pre-existing explanatory paradigm

In 1906, the year after the publication of *Three Essays on the Theory of Sexuality*, Freud appealed to his followers to supply his need of psychoanalytically inspired observations of children. Graf, one of his Wednesday evening friends, loyally reported on the romping of his youngest sprog. From a certain point on, this report became a case study. Little Herbert/Hans had turned phobic: afraid to leave the house and afraid of horses. Supervised by Freud, Graf hesitatingly took the first steps on the road to analysis with children. Failing as a father, he emerged as...an analyst. Not really, no. Rather a 'Sujet-(supposé)-savoir', a subject who is supposed to know but who forgot about the supposing part.

This case study enables us to demonstrate: 1) how the father establishes himself as a subject-who-knows with respect to sexual difference; 2) how and why this is exactly what Hans was looking for; 3) how the father appeared on the stage of hysteria. Concerning this last point: it is precisely in this case study where Freud classified the most frequent form of phobia as anxiety hysteria, that is, something which has the same structure as conversion hysteria. The only difference lies in the presence or absence of anxiety or conversion; moreover, clinical practice proves that those two are often mixed.[55]

The giraffe fantasy and the desire of the father

Central to this first analysis of a child, we find a fantasy featuring a giraffe. What is the story? Having entered the bedroom of his parents during the night, Hans explains the next morning that "In the night there was a big giraffe in the room and a crumpled one; and the big one called out because I took the crumpled one away from it. Then it stopped calling out; and then I sat down on top of the crumpled one".[56] From the child's comment, Freud concludes that he is relating a fantasy, not a dream.

This is right up the analyst's street, that is, the analyst Hans' father imagines himself to be. A more classical script could not be imagined: giving himself the role of father Laius, he straightaway recognises Oedipus-Hans taking possession of the crumpled mother giraffe (Jocasta), while the big father giraffe is reduced to the role of screaming observer. In its totality, he adds, the story is a reproduction of an almost daily scene: the little boy joins his mother in bed in the morning, encountering only feeble protests from his father that are invariably rejected by an irritated mother.[57]

Rereading the fantasy line by line, together with the ensuing dialogue, it becomes quite clear that a number of things are not what they are supposed to be. The interpretation of the father, as given above, is at the very least incomplete and probably wrong.

Let us listen first of all to the father's interpretations. "That same day his father discovered the solution of the giraffe phantasy". He *finds* them. Where does he find them? Sure enough not with Hans, because the dialogue on that page in no way endorses what the finder has found. The interpretation is an after-effect of an already established, pre-existing knowledge, and will be given from an S1-position, the one of the master: "In the train I explained the giraffe phantasy to him...". Freud warns us in several papers about explaining: the patient has to find the meaning of his symptoms for himself, the task of the analyst is to open the pathways leading thereto; the warning even appears in this very case study.[58] Many years later, Lacan warned against 'verbalism', seduction through significations; the analyst has to work in and with the signifier, without losing sight of the dimension of object *a*.

The interpretation from S1 charges the other with a knowledge, S2, the explanation. Consequently, we have to suppose the presence of a divided subject $ \mathcal{S} $ under the S1, at the place of the , because, obviously, we are in the discourse of the master. What is the of Hans' father as a divided subject? Throughout the case study, this becomes more and more obvious: the man just can't assume the position of the father. In the relationship with his wife, he is the one who is supposed to talk nonsense. It is also the father who loyally visits *his* mama in Lainz every Sunday, together with Little Hans. Without his wife, that is. And when the father asks Hans what he would do if he were papa, the child answers without hesitation that he would take mama along to Lainz.[59] Children have a good nose.

In the light of this $ - , the interpretation from S1 takes on more and more the bearing of a fantasy of the father, fulfilling his deepest wish: indeed, he would very much like to take the position of the Father of the Law, "the one who has rightful possession of the mother - and in peace, in principle" and is therefore envied and admired by the son.[60] Alas, in everyday life, Hans is not at all afraid of his father, on the contrary, he is afraid of his mother. It is her to whom he would like to give a good hiding, not his father.[61] Moreover, that father does not possess the mother "in all tranquillity", on the contrary, their divorce is on the way (see Freud's appendix to the case).

Truth will out. The beauty of the case is that the father, in spite of his wise explanation, reveals the in a spontaneous reaction: "On Sunday, 29th March, I went with Hans to Lainz. I jokingly took leave of my wife at the door with the words: "Good-bye, big giraffe!" "Why giraffe?" asked Hans. "Mummy's the big giraffe," I replied; to which Hans rejoined: "Oh yes! And Hanna's the crumpled giraffe, isn't she?" (see note 57).

Immediately following this reaction, the father supplies an explanation that no longer tallies with the above; he very patiently explains to Little Hans that he (the father) is the great giraffe, (long neck naturally equals long penis), that the small crumpled one is the mother (without a penis), and so on. Hans confirms all this in a typically hysterical style of complicity with the desire of his father - "The desire of the hysterical subject is to support the desire of the father" - in a way which is diametrically opposed to his first reaction.

The answer of Little Hans

Independently of his confirmation, Hans shows us the way to his : "Mummy's the big giraffe", to which Hans replied: "Oh yes! And Hanna's the crumpled giraffe, isn't she?". The big giraffe is the demanding mother whose phallic desire he has to fulfil, the small giraffe is Hanna, the new baby sister.

To interpret the fantasy further is difficult, almost impossible. The only thing we can point to with a reasonable amount of certainty is that Hanna is an episode in the castration history of Hans. All living things have a penis, he states, including his mother, whatever his old man may maintain.[62] But with Hanna he has to strain his eyes in order to be able to see her willy. The fantasy has to do with a defence against the threat of castration. If we were to try to interpret any further, we should make the same mistake as his father: enforcing an established knowledge.

This does not mean that we cannot discern other interesting material, based on other fragments in the case study. The plumber fantasy especially is very instructive.

The desire of the mother

As a first great Other, she articulates her desire for her child through her presence and absence. In the case of Hans' mother, this desire is massively phallic. Just read the case study: she pretends also to have a widdler, and confirms her position as the phallic mother. A widdler as big as a horse, Little Hans suspects.[63] Horse phobia.

Nevertheless, we have to wait for this phobia. At first, there seems to be no trouble whatever. It is only later on that anxiety erupts, and this is at a very definite point. Freud's first chapter ends with Hans' first, albeit defensive, recognition of sexual difference.[64] And chapter two starts with the onset of the phobia.

Together with Lacan, it is here that we have to situate the discovery of the lack of the mother. The mother - originally almighty - is affected in her power.[65] The child is confronted with S($\bar{A}$), the lack in the first great Other, but now specifically linked to gender. Primal repression has taken place, the imaginary phallus enters the game as the third term between mother and child.

This brings about a complete reversal of the situation. While the child partakes of his mother's power in the first situation (hence the feelings of omnipotence with neurotics and little children), in the second, he is reduced to the mere object *a* of the desire of the mother. For Freud, as for Lacan, this entails a confrontation with the castration complex. It is Lacan who situated this confrontation on a verbal level: "The privation of woman, that is the meaning of castration expressed in terms of lack of discourse" (La privation de la femme - tel est, exprimé en terme de défaut du discours, ce que veut dire la castration).[66]

In other words: an originally pleasurable and satisfying situation changes into one which provokes anxiety. Hence, Freud's thesis that the anxiety of Hans corresponds to a previous pleasure. The change has to do with a process of repression, more particularly, a primary repression.[67] The phobic anxiety functions as an outpost, signalling the danger of an anxiety-ridden enjoyment that is actually impossible. In Freud's terms: anxiety equals a desire that has become impossible to satisfy: Hans remains anxious, even when his mother accompanies him in the street.

There is a fairly well known controversy concerning the ambiguity of Freud's theory on anxiety. Initially, Freud was convinced that anxiety was nothing but transformed libido (this thesis is applied in the case study on Hans); later on, in *Inhibitions, Symptoms and Anxiety*, this is changed: anxiety is not transformed libido, but functions as a signal for something dangerous. In our opinion, the ensuing ambiguity can be understood as follows. In the transition from an originally satisfying but now anxiety-provoking situation, we recognise the first transitional situation for the child as we have described it in Freud's second theory: from the mythical first enjoyment of a non-divided subject and an almighty Other without any lack, to the state of division and loss, $ \$ \lozenge a $, where one has to content oneself with a merely phallic satisfaction. This is the 'transformation' of libido, the original enjoyment which has now become anxiety-provoking. The difficulties about its conceptualisation can also be explained: based on his univocal concept of pleasure, Freud was not able to make a differentiation between satisfaction and enjoyment. Nevertheless, it is also quite obvious here that Freud is on the brink of finding this differentiation, just as we have seen with *Beyond the Pleasure Principle*: with Little Hans, he observes that anxiety corresponds to a repressed desire, but is not the same, precisely because in between comes repression. Anyhow, it is important to see that the fundamental discovery lies beyond the controversy of 'first' or 'second' theory on anxiety: *that anxiety is directed to something that was originally a source of pleasure*. This pleasure has to be understood in terms of Lacan's 'jouissance de l'Autre', the child as a passive object of enjoyment of the Other.

As a matter of fact, about whose desire are we talking? 'Le désir de l'homme, c'est le désir de l'Autre', it is the desire of the first great Other, the mother, which has become dangerous for Hans after his discovery of her lack. Freud observes that the mother has facilitated the neurosis "on account of her excessive display of affection for him and her too frequent readiness to take him into her bed".[68]

Hans will elaborate this complex in another fantasy, expressing his anxiety in relation to his mother's desire as a first solution: "Daddy, I thought something: *I was in the bath, and then the plumber came and unscrewed it. Then he took a big borer and stuck it into my stomach.* Hans' father translated this phantasy as follows: '"I was in bed with Mummy. Then Daddy came and shoved me away. With his big penis he pushed me out of my place beside Mummy."' Let us suspend our judgement for the present."[69]

Freud's last remark is a necessary one. The interpretation given by the father can be criticised along the same lines as the one he gave concerning the giraffe fantasy. We have only to turn to the next page to learn more from Little Hans himself. He is frightened to be put into the bath by his mummy, he is afraid to fall into the tub. The ensuing dialogue is very instructive: '"Hans: It's only in the big bath that I'm afraid of falling in." I: "But Mummy bathes you in it. Are you afraid of Mummy dropping you in the water?" Hans: "I'm afraid of her letting go and my head going in."' (see note 69). In his eleventh seminar, Lacan typifies the phallic mother as the one who drops her child, the child object/abject.[70] Precisely the thing Hans is afraid of.

Primary anxiety, i.e. the anxiety that establishes an anxiety hysteria and precedes a phobia, can now be described as follows. The mother is affected in her omnipotence, because she desires the phallus. The introduction of the phallus between mother and child bares the lack of the Other. Through the confrontation with S($\cancel{A}$), Hans is notified that he has to fill in this gap in his capacity as object *a*. In the relationship between the divided subject - i.e. the desiring mother - and the lack in the Other, Hans disappears as a subject and is changed into her abject object. This can be understood in terms of the first part of the metaphor of the Name-of-the-father, in which the confrontation takes place between a mother's desire and a child:

$$\frac{\text{Desire of the mother}}{\text{Signified to the subject}}$$

This is alienation, Lacan's first operation of the process through which a subject has to constitute itself in the field of the Other: "if it appears on one side as meaning, produced by the signifier, it appears on the other as aphanisis".[71] Aphanisis or 'fading of the subject' is the lethal consequence of alienation. Indeed, as a subject he either disappears in the meaning of the field of the Other ('Desire of the mother' whose signified he becomes), or he stays out of it and vegetates in the Real as a mere 'being' without any signifier whatsoever.

As a solution, there is the operation of separation. The subject discovers the gap in the Other, and as an answer presents his own lack, the 'Veut-il me perdre?', 'Can he lose me?'.[72] This solution presupposes the presence of a fourth element, to which mother and child can direct their desire: the symbolic father. For Hans, this will not be sufficient. His phobia is precisely an attempt to supplement the failing paternal metaphor.

Phobia as a supplement to the Name-of-the-father

Freud described phobia as an evolving process in which anxiety hysteria turns more and more into a phobia, that is, chooses a phobic object. This enabled him to formulate a hitherto unknown clinical differentiation: on the one hand we have anxiety, and on the other we have the object as a screen, a protective bar against that anxiety. From which we can deduce a necessary therapeutic precaution: it is not wise to relieve somebody of his object of anxiety.[73]

Through Lacan, we can understand this phobic object as a phobic signifier. Obviously, this phobic signifier occupies a structural position which protects against anxiety.

The question now becomes: which anxiety? The answer is already in Freud: it is an anxiety which concerns a previous pleasure that is related to the mother, a pleasure that became anxiety-laden after primary repression and after the confrontation with castration - $S(\cancel{A})$ (see note 67). This is the 'enjoyment of the Other' from which the subject recoils and which terminates in satisfaction. From this point onwards, we have to make a differentiation between *enjoyment* as 'enjoyment of the Other' (*jouissance de l'Autre*), the complete fusion of a non-divided subject and Other, and 'phallic satisfaction' (*jouissance phallique*) which is inaugurated by the paternal metaphor, precisely as a protection against this enjoyment of the Other.

The further elaboration of this conceptualisation brings us to the idea that the phobic signifier functions as a form of protection against this anxiety-provoking enjoyment of the Other. As this protective function should be taken care of by the Name-of-the-father, we are confronted with at least two questions: 1) why is it that the paternal metaphor does not function normally for Little Hans? 2) how does the phobic signifier supplement this defect?

As benevolent as the father's intentions may be, he fails in his specific role as a father for Hans. His son will never receive a satisfying answer to his most important question: "But I belong to you?", that is, to his father.[74] Even more so: his role as a father is almost systematically passed over in silence throughout the case study. The most crucial passage in this respect starts with the chicken-and-egg enlightenment, in which Our Lord seems to be the decision maker, so that Hans has to conclude that both men and women can lay eggs and that he too will be able to have children just like a woman.[75] The father denies this and appeals once more to the Almighty as the One who has taken care of the matter in such a way that only women have children, apparently without any male interference whatsoever ("...if God did not wish it none would grow inside her"). The absolute limit is reached when Hans finally turns to his mother. From her, he learns that if the mama does not want a child, then God almighty does not want one either.[76]

In this way, Hans is compelled to feel completely at the mercy of his mother's desire, for whom apparently even God has to lower His divine head. Freud puts it as follows: "His father must have had something to do with Hanna's birth, for he had declared that Hanna and Hans himself were his children".[77] He 'had declared' that he'd had 'something' to do with it ... The symptomatic productions of Hans involving the 'wegen/Wägen dem Pferd' were interpreted by Lacan as an expression of the child's most central problem: to whom is he tied, to which chariot? The motherly or the fatherly one?[78]

How will the phobic signifier supplement this failure in the symbolic function of the father? To be more specific, what is so special about the signifier 'horse'? Freud considers the phobic object as a choice, and that is quite obvious at the beginning of the phobic development: "It may be remarked that the giraffe, being a large animal and interesting on account of its widdler, was a possible competitor with the horse for the role of bugbear;...".[79] If we remember the not unimportant fact that the family name, that is, the *father's* name is 'G(i)raf', the competition becomes more obvious and the choice even more enigmatic. At the beginning of the case study, the father had drawn a giraffe - and Hans obliged him by completing his drawing with a wiwimacher. The father has to be in possession of the phallus.

Nevertheless, Hans opts for the horse. We learn that, of all great animals, Little Hans definitely preferred horses, that it was his father who first played horses with him, that one of his little friends hurt himself while playing at being a horse. All this seems rather trivial, not of any real importance. One detail sticks out: there was one father - not Hans' father - who had warned the children against horses. A warning father. It becomes all the more interesting if we look at the moment when the anxiety turns into a phobia: after the observation of an omnibus horse *falling* in the street. Freud concludes that this accidental observation can only result in such an effect if the signifier 'horse' had previously acquired a certain signification for Hans.

About this previous signification, he remains rather vague. Our thesis runs as follows: the signifier 'horse' refers to the imaginary father, the one who has to take charge of the desire of the mother. And this primal father is none other than Freud himself.

In April 1903, a child was born into the Graf family. Freud knew them very well: the mother had been in analysis with him, the father attended the Wednesday evening meetings in Freud's home on a regular basis. When the child was three years old, Freud bought him a gift and worked himself into a sweat carrying the thing upstairs to their apartment: a rocking horse...[80]

A trivial phenomenon, one might remark. Certainly, as a fact. But facts exist only within the framework of a discourse. As a signifier, 'horse' was filled in by Hans as something in parental speech which referred to an external master figure, the one who had helped his mother, the one his father had asked for advice and the one to whom his own childish productions about his 'non-sense' were sent. *The one who knows*, the fourth point.

But if even this fourth point can come down (the falling horse - the falling object *a* of his mother - falling into the bath), what security is there left? No wonder the phobia erupted at that point. Indeed, it took the insight of a Freud to acknowledge that behind the superficial anxiety about biting horses lay a more fundamental anxiety: that even horses can *fall*.[81] That even they are not sufficient to respond to the lack of the mother.

Freud's intervention: guaranteeing the guarantee

Throughout the whole case study, Freud intervened only once in person. Needless to say, it was a weighty intervention; as a matter of fact, it was a construction: "Long before he (Hans) was in the world, I went on, I had known that a Little Hans would come who would be so fond of his mother that he would be bound to feel afraid of his father because of it; and I had told his father this".[82] What Freud is introducing here is nothing but the missing part of the paternal metaphor. The beauty of the case is that he not only introduced it for Hans, but also for his father: "and I had told his father this". Which, in view of the situation, was highly necessary.

The impact of this intervention on Hans can be measured by looking at the position he afterwards explicitly ascribed to Freud. "Does the Professor talk to God as he can tell all that beforehand?" And in the end, when the father - completely at a loss - asks him almost desperately what he is afraid of, the little boy answers without hesitation that he does not know it himself, but that one should ask the Professor because he will surely know the answer. He also expresses his hope that when everything is sent to the Professor in a letter, his 'non-sense' (the family nickname for his phobia) will be soon over. [83]

It is here that we are confronted with a surprising element, surprising, that is, for a 'classical' post-Freudian analysis: the Oedipal father is one *who has to know*.[84]

This can already be read in Freud himself: he noted that for Hans, his father was not only somebody who prevented him from being with his mother, he was also somebody who withheld a certain knowledge from him.[85] We will return to this important theme in a moment.

After Freud's intervention, Hans' treatment moves into overdrive. The father has been given a certain position by Freud, and Hans has heard this very well. This can be verified in the ensuing parts of the case study. Before Freud's intervention, the father only had a role as an accomplice in Hans' fantasies, while the Law was incarnated by an external agency, the policeman. This is the case in two fantasies which picture a misdemeanour carried out together with the father (entering a forbidden area in a park, breaking a window in a railway carriage) and which finishes each time with both of them being punished by the Law (see note 57). At the very moment of Freud's intervention, the father intervenes to deny that he was ever angry with Hans, arguing that he has never hit him (see note 82). Whereupon Hans immediately replies that of course he has been hit by him (even if only while playing). With this, Hans confirms Freud's construction: for him the father has to function as an authority. He will repeat this later on in an analogous discussion: when the father denies being angry, Hans replies: "Yes, it *is* true. You're cross. I know you are. It must be true".[86] In the aftermath of Freud's intervention, more and more of the knowledge originating with Freud is ascribed to the father.[87] Moreover, it is now possible for Hans to express his anxiety in a much clearer form: he is anxious when his father leaves the house, anxious that the man will not come back.[88] In the dialectical movement of the analysis, this can be understood as follows: now that the father has only just been established, Hans cannot afford to loose him.

Established in his function: as an incarnation of the Other, Freud had indeed established the second part of the Name-of-the-father. He had acted as a primal father whose intervention transformed papa Graf into his ambassador. primal father equals imaginary father. The symbolic father function, Lacan's Name-of-the-father was not set up. It could be written down as follows:

$$\frac{\text{Primal father S1}}{\text{Desire of the Mother}} \cdot \frac{\text{Desire of the Mother}}{\text{signified to the subject}} \Rightarrow S1 \quad \frac{(A)}{\text{phallus}}$$

Instead of:

$$\frac{\text{Name of the Father}}{\text{Desire of the Mother}} \cdot \frac{\text{Desire of the Mother}}{\text{signified to the subject}} \Rightarrow \frac{(A)}{\text{N.ofF. phallus}}$$

This implies that from here on, Hans has to behave as a divided subject in front of an S1. It is especially important to acknowledge which structure is introduced in this way by Freud; this is only possible with the Lacanian conceptualisation. Our thesis is that Freud introduces the Unconscious in Little Hans, thereby obliging him to make the transition to the hysterical discourse.

Freud introduces the Unconscious, he grafts it onto the chaos of Hans' current psychic life. Which chaos? The one of the signifiers, of language. The chain of signifiers which Hans has received through the parental discourse, lacks the necessary anchoring point. Freud provided this. He introduced an S1 as a necessary element to handle S2. For Lacan, this is precisely the discourse of the Unconscious, synonymous with the discourse of the Master; the S1, the 'l'au moins un', 'the at least one', $\exists x \overline{\Phi x}$, is a grounding element for S2, the storehouse of signifiers with its inherent lack.[89] The divided subject finds its origin in the same movement :

$$\frac{S_1 \longrightarrow S_2}{\mathcal{S} \quad // \quad a}$$

As a divided subject, Hans enters the normal social bonds of every speech-actor, that is, the discourse of the hysteric: Freud gave him a desire - an Oedipal one - and confronted him with a master who produces knowledge.

$$\uparrow \frac{\mathscr{S} \longrightarrow S_1}{a \quad // \quad S_2} \downarrow$$

This implies that Freud foisted the discourse of the hysteric on Hans forever. Indeed, the search for a master who knows was going to become an endless one. Freud was here doing what he proclaimed at the end of the *Studies on Hysteria*: "much will be gained if we succeed in transforming your hysterical misery into common unhappiness".[90] He had trivialised the hysteria, reducing it to common misery. This 'solution' is endless from a structural point of view since the master can never be master enough. Hans entered imaginary competition, what we like to call *The Guinness Book of Records-hysteria*, which is a typical masculine variant. Hans' treatment concluded with the fantasy in which a plumber takes away his widdler with a pair of pincers and replaces it with a bigger one. This is not enough in itself: his behind is also removed and replaced by a bigger one. The bigger the better. And Little Hans keeps on asking questions: "What are things made of?", or "Who makes them?". And when the father is bored with them and answers that he can't know everything, Hans reacts with: "Well, I thought as you knew that about the horse you'd know this too".[91]

There is a remainder.

The Oedipal myth in hysteria

In a first, non-analytical reading of the case study, a reading directed by an established knowledge, everything in Hans' analysis seems perfectly understandable. The boy wants to be with his mother, wants to cherish her. The father occupies the position of the feared and hated rival. The birth of Hanna in combination with the castration complex gives rise to a process of repression, which results in a phobic object: anxiety about a biting horse being the neurotic substitute for the father. The analysis aims at making conscious the basis of this anxiety, and so forth.

We hope that our previous elaborations have shown the untenability of this S2-type reading. The obvious question then is: where does the unmistakably real therapeutic effect come from? It is here that we have to give all credit to Freud's construction. We have already seen its effect through Hans' ensuing reactions: the father is introduced by Freud in his function, the second part of the paternal metaphor. From this intervention onwards, the Oedipus *begins* for Hans, with the father in the position which solicits the desire of the mother.

From this point of view, the Oedipal structure is not so much the cause of Hans' neurosis, as the solution for it. It is that which had to be introduced in order to liberate him from the dangerous relationship between mother, child and phallus. Hence his grateful confirmation of Freud's construction and his acceptance of the paternal interpretations concerning the giraffe and the plumber fantasy, as they bring him exactly what he needs in order to escape the deadlock.

In the meantime, we are ready for a major conclusion: the Oedipal structure is not so much that which grounds a neurosis, setting the scene for the necessary fight. On the contrary, this Oedipal structure reveals itself as a *necessary factor for security* for every neurotic. Once the Oedipal myth is set up, he is on safe ground, because he has left a threatening duality. From that point on, he can start a much more reassuring fight: that with a father who will never be father enough.

Assembling all these pieces forces us to rethink the role of the father in hysteria together with the Oedipal myth.

The primal father as keystone of the hysterical Oedipal fantasy: Totem und Taboo

Construction within the theory

Our previous section ended with a strange conclusion: the Oedipus complex is not so much the basis of every neurosis, as it is a necessary, fantasmatic construction built by the neurotic subject himself as a fortification against the desire of the first Other, the mother. This is strange in the light of the classical theory in which the Oedipal theory is usually considered as the ultimate explanation for every neurosis, including offshoots in the direction of psychosis.[92]

Hence, we now want to study Freud's theory of the Oedipus complex. Anybody undertaking that study is straightaway confronted with a strange fact: the concept is not elaborated theoretically as much as it is applied in practice. It is mainly conceptualised in a descriptive way, in which Freud explains the complex by referring to Sophocles' tragedy, as in his twenty-first lecture. He succeeds very well here in explaining the universal attraction exerted by this tragedy - everybody feels acquainted with Oedipus' feelings of guilt and desire - but the complex in itself remains almost unexplained.[93]

For want of a systematic elaboration, we have to look at the history of the concept. Freud's first ideas obviously concern something Real: the seduction and trauma theory depict a certain father as protagonist:

a perverse father, a father who is not good enough. In the second theory, with the discovery of the fantasy, the accent shifts to the Imaginary insofar as it aspires to the Symbolic register. The seduction scenes and traumas are fantasmatically elaborated neurotic constructions, around a kernel of the Real. It is within this framework that Freud developed the Oedipus complex. The castration complex followed years later.

The next theory, a third phase in his development, brings us the necessary tailpiece. It is our aim to discuss the how's and why's of this third phase, focusing on the function of Freud's *construction* in relation to hysteria.

Indeed, we are concerned with a construction in the psychoanalytic sense of the word. During the treatment, the analyst constructs a missing part of the history of a subject, in order to complete his anamnesis. This particular construction will become, both in practice and in theory, the most important tailpiece. It is here that Freud made a mistake in his argument: the necessary construction of the myth of the primal father remained for him within the field of the Imaginary. That is the reason why Freud became the primal father of psychoanalysis itself, the "at least one", $\exists x \, \overline{\Phi x}$, thanks to whom his sons can ground their work on an authority. This was clear in the case of the post-Freudians. Moreover, at this date, we can already be quite certain that the same thing will happen to the 'post-Lacanians'.[94]

Transition from the real father to the imaginary one: the family romance of the neurotic

In 1908 Freud wrote an introduction to a book by Otto Rank, *Der Mythus von der Geburt des Helden*. Written originally within this significant context, it was published separately as *Family Romances*. In our opinion, this small paper was the precursor of, as well as the transition to, the theory that he elaborated in 1912 in *Totem and Taboo*.

The opening sentence plunges us into the heart of the matter: "The liberation of an individual, as he grows up, from the authority of his parents, is one of the most necessary though one of the most painful results brought about by the course of his development".[95] In this paper, Freud elaborated an idea that he had formulated years before while discussing paranoia, but he now applied it in an adapted version to neurosis.[96] The central theme concerns the relationship between man and parental authority. That this 'parental' authority can be understood as a 'paternal' authority, becomes obvious as soon as one reads this short paper.

Freud drew an evolving picture. Initially, the parents incarnate the sole authority for the child, who has no thought of questioning their power. While growing up, the child will compare his parents with other adults, usually to the disadvantage of the parents. Often enough, at that very moment, there emerges a new kind of fantasy, called 'family romance'. The child imagines that his parents are not the 'real' ones, somewhere, sometime, there has been a substitution. There is a typical and recurring particularity to this: the 'real' parents are thought to be of a much higher standing. Freud adds that this fantasy is elaborated in the period during which the child has as yet no accurate knowledge of the sexual details concerning procreation. Once it has acquired this knowledge to a sufficient degree, the content of the fantasy changes. Indeed, the timeless 'Pater semper incertus est' is used by the child in order to exclusively substitute the *father figure* in his fantasy.

At that point, Freud returned to the afore-mentioned particularity: the child does not so much substitute the father, as put him on a much higher plane.[97] Indeed, he observes that the imagined father, the one of nobler origin, and so with a greater symbolic authority, resembles the real father on all accounts, except for the social standing.

The reason for this 'substitution' can also be found in Freud. It is an expression of the child's longing for that lost period in which it did not have to doubt the authority of the father. The fantasy is nothing but an attempt to make this period last a bit longer.

To put it differently, the child needs a father whose authority is beyond any doubt. When this authority inevitably fails in reality, the child will imagine one. Here, we find the same pattern as with infantile theories on sexuality: a certain father figure is set up beyond the real father. This is a phenomenon that can easily be observed. It is enough to visit the playground of any primary school to hear vehement discussions between young father supporters: "My father is the best, the strongest, the cleverest..." This raises an implicit question which Freud did not answer: *why* does the child need such a father figure?

Up till now, we can recognise a certain evolution, both in neurotic development and in the accompanying theory. Hysterical patients tell tales of seduction in which the father is featured as the main actor. While Freud accepted this as real in his first theory, he reached another level of conceptualisation once he recognised the importance of fantasy. The next stage gives us the discovery of the Oedipus complex and its accompanying fantasies. Nevertheless, on many points, the theory is not very convincing. First of all, the seducing father of the hysteric, whether real or imaginary, reveals himself in reality as a weak, ill, even impotent father. Secondly, the threats of castration which inaugurate the Oedipus complex, are usually uttered by women, while normally, one expects them from the father. This is not only the case with Little Hans, but also with the Wolf man and the Rat man. Thirdly, the pre-Oedipal period and the female Oedipus complex stay in the dark, to say the least. The next step in Freud's conceptualisation brings us to the afore-mentioned family romance, demonstrating that the neurotic subject ascribes all authority to the father figure.

Studying this development, one can't help but come to the conclusion that there is something wrong, something lacking, especially because of the observation that the Oedipal father figure, as an incarnation of the Law, is *imagined* by the child as a necessary complement to the real father. The cause of this process must presumably be looked for in the pre-Oedipal period, which, in its turn, makes a revision of the castration complex necessary.

When he got to this point, Freud could have theorised the necessity of this father figure for the hysteric. Instead, as an answer to the Oedipal family romance, he created an Oedipal family myth: *Totem and Taboo*.

Establishing the primal father

Totem and Taboo was considered, both by Freud and by his editors, as a study in the field of social psychology and social anthropology. Moreover, the last part of it - the essay on the primal horde and the murder of the primal father - had always remained Freud's favoured paper. He considered it the best he had ever written.[98] Leaving aside the eventual anthropological applications, we are convinced that this last essay goes beyond this field and fulfils a totally different function: *it is the necessary tailpiece to Freud's Oedipus complex*.

The book can be considered as one long run up, ending in a climax: *Die infantile Wiederkehr des Totemismus*, (The return of totemism in childhood), in which the myth of the primal horde, the primal father and his murder are developed. We will concentrate our attention on this last part.

Within the framework of the anthropology of that day the problem can be summarised as follows: what is the origin of those complicated structures of totemism, the ensuing taboos and the rules of exogamy? With his usual shrewdness, Freud reduced these massive problems to their bare essentials. He discovered quite soon that there were two major taboos: the taboo prohibiting the killing of one's totem animal, and the taboo prohibiting sexual intercourse with somebody of the same totem clan, incest.[99] Within the first taboo he studied the role of the 'kings' first of all; the inverted commas are necessary, because the study reveals a totally different picture from the one expected. The king is not an autocratic and almighty despot, on the contrary, he lives for his subjects who are really in need of him, because: "It is his person which, strictly speaking, regulates the whole course of existence".[100] If he fails in his task, he will be repudiated, eventually killed. Freud recognises here the attitude of the paranoiac towards his father-persecutor, based on the relation of overestimation between father and child.[101]

This means that the king occupies a very strange position. Being the guarantee for law and order, he is at once the most necessary and the most vulnerable person within society. When he fails in his task, the cornerstone falls away and society as a whole is doomed.

Immediately after this theme, Freud discussed the taboo on death. In this discussion, he formulated an idea that only received its full implementation with Lacan: that the taboo concerning a deceased person is concentrated on the *name* of the deceased. The punishment for speaking that name aloud is as severe as a case of murder. Obviously, there has to be a relationship between killing and speaking a name aloud. Moreover, being a clinician, Freud remarked that this taboo was not part of the work of mourning, but belonged to a reaction of fright.[102] Let us remark in passing that, as a Jew, he was quite prepared for this discovery: in the Jewish religion, the name of Jahweh may not be pronounced. The name is an integral part of the person and knowledge of this name implied a potentially deadly power over that person for the so-called primitives.[103]

The next step in Freud's argument concerned the relationship between the totem, the taboos and the king. The members of a certain totem clan *name* themselves after their totem, convinced as they are that they descend from this very totem. The associated interdictions concern in the first place the 'Eheverkehr', that is, *the sexual relationship*.[104] With respect to this idea of descent, Freud made an almost casual remark that went way beyond the anthropological ideas of that day. I have got the impression, he noted, that the ultimate source of totemism is the uncertainty of the primitives in questions of procreation, *and especially concerning the role of the father*. For Freud - and contrary to the anthropological ideas of his time - this had nothing to do with a supposed lack of intelligence on the part of the 'savages', for they knew the biological role of the father full well. No, there is another factor at play: "They seem to have sacrificed paternity for the sake of some sort of speculation designed to honour the souls of their ancestors".[105] We remind the reader of the fact that with the child too, the 'Pater semper incertus est' gave rise to elaborations of special constructions, starting with basic fantasies on infantile theories of sexuality and ending in the family romance. We can assume that there is a relation between the totem and the father promoted in these childish productions.

After having made a comparison with the case of Little Hans, Freud confirmed the equivalence of a series of terms: totem animal - king - father, in which we should not neglect the aspect of naming. In the case of an animal phobia, the child transfers a part of his feelings concerning his father onto an animal, just as a tribe operates the same shift onto their totem. What is remarkable is that in both cases - totem and phobic object - the father ersatz is feared as well as being respected and admired.[106] A case study by Ferenczi on little Arpàd highlighted a certain factor that we already saw at work in Little Hans. With this little boy, the phobia concerned hens and cockerels. There is no doubt whatsoever about the underlying motive: it concerns *the urge for knowledge concerning sexuality and procreation.*[107]

This implies that, once again, we are confronted with the same questions that were already asked during the infantile theories on sexuality and fundamental fantasies. What is a woman, what is a father, what sexual relationship is there between those two? In relation to these questions we are now able to add something of importance: *the construction of a particular father figure has everything to do with the impossible answer to these questions.*

The totem animal is the primal father from whom everybody descends and from whom one derives one's name. The two major taboos - taboo against killing the totem animal and the taboo against having sexual intercourse with somebody of the same totem group - now become intelligible: just have a look at Oedipus, killing his father and sleeping with his mother. Still, what remains unexplained is the origin, as such, of the totem and these two major taboos. Freud aimed explicitly at explaining this with his home-made myth. The story is well-known. In the primal horde, the united sons exterminated the father in order to have access to the women. The sense of guilt resulting from the murdrous deed gave rise to an a posteriori compliance with the Law. The totem was erected as a reminder of the primal father and the prohibition of incest was laid down, together with the injunction to exogamy. In this way, the *dead* primal father acquired a power that the living one never had: "The dead father became stronger than the living one had been...".[108]

In this way, Freud killed two birds with one stone: the solution to an anthropological problem simultaneously provided him with a reassuring explanation of the analogous situation on an individual level, the Oedipus complex. What was once real in the history of mankind is repeated in every human child, albeit on a smaller scale in a defensive manner.

Here, Freud reversed his course. Initially, he had discovered Oedipal feelings and situations in clinical practice, and this enabled him to explain the timeless attraction and fascination exerted by Sophocles' tragedy; now, he made use of a myth - a home-made one moreover - to explain recurring clinical phenomena on the individual level. This was not without gain. Besides the fact that this construction produced the necessary tailpiece for his Oedipal theory and made it coherent, it also yielded a major advantage in clinical practice: Freud had constructed that very father who is looked for by every neurotic. That this father is preferably a dead one, one who can no longer fail, was already known by the totem clans. Freud did not develop this idea to its ultimate limits; he stopped at the real father who was really killed.[109]

We want to take a closer look now at what we have called a reversal. There are three questions. First of all, where is the flaw in Freud's argument? We will demonstrate that this has much to do with his study of ambivalence and of the prohibition on incest. Secondly, how can the gain of Freud's construction be translated into clinical terms? Thirdly, what is the importance of all this for hysteria? This last question, will oblige us to examine the relation between the Law and the 'Il n'y a pas de rapport sexuel', together with the desire for knowledge about sexuality.

Ambivalence and prohibition on incest

In Freud's argument there are a number of strange elements which only become intelligible if one pursues another line of reasoning.

One of these elements concerns the ambivalence of the sons towards the primal father, mutatis mutandis, the ambivalence of the male child towards his own father. This ambivalence is supposed to consist on the one hand of love and admiration, and on the other hand of hate and aggression. In our opinion, these terms refer to adult affects, and are less appropriate in speaking of the emotional turmoils of childhood. Defining hate and love in themselves in relation to adults is problematic enough. With children, it seems more appropriate to think in terms of 'afraid of' and 'in need of'. The need for a certain figure is rebaptized in love, the 'afraid of' gives rise to hatred. We can then consider Oedipal ambivalence within neurotic structure as follows: the child is in need of a certain referential father figure of whom it is also afraid. We hope to make clear later on the gain of this way of putting it.

A second more strained argument concerns Freud's most central point: the origin of the prohibition on incest. After having murdered the primal father, the sons, assembled in brotherhood, are supposed to feel so guilty that they take the decision to establish the Law prohibiting incest, thereby proclaiming the women of their own clan as sexually forbidden. This renders the original aim of the murder completely redundant. This invocation of morality fits rather oddly within the framework of his argument. In order to explain the origin of the prohibition on incest, Freud thought it necessary to add a second argument. After the murder, and the subsequent disappearance of authority, all these brothers would have become rivals for the women they wanted, would therefore have killed each other, and destroyed society as such; so the only thing they could do to save the group was to install the prohibition on incest. This would not be possible "until they had passed through many dangerous crises".[110] Here, even Freud felt that something was awry in his argument. Besides the fact that the need for a double argument is always suspect - cf. the Jewish joke about the borrowed kettle - we can argue, as Lacan did in his critique of Kant, that a subject will not necessarily suspend his desire even if its consequence is death, let alone the eventual decline of the group. Much later, at the time of *Moses and Monotheism* - a paper which is in our opinion a revised version of *Totem and Taboo* - it was precisely on this point, between the real murder of the real father and the imaginary father, that Freud situated matriarchy. [111]

The combination of these two strained arguments brings us to the following thesis: what Freud was doing here was nothing but repeating the typical neurotic defence, in spite of the fact that he had raised this defence to the level of a mythical and grounding structure.

Our thesis can be explained as follows. What is the defensive aspect in the fantasy $ \$ \lozenge a$? Against what is the defence of the neurotic directed? Against the threatening Real, that is, the threat of being absorbed by the mother's desire, of being reduced to the abject object. The $\lozenge$ aims to ground the necessary distance between subject and object. To effect this separation, the child needs a third agency. In other words, *the prohibition on incest of the Oedipal period is first of all directed at the mother*. Our discussion of Little Hans demonstrated the clinical necessity of this separation through the function of the symbolic father. For the neurotic subject, this function is never sufficient. That is why he will continue to call on a father substitute, a super-father who can do the job. This figure is portrayed in every family romance, concerning which Freud had already noted that father figure imagined therein is always the real one, but magnified to unreal proportions. We could therefore describe the effect of the Oedipus complex as the spanning of a bridge between the dangerous enjoyment of a first great Other and an insatiable desire of the divided subject. Insofar as this takes place in a neurotic fashion, it implies the construction of an imaginary all-powerful father, which results in anxiety about an imaginary castration. Last but not least, we have to remark that, as a result of this set up and the consequent feeling of security, the subject is able to long for his mother. We can now put two remarks of Freud side by side: first of all, that a human being never abandons a previous source of pleasure; secondly, that a former source of pleasure can become an actual source of anxiety. Indeed, a child can only long for the former unity with its mother after being separated from her, that is, once the necessary security is set up. If this is not the case, it becomes a source of anxiety.

Freud's gain

This neurotic construction of an imaginary father as a necessary defence against the gaping desire of the mother was never recognised as such by Freud. He accentuated instead the second moment of the Oedipus complex. His treatment focused on the effects of, and the reactions to, the father figure as set up by the neurotic himself. Those effects are twofold: on the one hand, we have the castration complex arising together with castration anxiety; on the other hand the vicissitudes of a now safe desire for a definitively lost enjoyment in a former fusion with the mother. This particular desire contaminates every woman with the image of the mother. A woman is only safe insofar as she can be identified back to the mother, because this brings the assurance of regulation, law and order. Where this tracing back is not possible, there arises instead an ominous figure, an 'it', a threatening sphinx with a riddle in the place of desire: "Was will das Weib", "What does Woman want?".

The interpretations and constructions based on this theory yield an immediate gain in the clinic. We have already illustrated this with Little Hans: when Freud produced his construction, he installed the father function. This is precisely what the neurotic longs for, an element of certainty and security, something which brings about a separation and installs law and order, the king-totem who 'regulates the whole course of existence'. In this way, Freud confirmed and enforced the defensive fantasy. When necessary, he even handed it to the patient: 'Yes, there is The Father who...'. He constructed the Other of the Other as a necessary guarantee to answer the lack in the Other. With this, he remained within the boundaries of the neurotic, and especially the hysterical, line of thought. From a Lacanian point of view, *Totem and Taboo* is a typically neurotic product, whose content was dictated to Freud by his hysterical patients. As a specialist in myths, Lévi-Strauss criticised Freud's home-made myth in the same way: "In the one case, one goes from clinical experience to myths, and from myths to the structure ; in the other case, one invents a myth in order to explain the facts: instead of interpreting, one has done the same thing as a patient".[112]

From this point on, we can make a sharp differentiation between a remedial therapeutic discourse on the one hand and analytic discourse on the other. From this point of view, there is only one therapeutic discourse: the discourse of the master. If one wants to apply a 'supportive' therapy with neurotics, one is obliged to take the seat of the master, that is, one has to guarantee the existence of the primal father, usually by incarnating him. That is the explanation for why the transition from individual psychotherapy to a group formation is such an easy one, when the group clusters almost religiously around their incarnation of the primal father who is supposed to secrete knowledge about desire and enjoyment. The sixties were full of them, but the phenomenon itself is as old as time. The nineteenth century alienists were acutely aware of this necessary guarantee, and that is why they made codes of conduct for the therapist: to make sure that his mastery was never endangered. Nevertheless, as we have seen in our discussion of the theory of discourse, from the moment one speaks, failure is inevitable. Every therapeutic discourse produces a remainder, and it is there that the hysterical subject makes her appearance.[113]

The question is now: to what is this guarantee directed, what has the master to guarantee, following the footsteps of the primal father? It is here that full attention must be given to the symbolic father and his function.

Primal father, law and knowledge

In this study of 'basic' fantasies, infantile theories of sexuality, family romances (the individual myth of the neurotic), as well as the myth in *Totem and Taboo*, we have seen several recurrent elements. The point of application of these myths is always centred on *a (not) knowing with respect to sexual relations*. During the period when the child is unfamiliar with the procreative function, it substitutes both parents in its family romance. Once it has received the necessary enlightenment, it will seize the remaining weak point - 'Pater semper incertus est' - and it will replace only the father in its fantasy. In totemistic societies, the totem or primal father is considered as the progenitor, in spite of correct biological knowledge about procreation. The members of the totem, Freud said, honour in that way 'the spirit of their ancestors'.

A second constant is that in both cases, the individual neurotic and the totem clan, the father thus constructed has different proportions. In the family romance, he is promoted to a higher social level, in the myth, he becomes the universal ancestor from whom everybody is descended and after whom everybody is named. The most peculiar thing about this is that this super-father does not so much become a super authority, in the sense of a dictator, as that he becomes a founding father. This became very clear in ethnological studies where kings were seen to function as a guarantee for the normal course of daily life. *The primal father is a fundamental guarantee.*

A third recurring phenomenon is the difficulty in ascribing to the real father the function which normally belongs to the primal father. The members of a clan may very well elect a king who has to fulfil the role of guarantor, sooner or later the poor man has to fail and be replaced. In his fantasies, the child may blow the father up to phobic proportions if need be. And here Freud brought us that important discovery: it is only the *dead* father who can incarnate sufficient authority to fulfil his function.

In this way, the totem system reveals itself as a very interesting solution, because as a system, it leads to *a treaty with the father*: "The totemic system was, as it were, a covenant with their father, in which he promised them everything that a childish imagination may expect from a father - protection, care and indulgence - while on their side they undertook to respect his life, that is to say, not to repeat the deed which had brought destruction on their real father" (see note 110). The dead father as ultimate guarantee. This permits us to take the next step. Freud had already observed that for certain 'savages' speaking one's name aloud was equal to murder and severely punished. Hence: the name of the father and the dead father are on the same side, that of his symbolic function.

At this point, we can bring together a very important combination. One: the starting point is a not-knowing with respect to sexual activity. Two: the constructed father furnishes a fundamental guarantee. Three: this father is the dead father or the name of the father. Well then: both the members of the totem clan and the children of a family receive the name of the father. To put it clearly: *the Name of the father furnishes a guarantee against uncertainty as regards sexual relations.* This guarantee grounds the social model for the regulation of the relations between the different sexes and the different generations.[114] The Oedipal law is set up to regulate enjoyment.

In Freud, the symbolic father is lacking qua concept. In *Totem and Taboo* he was definitely on the way to formulating the father through his essence as signifier, but he never succeeded in doing so. He situated the primal father in the Real with his home-made myth, and eventually found him back in the Imaginary with the totemic system. In 1923, he grounded this phylogenetic myth in ontogenesis by formulating the idea of the formation of the Super-ego. This special formation originates in the early Ego and incarnates the father as an authority figure.[115] From this point in the theory the castration complex becomes increasingly important as the determining element in the Oedipus complex. The relationship between primal murder and name giving was already present in *Totem and Taboo*, but the step to the Symbolic order as such, to the grounding function of the name of the father, was not taken. Linked to this failure was another lack in the theory: in the first version of the myth there were neither mothers nor women, only 'females'.

As a signifier, this name of the father has a very special status: "the signifier in the Other, as locus of the signifier, is the signifier of the Other as locus of the law".[116] As a signifier, it belongs to the Other, to the locus or field of all signifiers. This 'belonging to' is transcended by its *function*: it grounds the Other as the place of the Law. The Name-of-the-father is the particular exception to the universal *which thereby establishes the universal*. We will try to make this difficult formulation more understandable by using two illustrations. The set of all possible sets by definition contains itself, yet stands outside itself in order to create the possibility of a universal set. The number 1 belongs to the set of so-called 'natural' numbers, but also stands outside this series because it is its necessary starting point. These examples illustrate how the Law operates: the grounding element covers the infinite. Any set added will always belong to the set defined as complete; any new number added to the series can always be expressed in terms of 'one'. In an analogous way the Name-of-the-father produces the anchorage of $\cancel{A}$, he is the back-up of the law which regulates the lack of the Other. The answer to that lack in the Other is the production of the phallus, which has to be understood in this context as the production of *difference*, that is, that which is the very basis of the system of signifiers, and thus of the Other. The Other is not complete, there is $\cancel{A}$. Whatever comes as a supplement in this endless series of signifiers, one thing is certain: it will always be taken up in terms of difference, that is, in terms of the phallus as the basis of that system, and will thus become part of the signifying system. The Name-of-the-father produces the phallus as the basis for the human symbolic signifying system. As a signifier, it is itself outside the series: $\exists\,x\,\overline{\Phi}\,x$, the founding exception. Hence its Lacanian name: 'l'au-moins-un', 'the at least one', the necessary exception to the rule. That is precisely why it creates the possibility of the signifying system, why it is necessary in order to allow the representation of a subject by a signifier. Furthermore: to allow representation by the signifier. This implies that human reality - being a symbolic reality - is assured by the Name-of-the-father and its production, the phallic signifier.

As a starting-point for our human symbolic culture, the law of the Name-of-the-father grounds all other laws. The totem system, Freud noted, laid the foundation of social organisation.[117] The Name-of-the-father grounds the Symbolic Order, S1 → S2, thereby creating the possibility of the discourses, those structures which enable our different social bonds to exist. Hence, the trespassing of this system implies a threat to the very existence of the social order, and all the more so if the trespassing concerns the founding law itself.[118]

Hysteric, law and truth
The symbolic function of the father establishes by convention the

law which regulates sexual relations. By convention: the human world is a conventional world; but even more so it is what Lacan calls 'le monde du semblant', the world of make-believe. It is here that the hysteric appears on the scene with what Lacan calls her typical love of truth. The role of hysteria in undermining social relations has been common knowledge for a long time. Israël remarks that it is possible to recognise hysteria as the common thread in many different revolutionary movements. The psychiatrist knows the commotion one hysterical patient can cause in an entire ward. The reason is less well known.

The hows and whys of this hysterical troublemaking can be read at length in Freud: "The asocial nature of neuroses has its genetic origin in their most fundamental purpose, which is to take flight from an unsatisfying reality into a more pleasurable world of phantasy. The real world, which is avoided in this way by neurotics, is under the sway of human society and of the institutions collectively created by it. To turn away from reality is at the same time to withdraw from the community of man".[119] The hysteric steps outside 'human society'; so there can be no normal circulation through the discourses and, consequently, no circulation through the social relations inherent in the discourses either.

In hysteria, sexual convention is put to the test. The hysterical subject sees through its fundamentalist character and detects its make-believe aspect; she attacks the inherent uncertainty at its base: the father and his followers, who are supposed to secure a guarantee that is always impossible to secure. The fact that she questions the 'collectively created institutions' based on it is only a consequence of a more fundamental question. Owing to the specific structure of the hysteric, her the revolutionary impact is rather small. She always succeeds in reinstating the master, thereby realizing the etymological meaning of the word 'revolution': return to the point of departure.

The series in which hysteria has to be situated can be described as follows. The lack in the Other is worked upon by primary repression and the symbolic father producing the phallic signifier: $S(\cancel{A})$ disappears under S^1. In this way, human reality is secured; according to Lacan, the Name-of-the-father is the binding ring which holds together the Real, the Imaginary and the Symbolic.[120] His function is the establishment of the Law in the Symbolic, by which the lack in the Other is covered. Freud had discovered this structural necessity in the clinic and had put it into words - "The myth is an attempt to give epic dimension to what is structurally at work".[121] This is of the myth of the primal horde as the foundation of Oedipus, providing the basis of human (h)order. Hence the obligation for Freud to presuppose an ever earlier repression, up to primary repression. Hence the Lacanian conclusion that family and society are effects of repression (and not the other way round), effects of the Law introduced by primary repression. Which Law? The one that regulates the relationship between the sexes: there is a sexual relationship by force of law.

The Name-of-the-father, as regulating principle of the Symbolic order, based on an exception, is a signifier. Its introduction takes place by way of a real figure - a father - who gives his name. It is here that the hysteric mounts the stage and exposes a double lack, highlighting two disjunctions. In reality, the father is always incapable of fulfilling fully his symbolic function. The hysteric can present herself as a solution for his impotence by filling his lack. Insofar as she tries to do this, she will be confronted with an impossibility: even a completed father is not able to take a position outside the phallically grounded symbolic order.

Both impotence and impossibility are covered by a make-believe world, a world that hysteria refuses and replaces with the truth, which is demonstrated in a symptomatic way: there is no sexual rapport.

For Freud, this was the end; a deadlock without any issue. The Oedipus complex ends on the rock where analysis stops: the castration complex, with masculine castration anxiety and feminine penis envy. As a new Sisyphus, he rolled this rock time and again over the top of the mountain without ever finding a moment of rest. On the way Sisyphus meets Oedipus, but this time in Colonus and it is a blind Oedipus who is at last able to see. Castration then evolved towards the fundamental *Ichspaltung*, while penis envy faded away in the elaboration of the pre-Oedipal period, in which the sphinx came up with a new riddle: "Was Will das Weib?"

CHAPTER 10.

THE ROCK OF CASTRATION

To listen or to read analytically implies paying special attention to the signifier whilst resisting the seduction of signification. This is not sufficient for, in the intervals between these signifiers, the strange alliance between subject and lost object makes its appearance. An analysis ought to focus on what is not revealed but, in this regard, it ought to aim at what is circumscribed as well as what is veiled by discourse.

Van Der Sterren has read the Oedipus Rex of Sophocles as an analyst. His conclusion is that translations and classical interpretations both favour the same omissions. When the original text states that Oedipus will cause the death of his parents (tous tekontas), half of the translations he consulted had translated this as the death of his father. It is also exclusively the death of the father that is stressed in the interpretations. Hence Van der Sterren concludes that the hostility between mother and son belongs to that part of the complex which is most defensively revised. With this discovery in mind, he continues his scrutiny of the text by looking at the role of the sphinx. It shows how the mother is doubled into two figures, Jocasta herself and the sphinx. "That is why the sphinx is the threatening and dangerous creature while Jocasta remains the attractive and loveable woman."[1] The relationship between the sphinx and Oedipus is dual and therefore mortal: if Oedipus does not succeed in solving the riddle he must die. Similarly, a correct answer entails her death. This riddle is linked by Van Der Sterren to the riddle of sexuality for the child.

So we have the murder of the father, the riddle the woman/mother poses for the son concerning sexuality, and a mortal relationship; but from our point of view, there are even more gaps. Freud's primary myth, which is the fundamental description of the Oedipus complex, contains a very remarkable omission. There is no mother figure in the horde. There is only a group of females, the totality of all women enjoyed by the primal father. Since this mother figure is lacking, it becomes all the more difficult to find the very foundation of the incest prohibition of the sons/brothers with respect to the mother. Lacan remarks that the Law thus inaugurated prohibits the enjoyment of all the women, that is, it prohibits the enjoyment that is reserved exclusively for the primal father.[2]

The mother is lacking; the only thing we find is a transition from all women to one woman, that is, to 'la pas-toute', the 'not-all'. There is yet another omission: the fundamental myth itself does not say anything about castration; neither does Sophocles' tragedy. Insofar as the idea of castration is mentioned in *Totem and Taboo*, it is done in a casual manner without ever being generalised. Even in *On Narcissism: An Introduction* Freud explicitly declined to make it general.[3]

These two omissions, mother and castration, are remarkable. Analytical praxis demonstrates time and again that what is omitted returns on the other side of the bar. In the discourse of the neurotic, castration only appears "as fear, avoidance, and this is precisely why castration stays enigmatic". The way in which castration appears in hysteria is typical for this form of neurosis: castration is avoided by placing it with the other - "Let us say that the hysteric is in need of a castrated partner". With his answer, that is his Oedipal theory, Freud followed in the footsteps of the hysterical subject: his Oedipal theory "was dictated by hysterics".[4]

This answer is *Totem and Taboo*, according to Lacan. Freud's attempt to avoid castration, precisely by stressing the murder of the primal father, also followed in the footsteps of hysteria. Let us recall that the dead father is a symbolic function. Beyond the murder of the primal father, beyond the neurotic attempt to set up the symbolic father function there is another theme which has to be defensively covered up by it: that of the mother and castration. These we still have to develop.

Beyond the father and his murder looms the sphinx. Freud discussed this in his elaboration of the so-called pre-Oedipal period in which the mother occupies the central place. This is where the enjoyment of the first Other is paramount. This enjoyment is situated in the Real, it provokes anxiety and calls for a defensive working over. We shall see that this defensive working over is nothing other than 'castration' because it entails a connection between an enjoyment which is non-signified and the phallic signifier, thus expressing the lack of the mother in terms of the phallus.

In its totality, this process is nothing less than the process of becoming a subject, the transition from the Real to the Symbolic. Ideally, the result is a divided subject, beyond symbolic castration, with a desire of its own that can be punctuated by phallic satisfaction. During this transition, the hysteric remains stuck in the Imaginary, and Freud with her. For both of them, the phallus does not become a symbolic identity. It remains an object of demand: penis envy. The father is the one from whom one expects it, the mother is the one who was not able to give it. Freud constructed the real antecedents for it, even rewriting the myth of the primal horde. Precisely on that point he created his own deadlock: castration as a biological bedrock.

The black continent

Hystorical version

When Freud was writing his autobiographical portrait in 1925, he devoted part of it to the Oedipus complex. A boy, in directing his sexual desire to his mother would thus necessarily develop hostile impulses towards the father-rival. The situation was supposedly the same with girls but the other way round: the father is the love object and the mother takes the position of rival. Ten years later, he added a footnote to this paragraph, in which he rejected the analogy between boys and girls with respect to Oedipal development described in the paper.[5] During this ten year interval he had been looking and searching for The Woman. What he found was The mother.

Most of the official as well as the unofficial historians agree on this part of Freud's theory, at least as far as the sequence is concerned. Most of the manuals and introductions on Freud describe his discovery of the pre-Oedipal period of the girl in identical terms. The founding father of psychoanalysis first of all discovered the masculine Oedipus complex. Only later did he incline his white-haired head towards the Oedipal vicissitudes of women, and, as a result, produced three famous papers.[6]

Strachey provides us with an enthusiastic appraisal of what he calls a first complete re-assessment of Freud's views on the psychological development of women.[7] Jones' description contains the same content - after the Oedipus complex of the man, Freud discovered the feminine version - but his controversy with Freud on this point forced him to react coldly and without enthusiasm.[8] Ellenberger hastened to demonstrate that Freud's ultimate discovery of the pre-Oedipal period as a determinant of the female Oedipus complex was not new at all, but was already present in Bachoven's theory on matriarchy.[9] We close the series with Juliet Mitchell who explained Freud's delay in his discovery of the female Oedipus complex: as a man, he could not have eyes or ears for what was really important for a woman. His discovery was nothing but a further development of what he had received as a gift from women analysts.[10]

The development of this part of Freud's work seems well known, especially since it gave rise to a violent controversy. Indeed, Freud not only discovered the importance of the pre-Oedipal mother-child relation and its effects on the Oedipal development of the girl, he also formulated a number of consequences for the process of becoming a woman, and these consequences constituted the most controversial part of psychoanalytic theory. To begin with, let us give a conventional summary.

For both boys and girls the mother is the first love object. For boys, she will remain the love object, both in the pre-Oedipal and in the Oedipal period. The intervention of the father results in a very clear-cut effect: the castration complex. Due to castration 'anxiety' the mother will be given up as an object, and an internalisation of paternal authority takes place. In this way, the Oedipus complex ends with the formation of the Super-ego.

For a girl things are much more complicated. During the pre-Oedipal period she has active love impulses towards her mother, just like the boy. How then does the shift to her proper love object, the father, take place? According to Freud, this is caused by her discovery of the penis and the emergence of 'penis envy'. The fact that she is not provided with a penis means that, besides feeling inferior, jealous and manifesting resistance to masturbation, the girl turns away in hostility from the mother to the father, hoping that she will receive from him what she lacks. The most remarkable difference with the Oedipus complex of the boy is that the female counterpart of castration anxiety, 'penis envy', becomes the *cause* of the installation of the Oedipus complex, whereas for the boy it actually inaugurates the end of the Oedipal period.[11]

Freud summarised the difference between the two genders in a double displacement which is only applicable to the girl. First of all she has to change her erotogenic zone: the phallic-clitoral one has to be exchanged for the vaginal one. Secondly, the object has to be changed; the father ought to take the place of the mother.[12] These two shifts can be explained further. The first one implies that the *active* masculine clitoris has to be exchanged for the *passive*, receiving, feminine vagina. The shift towards the father as object implies two further modifications. First of all, the penis, as the object originally desired from him, has to be changed into the desire for a child; secondly, this child should in the end be desired from a man, her man, who has taken the place of her father.

Considered in this way, becoming a woman is not only a very complex, but also a hopeless business. The attentive reader will have noticed that we are back to square one: we started with the mother, and finally, we have returned to the mother, to the girl herself who has become a mother. Moreover, the whole process is directed by the man/father who is in effect producing the woman/mother. Freud discerned three possible paths of development.[13]

The first path concerns a turning away from sexuality. Based on penis envy, not only is clitoral activity stopped, but sexual activity as a whole comes to a standstill. The result is sexual inhibition and neurosis.

The second path concerns the famous masculinity complex: "To an incredibly late age she clings to the hope of getting a penis some time. That hope becomes her life's aim; and the phantasy of being a man in spite of everything often persists as a formative factor over long periods."[14] Here the transition to passivity is refused.

The third possibility concerns the acceptance of passivity and the almost complete renunciation of activity. The phallic-active part is repressed, and insofar as this repression is not too severe, the way to femininity is clear. If this repression is too severe, however, one returns to the first path of development. Apparently, things have to be dosed very accurately. Where the dosage is correct, the girl will turn to her father.[15] The original desire for a penis has to be exchanged for the desire for a child, and later on, the father has to be exchanged for another man, who can then provide her with a real child. On the road to femininity, the girl emerges as a mother...

This is a conventional summary of Freud's theory. Based on his three papers on femininity, it is quite comparable with Juliet Mitchell's much more exhaustive treatment in her book. The fact that this author devotes more space and time to the subject does not conceal the fact that an aporia remains. This tragic impasse changes into a comic caricature once we start studying the subsequent controversy.

This controversy took off quite early on with a paper by Karen Horney. In a critique of Abraham's paper on the female castration complex, she reduced everything to facts, preferably biological facts.[16] Moreover, the discussion acquired moral overtones which would remain: the aim was to demonstrate that women are not at all inferior to men just because they do not have a penis. Men themselves are jealous because they can't bear children. Goal! Things became even worse when Helene Deutsch elevated the supposedly biological substratum to a normative teleological something: a woman, no, The Woman, was vaginally orientated and the presence of the all-too-masculine clitoris was just 'unfortunate' (sic). Jones tried to be the clever boy by referring to the Bible. The only result of this confusion of tongues was that Freud entered history as an exponent of phallocracy and misogyny.[17]

As far as the opening question is concerned - how does the 'becoming' of a woman take place? - we can only produce a negative answer at this stage, based on the deadlock of our summary above. If a girl wants to become a woman, she apparently has to take leave of her mother. And it is precisely on this point that the hysteric comes to grief.

Analytical reading

The Oedipus complex is preceded by a pre-Oedipal period which casts the mother as the central character. She is the first love object for every child, independently of their gender. This first relationship is a peculiar one. On the one hand the mother appears as the incarnation of power, present or absent, refusing or giving. On the other hand, we find the child in the passive position in which it has to undergo everything. The so-called feelings of 'omnipotence' of an adult neurotic do not go back to a supposed infantile omnipotence, but to an infantile identification with the *mother's* omnipotence. To state it more clearly: to an identification with the phallic mother.[18] Paranoia shows us the pathological forms this relationship can take, more particularly in the fear of being killed by the mother, of being devoured, of being poisoned.[19]

Thus, the first relationship of man concerns an opposition between activity and passivity; this is before there is any trace of the Oedipal structure, that is, before castration. Freud remarked that passivity always entailed a certain reaction, an active repetition of the things one had to undergo passively.[20] This is also true for the pre-Oedipal mother-child relationship. The child wants to perform actively what it had to endure passively from the mother. A first transition concerns the step from being suckled to active sucking which can take on an oral-sadistic dimension. The duality in this is unmistakable; the aggressive oral-sadistic impulses towards the mother have found their counterpart in the fear of being killed by her.

We can now recall Freud's earlier opposition between active and passive. Comparing notes shows us that there is a shift in signification. In his earliest conceptualisations, active-passive stood for masculine-feminine, with 'passivity' as the most difficult component. Indeed, it was meant to represent femininity on the psychological level, but in the final analysis, it only demonstrated the lack of a specific signifier for the woman. The way in which Freud used the opposition at this point implies the addition of a very important component: passivity also denotes a certain enjoyment in the mother and child relationship. The attempts of the child to make the transition to the pole of activity must be understood as a running away from the position of passive object of enjoyment to an active form of pleasure. As a preliminary conclusion we can say that at this point in Freud's theory, there emerges a relationship between the lack of a signifier for a woman, passivity as a substitutive signifier and a certain attitude towards enjoyment.

This is a preliminary conclusion, because there is more to it. Freud discovered that the girl gives the pre-Oedipal mother a position he knew well: the seductive one. The mother 'seduces' the child to a certain form of enjoyment against which it will rebel. It is only later on, in the Oedipal period proper, that the father will be assigned this position fantasmatically. At last, Freud had discovered a real basis for the trauma and for seduction.[21]

The pre-Oedipal series can be completed. The child is a passive object of the mother's enjoyment, and that is the reason why the daughter will charge the mother with seduction. While we could read passivity in Freud's first conceptualisations as the lack of a signifier for woman, we can now enlarge this same concept of passivity to include the idea of an enjoyment outside the signifier. Both readings imply a certain understanding of Lacan's $S(\cancel{A})$, the lack of a signifier for the woman is thereby connected to a form of enjoyment outside the phallic order, one that cannot be signified. In both theories the core is a traumatic Real: the child runs away from a passive enjoyment. The direction in which it flees points towards the father, that is towards the Symbolic.

The question we have to ask at this point is twofold: why does the girl run away from this passive enjoyment, and why does she flee to the father? Freud's answer can be seen in his formulations on the feminine castration complex: penis envy. The narcissistic injury felt by the girl when she discovers her lack of a penis makes her turn away in hostility from her mother to her father. As well as the ensuing impasse, there follows the three possible developments, which are elaborated by Freud.

An impasse is often the result of a mistaken premise. Penis envy as a motive for a change of object has to be examined a bit further. There are two remarkable things about it. First of all, what is described as the effect of this penis envy - turning away from the mother and turning towards the father - does not actually begin when the girl discovers that she has no penis. For both sexes, the castration complex is fully implemented once the castration *of the mother* is discovered, that is, the moment that the mother loses her omnipotence.[22] In other words, the girl does not turn to the father because she herself has no penis, but because she has discovered that the mother is castrated and shows a lack. Secondly, insofar as Freud discussed penis envy as a motive for the turning away from the mother, he always took care to mention a number of other motifs which were usually neglected. *Before* there is any mention of penis envy at all, the child already makes attempts to leave the passive position in relation to the mother and to make the transition to the active one. Precisely in this transition there is a much more basic motive for the change of object: the first mother and child relationship, with the child as a passive object of enjoyment of this first Other, is dual-imaginary and as such deadly for the becoming of a subject. No wonder that it was precisely at this point that Freud discovered a primary form of anxiety: the fear of being killed by the mother, of being poisoned or devoured. This primary anxiety later merged with castration anxiety, because the latter re-worked the first one - 'nachträglich'. Hence, Freud's thesis that fear of death and castration anxiety can be seen as synonymous.[23]

This means that penis envy as well as the turning towards the father appear in a new light. The daughter turns away from the mother to the phallophoric father with a definite goal: to acquire that which could fill up the gaping desire of the mother, the lack of the first Other. Lacan explains this in a very plastic way: "Her role concerns her desire, which is something that never leaves one untouched: her desire as a big crocodile, between whose jaws one is stuck, and which she could shut... However, there is a roll, of stone naturally, potentially keeping the jaws apart: this is the phallus which protects you in case these jaws should close."[24]

The child runs away from the mother to the father. Such a statement inevitably gives rise to a number of psychologising interpretations. These can be avoided by using another formulation. The child leaves the Real for the Symbolic, the Real has to be conquered by the Symbolic. The link between those two orders is the fundamental signifier denoting difference, the one which grounds the symbolic order: the phallus. The mother's body is the order of the Real, while the symbolic father function has to introduce the phallic signifier.[25]

Considered in this light, the pre-Oedipal period can be inscribed in the history of the becoming of a subject as Lacan constructed it. A schema we have used earlier demonstrates this inscription:

A	S	Enjoyment - the Other of the body
a	$\not{A}$	Anxiety - the Other of the signifier
$\not{S}$		Desire - the divided subject and the law

This Lacanian schema can be crossed by means of the Freudian theory of the psychosexual development of the child. We write 'crossed' because there is no linear similarity. Freud noted that the first opposition to be set up was the one between object and subject, while the second one concerned activity versus passivity. Every child has to acquire an ex-sistence (sic: from the Latin *ex-sistere* - a famous Lacanian pun) outside the Real of the mother's body, outside that relationship in which it functions as a passive object of the Other's enjoyment. In this respect, the first Other is the Other of the body, without a lack, in the Real: A. The birth of the child has to be followed by the birth of the subject, or else the original intra-uterine relationship cannot be broken out of. The transition to this subject-object separation implies the existence of the mother as a separate subject: she loses her position of omnipotent mother and shows a lack with which the child is confronted. The mother thus becomes the first Other of the signifier, $\not{A}$, with a lack, *a*. The child's confrontation with this figure is the same as Oedipus' meeting with the sphinx. Insofar as this riddle is not expressed in signifiers it becomes the moment of supreme anxiety. According to Freud, the third opposition which has to be introduced during sexual development concerns the opposition between the male genital apparatus and castration. Later on, at the time of puberty, this has to change - Freud said - to masculine versus feminine.[26] It is at this point that the paths of Freud and Lacan diverge.

In Lacan we find two possibilities: either becoming a subject with a desire of one's own based on symbolic castration, or opting for dependency of one's neurotic desire on the Demand of the Other. In this last case, the effect of the Oedipal structure is restricted to the Imaginary, to imaginary castration. The object *a* of desire is translated in an imaginary-phallic way,

$$\frac{a}{-\phi}$$

whichever of the four objects it may be. The subject's desire remains alienated from that of the Other. Castration is avoided, refused, because the lack is unbearable. As we have already seen, this refusal is often a hysterical one, creating a master, exposing his lack and putting the blame on him as the cause of castration. In spite of this refusal the hysterical subject is irrevocably confronted with her own lack, with imaginary castration. The unbearable nature of this confrontation gives rise to a number of hysterical exploits in order to blur and disguise, even deny, her own faults, in a typical movement reminiscent of a fly-wheel that ends with assigning guilt to the other. A second consequence is the quasi-permanent state of dissatisfaction. Hysterical lack cannot be filled by anything or anybody. The whole process remains in the Imaginary. In the case of symbolic castration, however, the lack is traced back to its origin: the signifier dividing the subject. The liberation from the obligation to be 'complete' opens up the possibility of desire, creation and pleasure.

Freud never made this distinction. The mediating function of the Symbolic was lacking in his theory, and this obliged him - in perfect analogy to hysteria - to put the emphasis on the imaginary father and the refusal of imaginary castration. The impossible Real turned into a defensive Imaginary from which the fantasy tried in vain to reach the Symbolic. A lack of mediation through the Symbolic is often enough 'realised' in the Real: the primal father and the original murder were once real, penis envy is directed to the real organ which ideally is exchanged for a real, male child. Freud's outline of the process of becoming a woman has to be read as an elaboration of three hysterical variants.

The hysterical continent

Apparently, there was not much room for hysteria in Freud's study of the process of becoming a woman. He explicitly aimed at solving "the problem of femininity". The newly discovered pre-Oedipal period belonged to "the prehistory of woman".[27] In all of his three papers, hysteria appears only twice. These two appearances are, however, anything but unimportant.

A first point concerns the pre-Oedipal attachment of the daughter to the mother: "Among these is a suspicion that this phase of attachment to the mother is especially intimately related to the aetiology of hysteria, which is not surprising when we reflect that both the phase and the neurosis are characteristically feminine,...".[28] It is precisely this period that is very hard to dig up "...that it was as if it had succumbed to an especially inexorable repression". We have already seen that this refers to primary repression, as the leaving behind of the lack of the first Other. Freud postulated a close relationship between hysteria and femininity, but he did not elaborate it any further.

The second reference endorsed this idea of a narrow relationship. The hysterical fantasy about seduction by the father goes back to a pre-Oedipal reality: "I was driven to recognize in the end that these reports were untrue and so came to understand that hysterical symptoms are derived from phantasies and not from real occurrences. It was only later that I was able to recognize in the phantasy of being seduced by the father the expression of the typical Oedipus complex in women. And now we find the phantasy of seduction once more in the pre-Oedipus prehistory of girls; but the seducer is regularly the mother".[29] It is important to see that this passage contains a remarkable displacement. The starting point is hysteria as seduction by the father. This fantasy, originally solely hysterical, is suddenly changed into "Den Ausdruck des *typischen* Oedipuskomplexes beim *Weibe*" (the expression of the *typical* Oedipus complex in *women*), which is then retraced to "in der prä-ödipalen Vorgeschichte der *Mädchen*" (the pre-Oedipal prehistory of *girls*). Inconspicuously, hysteria and femininity have become synonyms.

Freud felt there was something wrong with this shift towards generalisation and in the next paragraph he felt obliged to justify and defend his theory. It is likely, he wrote, that some people will remark that in reality one cannot observe much of this pre-Oedipal sexual relationship between mother and child. He then went on to produce two arguments, which are true enough when taken by themselves, but whose juxtaposition evokes the joke of the borrowed kettle. First of all, one has to have a talent for observation if one wants to see something with children. Secondly, a child can express almost nothing of its sexual desire; hence the fact, said Freud, that the theory he had just produced was largely based on the analyses of adult female patients, with whom he could study *a posteriori* the residues and consequences of this early period, sometimes in an especially clear and rich form. He concluded that pathology, in its extreme form, always succeeded in demonstrating relationships that stay in the dark with normality. In view of the fact that his research did not contain cases of severe pathology, the generalisation seemed justified to him.

This aspect of hysteria becomes all the more clear when we focus on Freud's clinical starting point: women with a strong attachment to the father, beyond whom he discovered - to his surprise - an equally strong attachment to the mother.[30] It seems as though the father has inherited this attachment, and it is precisely with this inheritance that things go wrong, especially when the next change of object has to take place, that is, when the man-husband has to take the place of the man-father. During this exchange, the preponderance of the first, pre-Oedipal attachment to the mother becomes apparent and the husband inherits this burden. "The husband of such a woman was meant to be the inheritor of her relation to her father, but in reality he became the inheritor of her relation to her mother".[31] This can be reformulated in Lacanian terms: in the process of becoming a subject, the desire of the mother should be exchanged for a desire of the subject's own and this is thanks to the intervention of the name of the father as described in the paternal metaphor. In the cases described above, there is ample evidence that the attachment to the desire of the mother is only metonymically displaced towards the father, that the process described in the metaphor does not take place. Consequently the way back to the first object is never blocked.

Considering the three possible developments Freud sketched, it is no wonder that each one of them concerns a hysterical development. Freud's black continent reveals itself as a hysterical one.

The first path concerns an almost total turning away from sexuality, based on penis envy. If they can't acquire a penis, they just don't want the rest of it either. Freud calls this path the neurotic one, characterised by massive sexual inhibition. hysterical dissatisfaction is a prime example.

The second path gives rise to the masculinity complex: the hysteric is as bold as any he-man. This vindicatory variant of hysteria was traced back by Freud to an identification with the father or with the phallic mother, resulting in latent or even manifest homosexuality. The series starts with Dora and her 'gynaecophilic' love for Mrs K. and ends with the young homosexual woman and her 'cocotte'. The basis still remains penis envy, in the form of a refusal to renounce clitoral activity.

The third path is the one which opens up the possibility of becoming a woman. This path is the most interesting because it shows us both the script of the typical hysterical fantasy and its failure. It also illustrates very convincingly how Freud followed in the footsteps of hysteria itself in the development of his theory. The girl was supposed to change into a woman the moment passivity gained the upper hand, although the masculine-active part was not supposed to disappear completely. This enabled the girl to make the transition from the mother to the father, albeit still retaining the demand for a penis. Lastly, the father had to be exchanged for the man-husband and the penis for a child, preferably a *male* child.

Hysterical phantasy: the hysteric addresses herself to the father-man-master who has to make the woman, who has to give to her what she is lacking in order to become The Woman. Failure: its ultimate result is that the hysteric becomes a mother, that she falls back to the first identification with the mother. Anna O. had addressed Breuer with her demand for becoming a woman, to the point of hysterical pregnancy, but this did not prevent her from falling back to the first identification with the mother years later. While in her case, the end was a relatively happy one, this was not so with Dora. The fact that her question remained unanswered, by her father, by Mr K. and by Freud, resulted in her becoming a caricature of her mother.

Freud himself was aware of the fact that something somewhere was wrong. He recognised that the result of the third path was more often than not a regression to the first identification with the mother, thus making the matrimonial relation of the daughter into a pitiful repetition of the parental failure. Insofar as this was not the case, the marital ship had to negotiate yet another reef. Indeed, the happy end, the longed-for son as the metonymic substitute of the penis, filling the lack of the new mother, produced the effect of concentrating all the love on the baby son, the love that the man-father had reserved for himself. In this respect, Freud can be said to have started a doxology on this love between mother and son, as the most perfect love there can be. The son as answer to the lack of the mother, to be 'everything' for one's mother.[32] Here, we ought to open a paragraph on masculine hysteria...

The man who was supposed to make the woman came to the conclusion that he had created a mother. Freud's sober conclusion was that "One gets the impression that a man's love and a woman's are a phase apart psychologically".[33] There is no sexual rapport.

Oedipus revisited: Moses and the reintroduction of the father

Angry young (wo-)men - hysteria

It is thought that Freud first of all discovered the Oedipus complex on the side of the man and that *Totem and Taboo* was an anthropological application of this discovery, an excursion of 'applied psychoanalysis' into anthropology. It was only later that Freud was supposed to have concentrated on the feminine Oedipus complex, resulting in the discovery of the importance of the pre-Oedipal period in the process of becoming a woman.

We have demonstrated that Freud's first conceptualisation of the Oedipal period was not in fact the masculine version of this complex, but the hysterical version in which Freud followed in the footsteps of the hysteric in creating a certain solution for a problem that he did not yet know to its full extent. This solution consisted in introducing a particular father figure. Introducing such a figure did not take place without difficulties, and *Totem and Taboo* was Freud's answer to them. With this myth he provided a guarantee for the existence of the particular father figure needed by the neurotic subject for the solution of his problem.

The nature of this problem was not very clear in the first Oedipal theory. Prohibition of incest in relation to the mother was not accounted for by the myth of the primal horde. Conversely, there emerged another 'prohibition', the prohibition against enjoying all women, against enjoying The Woman as a totality. The discovery of the pre-Oedipal period as the relationship between mother and child allows us to understand this prohibition as a protection. The first form of enjoyment entails the risk of the subject disappearing in the Real of the mother's body. The Woman as totality is precisely made such by using the child as object.

This implies that the second part of Freud's Oedipal theory, the so-called discovery of the feminine Oedipus complex, should also be understood differently. It was not his discovery of a masculine Oedipus followed by a feminine one. Rather, it was a formulation of the hysterical Oedipus complex in two stages. First of all, he established the defensive final period. Next, he discovered what this defensive period was directed against.

The starting point was the relationship between the first Other and the infant, characterised by an enjoyment beyond the signifier and described by Freud as passivity. We have seen that this term permits a double interpretation of the traumatic Real. Both of them are an interpretation of Lacan's S($\cancel{A}$). At first Freud took passivity to be the passive sexual trauma, and passivity became a substitute concept for femininity, for the lacking signifier. With the discovery of the pre-Oedipal period, 'passivity' came to denote that form of enjoyment in the mother and child relationship from which the child wants to run away. The mother in this case is assigned the position of seductress. The two traumas meet each other at the point where the lack of a signifier for femininity is also the lack of the mother, with the child running the risk of becoming the eventual filling.

The function of the symbolic father is to provide the full stop, resulting in symbolic castration and the introduction of the phallus as a signifier, grounding the symbolic system of exchange. The child is taken into language and acquires a desire of its own based on this division. The dimension of incompleteness is thereby opened up and secured: the Symbolic is by definition incomplete, but this incompleteness can always be expressed in terms of S1. Desire keeps shifting, but intermittent phallic pleasure provides a scansion.

With hysteria, this full stop has a different dimension. Another father figure is introduced, one who has to deliver the answer to the lack of the mother. But both this lack and the answer to it remain at the level of the Imaginary. The transition to symbolic mediation does not take place, obliging the Imaginary to enter into a coalition with the Real. The father and the penis acquire a dimension of reality which is not transcended by the Symbolic. The hysteric will go on looking for the master - an abstract figure, and the starting point for all possible discourses - in reality.[34]

This different dimension is best expressed in terms of the discourse of the hysteric and the matheme of hysterical fantasy.

$$\text{impossibility}$$

$$\uparrow \quad \frac{\cancel{S}}{a} \xrightarrow{\quad} \frac{S_1}{S_2} \downarrow \qquad \frac{a}{-\phi} \Diamond \text{ A}$$
$$// \quad$$

$$\text{impotence}$$

The hysterical subject runs away from the lack of the first Other, the mother, towards the second Other, the father. The goal of the flight is to attain protection against enjoyment. The structural formula of the hysteric's discourse demonstrates that, in order to conserve the impossibility of this enjoyment, the hysteric endorses the disjunction of impotence. In Lacan's words: "the hysteric's desire is to sustain the desire of the father in its status". Which status? Clinical practice yields only one answer: the status of impotence. The father of Dora, of Anna O, of... can always be characterised by this 'Unvermögen'. As long as this impotence is preserved, as long as the chain of signifiers, S_2 , cannot answer for object a, impossibility is retained, $\emptyset$ is saved from being swallowed by the Other.

The hysteric's phantasy displays the pathological variant. In order to maintain the impotence of the Other, the hysteric presents herself as what might fill his lack but never succeeds in doing so. The lack of the Other, object a, cannot be expressed in terms of signifiers, of Φ. What the hysteric presents to the other is:-

$$\frac{a}{-\phi}$$

thereby confirming imaginary castration. Hence, hysteria can be characterised as the neurosis in which the problem of castration is 'solved' by pointing to the castration of the Other.

Up to now, we have argued that the 'masculine' version of the Oedipus complex is nothing but the hysterical end point. This thesis is illustrated at its best with something which we still have to elaborate further: that both the theory and the hysterical subject are stranded on the same rocks, the father and castration.

Let us first correct a misconception about the origin of Freud's theory. Freud has been accused of having developed only the masculine Oedipus complex for years, while brushing aside the female version as 'analogous' before changing his mind. From our point of view, Freud's first conception is correct: his first Oedipal theory is valid for both man and woman, on condition that we replace 'woman' by 'hysteric'. In hysteria, the subject opts for the *masculine* line of development. It is no coincidence that Lacan, in his schematic representation of the process of sexuation, places the hysterical subject on the masculine side.[35]

This masculine version results - like the hysterical one - in the creation of a super father, who is all the more necessary for the man to the extent that he is *not* obliged to give up his first object. Hence, the relationship between mother and son asks for a special safeguard, a special father, "a father who already knew long before that...". For man, the castration complex together with the introduction of the Super-ego, ought to entail the absolute decline of the Oedipus complex. Nevertheless, every man needs years to take his distance from this patriarch, to make the differentiation between Law and representative of the Law. The 'angry young men movement' is valid for both the man and for the hysteric who has chosen the masculine side. Due to the structure, such a revolution can only confirm the master in the Imaginary. Its result is an endless competition, *the Guinness Book of Records*-hysteria. Freud himself needed another twenty years before he could give this paternal moloch some nuances. The result can be read in his study of Moses.

Moses: "credo quia absurdum"

One of Freud's last publications is a bundle of three essays: *Moses and Monotheism: Three Essays*.[36] Nowadays, this is one of the least read of Freud's works. It is considered as a product of the anti-Semitic climate of the time. At most, it is thought to be a sequel to his earlier anthropological-historical study, *Totem and Taboo*.

More than a sequel, it is a supplementary correction to this work, which has to be situated in the clinical sphere. Freud changed the foundation of the Oedipus complex on three crucial counts. The first one concerns the place of the mother. The second one treats of the son as the one who brings in the father. The third concerns castration. These three changes are situated by Freud within the framework of a historical interpretation of a religion. Nevertheless, a reading of the text soon demonstrates that he transcended this dimension on every page and elaborated an essay with important clinical repercussions.

The difficulties concerning the construction and deconstruction of the imaginary father - both for men and for hysterical subjects - is very well illustrated by this rewriting of the myth of the primal horde. Freud's first version of it made no room for the mother. The primal father was real for him, the primal murder really took place in the mists of time. The remembrance of it, heavy with effects, was conserved in one way or another in the unconscious. The final sentence runs as follows: "...in the beginning was the Deed": humanity started off with parricide. We read the opening sentence of *Moses and Monotheism* as its correcting sequel: "To deprive a people of the man whom they take pride in as the greatest of their sons is not a thing to be gladly or carelessly undertaken, least of all by someone who is himself one of them".[37]

We prefer to see *Moses and Monotheism* as a failed rewriting of *Totem and Taboo*. Rewriting, because the pre-Oedipal period and the mother receive a place at last. Failed, because it does not really know what to do about the father figure and castration - a perfect analogy with the clinical effects of hysteria. Freud attempted to deconstruct the imaginary father, but this did not prevent it having the same effect as its construction, namely, the confirmation that it concerns a statue, an artefact.

There is another important difference with *Totem and Taboo*. When Freud had finished the third essay in 1912, he considered it the best he had ever written, and he always kept to this opinion. *Moses and Monotheism*, and especially the third essay, was depicted by him as the worst thing he had ever written. This is a strange reversal, which cannot be considered in isolation from its counterpart, all the more because it is a reworking of this counterpart. Just like *Totem and Taboo*, *Moses and Monotheism* consists of three parts, but that is the end of the analogy as far as structure is concerned. The assured building up towards a certain climax in the first work becomes a stammering repetition in the second. The third essay is an attempt to rewrite the second one, while in the first one there are elements which are only justified in the ulterior essays. The reasons for this literary failure have to be looked for in the subject, not in the circumstances in which it was written.[38]

The central subject of the book is the rewriting of the myth of the primal father. While *Totem and Taboo* was solely concerned with the effect of paternal power on the sons, this paper is concerned with the effect of patriarchy on the female order, matriarchy. Freud began it twice without ever reaching an end.[39] In both these attempts, Moses is wandering around as a go-between, a mediator between an originally real, all too real, primal father on the one hand, and on the other hand a kind of imaginary primal patriarch who almost reaches the dimensions of the symbolic father.

The myth of the primal horde is here depicted in stages. The first stage only contains the primal father and his females; there are no mothers and language is absent. In the second stage the murder of the primal father occurs and unexpectedly results in the establishment of matriarchy. The third stage gave Freud a lot of trouble. As a transitional phase it contains a strange mixture of matriarchy, mother goddesses, clans of brothers and an emerging totemism. The fourth and last stage brings the reintroduction of the primal father-patriarch thanks to an intermediate figure: the son.

Reading this twice repeated periodical table yields the following result: it only makes sense insofar as it is read backwards, and secondly, it is related to the seemingly secondary digressions concerning language and the origin of culture scattered in between.

Let us start with the reversed reading, in which every phase receives its importance from the next one. The first stage is the most unequivocal, that is, the most idiotic in the properly etymological sense of the word. There is no language, only the Real 'is'.[40] It is only in the second stage that the first one receives a meaning and this is due to the way in which it disappears: the murdered male animal becomes a primal father whose vanished authority permits the eruption of a power previously bridled by him: matriarchy. Just as one has to be read from two, the second stage - matriarchy - only receives meaning and weight by the way it disappears in the third. Already in *Totem and Taboo* Freud had mentioned an interval full of difficulties between the primal murder and the appearance of feelings of guilt, incest prohibition and the obligation to exogamy. That same interval is here elaborated as the third stage. The disappearance of paternal authority sets free a previously chained power - matriarchy - which calls for countermeasures to bridle it once again.[41] According to Freud, this happens thanks to the intervention of the son-hero who re-installs the function of the father. Alongside primal mothers and goddesses, masculine son-gods make their appearance and will themselves eventually take on a patriarchal style.[42] The transition to monotheism takes place through a mediator - Moses, Christ - who will re-establish paternal authority once again. This is the last phase.

The hysterical clinic is easy to recognise in the two last stages. Little Hans has to bring in the father-patriarch in order to escape from matriarchy, from the big maternal bathtub in which he risks disappearing. Dora dreams about a father who saves his children from a house in flames, and this against the mother. Anna O. imagines stories in which the daughter acts as the one who saves the father, with a happy end containing the disappearance of the mother.

At this 'familiar' juncture, it is not difficult to see that Freud was preparing to differentiate between the symbolic paternal function on the one hand and the imaginary father constructed by the neurotic on the other. Freud's fourth stage, monotheism proper, treats of a symbolic principle, through which a treaty, a pact is entered into with a founding figure.

Nevertheless, Freud never succeeded in making the proper differentiation between the principle, the bearer of this principle and the imaginary construction of a father as the neurotic bridge between those first two. In his deconstruction of this imaginary father - as in the opening sentence - Freud kept on turning in circles. He wrote that his construction of Moses - to be compared with his construction in the case study of Little Hans - does not suffice to explain the introduction of monotheism. There has to be something that goes beyond it, he said. In this, he formulated his own mistake: his creation of Moses implied a falling back on the myth of the creator, the hero.[43] Indeed, when he continued to look for the differentiating traits of the "great man", this search inevitably brought him back to the father. *Petitio Principii*: the figure of Moses is able to re-establish the father because he himself is a representative of the father. The confusion between imaginary and symbolic father continued. Probably, he said, it was not easy for the Jewish people to make a differentiation between the image of the man Moses and God.[44] Neither was it for Freud himself. Slightly further on in the text a sentence appears in which the opposition between those two is clearly expressed: "That religion brought the Jews a far grander conception of God, or as we might put it more modestly, the conception of a grander God".[45]

This sober realisation came from the clinician who saw in his practice mainly 'the conception of a grander God', of an imaginary father who could never be grand enough. The 'far grander conception of God' was the furthest step Freud would ever make in the direction of the discovery of a principle which grounded the symbolic.

As a result of the fact that Freud was never able decisively to formulate this principle, he was compelled to formulate ethical conclusions about truth and justice. In his opinion, spiritual progress (*Das Geistige*) and culture cannot be accounted for by reference to the father because paternal authority is precisely inaugurated by this progress. The reason for this was not clear to him but it allowed him to formulate its consequence all the better: "*Credo quia absurdum*".[46] A principle is always arbitrary, just like the language in which it is expressed. The grounding principle here is language itself, of which the name of the father furnishes the basis, transforming the real father into its representative. The mixing of the two forced Freud into his 'credo'. He applied this also to the moral rules imposed by patriarchy, by which a moral and social order is installed based on incest prohibition and rules of exogamy.[47] These rules too are arbitrary, 'on principle', and one has to believe them, '*credere*'. Their arbitrary character showed itself for Freud more than convincingly in the ample possibilities for transgression. Even the argument based on biology, that incest was lethal for the species, was dismissed by him:[48] likewise the oft repeated statements about these rules being 'eternal truths'. Freud had enough clinical experience to know that the average human does not tolerate much truth and usually runs away as fast as possible if the dose becomes too great.[49]

It is remarkable that Freud's conclusion in this respect ended on the same point as the one he had already recognised in Dostoyevsky in an analogous context: the submission to a father figure within a religious context.[50] In this paper, Freud depicted the typical sequence of Dostoyevsky's attitude towards the father: construction of, rebellion against, submission to. It was precisely this endpoint that brought him to the conclusion that Dostoyevsky had remained neurotic. This paper brings us to an aspect we still have to develop: the murder of the father. In *Moses and Monotheism*, Freud stuck to his opinion that this murder did really happen. This confronted him with another problem: he had to explain how the memory of this murder was stored in the individual memory, and in such a way that even in (post)modern times its effects are still at work. This brings us back to the first and second stages of his myth, and especially to his casual remarks concerning language and the origin of culture.

The two last stages, in which matriarchy is subjected to the Law, reintroduce the father-patriarch through the son. Its starting point is reconstructed in a retroactive way: once upon a time there was a primal father who was killed by his sons, after which matriarchy took root. Hence, *re*-introduction by the son. This is where Freud situated the idea of the 'hero' and of 'tragic guilt'. One of the sons took the burden of guilt on his shoulders, thereby exonerating the others. The strength of drama, epic and tragedy lies precisely in the rewording of this theme.[51] Through the intervention of the son, the father-patriarch was back in office. Every neurotic personally picks up this thread of what is stored in the collective memory of humanity. In order to explain this transition from the phylogenetic level to the ontogenetic one, Freud had to appeal to the "phylogenetic, archaic heritage in the unconscious".[52]

Before dismissing this argument as facile, it is more than worthwhile to examine how Freud elaborated this phylogenetic heritage. He formulated it after making a digression on the function of memory and repression. Its conclusion was that consciousness can only take place through language. Then followed the idea of 'archaic heritage', which he immediately linked to the acquisition of language. Freud discovered 'the universality of symbolism in language' and concluded that the acquisition of language as such belonged to this phylogenetic heritage. Language contains an 'original knowledge' that is not acquired, that consists of "thought-connections between ideas - connections which had been established during the historical development of speech and which have to be repeated now every time the development of speech has to be gone through in an individual". If it is possible to conserve this in phylogenetic memory, then the same is true of the memory of the primal murder. His conclusion: "After this discussion I have no hesitation in declaring that men have always known (in this special way) that they once possessed a primal father and killed him."[53]

Freud here puts two points together: the acquisition of language and the primal murder. His clinical genius sensed the relationship between those two themes. This becomes all the more clear the moment he takes up his earliest aetiology of the neuroses once more and in such a way that there cannot be any doubt about his loyalty to it. Whilst he doubted his trauma theory because of the absence of objective possibilities of verification of the traumatic, he now simply reversed matters and produced a definition from the point of view of the subject: at the base of every neurosis there is always something traumatic, *because it is traumatic for the subject*. And why is this so? Because it always concerns something that took place *during the period of acquisition of language, something for which words were lacking*.[54]

In this way everything crystallises around one central point: trauma, primal murder, phylogenetic heritage, language acquisition. Freud had already written that for the primitives, calling out a name was deadly and therefore forbidden. The same was true for Jewish monotheism in which the pronunciation of the name of the grounding god is forbidden, which is why Freud assumed that Moses' scribes were the inventors of the alphabet, that is, the inventors of a language with signifiers, one freed from its imaginary character.[55] For Freud this language revealed itself as the most important point in what he called the *'Menschwerdung'*, becoming human. Its consequence is a *'Triebverzicht'*, renunciation of the drive, and the 'triumph of the spiritual over the sensual'. This was not yet enough in his opinion because the acquisition of language does not prevent the 'omnipotence of thoughts'. The next step was the introduction of patriarchy over matriarchy, which resulted in a new form of jurisdiction. The 'triumph of the spiritual' was thus aligned with a *'Kulturfortschritt'*, a further step in the development of culture, simply because paternal lineage is always an assumption based on premises, contrary to maternal descent which is perceptually verifiable.[56]

It is not surprising that the impact of this very important part of psychoanalytic conceptualisation was bound to be misunderstood. What Freud discovered here was nothing less than the becoming of a subject, that is, the transition from a 'biological' and 'natural' being to a 'cultural' and speaking human being, the transition from the Real of the complete body to the Symbolic of lack and desire. What has been read and understood is that Freud was a phallocratic patriarch who amassed theoretical arguments in order to put down matriarchy and 'therefore' every woman. What people will continue to believe they understand concerns actual fathers and mothers with whom everyone of us still has to settle accounts, either in the negative or in the positive sense.

Lacan can help us to bridge Freud's phylogenesis and ontogenesis. The bridge is language itself which is acquired in two stages. Originally for the subject signifiers are ordered in a binary way as in the Freudian "fort-da". Based on this absence or presence of the omnipotent mother as the first Other, this sequence of signifiers does not, however, show the regularity of law. Its regulation is only introduced by a third term, the Name-of-the-Father and the phallus, through which language transcends the system of signs and becomes a symbolic chain of signifiers. The primal murder Freud considered as real repeats itself with each human child when it learns to speak. "The word is the murder of the thing". The name of the father as symbolic father is henceforth the dead father. Dead because it concerns a symbolic function, to which the real father has the same relationship as every subject to any signifier: he disappears beneath it. The fact that he can pop up again with any other signifier forms part of the neurotic drama. For neurotics, the real father has to coincide with the symbolic father; and that is why the imaginary father is constructed.

It is with this imaginary father that Freud came to a standstill, resulting in his *credo quia absurdum*. The other consequence is as follows: in this revised version of the Oedipal structure the idea of castration cannot keep the same status. Whilst it did not occupy much space in the first theory and was only introduced later on as a threat, a feared punishment, all this becomes much more complicated in the second version. If the murdered primal father is restored to his power through his son in order to bridle matriarchy, what happens to the idea of castration? In the Moses paper, the alteration of the concept is only hesitantly introduced. Here and there, we find the classical use: castration as threat, as punishment, albeit in a weaker form. Freud is telling us that there other ways the primal father can punish his sons apart from castration; he can restrict himself to killing them or throwing them out.[57] Alongside the familiar wording of the castration complex, something different appears. Circumcision, as a weakened form of castration, is the sign of a treaty with the founding god.[58] Castration signs the treaty with the father. The intervention of the symbolic father is symbolic castration. For Freud, it became a bedrock.

The rock in the black continent

"It is only by understanding this position - the recognition of desire as an unsatisfied desire - that the analyst gains access to hysterical symptoms and their evolution. It is in this respect that the hysterical subject was Freud's teacher and that we can learn, even today, about the functioning of unconscious desire in the linkage of the divided subject to its inner objects. *But even this veils something that lies beyond, the problem of castration.*"[59]

Hysteria still has something to teach us, something beyond desire and its object, something that only makes its appearance in a veiled form. This is the most difficult point in the entire theory, because it is in itself the cause of the absence of totality: castration.

Insofar as we have formulated the classical interpretation of the Oedipus complex for hysteria in a different way, we have to ask the question how the castration complex receives a place in this reformulation. The history and function of this complex are fairly well known. The most remarkable thing about the history of the Oedipus complex is that its generalisation came rather late, as late as 1923 when Freud assigned it a fundamental role.[60] Its function can be stated as follows. The boy fears the father, fears castration as the paternal punishment for his forbidden desire for his mother. The girl develops a penis envy, a tendency to compensate for her phallic lack by looking to her father for an answer. The possible lack of a penis is paramount for both sexes. We have already met this idea earlier in Freud when he discovered the primary phantasy about castration as the infantile explanation for sexual difference.

We have defined the hysterical Oedipus complex in two stages. The first period showed us a turning away from the mother, away from the lack of the first Other. The pre-Oedipal relationship between mother and child contains a form of enjoyment in which the child runs the risk of disappearing. By way of solution, the hysterical subject constructs an imaginary father who has to provide an answer for the lack of the first Other. This is the second period. With this hysterical Oedipus complex, anxiety is situated primarily on the first level, where the child is confronted with the desire of an incomplete Other. All the same, clinical practice shows us another anxiety, this time directed towards the father figure as introduced in the second stage. This anxiety - called castration anxiety - is thus associated with an imaginary figure. The same is true of the penis envy of the girl.

With this reformulation in hand, we now want to study the theoretical and clinical implications of castration.

The impasse of the Real

The solutions proposed by Freud for the 'feminine' Oedipus complex ended in an impasse. All three were guided by penis envy. Complete sexual inhibition ends in neurosis, the masculinity complex sticks to the penis-clitoris, and the third method only reaches a happy end on condition that the desire for a penis is exchanged for the desire for a child, preferably a male child.

Considered in this way, Freud could not avoid asking himself what made an analysis efficient, what the chances of ending a treatment were. To this central question of *Analysis Terminable and Interminable*, he produced a pessimistic answer,[61] which is well-known: every analysis ends on a biological bedrock, castration anxiety for the man, penis envy for the woman. Beyond that, nothing is possible. The hallowed status of this answer does not excuse us from the obligation to read this paper very carefully.

Freud isolated three determining factors relating to the success or failure of an analysis: the influence of the traumatic aetiology, the strength of the drives and the alterations in the Ego.[62] The first two need to be discussed together as the traumas which are important psychoanalytically are always situated in the sexual field. The last factor, the alterations in the Ego, constitutes a completely different category, an opening towards a new register.

An analysis which is completed successfully presupposes that the analysand remains free from all neurotic symptoms afterwards. When Freud looked back on his practice, he had no difficulty in finding a number of cases in which the analysis seemed to him to have ended successfully, but this did not prevent the patient from becoming openly neurotic again, sometimes many years later. Freud stated that normally a neurosis breaks out or starts again in those periods of life during which the drives undergo a somatic change: puberty and menopause. He considered this as the effect of the 'quantitative' factor, the combination of the strength of the drives and the traumatic impact. An analysis is supposed to provide a solution to it, he said, by revising and correcting the original process of repression. Nevertheless, his experience proved that this was almost impossible.[63]

Beyond this biological terminology - menopause, puberty, strength of the drive - something else emerged. A neurosis always breaks out during a confrontation with the problem of sexual identity. This is best illustrated by one of Freud's examples. One of his hysterical patients remained free from neurosis for a considerable number of years, and this "in spite of a number of actual traumatic circumstances". Nevertheless, at a given moment the neurosis broke loose in all its strength, and this time in a definitive way.[64]

The moment was not accidental: the neurosis broke out when a growth was discovered which necessitated a hysterectomy. The result was a questioning of sexual identity, which was here unmistakably the determining factor.

At this point, we can highlight Freud's pessimism vis-à-vis the correction of the original process of repression. Insofar as this concerns primary repression - Freud did not say it concerned 'secondary repression', he talked of 'original' repression - it concerns the irremediable lack of a specific signifier for femininity. The symbolic order is lacking in comparison to the Real, lack which is 'solved' by the hysteric by means of an imaginary superstructure. The moments when neurosis erupts always entail a confrontation between an impulse from the Real of the drive - puberty, masturbation, marriage, illness, menopause - and a lack in the Symbolic. Neurosis is an attempt to bridge this by way of the Imaginary. The therapeutic effect of an analysis can be measured by the way in which it questions the neurotic answer to this lack in the Symbolic and the way in which it eventually puts itself forward to mend this lack.

The stumbling block for Freud was the castration complex. In a lecture about this subject, André stressed the fact that the way an analysis ends is determined by the analyst's conception of castration.[65] If we apply this idea to Freud it becomes clear that his conception causes both his theory and practice to end up in an impasse, determined by biological realities desired or avoided in the imaginary.

In his practice Freud complained that when one is trying to persuade a woman to abandon her wish for a penis on the ground of its being unrealisable, or when one is seeking to convince a man that a passive attitude to men does not always signify castration, one gets the impression of preaching in the desert. Analysis becomes interminable.

In the theory, with the 'envy for the penis' and the 'masculine protest', Freud struck through all the psychological strata and hit the biological bedrock. "The repudiation of femininity can be nothing other than a biological fact, a part of the great riddle of sex".[66]

Both in practice and in theory, Freud had made the very same development as the hysteric, except that he pushed further into the Imaginary, right up to biologically determined realities. If one follows this line of reasoning, one might as well move the couch to the attic, together with the books. Indeed, from this point of view, salvation is to be expected only from the kinds of questionable organ displacements for which Marie Bonaparte set the standard.[67]

Freud's pessimistic conclusion does not prevent us from finding some clues which point back to his earlier conceptualisations; these clues will bring us to another theory and therefore another practice.

When we read Freud's wording of his impasse, something stands out which concerns the link to his previous conceptualisation. The bedrock upon which every analysis stalls gives rise to the idea of a common principle for both sexes: "Something which both sexes have in common has been forced, by the difference between the sexes, into different forms of expression".[68] The common point, the hidden principle is the 'repudiation of femininity', and in this paper the repudiation is traced back to a repudiation of *passivity*. This implies that we have to link it to the whole of the pre-Oedipal problematic, something not done by Freud, in combination with the concept of passivity.

Freud had isolated three factors pertinent to the success of an analysis. As the first two already seemed sufficient to abandon all hope of success, the third seemed relatively unimportant. The so-called 'alterations in the Ego' were discussed by Freud as an aside, apparently unconnected to the previous topic. Individual constitution played a role as well as upbringing. During the developmental process, defences are erected, and these are held responsible for the alterations in this Ego. The central process of defence is of course repression. Freud used a metaphor in which he compared repression to censorship which omitted parts of a text: omission, something lacking. Its motive was that "The psychical apparatus is intolerant of unpleasure; it has to fend it off at all costs, and if the perception of reality entails unpleasure, that perception - that is, the truth - must be sacrificed".[69]

This formulation rings a bell: it is the very one Freud used in several places to describe the discovery of castration, the lack of a penis in women. There too, perception was typically falsified by 'omission'. This third factor which determines the success or failure of an analysis has to be linked to castration theory. 'Alterations in the Ego' are also connected to it.

This opened a path of thought which *Analysis Terminable and Interminable* did not pursue. In order to find its ulterior development, we have to consult Freud's unfinished papers. They will show us that castration can be understood in a different way, thereby giving a new direction to the idea of the end of the treatment.

Of feminine privacy[70]

In 1919 Freud published a paper in which he looked for the sources of 'Das Unheimliche', 'The uncanny'. Using linguistic analysis he discovered that 'heimlich' and 'unheimlich' share the same meaning, that which is familiar can become a source of anxiety if it contains something that has to be kept hidden because of a certain danger.[71] Freud succeeded in isolating two great categories at the root of this feeling. In the first, the castration complex is central, and the mother's genitals function as an all-too-well-known yet radically unknown 'heim'. The second source concerns the return of the infantile phantasy of the omnipotence of thought. In the normal course of events this stage is transcended, but when it recurs, it becomes a source of 'Unheimlichkeit'.[72]

Further analysis of these two sources brings up new material. Freud depicted the connection between castration and the 'uncanny' by using Hoffman's tale of the Sandman. In this story, the specific way in which castration makes its appearance is very remarkable indeed: it concerns the loss of the eyes. This loss is supposed to be a substitute for castration and is thus as much feared as castration itself. Freud referred to Sophocles, where he found the same substitution: Oedipus tore out his own eyes by way of punishment for his forbidden relationship with his mother. On the basis of this classical model, Freud could generalise: being blinded was a substitute for being castrated, the fear of it can be traced back to castration anxiety.[73]

This substitution is rather strange, to say the least. If the 'uncanny' component of the castration complex goes back to the fact of having *seen* the mother's genitals, the lack of a penis, then tearing out one's eyes does not seem to be the first substitution at hand. Being blinded calls to mind instead a defence *against* a having seen, against something that one does not want or cannot see. This is more evident when we recall Freud's formulation of 'the uncanny': something familiar in which something unfamiliar and dangerous is hidden. Years before, Freud had applied this to hysterical blindness, in which perceptual contents that were 'dangerous' for the subject had to be avoided.[74] Moreover, we can apply the same thing to Oedipus: he tore out his eyes, so he said, in order not to see her any more, the one he had seen far too much, his mother.[75]

So, to be blinded is a defence against that which it is forbidden to see. We can extrapolate this idea further if we take into account Freud's clinical descriptions about the onset of the castration complex. Freud always presented this clinically in *visual* terms, and in a very particular way. The little boy sees the female genitals but falsifies his perception: what he observes is the lack of a penis. The little girl sees the penis and wants to have one herself. Hence, the starting point of the castration complex is the fact of *not* having seen the female genitals. The only thing that has been 'seen' is the lacking penis, either because it still has to grow, or because it has been taken away.

At this point, we have to make a differentiation between anxiety, castration and being blinded. The idea of castration, as it arises in the infant's world, is first of all an *interpretation* of the female genitals, one that makes them disappear in such a way that they are never seen. The castration complex covers the mystery of femininity.[76] If the female genitals can no longer be seen in terms of castration, then what threatens to emerge is another perception, against which being blinded is the last line of defence. Therefore anxiety has to be understood primarily as a reaction to what lies *beyond* castration, to something against which both the interpretation of castration as well as blindness form a bar. This 'something' is the mother's lack beyond the phallic order. It entails a confrontation with enjoyment in the Real, one that threatens to take in the child as a passive object.

As the first source of the uncanny, the castration complex shows itself especially '*unheimlich*' at the point where it might fail. Freud's second source dealt with the omnipotence of thoughts, in which wishes and reality come together. Based on his description, we can trace this omnipotence back to the period before the splitting between subject and object, when the other functioned as a double in a very particular way. The double is not yet recognised as another and the 'Spaltung', from which the Ego-Ideal will emerge, has not yet taken place. It is the period in which the Ego is not yet differentiated from its counterpart and the 'Umwelt'.[77] In other words, this source of 'the uncanny' can also be traced back to the mother. The feelings of omnipotence of the neurotic have their origin in an identification with the almighty mother during the time before castration. It is an identification which, once the Oedipus complex has been passed through, is supplanted by another identification, the one of the Ego-Ideal.

Considered in this way, Freud's twofold sourcing of 'Unheimliche' points to the Real of the first Other. The second source harks back to the period before the lack in the first Other. The castration complex, which treats this lack in phallic terms, has to be situated in its aftermath. The effect of 'Unheimlichkeit' is produced in the moment when the defensive layers are broken through and the Real risks appearing in its naked form. Here, we recognise Freud's earlier formulations about the traumatic Real as the kernel which is not psychically worked over and around which the pathogenic material is arranged. This traumatic Real has to be understood as the lack of the Other which is still outside the phallic order.

We are now in a position to understand two other points of Freud's paper which would otherwise remain almost incomprehensible. The first one concerns something that Freud considered to be a general feature requiring special attention: "This is that an uncanny effect is often produced when the distinction between imagination and reality is effaced, as when something which we have hitherto regarded as imaginary appears before us in reality, or when a symbol takes over the full functions of the thing it symbolizes, and so on".[78] The 'uncanny' makes its appearance when the Real emerges through the rupture of the fantasy, when the Imaginary no longer fulfils its defensive function.

The second point concerns the way this paper fits into the greater unity of Freud's evolving work. Halfway through the paper, Freud apologised because he could not completely develop the link between the 'uncanny' and its infantile determinants. He referred the reader to a forthcoming paper and a central concept which was going to be developed in it. The book in question was *Beyond The Pleasure Principle*, and the concept repetition compulsion, that which goes beyond the pleasure principle.[79] This is of capital importance. Freud was saying that the 'uncanny' has to do with what lies beyond the pleasure principle, beyond phallic pleasure. It has to be linked to another enjoyment, one that lies outside the signifier, in a threatening Real. In our earlier elaboration we were able to describe the function of this repetition compulsion as the 'binding' of this Real, linking it to signifiers, where signifiers were lacking to start with.[80]

Castration now appears in a totally different light. Castration *protects* against the mystery of femininity and forms the line of rupture between two forms of pleasure. The first form belongs to the Real, is traumatic and makes the subject disappear, fade away in the Other; hence, its double name: the enjoyment of the Other, the other enjoyment. The second one is lawfully signified; unknown enjoyment is worded through the phallus and is inscribed in the phallic pleasure principle; hence its name: phallic pleasure or phallic enjoyment. The phallus, the signifier of this putting into words, has to be introduced by the father, thereby opening the possibility of interpreting the lack of the mother in phallic terms, in terms of castration. In this sense, castration becomes *the condition* for phallic pleasure.

How does this tally with the idea of the father as the bogey man who punishes with castration? There is another dimension of castration, already commented upon by Freud in his paper on Moses, in which circumcision, as symbol of castration, functioned as a token for the treaty with the father/god. This can also be found in other parts of his work.

Three years after the publication of *The Uncanny*, Freud wrote a draft for something he planned to develop at a later date. The manuscript entitled *Medusa's Head* was published after his death. One and a half pages long, this draft contains Freud's most advanced ideas about castration, together with *The Splitting of the Ego in the Process of Defence* and *An Outline of Psychoanalysis*. It is typical that these papers remained unfinished and were only published posthumously, typical because of the difficulties Freud had with this concept and its redefinition.

The paper straight away introduces us to familiar surroundings. The fear evoked by the perception of Medusa's snaking hair is traced back to castration anxiety "...linked to the sight of something". One would expect the snakes to be phallic symbols, and this is indeed the case. The apparent contradiction - symbolising both castration and phallus - is solved by Freud in an elegant way: "...however frightening they may be in themselves, they nevertheless serve as a mitigation of the horror, for they replace the penis, the absence of which is the cause of the horror. This is a confirmation of the technical rule according to which a multiplication of penis symbols signifies castration".[81]

A technical rule stating that the multiplication of penis symbols signifies castration and therefore evokes castration anxiety, but at the same time also mitigates this very anxiety because this multiplication replaces the lacking penis. It is clear that Freud was not afraid of paradoxes. Before calling logic to our aid it seems appropriate to stress the fact that Freud is commenting upon a clinically verifiable phenomenon. In a methodologically rigorous study, Wisdom remarked that in hysteria those parts of the body which are subjected to conversion can signify both the penis and castration.[82] Using logic to throw out the bath water of the expression implies in this case that clinical practice ends up as the baby.

Another piece of clinical practice gives another formulation of Freud's expression. In 1919 he added a few supplementary paragraphs to *The Interpretation of Dreams*. The title was: *Die 'grosse Leistung' im Traume, A 'great Achievement' in a Dream*, and the text of the dream was as follows: "A man dreamt that *he was a pregnant woman lying in bed. He found the situation very disagreeable. He called out: 'I'd rather be...'* (during the analysis, after calling to mind a nurse, he completed the sentence with the words 'breaking stones').*Behind the bed there was a map on the wall, the bottom edge of which was kept stretched by a strip of wood. He tore the strip of wood down by catching hold of its two ends. It did not break across but split into two halves lengthways. This action relieved him and at the same time helped on delivery.*" Immediately after the dream which the patient interpreted - without any help, Freud added - the tearing down of the *'Leiste'* (frame) as a great *'Leistung'*, achievement. "He was escaping from his uncomfortable situation (in the treatment) by tearing himself out of his feminine attitude..." Freud thought that the splitting into two halves lengthways of the wooden frame was a doubling of a penis symbol, and hence referred to castration, all the more so because the signifier *'Leiste'* also means 'groin' in German. The last sentence of the interpretation was as follows: "...that he had got the better of the threat of castration which had led to his adopting a feminine attitude".[83]

From our point of view, this dream represents the birth of a subject, what can rightly be called 'a great achievement'. The picture at the start shows us the analysand as a pregnant woman, as being taken in by the Real of the body of the first Other. "He found the situation very disagreeable". The final situation is a birth, from which the subject steps out as freed. In between we find castration, as a method through which he "tears himself out of his feminine attitude". As in the case of

Medusa's snake hair, the doubling of the penis results in a lessening of anxiety. The dreamer does not so much go beyond 'the threat of castration which had led to his adopting a feminine attitude', as that he transcends that feminine attitude precisely thanks to castration. The non-signified desire of the pregnant woman-mother at first sucks him into the Real, into the enjoyment of the first Other of the body. Castration is a defensive interpretation, because as a result of it, the mother's desire is linked to a signifier, that is, to the phallic order. The remaining piece of traumatic Real acquires phallic signification, the first enjoyment provoking anxiety is turned into a safer phallic pleasure.

Primary anxiety is not directed towards castration, but to the Real that lies beyond castration, i.e. beyond the signifier. Castration is what transforms this primary enjoyment in a retroactive way into a lawfully signified and thus workable form. The feeling of '*Unheimlichkeit*' is just like anxiety a signal that the Real is about to erupt, that castration is in danger of failing in its function. As a reaction, the defensive phallic interpretation is doubled: it is not the female genital that is seen, but the absence of a penis which can still grow, if need be, and multiply a hundredfold into snake hair. Beyond castration lies the *Beyond The Pleasure Principle*, the other enjoyment that does not square with phallic enjoyment, because it is not linked to signifiers.

Pieces for a new theory, another practice

The subject comes into existence when the infant is severed from the Real and enters the human symbolic world. The price it has to pay is its own division, *Die Ichspaltung im Abwehrvorgang*, 'The splitting of the Ego in the Process of Defence', symbolic castration. As a subject, it is divided between a truth that it disavows and a conviction to which it clings,

$$\uparrow \frac{\cancel{S}}{a} \longrightarrow S_1$$

the defence is directed towards an anxiety-provoking Real that loses its traumatic power when it becomes signified. At the same time and in the same process, primary enjoyment is left behind and primary anxiety can be worked over in the first symptoms.

That is what Freud wrote on 2nd January 1938. The Ego is split under the impact of a psychic trauma. During an experience of enjoyment, the child becomes frightened by something that entails a 'real danger'. The division of the Ego can give rise to two possible reactions. Either 'reality' is put aside and one continues as usual. Or 'the danger of reality' is acknowledged: as a consequence anxiety is changed into a workable symptom.[84] The traumatic experience is the observation of the female genitals together with the threat of castration which is 'as usual, ascribed to the father'. The child then 'understands' the absence of the penis in women and therefore renounces a certain form of enjoyment - "in other words, he gives up, in whole or in part, the satisfaction of the drive".[85] The father comes to the fore as the feared agent of punishment. This punishment is supposed to be castration, hence the anxiety is castration anxiety. 'Supposed to be'. "This fear of his father, too, was silent on the subject of castration: with the help of regression to an oral phase, it assumed the form of a fear of being eaten by his father".[86] The child-eating giants from fairy tales do not castrate, they just devour. Primary anxiety concerning the enjoyment of the first Other is shifted to the second Other, where it becomes workable. Anxiety in relation to the father as this second Other stems from primordial anxiety.

Freud generalised the division of the subject in his *Outline*, but as with his other last papers, the theory remained unfinished. Freud ended with the idea that *Ichspaltung*, 'the splitting of the Ego' is followed by the formation of the Super-ego, the agency which helps the ego in living up to its norms and imperatives. What was surprising was the recurring severity of this Super-ego which always exceeded the real severity of the father.[87] Maturity now consisted in the deconstruction of this hyper-severe Super-ego, and this was the last hurdle in the Oedipus complex: "After the paternal agency has been internalized and become a Super-ego, the next task is to detach the latter from the figures of whom it was originally the psychical representative".[88] This apparently innocent little phrase marks the difference between a neurotic and a non-neurotic subject, between a subject who has assumed symbolic castration and a neurotic who keeps on avoiding imaginary castration.

It was Lacan who took up this line of thought. Symbolic castration became the signing of a treaty with the symbolic father, a necessary condition for desire and pleasure. The introduction to the Symbolic *is* castration: "Castration, a symbolic function, can only be understood from the point of view of a signifying articulation (...) castration is the real operation introduced in the relation between the sexes by the impact of any signifier. And it is obvious that it also determines the father as this impossible real we have described." [89] The signifier and its legitimate rule protect against the other enjoyment and open the gate to desire and phallic enjoyment. Between those two forms of enjoyment comes symbolic castration: "Castration means that jouissance must be refused so that it can be reached on the inverted ladder of the Law of desire."[90] The symbolic father function is what links desire to the Law. Which Law? The one of the signifier, stating that the lack is a definitive one, that the real beyond the signifier is forever lost.

Neurosis is located in the gap of this difference between the symbolic father function and the real father. This latter is also subject to splitting, is also a divided subject, lacks and desires. Therefore his position is an impossible one: as a representative of the symbolic order, he cannot coincide with his function. The impossible relation between symbolic father function and real father results in the neurotic construction of an imaginary father image which is cause of this privation, of imaginary castration. In neurosis, the lost Real - 'l'a-chose'[91] - is turned into a missing object, that is, an object of demand. The master has to provide what is missing in order to alleviate the lack.

Beyond any Imaginary stopgaps, this lack is constitutive for the human being as a divided subject in the Symbolic. It is precisely this lack that makes creation possible, in the sense of giving meaning, and this includes the creation of a sexual rapport. The lack discovered first, that of the Other of the body, has to be signified via the second Other so that fear of enjoying can be transformed into phallic enjoyment via castration. Hence the designation of the lack is a signifier signifying that there is something lacking in the Symbolic: S($\cancel{A}$). The Symbolic is incomplete, there is the 'pas-tout', the 'not-all'. This is where the woman comes in. 'The Woman does not exist' as a statement is the effect of the phallically grounded symbolic system. Her desire becomes an enigma - 'Was will das Weib?' - if taken as a desire for a missing signifier. From this point on all interpretations are possible. Pathology is the demand for the one and only interpretation.

In the Symbolic, The Woman does not exist. Hence, there is no sexual rapport possible between two sexes which are differently signified. The only rapport that is possible is the one given by speech: "...que le rapport sexuel, c'est la parole elle-même."[92] Via metaphor, speaking embraces the dimension of creation, the possibility of preparing the ground for new significations. Hence, for Lacan, metaphor is the sole entry to a discourse beyond the world of make-believe, "qui ne serait *pas du semblant*".[93] Here, the unifying effect for the woman of the demand for a penis shifts towards the enigma of an unknown interpretation.

CONCLUSION

From Freud's hysteric to Lacan's ~~The~~ Woman

Freud's first psychoanalytic conceptualisation about hysteria concerned the 'Spaltung' (splitting) of the hysterical subject, based on an unbearable desire. His very last ideas aimed at a general theory of the division of the subject, linked to castration.

In between lay the long road along which Freud travelled as theorist and practitioner behind his hysterics. When he departed from the straight track, they would make sure he retraced his steps and reworked his theory. Eventually, the two of them stumbled on the same spot.

On this road, a lot of luggage got lost and was picked up again later, sometimes decades later. Moreover, after Freud, it got lost again. This was especially true for the idea of the traumatic Real as aetiological basis of hysteria. Freud's search for the Real was broken off by the discovery of that with which every neurotic covers the Real: the fantasy. In his theory, the concept of fantasy acquired for a long time the same function as it has in neurosis: forgetting the Real. Neurosis was understood as a pathological system of wish fulfilment in which the pleasure principle did not follow the right paths. The mechanisms of defence, with repression at the top of the list, acted as cause.

Nevertheless, the cause of the cause proved troublesome. The unpleasure that was supposed to be at the root of repression covered a strange form of pleasure, taking on another form which ignored the laws of pleasure and the principle of constancy. Moreover, repression seemed to be linked to the process of sexualisation, the process of becoming of man or woman; the latter being especially difficult. Freud reluctantly concluded that in the psyche the idea of traumatic 'passivity' was the least inappropriate representation of what it took the place of: 'femininity'.

Freud's own analysis ran right through all these discoveries. Its effects were obvious. Following the death of his father, he loosened his ties with Fliess, the recipient of his transference, and abandoned the position of pupil. After his first period of discovery, in which he allowed himself to be surprised by what he was told, he put on the master's hat and started to teach, turning discovery into its opposite. He built up his theory into a closed totality. The knowledge he originally received from his practice of listening was transformed into an imperative, an enforced yoke. The earlier questions received the kind of solution which obliterated the questions themselves. Freud knew how one ought to desire, knew which pathways took one to the pleasure principle. His theory formed a consistent model. What was opposed to it was either neurosis or resistance, two concepts which became quasi-synonymous. The treatment was turned into an excercise in didactics, the teaching became a treatment.

In a second movement which was a renewed confrontation with hysteria, the theory seemed to fail. The success of the didactic element did not prevent the yoke of the treatment being refused. The two basic principles of pleasure and constancy became an illustration of Charcot's famous words: "*La théorie, c'est bon, mais ça n'empêche pas d'exister*". Beyond them, something different ex-sists, something that does not obey the same laws. Again, Freud was confronted with the Real and with the trauma. He discovered repetition compulsion and its aim: to put the non-signified into words, to force the un-bound primary processes, via a binding process grounded in an energetics, into the laws of the pleasure principle and the secondary process. Beyond this pleasure principle, there lay another form of enjoyment, unbound, non-signified, Real.

Thence, the theory fell back to ever more primary concepts. The most important concepts from the first period received the prefix 'Ur'(primary). repression was changed into primary repression constituting the border between the non-symbolised and the symbolic Order with its '*Bejahung*'. The three primary fantasies are all attempts to signify a certain aspect of that Real. The difficult relationship between the Symbolic and the Real is crystallized in two points: the sexual identity of the woman and the function of the father. The primary fantasy about castration can only provide a woman with a negative sexual identity. The solution is therefore found in the dreamt-of father who has to evoke desire in the child: it is the primary fantasy about seduction. The result aims at the establishment of sexual rapport: it is the fantasy of the primal scene.

Infantile sexual theories and primary fantasies are attempts by the child to bridle the Real where the Symbolic fails. These attempts give rise to a never-ending displacement in the Imaginary, precisely because of the lack of a Symbolic anchorage. For each pathology, this lack focuses on the father figure. Specifically for the hysterical subject, it is from this father figure that an answer is expected about questions of sexual identity, sexual rapport and the regulation of desire. The real father appears insufficient, thus necessitating the creation of an imaginary father image. Within the imaginary order, this creation becomes endless: large, larger, largest, but never large enough.

Freud heard this appeal to the father. He therein followed hysteria, not by interpreting this appeal in the treatment and bringing it into a theory based on this practice, but by himself incarnating this father figure in the cure and by constructing a theory as a guarantee for the response to this appeal. *Totem and Taboo* gave substance to the primal father needed by the neurotic, the one exception to the law which grounds the law itself. Desire thereby seems regulated, and sexual rapport guaranteed. Nevertheless, in the treatment, difficulties around the construction of a father figure kept popping up. Either he was not big enough, with the result that the hysterical search continued, or he was too big, with the result that he had to be obsessionally destroyed.

Clinically the theory yields a number of thoughts over and above this construction. In Freud's myth about the primal horde there is no room for a mother figure. incest prohibition appears first of all as a prohibition to enjoy in the way the primal father does, it is the prohibition against enjoying all women, against enjoying The Woman as a whole. The problem of castration is only spoken of indirectly. Freud situated his myth in the Real, as if it really happened, while its heritage has been kept alive in the unconscious and takes care of the regulation of desire in each human child.

A prohibition which enforces a regulation of enjoyment in the Real is a prohibition which promotes security. The Oedipus complex, in Freud's first version, is therefore a structure providing security, a defensive endpoint which was avidly expected by the neurotic. Its starting point, that against which the defence was directed in the first place, remains hidden if not lacking in this first version.

What Freud discovered as the pre-Oedipal period in the female Oedipus complex was nothing but the formulation of what had to be hidden, the starting point of the hysterical Oedipus complex. The mother then gained a new status, not as a psychologised mother, but as the first Other, the reservoir of signifiers, the mother tongue. At first she remained the Other of the body, the Real. The primary mother and child relationship begins as a continuation of the intra-uterine relationship, in which the child enjoys the Other of the body by forming a unity.

Enjoyment and unity are lost in the acquisition of language. The mother becomes the first Other of the signifier, revealing both lack and desire. This lack is threatening for the child because it cannot discover any regularity in the *fort-da*, in the binary structure of presence and absence of the first Other of the signifier. It is turned into a passive object of enjoyment that completes the Other. Anxiety is the only reaction.

For a subject to escape the lethal reduction to what fills up this lack, a regularity in the signifier has to be imposed, an anchorage point through which signification can come into being. It is here that the father has to make his appearance as a representative of the law, as the one who subjects enjoyment to the law of the phallic signifier.

In a first movement Freud had discovered and verified the necessary terminus of the Oedipal structure for the neurotic: the primal father. In a second movement he supplied its starting point in which the mother is the central figure. In both cases he followed hysterical displacements into the Imaginary which resulted in an impasse. Symbolic father function and imaginary father image fused together in the *Credo quia absurdum*. The phallus as signifier for the lack of the first Other appeared only in its imaginary form: castration anxiety and penis envy.

The process of becoming a woman depicted by Freud can be understood in terms of three lines of hysterical development. With the first two, he brought hysterical desire to a seemingly biologically determined impasse, which one could say his theory precisely imposed: penis envy, the envy for the organ. The imaginary object which always fails to appear at the end of the metonymy of desire received a consistency, a dimension of reality, which is still hard to discard. The third line of development - being the least of three evils - entailed a return precisely to what had to be avoided, the mother.

Freud had followed his hysterical patients faithfully, both in his theory and in his practice. He therefore had to face the same deadlock, in which the treatment became interminable while the theory had to abandon the psychical realm. It had been the most fruitful failure in the history of the human sciences. Realising hysterical structure up to its very limit was the *conditio sine qua non* for creating the possibility of going beyond it. A closed paranoid system would have made this impossible. Beyond this impasse, we find that Freud sowed the seeds for a new theory, another practice. Castration became the symbol of a treaty with the father, became the cause of an '*Ichspaltung*', splitting of the Ego, beyond the Imaginary. The craved-for illusion of totality was changed into a grounding lack, opening up possibilities of creation.

Lacan developed the consequences of Freud's last beginnings. The three registers were his conceptual knife enabling him to dissect clinical practice in such a way that it honoured Freud's theory. The four discourses offered a rigorous formalisation of the transference. On this basis the psychoanalytic conceptualisation of hysteria could be formulated in a clear way. The hysteric opts for a masculine line of development and can only inscribe herself phallically in a negative way. This explains a certain monotony in hysteria: everything is reduced to the demand for an object that should fill up the lack, yet it is never enough. Beyond that, there is another possible rapport for a woman with the big Other. The Woman does not exist, for lack of a unifying signifier. Hence, ~~The~~ Woman is not only subject to the phallic signifier, but also to the signifier of lack. The combination of the symbolic phallus Φ and $S(\cancel{A})$ results in the fact that ~~The~~ Woman, the becoming of a woman, is a meaningful process which is based on metaphor. hysteria, on the contrary, is a fixation which refuses meaning, based on metonymy.

Analysis and Hysteria

Hysteria is the name of the age old relationship between man and woman. Eve offered Adam the apple of the tree of wisdom, hoping that it would result in knowledge. The very next instant both of them found themselves outside paradise.

The hysteric wants to fill in the lack of the Other and appeals to the master. He has to produce what she lacks, he has to guarantee a wholeness. In exchange, she offers herself as the answer to a question she has asked in his place, an answer she refuses beforehand: "It is not *that* which...". At the same time, in a tacit conspiracy, the lack is never brought to the negotiating table. The shadows in the shadow play can be substituted but the filling up remains. If an analysis is reduced to such a shadow play, its failure will also tread the same well-worn paths. The hysterical solution has to be avoided. Psychoanalysis does not make the woman, nor the master. Insofar as the analytic treatment of hysteria aims at something beyond the classical impasse, it can reach this only by listening to its causality. The imaginary consistency of the object demanded has to make a place for what it hides: a divided subject. The way to this is the wording of the function of this object. This leads to the fantasy which is the scenario that always places desire beyond the realm of the present - not now, then perhaps, maybe later - as a scenario which makes the subject disappear in the object - the dreamt-of unity, with an excess of enjoyment which leaves no room, neither for the subject, nor for the other as subject.

Beyond this deceitful unity, analytical discourse aims at the difference between two subjects, each of them with a rapport of their own towards the lack and thus each of them with their own desire.

At this point many are tempted to evoke the mirage of the man as a privileged being who, by way of the phallus, has a privileged place with respect to desire and enjoyment. For both sexes, the phallus functions as a signifier. The man can inscribe himself as a categorical being under that one signifier, the woman cannot. The transformation of this fact into the idea of a privileged position is nothing but a hysterical reaction which is totally at odds with clinical practice. The study of neurosis in men yields more than sufficient proof of the contrary. The presence of such a signifier does not prevent its bearers from getting involved in an endless imaginary phallic competition, does not prevent them from creating - in order to guarantee it - an authority which most of them will never get rid of any more, does not prevent them, as categorical beings, of displaying a boring monotony.

As a woman, the hysteric has chosen the masculine side, and hence, she becomes either its caricature or a complaint against this caricature. There where a woman transcends hysterical structure, she escapes being reduced to an ever absent signifier. Only there the difference with man can become clear.

We have but to look at the difference in their respective relation towards law and authority. With a man as with a hysteric, this relation is always a special one. Owing to their subjective structure, both of them are in need of an authority who has to provide the necessary certainty for the impossible, but for that same reason this certainty always remains contestable. The Super-ego, as heir to this home-made authority, is a typically masculine formation determining a typically masculine neurosis, obsessional neurosis. In the process of becoming a woman, there is no motive for the installation of such a Super-ego as heir to the imaginary father, and this colours the woman's relationship with the law very strongly. The fact that this colouring gave some analysts the idea that a woman does not have a Super-ego - echoing earlier theological discussions about whether or not woman had a soul - demonstrates clearly the necessity man has for an authority and his confusion when confronted with a being who has no need of it. Kafka's figure in *Vor dem Gesetz*[94] is, together with the soldier, a man - any other situation is unthinkable. For Lacan, The Woman is the only being who is both inside and outside the law at the same time, thereby relativising it.

A second difference we can look at, but in a formal way without any definite elaboration of content, is that in the process of becoming a woman, we find another form of creativity. Not reduced to a category and having a different relationship towards the law and authority, women have many possibilities open to them with respect to this process of becoming. It has been said that this process can be understood in terms of sublimation. We will only retain the following: that this process is always unique, not to be transferred or repeated in its content. There are many neurotic detours in this, not all of them necessarily pathological. It is still best to counter the lack of one signifier with another signifier. This is the point in which the alienating attraction of every ideology and every mythology is greatest. Different though they may be - from mother at home to liberated 'femme fatale' they - they all have one feature in common: that they are reductive.

The aim of psychoanalysis is best described as negative: it ought not to deteriorate into a system which presents itself as an answer to the lack of a signifier. A classical metaphor describes the neurotic as somebody who keeps on trying to pack his suitcases, hoping he will one day be able to leave. A psychoanalysis is the unpacking of those suitcases and going over its contents so that indeed one day a journey without superfluous luggage can be attempted. At the very point where the journey begins the analyst has to be left behind, if need be, as the last piece of superfluous luggage.

NOTES

FREUD'S ENCOUNTER WITH HYSTERIA: DESIRE

1   M.Solms is preparing an edition of these relatively unknown Freudian papers.

2   Freud, *Hysteria* (1888b).S.E. 1, p. 41.

3   Ibid., p. 41.

4   Ibid., pp. 43-44, p. 46 and p. 52.

5   Freud, *Preface to the translation of Bernheim's "De la Suggestion"* (1888). S.E. 1, p. 83.

6   Freud, *Review of August Forel's "Hypnotism"* (1889a). S.E. 1, p. 100.

7   Freud, *Psychical (or Mental) Treatment* (1890a), S.E. 7, pp. 291-293.

8   Didi-Huberman, *Invention de l'hysterie, Charcot et l'iconographie photographique de la Salpêtrière*, Paris, Macula, 1982, pp. 1-303.

9   Freud, *A Case of Succesful Treatment by Hypnotism* (1892-1893). S.E. 1, p. 122

10 In the *Standard Edition*, "Erregungszuwachs" is translated by "accretion of excitation". S. Freud, *Preface and footnotes to the translation of Charcot's "Leçons du Mardi de la Salpêtrière* (1892-94). S.E. 1, p. 137. Difficulties about the footnotes are discussed by Strachey in his introduction, o.c., p. 132.

11 In German: "Vorstellung", means 'idea'as well 'as 'representation'. The central element in the German academic psychology of that time was indeed the "Vorstellung", which is generally translated as idea, thereby losing the connotation of representation. From a Lacanian point of view, the best translation is of course 'signifier'.

12 Freud, *On the Psychical Mechanism of Hysterical Phenomena: Preliminary Communications* (1893a). S.E. 2, pp. 8-12.

13 Freud, *The Neuro-Psychoses of Defence. An Attempt at a Psychological Theory of Acquired Hysteria, of many Phobias and Obsessions and of certain Hallucinatory Psychoses* (1894a). S.E. 3, p. 60.

14 Freud, *On the Grounds for detaching a Particular Syndrome from Neurasthenia under the description "Anxiety Neuroses"* (1895b). S.E. 3, pp. 114-115.

15 Freud, Ueber Hysterie (1895g). *Wiener klinische Rundschau*, IX, 1895, pp. 662-663, pp. 679-680, pp. 696-697. Not included in the G.W., nor in the S.E. We discovered this text thanks to J. Quackelbeen. The quotation is on page 696 of the original text.

16 Freud, *Aus den Anfängen der Psychoanalyse (1887-1902). Briefe an Wilhelm Fliess*. Frankfurt, Fisher Verlag, 1975, pp. 297-385.

17 Claes, *Psychologie, een dubbele geboorte*. Kapellen, De Nederlandse Boekhandel, 1982, pp. 145-189.

18 Russelman, *Van James Watt tot Sigmund Freud, de opkomst van het stuwmodel van de zelfexpressie*. Deventer, Van Loghum Slaterus, 1983, p. 204. This study leads to a cul-de-sac. For a Lacanian lecture which opens new perspectives outside the artificial deadlock we refer to a paper by J. Quackelbeen: "Welke plaats geeft Lacan aan de psychische energie, het affect en de drift? Television IV". *Rondzendbrief uit het Freudiaanse veld*, 1983-84, jrg. III, nr. 3, pp. 5-26.

19 Freud, *The Unconscious* (1915e). S.E. 14, p. 178.

20 Freud, *Studies on Hysteria* (1895d). S.E. 2, p. 67, footnote 1.

21 Lacan, Le Séminaire, Livre III, Les Psychoses, pp. 303-304. *The Seminar of J.Lacan, Book III, The Psychoses*, translated by R.Grigg, New York, Norton, 1993, pp. 266-277.

22 Freud, S.E. 1, letter 72, p. 267.

23 J.Lacan, *Le Séminaire, Livre XVII, L'envers de la psychanalyse (1969-1970)*, Paris, Seuil, 1991, chapter XI, pp. 175 ff.

24 Far from being introduced by Lacan, this problem is already present in Freud's early work, where he compares 'normal' with 'hysterical' repression. The difference between those two would be purely quantitative, although Freud did not like the idea of a 'constitutional' factor. He never found a satisfying answer to this question; moreover, his last paper, *Splitting of the Ego in the Process of Defence*, can be considered as a generalisa-

tion of the process of defence way beyond hysteria, even situating this process at the basis of psychological development.

25 Freud, *Psychical (or Mental) Treatment* (1890a). S.E. 7, p. 292.
26 Micale, *Approaching Hysteria. Disease and its Interpretations*, New York, Princeton University Press, 1995. Libbrecht, *Hysterical psychosis, a historical survey*, London, Transaction publishers, 1995.
27 Plato, *Timaeus*, part III, 91 c.
28 See Charcot's foreword in: Janet, P.M.F., *L'état mental des hystériques*. Paris, Rueff, 1894.
29 Wajeman, *Le maître et l'hystérique*. s.l., Navarin, 1982, part IV.
30 Freud, *On the Grounds for detaching a Particular Syndrome from Neurasthenia under the description "Anxiety Neuroses"* (1895b). S.E. 3, p. 114-115.

FROM TRAUMA TO FANTASY: THE REAL AS IMPOSSIBLE
1 This differentiation was systematized in *The Neuro-Psychoses of Defence* (1894a). S.E. 3, pp. 46-47. Freud takes it up again in the *Studies on Hysteria* (1895d). S.E. 2, p. 285.
2 Freud, *Studies on Hysteria* (1895d). S.E. 2, p. 10.
3 Ibid., p. 286. Lacan, subversion du sujet et dialectique du désir, in: *Ecrits*. Paris, Seuil, 1966, p. 795.
4 Freud, *Studies on Hysteria* (1895d). S.E. 2, pp. 286-287.
5 Ibid., p. 116 and p. 122.
6 Ibid., p. 67, footnote.
7 Ibid., p. 302.
8 Ibid., p. 69.
9 Ibid., pp. 288-289.
10 Ibid., p. 289.
11 Ibid., p. 53, footnote 1.
12 Ibid., p. 280.
13 Ibid., p. 110.
14 Ibid., pp. 74-75, footnote 2 and S. Freud, *The Aetiology of Hysteria* (1896c). S.E. 3, pp. 195-197.
15 Ferenczi, Confusion of Tongues between the adult and the child. *Int.J.Psychoanal.*, 1949, XXX, pp. 225-230. Freud, *Aus den Anfangen der Psychoanalyse, Briefe an W. Fliess*. Frankfurt, Fisher, 1975, letter 29, 30 and 31 to Fliess, pp. 112-114. In this respect, see also one of Freud's original French papers, wherein he writes: "expérience de passivité sexuelle avant la puberté: telle est donc l'étiologie spécifique de l'hysterie". (*Heredity and the Aetiology of the Neuroses* (1896a). S.E. 3, p. 152.)
16 Freud, *Aus den Anfängen der Psychoanalyse*, o.c., letter 12, p. 68; see also letter 59.
17 Freud, *Project for a Scientific Psychology*, S.E. 1, p. 356.
18 Ibid., letter 52, S.E. 1, p. 239. As a matter of fact, this is the further elaboration of an earlier discovery: "..., wie der Hysterie immer ein Konflikt zu grunde liegt (der sexuellen Lust mit der etwa begleitenden Unlust)", *Aus den Anfängen*, o.c., letter 38, p. 121.
19 Freud, *Studies on Hysteria* (1895d). S.E. 2, p. 134, footnote 2. S. Freud, S.E. 1, letter 69, p. 259.
20 Freud, S.E. 1, letter 59, p. 244.
21 Ibid., letter 61, pp. 247-248.
22 'primal scene' here has the meaning of 'first scene'; only later will this indicate the parental coitus. S.Freud, *Draft L*, S.E. 1, pp. 248 - 250, *Draft M*, ibid., p. 252.
23 Ibid., *Draft M*, p. 250.
24 Freud, S.E. 1, letter 69, p. 260.
25 Freud, S.E. 1, letter 71, p. 265.
26 Freud, S.E. 1, letter 75, p. 270.
27 Freud, S.E. 1, *Draft K*, p. 288, italics by Freud.
28 Ibid., *Draft E*, p. 192.

29   Ibid., letter 84, p. 274
30   Freud, *Aus den Anfängen der Psychoanalyse*, o.c., letter 80, p. 207.
31   Ibid., letter 94, p. 255 and letter 96, p. 227.
32   Freud, S.E. 1, letter 101, p. 276.
33   Freud, *The Interpretation of Dreams* (1900a). S.E. 5, respectively p. 525 and p. 604.
34   Lacan, *Le Séminaire, Livre XI, Les quatre concepts fondamentaux de la psychanalyse (1964)*, p.
      118. *The Four Fundamental Concepts of Psycho-analysis*, Harmondsworth, Penguin, 1991,
      p.129.
35   Lacan, *Le Séminaire, Livre I, Les écrits techniques de Freud (1975)*, p. 47. *The Seminar of
      J.Lacan, Book I, Freud's Papers on Technique 1953 - 54*, Cambridge, Cambridge University
      Press, 1988, translated by J.Forrester, p.36.
36   Freud, S.E. 1, letter 69, p. 260.
37   Freud, S.E. 1, Letter 52, p. 239.
38   Freud, S.E. 1, Letter 69, p. 259-260.
39   Ibid., letter 102, p. 278.
40   Freud, *Studies on Hysteria* (1895d). S.E. 2, p. 161.
41   Freud, S.E. 1, letter 125, p. 280.
42   Ibid., *Draft N*, p. 256, our italics.

THE THEORY OF REPRESSION: THE IMAGINARY AS DEFENCE

1   Freud, *On the History of the Psycho-Analytic Movement* (1914d). S.E. 14, p. 16.
2   Freud, *The Neuro-Psychoses of Defence* (1894a). S.E. 3, p. 48.
3   Freud, *Heredity and the Aetiology of Defence* (1896a). S.E. 3, p. 147.
4   Freud, *Further Remarks on The Neuro-Psychoses of Defence* (1896b). S.E. 3, p. 166.
5   Freud, *The Aetiology of Hysteria* (1896c). S.E. 3, pp. 189-221 and S. Freud, *Sexuality in the
      Aetiology of the Neuroses* (1898a). S.E. 3, pp. 261-285.
6   Ibid., p. 282.
7   Respectively *The Psychical Mechanism of Forgetfulness* (1898b). S.E. 3, pp. 289-297; *Screen
      Memories* (1899a). S.E. 3, pp. 301-322
8   Ibid., p. 291
9   Ibid., p. 296.
10   Ibid., p. 308 and p. 310-311.
11   Freud, *My Views on the Part played by Sexuality in the Aetiology of the Neuroses* (1906a). S.E.
      7, pp. 274-275.
12   Freud, *Draft K*, S.E. 1, pp. 221-222.
13   See bibliography: E. Ville, B. Grunberger, J. Marmor, A. Lazare, A. Sugarman and W.
      Reich.
14   See bibliography: O. Sachs, J. Neu, A. Silber, M. Klein.
15   Freud, *Draft K*, S.E. 1, p. 228.
16   This can be found in his papers of 1927 and 1933 (see our bibliography). If Jones had
      read the Bible more carefully, he would not have used it as an argument. Indeed, in
      Genesis II, woman is called 'Icha', in Hebrew the female variant of 'Ich'. 'Ich' stands for
      man...
17   Freud, *Aus den Anfängen der Psychoanalyse, Briefe an W. Fliess*. Frankfurt, Fisher, 1975, let-
      ter 123, p. 259. Later on, Freud aptly used the metaphor of the 'black continent'.
18   Freud, *Three Essays on the Theory of Sexuality* (1905d). S.E. 7, p. 219, footnote. In 1924,
      Freud confirmed this in a final sentence added to the second part of the first essay (S.E.
      7, p. 160).
19   Freud, *Draft M*, S.E. 1, p. 251.
20   Ibid., *Draft K*, pp. 228-229.
21   The "Ia sexual scene" refers to the traumatic nucleus which lies beyond verbal represen-
      tations.
22   Ibid., letter 46, p. 230.

23   Ibid., letter 52, pp. 235.
24   Ibid., *Draft K*, pp. 228-229.
25   Ibid., letter 59, p. 244. Cfr.: Ibid., letter 59, p. 244; letter 61, p. 247 and S. Freud, *Aus den Anfängen der Psychoanalyse*, o.c., letter 62, p. 173.
26   This is the borromean knot, in which the circle of the Imaginary covers the circle of the Real. The circle of the Symbolic covers the Imaginary one, but is itself covered by the circle of the Real drawing of the knot: This is one of those Lacanian topological figures which enable us to understand a number of clinical phenomena from a formal point of view. For instance, the impact of the father figure is often paradoxical as long as one works with pure clinical data. Once one understands this data in terms of the real father, the symbolic father function, and the imaginary father image, things become clearer.

27   Freud differentiated between two forms of conversion: motor (i.e. all 'classical' forms) and sensory conversion. This last form is hysterical hallucination. Both of them are fundamentally alike for Freud: they are literally 'realisations', taking the place of a psychical working-over or processing. For the reference see: S. Freud, *The Neuro-Psychoses of Defence (1894a)*. S.E. 3, p. 49.
28   Freud, *My views on the Part played by Sexuality in the Aetiology of the Neuroses* (1906a). S.E. 7, p. 278; *Three Essays on the Theory of Sexuality* (1905d). S.E. 7, p. 167.
29   For the differentiation between symbolic and imaginary interpretation, see J. Lacan, *Télévision*. Paris, Seuil, 1973, p. 18 ff.
30   Freud, *Studies on Hysteria* (1895d). S.E. 2, p. 69.
31   Freud, letter 61, S.E. 1, p. 247; Ibid., *Draft M*, p. 252; *Draft L*, p. 248.
32   Ibid., letter 52, p. 239. Ibid., letter 61, p. 247-248.
33   Ibid., letter 75, p. 268-269.
34   Ibid., letter 69, p. 260; letter 57, p. 244; letter 102, p. 278.
35   Ibid., letter 125, p. 280. Freud, *Aus den Anfängen der Psychoanalyse*, o.c., letter 91, p. 220.Freud, *Draft M*, S.E. 1, p. 252 and *Draft N*, p. 256-257.
36   Ibid., letter 75, p. 270, italics by Freud.
37   Freud, *Aus den Anfängen der Psychoanalyse*, o.c., letter 141, pp. 280-281 and letter 145, p. 287.
38   Freud, *Three Essays on the Theory of Sexuality* (1905d). S.E. 7, p. 219. This part of Freud's text is entitled: "The differentiaton between man and woman".
39   Freud, *Aus den Anfängen der Psychoanalyse*, o.c., letter 113, p. 249.
40   Ibid., letter 71, p. 194.
41   Ibid., letter 81, p. 208.
42   Freud, *Three Essays on the Theory of Sexuality* (1905d). S.E. 7, pp. 142-143. The original title of this part runs as follows: "Heranziehung der Bisexualität", which is abbreviated in the translation to "Bisexuality". It can be considered as an illustration of Freud's rejection of the idea of androgyny.
43   Ibid., p. 221.
44   Ibidem.
45   Freud, *On the Sexual Theories of Children* (1908c). S.E. 9, p. 217.
46   Freud, *Hysterical Phantasies and their Relation to Bisexuality* (1908a). S.E. 9, pp. 157-166.
47   Freud, *Some General Remarks on Hysterical Attacks* (1909a). S.E. 9, p. 234.
48   Freud, *Three Essays on the Theory of Sexuality* (1905d). S.E. 7, pp. 181-182.
49   "Everything relating to the problem of pleasure and unpleasure touches upon one of the

sorest spots of present-day psychology", Ibid., p. 209.
50   Freud, *Three Essays on the Theory of Sexuality* (1905d). S.E. 7, p. 170; p. 176, footnote 2; p. 205, footnote 1. With respect to Moebius, see: Ibid., p. 171.
51   Freud, *Three Essays on the Theory of Sexuality* (1905d). S.E. 7, p. 191.
52   Ibid., p. 236.
53   See: P.Verhaeghe, *Neurosis and psychosis: Il n'y a pas de rapport sexuel*, CFAR-seminar dd. 27 May 1995, paper published in the *Journal of the Centre for Freudian Analysis and Research no 6.*, London 1996
54   Freud, *Three Essays on the Theory of Sexuality* (1905d). S.E. 7, p. 183.
Ibid., p. 170. See also: S.Freud, *My views on the Part played by Sexuality in the Aetiology of the Neuroses* (1906a). S.E. 7, p. 271.

DORA: THE LACK IN THE SYMBOLIC
1   Freud, *Fragment of an Analysis of a Case of Hysteria* (1905e). S.E. 7, pp. 7-8, p. 10 and p. 16.
2   Ibid., pp. 13-16, p. 111. Freud, *A letter from Freud to Theodor Reik* (appendix to "Dostoyevsky and Parricide", 1928b). S.E. 21, p. 196.
3   Freud, *Fragment of an Analysis of a Case of Hysteria* (1905e). S.E. 7, p. 11.
4   Freud, *The Handling of Dream-Interpretation in Psycho-Analysis* (1911e), S.E. 12, p. 92.
5   Everybody knows Freud's favourite quotation of Charcot: "La théorie c'est bon, mais ça n'empêche pas d'exister". J. Quackelbeen has drawn our attention to the lesser known sequel which is by Freud himself: "...If one only knew *what* exists!". S.E. 1, p. 139.
6   S.Freud, S.E. 1, letter 72, p.267.
7   Freud, *Fragment of an Analysis of a Case of Hysteria* (1905e). S.E. 7, p. 29 and p. 95.
8   Freud, *The Psychopathology of Everyday Life* (1901b). S.E. 6, p. 241.
9   Freud, *Fragment of an Analysis of a Case of Hysteria* (1905e). S.E. 7, pp. 105-106.
10   Ibid., p. 45, p. 59 and pp. 69-71. Freud, *"Wild" Psycho-Analysis* (1910k). S.E. 11, pp. 225-226.
11   Freud, *Fragment of an Analysis of a Case of Hysteria* (1905e). S.E. 7, pp. 22-23, p. 73, footnote 1 and p. 78.
12   Ibid., p. 31 and p. 36, footnote 1.
13   Ibid., p. 21. Freud, *The Interpretationof Dreams* (1900a). S.E. 4, pp. 256-265.
14   Freud, *Fragment of an Analysis of a Case of Hysteria* (1905e). S.E. 7, pp. 56-59.
15   Lacan, *Le Séminaire, Livre I, Les écrits techniques de Freud* (1953-1954), pp. 78-80. *The Seminar of J.Lacan, Book I: Freud's Papers on Technique 1953-54*, translated with notes by J.Forrester, Cambridge University Press, Cambridge, 1988, pp. 65-67.
16   Lacan, *Le Séminaire, Livre IV, La relation d'objet* (1956-1957), Paris, Seuil, pp. 179-195.
17   Ibid., pp. 198-214.
18   Freud, *Fragment of an Analysis of a Case of Hysteria* (1905e). S.E. 7, p. 120, footnote 1.
19   Cf. Lacan: "Ceci ressortit, dirons-nous, à un préjugé, celui-là même qui fausse au départ la conception du complexe d'Oedipe en lui faisant considérer comme naturelle et non comme normative la prévalence du personnage paternel: c'est le même qui s'exprime simplement dans le refrain bien connu: 'Comme le fil est pour l'aiguille, la fille est pour le garçon'". In "Intervention sur le transfert", *Ecrits*, Paris, Seuil, 1966, p. 223.
20   Freud, *Fragment of an Analysis of a Case of Hysteria* (1905e). S.E. 7, pp. 60-63.
21   Ibid., p. 105.
22   Ibid., pp. 24-28.
23   Ibid., pp. 70-71, footnote 1.
24   Ibid., p. 67.
25   Ibid., p. 77.
26   Ibid., pp. 96-100.
27   Ibid., p. 114.
28   Ibid., pp. 46-47.
29   Ibid., p. 51, p. 88 and p. 110.

30   Ibid., pp. 51-52.
31   Ibid., p. 98.
32   Ibid., p. 104, footnote 1. Rogow, Dora's brother. *International Review of Psychoanalysis*, 1979, nr. 6, pp. 239-259.

THE GREAT CONFUSION
1   The literature is more than abundant. The papers quoted below aim to give a representative sample from the major journals.
     Head, An address on the Diagnosis of Hysteria. *British Medical Journal*, 1992, 1, pp. 827-829.
     Riese, Wandlungen in den Erscheinungsformen der Hysterie. *Medizinische Welt*, 1927, 1, pp. 1160-1161.
     Codet, Le problème actuel de l'hystérie. *Evolution Psychiatrique*, 1935 (2), pp. 3-44.
     Cenac, L'Hystérie en 1935. *Evolution Psychiatrique*, 1935 (4), pp. 25-32.
     Nyssen, Le problème de la constitution et du caractère hystérique. *Acta Neurol.Psych.Belg.*, 1984, 48, pp. 47-56.
     Ajuriaguerra, Le problème de l'hystérie. *L'encéphale*, 1951, I, pp. 50-87.
2   Freud, *Charcot* (1893f). S.E. 3, p. 22.
3   Slater, Hysteria 311. *Journal of Mental Science*, 1961, 448, pp. 359-381. Slater, Diagnosis of Hysteria. *Britisch Medical Journal*, 1965, I, pp. 1395-1399. Slater, A follow-up of patients diagnosed as suffering from 'hysteria'. *J.Psychosom.Res.*, 1965, 9, pp. 9-13. The quoted conclusion can be found in the second paper on p. 1399.
4   Whitlock, The Aetiology of Hysteria. *Psychiat.Scand.*, 1967, 43, pp. 144-162. You can find the quotation on p. 148.
5   Gachnochi and P. Prat, L'hystérique à l'hôpital psychiatrique. *Perspectives Psychiatriques*, 1973, 44, pp. 17-27.
6   Perley and S.B. Guze, hysteria: the Stability and Usefulness of Clinical Criteria. *New.Eng.J.Med.*, 1962, 266, pp. 421-426.
7   Lewis, Survivance de l'hystérie. *Evolution Psychiatrique*, 1966, 31, pp. 159-165.
8   Chodoff, A re-examination of some aspects of conversion hysteria. *Psychiatry*, 1954, 17, p. 75. Satow, Where has all the hysteria gone? *The Psychoanalytic Review*, 1979, 4, p. 469.
9   DSM-III, *Manuel Diagnostique et Statistique des Troubles Mentaux*. Paris, Masson, 1983, pp. 1-535.
10   Chodoff and H. Lyons, Hysteria, the hysterical personality and hysterical conversion. *Psychiatry*, 1958, 114, pp. 734-740.
11   Trillat, Regards sur l'hystérie. *Evolution Psychiatrique*, 1970, 19(2), pp. 353-364.
12   Lazare, G.L. Klerman and P.J. Armor, Oral, obsessive and hysterical personality patterns. *Archives of General Psychiatry*, 1966, 14, pp. 624-630.
13   Zetzel, The so-called good hysteric. *International Journal of Psychoanalysis*, 1968, 49, pp. 256-260.
14   Kernberg, Borderline personality organisation. *Journal of the American Psychoanalytic Association*, 1967, 15, pp. 641-685.
15   Easser and R. Lesser, Hysterical personality: a re-evaluation. *Psychoanalytic Quarterly*, 1965, 34, pp. 390-405.
16   Sugarman, The Infantile personality: orality in the hysteric revisited. *International Journal of Psychoanalysis*, 1979, 60, pp. 501-513.
17   Maleval and J.P. Champanier, Pour une réhabilitation de la folie hystérique. *Annales Médico-psychologiques*, 1977, 2, pp. 229-272. Maléval, *Folies hystériques et psychoses dissociatives*. Paris, Payot, 1981. An excellent account of the history of this concept can be found in: K.Libbrecht, *Hysteric>al psychosis, a historical survey*, London, Transaction publishers, 1995.
18   Clavreul, *L'ordre médical*. Paris, Seuil, 1978, p. 206.
19   Lacan, *Le Séminaire, Livre XI, Les Quatre Concepts Fondamentaux de la Psychanalyse* (1964),

Paris, Seuil, 1973, p. 9, a.f.

20   Chodoff and Lyons, o.c. p. 735.

21   Dresen-Coenders, Het verbond tussen heks en duivel. Baarn, Ambo, 1983, p. 26. Freud
      also remarked on the relation between witch and hysteria, including the importance of
      the "Malleus Maleficarum". See: Freud, letter 56 and 57, S.E. 1, p. 242 and p. 244.
      Clavreul, o.c.

22   Wajeman, La médicalisation de l'hystérie. *Ornicar? Analytica*, 1, s.d., pp. 38-55.

23   Israel, *Hysterie, sekse en de geneesheer*. Leuven/Amersfoort, Acco, 1984. Shoenberg, The
      Symptom as stigma or communication in hysteria. *International Journal of Psychoanalytic
      Psychotherapy*, 1975, 4, pp. 507-516.

24   Lazare, The hysterical character in psychoanalytic theory. *Archives of General Psychiatry*,
      1971, 25, pp. 131-137. Pouilhon, Doctor and patient: same and/or other? (Ethnological
      remarks). *The Psychoanalytic Study of Society*, 1972, 5, pp. 9-32. Shoenberg, o.c.

25   Shoenberg, o.c., pp. 513-515.

26   Deutsch, Apostille au 'Fragment de l'analyse d'un cas d'hystérie de Freud. *Revue
      Française de Psychanalyse*, 1973, 3, pp. 407-418.

27   Israel, o.c., p. 116.

28   Major, *Rêver l'autre*. Paris, Aubier Montaigne, 1977, p. 20.

29   For Charcot, see: P. Pichot, Histoire des idées sur l'hystérie. *Confrontations Psychiatriques*,
      1968, 1, pp. 9-28. For Anna O., see: Breuer, *Studies on Hysteria* (1895d). S.E. 2, p. 21 and
      p. 46. For Justine, see: H. Ellenberger, *The Discovery of the Unconscious*. New York, Basic
      Books, 1975, p. 369. For Emmy von N., see: S. Freud, *Studies on Hysteria* (1895d). S.E. 2,
      p. 63.

30   Foucault, *Histoire de la folie*. Paris, Gallimard, 1972, p. 270.

31   Carter, *On the Pathology and Treatment of Hysteria*. London, Churchill, 1853, p. 110.

32   Hollender, Conversion hysteria, a post-Freudian reinterpretation of 19th Century
      Psychosocial Data. *Archives of General Psychiatry*, 1972, 26, p. 314.

33   Wajeman quoting Gilles de la Tourette, o.c., p. 48.

34   Israel, La victime de l'hystérique. *Evolution Psychiatrique*, 1968, 31, pp. 517-546.

35   Veith, *Hysteria, the History of a Disease*. London, Phoenix Books, 1970, p. 6 and pp. 98-99.

36   Freud, letter 52, S.E. 1, p. 239.

37   Miller, D'un autre Lacan - Intervention à la 1re rencontre internationale du champ freu-
      dien, Caracas, 1980. *Ornicar?*, Spring 1984, 28, pp. 49-57.

38   Miller, Liminaire. *Ornicar?*, Autumn 1984, 30, pp. 5-6.

39   Bram, The gift of Anna O. *British Journal of Medical Psychology*, 1965, 38, pp. 53-58. This
      rewriting of the history of psychoanalysis reminds me of Orwell. Contemporary psy-
      chiatry is at a loss with a number of patients: borderline, schizophrenia, narcissistic neu-
      rosis, hysterical psychosis... One can read an excellent review of this confusion in: H.
      Van Hoorde, De hysterische psychose, nosologische struikelsteen en eerherstel?
      Psychoanalytische Perspectieven, 1984, 6.

40   Miller, Liminaire. *Ornicar?*, Summer 1984, nr. 29, pp. 5-6. Quackelbeen, Naar een
      vernieuwde visie op de hysterie. *Psychoanalytische Perspectieven*, 1984, nr. 6, p. 25.

LACAN AND THE DISCOURSE OF THE HYSTERIC

1   Freud *Studies on Hysteria* (1895d) SE2, p529

2   Lacan *Le Seminaire, livre III, Les Psychoses* (1981) Paris, Seuil, p23

3   As we consider this theory to be a condensation of Lacan's evolution, every biblio-
     graphic reference to a particular piece of work is to limited. The theory itself was formed
     during the seminar of 1969-1970, *L'envers de la Psychanalyse* (Paris, Seuil, 1991),
     Radiophonie (Scilicet, 1970) and the next seminar *D'un discourse qui ne serait pas du sem-
     blant*. A further elaboration can be found in *Encore* the seminar of 1972-1973 (Paris, Seuil,
     1975

4   Lacan, *Seminaire XVII, L'envers de la psychanalyse* (1969-1970), Paris, Seuil, p11

5   Freud *Introductory lectures on psycboanalysis* (1916-1917) S.E. 16, p 285
6   Lacan, o.c. p 39 and p 38
7   Kierkegaard, *La repetition. Essai d'experience psychologique par Constantin Constantius* (translated from the Danish by P.H. Tisseau) Felix, Paris 1993 passim
8   Cf: The eleventh seminar, in which Lacan described the unconscious as a process of "beance causale", a gap with a causal function, a particular movement of opening and closing.
9   For a further elaboration, see: P. Verhaeghe, Psychotherapy, Psychoanalysis and Hysteria. *The Letter*, Autumn 1994, nr.2, pp 47-68
10   Freud, *Project for a Scientific Psychology* (1950a) S.E. 1, pp317-320. Of course this idea returns throughout the whole of Freud's work.
11   That is why the psychotic patient is so uncanny to us: we do not share the same social bonds. The psychotic does not share the discourses, due to his Oedipul solution that lies outside the discourse of the master, and hence outside the very structure of discourse.
12   Lacan, o.c. p 12
13   Lacan, o.c., p 178
14   Lacan, o.c., p 68
15   Freud *Fragment of an analysis of a case of Hysteria* (1905e) S.E. 7, p 105
16   Lacan, o.c. p. 239
17   The expressions "good or bad hysteric" were naively coined by E. Zetzel in her paper: *The so-called Good Hysteric* Int.J.Psychoanal., 1968, 49, 256-260. The difference between the hysteric as a saint or a witch was less naively described by G. Wajeman, *Le maître et l'Hysterique.*, Paris, Navarin, 1982, pp 1-287
18   Ibid, p26
19   J.Lacan, o.c., p.208
20   Lacan, *Le Seminaire, Livre XX, Encore*, Paris, Seuil, p74
21   Freud *Fragment of an analysis of a case of Hysteria* (1905e) S.E. 7, p 100
22   Lacan, *Seminaire XVII, L'envers de la psychanalyse* (1969-1970), Paris, Seuil, p205
23   J.Lacan, o.c., p.205
24   J.Lacan, o.c., p.79
25   J.Lacan, o.c., p.151
26   Lacan, Radiophonie, *Scilicet*, 1970, nr.2/3, p88
27   Lacan, *Le Séminaire, Livre XI, Les Quatre Concepts Fondamentaux de la Psychanalyse* (1964), Paris, Seuil, 1973, p. 106, Lacan, *Seminaire XVII, L'envers de la psychanalyse* (1969-1970), Paris, Seuil, p99
28   The core of this idea is elaborated in his book on hysteria, S. Andre *Que veut une femme?* Paris, Navarin editeur, 1986

FREUD'S SECOND THEORY OF HYSTERIA
1   Haley, *De machtspolitiek van Jezus Christus*, Amsterdam, Alpha boeken, 1972 (originally: *The power tactics of Jesus Christ*).
2   Freud, *Remembering, Repeating and Working-Through* (Further Recommendations on the Technique of Psycho-Analysis, II)(1914g). S.E. 12, pp. 147-148.
3   Freud, *Lecture 'On the Psychical Mechanism of Hysterical Phenomena'* (1893h). S.E. 3, pp. 27-39.
4   Breuer, *Studies on Hysteria* (1895d). S.E. 2, p. 192.
5   Freud, *Project for a Scientific Psychology* (1950). S.E. 1, pp. 295-296.
6   Fechner, *Einige Ideeen zur Schöpfungs- und Entwicklungsgeschichte der Organismen.* Leipzig, Breitkopf und Härtel, 1873.
7   Fechner, Ueber das Lustprinzip des Handelns. *Zeitschrift für Philosophie und Philosophische Kritik*, Halle, 1848.
8   Freud, *The Interpretation of Dreams* (1900a). S.E. 4-5, p. 599 and p. 574.
9   Israel, *Hysterie, sekse en de geneesheer*, Leuven/Amersfoort, Acco, 1984, p. 109 (originally:

L'hystérique, le sexe et le médecin).

10 This idea of prophylaxis was explicitly mentioned by Freud during the second international psychoanalytical congress of Nuremburg. See: S. Freud, *The Future Prospects of Psycho-Analytic Therapy* (1910d). S.E. 11.

11 Lacan, *The Seminar, Book I, Freud's Papers on Technique* (1953-1954). Cambridge, Cambridge University Press, p. 271.

12 Freud, *A Childhood Recollection from Dichtung und Wahrheit* (1917b). S.E. 17.

13 Freud, *Remembering, Repeating and Working-Through*, o.c., pp. 150-151.

14 Ibid., p. 156.

15 Freud, *Inhibitions, Symptoms and Anxiety* (1926d). S.E. 20, p. 159.

16 Lacan, *The Seminar, Book III, The Psychoses* (1955-1956). New York, W.W. Norton & Company, p. 164.

17 Freud, *A Case of Paranoia Running Counter to the Psycho-Analytic Theory of the Disease* (1915f). S.E. 14, p. 269.

18 Freud, *Remembering, Repeating and Working-Through*, o.c., p. 149; see also S.E. 12, p. 141, for the editorial footnote 1.

19 Freud - L.A. Salomé, *Briefwechsel*. Frankfurt, Fischer, 1980, p. 28.

20 Freud, *Instincts and their Vicissitudes* (1915c). S.E. 14, p. 121.

21 Freud, *The Uncanny* (1919h). S.E. 17, p. 238.

22 Freud, *Beyond the Pleasure Principle* (1920g). S.E. 18, p. 17.

23 Ibid., pp. 18-19.

24 Ibid., p. 21.

25 Ibid., pp. 52-55.

26 Ibid., p. 55.

27 "La petite mort" is a French expression for orgasm, condensing orgasmic moment and experience of death.

28 Ibid., p. 63.

29 Freud, *The Economic Problem of Masochism* (1924c). S.E. 19, pp. 159-161.

30 The "Project"-description about an original satisfaction which functions as a standard of comparison for all later satisfactions, is not an isolated one. The idea recurs in several other Freudian papers. S. Freud, S.E. 1, pp. 317-319; S. Freud, *The Interpretation of Dreams* (1900a). S.E. 4-5, p. 598; S. Freud, *Negation* (1925h). S.E. 19, p. 238.

31 Freud, *Female Sexuality* (1931b). S.E. 21, p. 234, p. 226.

32 Freud, *Some Psychical Consequences of the Anatomical Distinction between the Sexes* (1925j). S.E. 19, p. 248.

33 L.Israël and L.Gurfein, Le vieillissement de l'hystérique, in: *Evolution psychiatrique*, XXXV (II), 1970, pp. 372 - 73.

34 Balint, Early developmental states of the ego. Primary object love (1937). *International Journal of Psycho-Analysis*, 30,1949, p.269-272.

35 Winnicott, transitional objects and transitional phenomena, a study of the first not-me possession. *International Journal of Psycho-Analysis*, 1953, XXXIV, pp. 95-96.

36 Peto, Body image and archaic thinking. *International Journal of Psycho-Analysis*, 1959, 40, resp. p. 223, p. 226, p. 228.

37 Lorré, Psychose en pseudo-psychose: onderscheid in de spiegelopstelling. *Psychoanalytische Perspectieven*, nr. 7, 1985, pp. 129-140.

38 -C. Maleval, *Psychoses dissociatives et délires hystériques*. Paris, Payot, 1981.

39 Freud, *Project for a Scientific Psychology* (1950). S.E. 1, p. 319 and *The Interpretation of Dreams* (1900a). S.E. 4-5, p. 565.

40 Lacan, *The Seminar, Book IX, The Four Fundamental Concepts of Psycho-Analysis* (1964). London, Penguin Books, p. 271.

41 Lacan, Proposition du 9 octobre 1967 sur le psychanalyste de l'Ecole. In: *ECF, Annuaire et textes statuaires*, Paris, ECF, 1982, p. 28.

42 Freud, *The Theme of the Three Caskets* (1913f). S.E. 12, pp. 289-301.

CONSEQUENCES OF FREUD'S SECOND THEORY: PRIMARY PHEMOMENA

1   Freud, *Psycho-Analytic Notes on an Autobiographical Account of a Case of Paranoia (Dementia Paranoides)* (1911c). S.E. 12, pp. 66-67. Freud, *repression* (1915d). S.E. 14, p. 148. Freud, *The Unconscious* (1915e). S.E. 14, p. 181.

2   Laplanche & J.B. Pontalis, *Vocabulaire de la psychanalyse*. Paris, P.U.F., 1976, p. 397.

3   Freud, *The Unconscious* (1915e). S.E. 14, p. 181.

4   Freud, *Psycho-Analytic Notes...*, o.c., S.E. 12, pp. 66-67.

5   Freud, *Inhibitions, Symptoms and Anxiety* (1926d). S.E. 20, p. 94.

6   Freudian castration is indeed rewritten by Lacan. We will see later on that symbolic castration can be equated with the division of the subject caused by the introduction into language.

7   Lacan, Propos sur la causalité psychique. In: *Ecrits*. Paris, Seuil, 1966, p. 183.

8   Freud, *Analysis of a Phobia in a Five-Year-Old Boy* (1909b). S.E. 10, p. 7, p. 10, p. 17 and p. 18.

9   Ibid., pp. 20-21.

10   Lacan, *Le Séminaire, Livre IV, La Relation d'objet* (1956-1957). Paris, Seuil, 1994, pp. 319-335.

11   Lacan, The Signification of the Phallus. In: *Ecrits. A Selection*. New York, W.W. Norton & Company Inc., 1977, p. 285.

12   Freud, *Analysis of a Phobia in a Five-Year-Old Boy* (1909b). S.E. 10, p. 14.

13   André, *L'Ordre du Symbole*. Lecture in Gent, d.d. February 2, 1983. Guiraud, *Dictionnaire historique, stylistique, rhétorique, étymologique de la littérature érotique*. Paris, Payot, 1978. Quackelbeen, *Zeven avonden met Jacques Lacan. Psychoanalytische commentaren bij 'Télévision'*. Gent, Academia Press, 1991, p. 56.

14   Gorman, Body Words. *The Psychoanalyic Review*, vol. 51, 1964-65, pp. 15-28.

15   Lacan, *D'un discours qui ne serait pas du semblant*. Unpublished seminar, 1970-1971, June 9 and 16, 1971.

16   Lacan takes this position in reaction to a question by F. Dolto. Lacan, *The Seminar, Book XI, The Four Fundamental concepts of Psycho-Analysis* (1964). London, Penguin Books, 1979, p. 64.

17   Wisdom, A methodological approach to the problem of hysteria. *International Journal of Psycho-Analysis*, vol. 42, 1961, p. 227 and p. 233. At this point one of the most confusing things appears for the reader who is less familiar with Lacan, although acqainted with the psychoanalytic theory of 'the symbol'. What is the relation between the symbolic order of Lacan and the symbol in the more Freudian sense? Roughly speaking, the Freudian symbol, that has to be analyzed or interpreted, is in Lacanian terms part of the Imaginary. For Lacan, a symbol within a neurotic context will always be an 'understanding' of something, i.e., a fixation of a signification on a signifier where it does not belong, Freud's 'falsche Verknüpfung'(false connection). After an analysis, that is, after the interpretation and its 'durcharbeitung' (working through) by the subject, this symbol will be part of the Symbolic. The principal difference with the Imaginary is that in the Symbolic the free flow of signifiers has become possible again.

18   Mitchell, *Psychoanalysis and Feminism* London:Penguin Books 1990 p. 299

19   Freud, *From the History of an Infantile Neurosis* (1918b). S.E. 17, pp. 57-60.

20   Freud, *A Case of Paranoia Running Counter to the Psycho-Analytic Theory of the Disease* (1915f). S.E. 14, p. 269.

21   Freud, *Introductory Lectures on Psycho-Analysis* (1916-17). S.E. 15-16, p. 371.

22   Freud, *From the History of an Infantile Neurosis*, o.c., S.E. 17, p. 119.

23   Freud, Draft L, S.E. 1, p. 248.

24   The difference between the basic fantasy and the 'manifest' variations based upon it - the daydreams - asks for a detailed study which goes beyond the scope of the present work. The necessity for such a study is for example revealed by a lecture of Michel

Silvestre, "*L'aveu de fantasme*" wherein he, amongst other things, questions how it is possible that a fantasy can just as well determine a dream as appear in a daydream. This results for him in insoluble difficulties concerning the relation between the unconscious (the dream) and the conscious (the daydream). If one considers the basic fantasy as a generating structure at the base of all symptoms including the daydream, this difficulty ceases to exist.

If one were to venture upon this detailed study mentioned above, the emphasis should first of all be put on the position of the subject as the differentiating feature between these two kinds of fantasies (basic and daydream). A second emphasis should be placed on the relationship between the basic fantasy as constitutive element on the one hand and the symptoms that are determined by it on the other. Finally, this study should enable us to reconsider the aim of psychoanalysis, in the sense of the installation, as a result of the treatment, of a new relation between the subject and his fantasy. This does not imply that a patient after his analysis would no longer have any fantasies at all, nor does it mean that he/she could now consciously live out his/her previously defensive repressed fantasies. Each *a priori* normalisation of this relationship must necessarily reduce analysis to an 'orthopedia of the soul', but an explicit rethinking of this relationship - beyond any idea of 'adaptation' - can only be to the benefit of the analytic discourse. Let us not forget that the object *a* functions as agent in this discourse. It is precisely this new relationship between $\mathcal{S}$ and basic fantasy that we aim at when we state above that the (elaboration of the) basic fantasy can be considered as the result of an analysis. With this, we do not imply that it has to be 'discovered' within the cure, but that it can be constructed throughout the course of the sessions. In our opinion, this is the principal purpose of what Lacan called 'la traversée du fantasme', the journey through the fantasy.

One misconception has to be mentioned: the elaboration of the fantasy in the analytic cure should not be considered in terms of a mere 'confession' of its content, thus reducing the subject to what M. Foucault in his history of sexuality calls 'une bête de l'aveu'. After a confession, there can only follow penance and punishment, accompanied by a relief which makes clear that the principal salvation of an absolution is expected in the name of Freud as a new father-moloch: psychoanalysis as a scientifically grounded excuse.

Silvestre, *L'aveu de fantasme*. Lecture on the congress of "Ecole de la Cause Freudienne", Paris, 13 and 14 October 1984, publication in preparation.

Miller, D'un autre Lacan, Intervention à la première Rencontre internationale du Champ freudien, Caracas, 1980. *Ornicar?*, Spring 1984, nr. 28, pp. 49-59.

Miller, Symptôme-Fantasme. *Actes de l'Ecole de la Cause Freudienne, Vol. III*, Oct. 1982, pp. 13-19 (discussion included).

Soler, Transfert et interprétation dans la névrose. *Actes de l'Ecole de la Cause Freudienne*, June 1984, pp. 7-9.

25   Freud, *The Sexual Enlightment of Children* (1907e). S.E. 9, p. 131. Freud, *Analysis Terminable and Interminable* (1937c). S.E. 23, pp. 233-234.

26   Freud, *Three Essays on the Theory of Sexuality* (1905d). S.E. 7, p. 195, added in 1915 and p. 226, footnote 2, added in 1920.

27   Freud, *Three Essays on the Theory of Sexuality (1905d)*. S.E. 7, p. 195, added in 1915. This also has been mentioned in: *On the Sexual Theories of Children* (1908c). S.E. 9, p. 212 seq. and in: *Analysis of a Phobia in a Five-Year-Old Boy* (1909b). S.E. 10, p. 132.

28   Freud, *Some Psychical consequences of the Anatomical Distinction between the Sexes* (1925j). S.E. 19, p. 252, footnote 1. Freud, *On the Sexual Theories of Children* (1908c). S.E. 9, pp. 215-216.

29   In another paper (*Neurosis and Psychosis: il n'y a pas de rapport sexuel*), to be published in the CFAR-Journal, London) we have argued that penis envy is first of all an 'affliction' that afflicts the male... This is quite coherent with the above, as the hysteric identifies

with the masculine part in the gender.

30   Freud, *Three Essays on the Theory of Sexuality* (1905d). S.E. 7, p. 197, added in 1915.

31   Freud, *"Civilized" Sexual Morality and Modern Nervous Illness (1908d)*. S.E. 9, p. 195. Freud, *On the Sexual Theories of Children* (1908c). S.E. 9, pp. 221-223.

32   Freud received this 'recipe' from Chrobak. The history of the treatment of hysteria shows that this prescription is as old as the hills and has been carried out in different manners. The reactions to it - unbelief, moral indignation, ridiculization - obscure any notice of the structure wherein this recipe appears as a 'cure', that is, inevitable as well as bound to fail. The hysteric is in search of The Man, beyond any castration, because he is the one who could offer a possibility for a feminine sexuation. However, The Man beyond castration can only provide a confirmation of the cult of the phallus - see the lingam in the East. This confirmation provides in the end precisely the failure of the object in view: the resulting monosexuality confirms the lack of the sexual relation. The core of every treatment with hysterical patients lies in the avoidance of this typical hysterical solution, which is doomed to fail for structural reasons; hence, the therapist may not assume the position of the master.
     Freud, *On the History of the Psycho-Analytic Movement* (1914d). S.E., p. 14.
     Quackelbeen, Hysterie: tussen het "geloof in de Man" en de "kultus van De vrouw". *Psychoanalytische Perspectieven*, 1984, No. 6, pp. 123-1398.

33   Lacan, *The Seminar, Book I, Freud's Papers on Technique* (1953-54). Cambridge, Cambridge University Press, 1988, pp. 190-191.

34   Klein, *passim*. Bettelheim, *Uses of Enchantment. Meaning and Importance of Fairy Tales*. Freud, *On the Sexual Theories of Children* (1908c). S.E. 9, p. 211.

35   Freeman, *L'histoire d'Anna O*. Paris, P.U.F., 1977, pp. 1-326 (originally published in English). The interpretation in the text is entirely ours.
     After having finished our study, we came upon other interesting material, which we have used in another publication: P. Verhaeghe, Les fantasmes de l'hystérique, ou l'hystérie du fantasme, in *Quarto, Bulletin de l'Ecole de la Cause Freudienne en Belgique*, 1986,nr. 24, pp. 35-42. Below, we mention the bibliographical references of this often difficult to obtain material:
     Abrahams, Beth-Zion (ed.), *Glückel of Hameln: Life 1646-1724*. New York, th. Yoseloff, 1963.
     Bertha Pappenheim zum Gedächtnis. *Blätter des Jüdischen Frauenbundes*, XII, July/August, 1936, Berlin.
     Edinger Dora, *Bertha Pappenheim, Leben und Schriften*. Frankfurt am Main, Ner-Tamid Verlag,1963.
     Edinger Dora, *Bertha Pappenheim, Freud's Anna O*. Highland Park, Illinois, Congregation Soles, 1968.
     Löwenthal, Marvin (ed.), *Glückel of Hameln: Memoirs*. New York, Harper and Brothers, 1932.
     Ellenberger, H.F. The Story of "Anna O": a critical review with new data. *Journal of the History of the Behavioral Sciences*, Vol. VIII, July 1972, nr. 3, pp. 267-279.
     Jensen, E.M., Anna O - Ihr Späteres Schicksal, *Acta Psychiatrica et Neurologica Scandinavica*, Vol. 36, 1961, pp. 119-131.
     Jensen, E.M., Anna O: A study of her later life. *Psychoanalytic Quarterly*, Vol. 39, nr. 2, 1970, pp. 269-293.
     Karpe, R., The Rescue Complex in Anna O's Final identity. *Psychoanalytic Quarterly*, Vol. 30, 1961, pp. 1-27.
     Pollock, G.H., Glückel von Hameln: Bertha Pappenheim's Idealized Ancestor. *American Imago*, 1971, nr. 28, pp. 216-227.
     Berthold, P., *In der Trödelbude. Geschichten*. Lahr, Druck und Verlag von Moritz Shauenburg, 1890.
     Berthold, P., Frauenrecht. *Ein Schauspiel in drei Aufzügen*. Dresden, Pierson, 1899.

Berthold, P., (Bertha Pappenheim), *Zur Judenfragen in Galizien*. Frankfurt am Main, Druck und Verlag von Gebrüder Knauer, 1900.

Pappenheim, Bertha, *Die Memoiren der Glückel von Hameln*. Autorisierte Uebertragung nach der Ausgabe des Prof. David Kaufman von Bertha Pappenheim. Wien, Verlag von Dr. Stefan Meyer und Dr. Wilhelm Pappenheim, 1910.

Pappenheim, Bertha, *Tragische Momente. Drei Lebensbilder*. Frankfurt am Main, Verlag von J. Kauffmann, 1913.

Pappenheim, Bertha, *Kämpfe. Sechs Erzählungen*. Frankfurt am Main, Verlag von J. Kauffmann, 1916.

Pappenheim, Bertha, *Sisyphus-Arbeit. Reisebriefe aus den Jahren 1911 und 1912*. Leipzig, Verlag Paul E. Linder, 1924.

Pappenheim, Bertha, *Aus der Arbeit des Heims des Jüdischen Frauenbundes in Iseberg 1914-24*. Frankfurt am Main, Druckerei und Verlagsanstalt R. Th. Hauser & Cie, 1926.

Pappenheim Bertha *Sysiphus-Arbeit. 2. Folge*. Berlin, Druck und Verlag Berthold Levy, 1929

Pappenheim, Bertha, *Allerlei Geschichten. Maasse-Buch*. Nach der Ausgabe des Maasse-Buches, Amsterdam, 1923, bearbeitet von Bertha Pappenheim. Herausgegeben vom Jüdischen Frauenbund. Frankfurt am Main, J. Kauffman Verlag, 1929.

Pappenheim, Bertha, *Zeenah U.-Reenah. Frauenbibel*. Nach dem Jüdisch-deutschen bearbeitet von Bertha Pappenheim. Herausgegeben vom Jüdischen Frauenbund. Frankfurt am Main, J. Kauffman Verlag, 1930.

Pappenheim, Bertha, *Gebete*, Ausgewählt und herausgegeben vom Jüdischen Frauenbund, Berlin, Philo Verlag, 1936.

Pappenheim, Bertha und Rabinowitsch, Sara, *Zur Lage der Jüdischen Bevölkerung in Galizien. Reise-Eindrücke und Vorschläge zur Besserung der Verhältnisse*. Frankfurt am Main, Neuer Frankfurter Verlag, 1904

36 Translator's Note: In French in the original; this expression has an equivocal meaning, difficult to render in English: 'She makes the man' and 'She pretends to be a man'. The same has been indicated by André with respect to Elisabeth von R, in his *Que veut une femme?*, Paris, Navarin, Bibliothèque des Analytica, 1986, pp. 119-131. We have borrowed the expression "elle fait l'homme" from C. Soler, *Abords du Nom du Père. Quarto*, VIII, 1982, p. 64.

37 Israel, *L'hystérique, le sexe et le médecin*. Paris, Masson, 1980, p. 96. Here Israel formulates one aetiology for hysteria: that the woman-mother did not make the man-father, i.e. she did not permit the father to fulfil his symbolic function, so that her daughter has to do it in her place. We agree, but want to add a particular nuance in order to point out the difference from psychosis. The difference between psychosis and hysteria at this point is that the mother of a future psychotic has no desire beyond the child: either the child fills up entirely her desire, without any reference to something else, or the child forms a part of her own flesh, without any possibility of an existence as a subject in the Symbolic. In both psychotic situations - which add up to the same thing - the essential references to the concrete father as well as to the function of the father are missing. In case of hysteria, the father figure appears differently: here, the mother actually has a desire outside the child, but the concrete father is defined as being inadequate to fulfil even the slightest part of this desire. There is an actual reference to 'something' outside father and child that could come up to this desire, so that the dimension of desire itself is signified to the child. Precisely therefore, it will not become psychotic. In clinical practice with children, this difference can easily be noticed.

38 Translator's note: in the original 'Vermogen', meaning 'fortune' as well as 'sexual potence'.

39 J.Lacan, *D'un discours qui ne serait pas du semblant*. Unpublished seminar, 1970-1971, lesson of January 20 and February 17, 1971. Apparently, this warning against this misconception was not enough. It is repeated at least twice later on.

Lacan, *Le Séminaire, Livre XX, Encore* (1972-1973). Paris, Seuil, 1975, p. 68 and p. 75.

Lacan, *Le Séminaire, Livre XXII, le Sinthome* (1975). *Ornicar?*, nr. 9, 1977, p. 36 and p. 39.

40   In this respect, it becomes quite clear why Lacan warned the analysts on a very important point, while explaining the analytic discourse: "Il doit se trouver à l'opposé de toute
volonté au moins avoué, de maîtrise". Indeed, an analyst who endorses the impression
that he effectively *knows* in matters of desire and enjoyment, changes very fast into a
guru. The subsequent history of (post)Lacanian psychoanalysis demonstrates that a
number of his pupils did not hear the warning, thereby once again proving the gap
between knowledge and truth.

41   Lacan, *Le Séminaire, Livre XX, Encore*, o.c., p. 90.

The hysterial 'solution' becomes a deadlock wherein the subject is wavering between
two possibilities. A title of a paper by J.Quackelbeen summarises the hysterical peripat-
ics: *"Tussen het 'geloof in De Man' en de 'kultus van De Vrouw'"*., "Between the belief in The
Man and the cult of The Woman".

42   Lacan, *Le Séminaire, Livre XX, Encore*, o.c., p. 83 and p. 87.

This development was already announced in a footnote added in 1966 to the R-scheme
of "On a question preliminay to any possible treatment of psychosis" (*Ecrits. A Selection*,
New York, W.W. Norton & Company Inc., 1977, p. 223). There, fantasy is defined as a
screen across the Real, a screen whose border runs along the Imaginary to the Symbolic,
turning back to the Imaginary, in an endless movement; this is the structure of the
Moebius-string. In an earlier paper, "The direction of the treatment and the principles of
its power" (Ecrits, A Selection, o.c., p. 273) he defines fantasy as follows: "However, once
it is defined as an image set to work in the signifying structure, the notion of the unconscious phantasy no longer presents any difficulty." In his exposition for television he
will elaborate this "Il n'y a pas de rapport sexuel" with the categories of the coincidence,
the necessity and the impossibility. J. Quackelbeen has further formulated this elaboration in his comment on *Télévision*, in a paper published in *The Letter*, No. 1.

43   Two remarks concerning this object *a*.

The first is related to a historical repetition. As we have demonstrated throughout our
study, post-Freudianism goes only back to Freud I, in spite of Freud II. As far as the concept of fantasy is concerned, this implies that in the ego-analytic praxis fantasy has seldom or never been considered as a basic structure, as is the case with Freud II; they stick
to interpretations and the analysis of resistances. Strangely enough, the same phenomenon is repeated with Lacan. The rapidly increasing success of his work in the sixties
was focused on one aspect only, the signifier. Everywhere within the French intellectual
circles, the importance of the signifier was acknowledged, everything was explained by
it. In other words, only one half of Lacan and his 'retour à Freud' was absorbed. The
other half was brushed aside. Already in his famous 1971 lecture, Leclaire made an
appeal not to brush aside what he called Lacan's 'discovery', in his own school. The following discussion was surprisingly vehement and especially ad hominem. His appeal
not to put aside this object *a* in matters of theory and practice was repeated in 1980 by
J.-A. Miller on the first International Congress in Caracas. Before an international audi-
ence, Lacan's heir expounded the following: that too much stress was placed on the
'Lacan of the signifier', whereupon 'the other Lacan' was neglected, namely the Lacan
of object *a*.

Our second remark concerns the expression 'Lacan's discovery', which brings up the
supposition of the absence of this concept in Freud. Lacan has corrected this expression
of Leclaire in the discussion following the lecture. He calls object *a* his 'construction'
based on what is already implicitly available in Freud. Beyond this subtle nuance - discovery or construction - we wish to point out that indeed there are in Freud many arguments to be found preparing the way for this object *a*, but we think that Lacan's 'retour
à Freud' deserves an extension here: once returned he has made the disclosed talents
profitable, at least with as a result a surplus value - 'la plus-value': object *a*.

Leclaire, L'objet "*a*" dans la cure. *Lettres de l'Ecole Freudienne de Paris*, No. 9 (Congrès de L'E.F., Aix-en-Provence, May 1971), Dec. 1972, pp. 422-450 (discussion included).

44   Lacan, *L'Angoisse* (1962-63). Unpublished seminar, lesson of March 6 and 13, 1963.

45   Lacan, *Le Séminaire, Livre XX, Encore*, o.c., p. 77. Lacan, The subversion of the subject and the dialectic of desire in the Freudian unconscious. In: *Ecrits, A Selection*, o.c., p. 320.

46   Lacan, *L'Angoisse* (1962-1963). Unpublished seminar, lesson of May 15, 1963.

47   Here we can point out an addition of Lacan to Freud's clinic. The latter related fantasies to things early heard or seen which were only understood in retrospect. Lacan not only mentions "matters early heard and seen", but also and especially things the child didn't hear, things which weren't even mentioned, but that nevertheless appeared in speech, more precisely in the gaps between the spoken words. Nothing is more significant than the omitted, it gives a particular flavour to what is present.
With Little Hans, this is very obvious: the boy continuously asks his father during a certain period who or what his father actually is ("But I belong to you?", see the following section on the primal father). The harrowing is that he never receives an appropriate answer. At least part of his neurosis finds its origin in this omission. Another case in which the absence of elements in the parental speech is central, with a discussion of its pathogenic effects, is discussed in the very interesting paper by Suzanne Hommel: Une Rencontre avec le réel, originally published in: *Actes de l'Ecole de la Cause Freudienne*, vol. III, 1982, and reissued in: *Ornicar?*, nr. 31, 1984, pp. 138-143.

48   Lacan, *Le Séminaire, Livre XX, Encore*, o.c., p. 114.

49   Lacan, *L'Angoisse* (1962-1963). Unpublished seminar, lesson of July 3, 1963.

50   It is not so much a process of translation as a process of verbalisation of something nonverbal. The attentive reader will already have recognized this process: it is the very same that we have discovered at the base of Freudian hysteria, the primary experience of anxiety etc., first of all denominated by Freud as a 'primary defence', later on rediscovered as 'primary repression'. Lacan himself did not make this connection. We have elaborated its metapsychological and clinical consequences in another book: *Klinische Psychodiagnostiek vanuit Lacans discourstheorie (Clinical psychodiagnostics based on Lacan's theory of the four discourses)*.

51   Lacan, The subversion of the subject and the dialectic of desire in the Freudian unconscious. In: *Ecrits. A Selection*, o.c., p. 321.

52   Lacan, Position de l'inconscient. In: *Ecrits*, o.c., pp. 835-844 and p. 823. See also, J. Lacan, *The Seminar, Book XI, The Four Fundamental Concepts of Psycho-Analysis* (1964). London, Penguin Books, 1991, pp. 203-215.

53   Lacan, *Le Séminaire, Livre XX, Encore* (1972-73), o.c., p. 75.

54   Lacan developed this formula in his seminar on transference. The most remarkable thing about this formula is that it disappeared afterwards. For example, it is completely missing in S. André's book about hysteria. The study by Melman contains a separate chapter about hysteria and fantasy, but the usual formula is used. C. Calligaris succeeds in developing a formula of his own, but he doesn't breath a word about Lacan's formula. Where mentioned, the formula is indeed a mere mentioning, without any elaboration, explanation or application.
Lacan, *Le Séminaire, Livre VIII, Le Transfert* (1960-1961), Paris, Seuil, 1991, lesson of April 19 and 26, 1961.
André, *Que veut une femme?*, Paris, Navarin, Bibliothèque des Analytica, 1986.
Ch. Melman, *Nouvelles Etudes sur l'Hystérie*. Paris, Ed.J.Clims, 1984, pp. 1-296.
Calligaris, *Hypothèse sur le fantasma*. Paris, Seuil, 1983.
Chemama, A propos du discours de l'hystérique. *Lettres de l'Ecole Freudienne de Paris*, nr. 21, 1977, pp. 311-326.
Leres, Proposition pour un article 'Hystérie'. *Lettres de l'Ecole Freudienne de paris*, No. 15, 1973, pp. 245-250.
Lemoine, L'hystérie, est-elle une structure nosographique? *Actes de l'Ecole de la Cause*

Freudienne. Premières journées d'études consacrées à la clinique psychanalytique d'aujourd'hui, Paris, Feb. 1982, pp. 13-19, discussion included.

55 Freud, *Analysis of a Phobia in a Five-Year-Old Boy* (1909b). S.E. 10, p. 115. The appellation 'anxiety hysteria' was initially used in Freud's preface in Stekel's book, *Nervöse Angstzustände und ihre Behandlung*, 1908.

56 Freud, S.E. 10, o.c., p. 36.

57 Freud, S.E. 10, o.c., p. 23 and p. 121.

58 This reminds one of course of Lacan's "Gardez-vous de comprendre!" Other Freudian papers wherein the warning appears: *The Future Prospects of Psycho-Analytic therapy* (1920d), *Wild Psycho-Analysis* (1910k), *On Beginning the Treatment (Further Recommendations on the Technique of Psycho-Analysis)* (1913c), *Remembering, Repeating and Working-Through (Further Recommendations on the Technique of Psycho-Analysis)* (1914g).

59 Freud, S.E. 10, o.c., p. 89.

60 Lacan, *The Seminar, Book III, The Psychoses* (1955-56). New York, W.W. Norton & Company, 1993, p. 204.

61 Freud, S.E. 10, o.c., p. 81.

62 Freud, S.E. 10, o.c., pp. 32-33.

63 Ibid., respectively p. 7 and p. 10.

64 Ibid., p. 21.

65 Especially in matters of phobia, this is elaborated by Lacan in the 3rd and 4th lesson of his Seminar "La relation d'objet" (December 5 and 12, 1956).

66 Lacan, *Le Seminaire, Livre XVII, L'envers de la psychanalyse* (1969-70). Paris, Seuil, 1991, p. 180.

67 Freud, S.E. 10, o.c., p. 58, footnote 1. In *Totem and Taboo* Freud will face the same problem, especially when he questions the reason of the motivating anxiety in relation to an act which must have been pleasurable, but is now loaded with a taboo (S.E. 13, p. 69).

68 Freud, S.E. 10, o.c., p. 27.

69 Freud, S.E. 10, o.c., pp. 65-66.

70 Lacan, *L'Angoisse* (1962-1963). Unpublished seminar, lesson of January 23, 1963.

71 Lacan, *The Seminar, Book XI, The Four Fundamental Concepts of Psycho-Analysis* (1964). London, Penguin Books, 1979, p. 210.

72 Lacan, *The Seminar, Book XI, The Four Fundamental Concepts of Psycho-Analysis*, o.c., pp. 214-215. This idea appears already in the Seminar *La relation d'objet*, and especially in the lesson of February 6, 1957. There also, he differentiates between two periods in the relation of the child and the lack of the mother: a first one wherein an 'identification primaire' takes place and wherein the child fills up the gap; a second one, where the child presents his own lack, pointed out as the basis of every infatuation. In our opinion, these two will eventually become respectively the alienation and the separation. It is remarkable to see that also in the quoted passage from the eleventh seminar, there is no real solution offered for the alienation; the separation is only indicated, but not worked out. In our view, it is exactly at this point that the metaphor of the Name-of-the-Father should appear as the separating instance. This is confirmed by a short passage from 'Position de l'Inconscient', in: *Ecrits*, o.c., p. 849.

73 Freud, S.E. 10, o.c., pp. 116-117.

74 Freud, S.E. 10, o.c., p. 87.

75 Ibid., pp. 85-88.

76 Ibid., p. 91.

77 Freud, S.E. 10, o.c., pp. 133-134.

78 Lacan, *Le Séminaire, Livre IV, La relation d'objet* (1956-1957). Paris, Seuil, 1944, pp. 116-117.

79 Freud, S.E. 10, o.c., p. 122.

80 Graf, Reminiscences of Professor Sigmund Freud. *Psychoanalytic Quarterly*, 1942, II, pp. 465-476, and p. 474: "On the occasion of my sons third birthday, Freud brought him a rocking horse which he himself carried up the four flights of steps leading to my

house!".

81   Freud, S.E. 10, o.c., p. 125.
82   Ibid., p. 42.
83   Freud, S.E. 10, o.c., pp. 42-43, p. 48 and p. 61.
84   The so-called 'classical' analysis is indeed *not* a Freudian one, which is a surprise to the well-read ego-analyst: Lipton, *The Advantages of Freud's Technique as shown in his Analysis of the Rat-man*. The title of his paper speaks for itself. Lipton, The advantages of Freud's technique as shown in his analysis of the Rat-man. *International Journal of Psychoanalysis*, 1977, nr. 58, pp. 255-273.
85   Freud, S.E. 10, o.c., p. 134.
86   Ibid., p. 83.
87   Two expressions of Hans in relation to his father are typical in this respect: "You know everything; I didn't know anything" (S. Freud, S.E. 10, o.c., p. 90) and "You know better, for certain." (ibid., p. 91).
88   Ibid., p. 45.
89   Lacan, Proposition d'Octobre 1967 sur le psychanalyse de l'Ecole. *Scilicet*, 1968, No.1, pp. 14-30. For an accompanying comment, see J.-A. Miller, De la fin de l'analyse dans la théorie de Lacan. *Quarto*, VII, pp. 15-24, and especialy p. 22.
90   Freud, *Studies on Hysteria* (1895d), S.E. 2, p. 305.
91   Freud, S.E. 10, o.c., pp. 98-100. The typical continuous questioning of children at a given period of their language development, is discussed by Lacan as a try-out of the boundaries of the Other, of the possibility of representation in language, this means of his/its lack. Doing this via the other, i.e. the father and the mother, and thus ultimately via the lack of the other, brings us back to the hysterical problem. Lacan, *Le Séminaire, Livre VIII, Le transfert* (1960-1961). Paris, Seuil, 1991.
92   The study of psychosis provides us with the best example of the dominant nature of this Oedipal interpretation, as well as of its faulty character. For half a century, studies on Schreber have focused on the role of the father in the genesis of the psychosis of the son. Schreber senior is depicted as a tyrant, a Prussian fanatic of living-room-gymnastics with a preference for designing apparently sadistic 'pedagogical' instruments etc. There were even two successful plays based upon this idea during the anti-psychiatric wave of the seventies. This interpretation of psychosis is nothing but a *neurotisation* of psychosis: if the Oedipal father-tyrant gets somewhat too 'tyrannical', exceeds a certain limit, then his children become no longer neurotic, but they also cross a border - the 'borderline' - and become psychotic. This theory is wrong, and can only be maintained insofar as one discards clinical reality. Based upon newly found historical material about Schreber, J. Quackelbeen has shown convincingly that firstly the mother is central in a way that has never been revealed until then; secondly, that the father was not at all the house- garden- and kitchen- tyrant he is so often claimed to have been, but rather an absent shadow who was hiding for hours in his room. The fact that his name became fairly well-known, has to be put entirely down to the mother, who after his death, through a good policy and a bit of luck, promoted him up to unknown heights. In this regard, the 'Schreber-Forschers' have helped her very well.
     Quackelbeen (ed.), Schreber-Dokumenten I, *Psychoanalytische Perspectieven*. 1981, No. 1,pp. 1-164.
     J.Quackelbeen (ed.), Schreber-Dokumenten II, Nieuwe teksten van Paul Schreber. *Psychoanalytische Perspectieven*, 1983, No. 3, pp. 1-123.
     Quackelbeen, Forclusion. *Psychoanalytische Perspectieven*, 1983, No. 3, p. 142.
     Schreber, Rimes à sa mère, translated and annotated by J. Quackelbeen. *Ornicar?*, 1984, nr. 28, pp. 19-31.
     Quackelbeen, Notes sur les Rimes à sa mère. *Ornicar?*, 1984, nr. 28, pp. 32-37.
93   Freud, Letter 71, S.E. 1.
94   Freud, *Introductory Lectures on Psycho-Analysis* (1916-17). S.E. 15-16, 21th lecture.

The tragi-comic fate of the psychoanalytic movement is that it exerts a very strong attraction to the likes of Little Hans or Dora, that is, to the passive-hysterical character who, due to its subject structure, is in dire need of an S₁ figure. This results in the historically verifiable fact that most of the analytical societies end as a variation on the primal horde-myth, providing in the meantime a painful illustration of Karl Kraus' sneering remark about psychoanalysis being the disease that it pretended to cure. Beyond this phenomenon, that is, beyond this inappropriate application of the signifier of psychoanalysis, the theory on the four discourses provides us with the possibility of making sharp differentiations. In view of the above mentioned problem, the important question to ask concerns the position taken by the S1.

95   Freud, *Family Romances* (1909c). S.E. 9, p. 237.
96   Freud, letter 57 and Draft M, S.E. 1.
     Freud, *Aus den Anfängen der Psychoanalyse, Briefe an W. Fliess*. Frankfurt, Fisher, 1975, letter 91.
97   Freud, *Family Romances* (1909c). S.E. 9, p. 214.
98   Respectively: S.E. 13,pp. X-XI and S.E. 15, p. 9.
99   Freud, *Totem and Taboo* (1912-13). S.E. 13, p. 31.
100 Ibid., p. 43.
101 Ibid., p. 50.
102 Freud, S.E. 13, o.c., pp. 54-57.
103 Ibid., p. 181.
104 Ibid., respectively p. 104 and p. 107.
105 Ibid., p. 118.
106 Ibid., p. 129.
107 Freud, S.E. 13, o.c., pp. 131-132.
108 Ibid., p. 143.
109 Lacan, On a question preliminary to any possible treatment of psychosis. In: *Ecrits. A Selection*, o.c.,p. 199.
110 Freud, S.E. 13, o.c., pp. 143-145.
111 Lacan, Kant avec Sade. In: *Ecrits*, Paris, Seuil, 1966, pp. 781-782.
112 Lévy-Strauss, *Les structures élémentaires de la parenté*. Paris, Mouton, 1949,p. 611. (Our addition between brackets.) Lacan, *D'un discours qui ne serait pas du semblant* (1970-71). Unpublished seminar, lesson of June 9, 1971.
113 It would be quite interesting to study the different schools of psychotherapy in function of the remainder they produce, because it is with this remainder that the patients identify themselves.
114 Freud, S.E. 13, o.c., p. 107: "Of these norms, those governing marriage relations were of first importance". In this way, the human child is offered, through the Name-of-the-father, a guarantee about the sexual relation. However, this certitude is precarious, because it rests upon a certain sort of convention. The consequence is that things can be reversed just as well: namely that a child or producing a child can function for certain couples as a proof of their (sexual) relationship. The pathological effects on the development of the child, fathered for this purpose, is well-known to most therapists.
115 Freud, S.E. 13, o.c.,p. 100. Lacan, *Ecrits*, o.c., p. 188 and p. 432.
116 Lacan, On a question preliminary to any possible treatment of psychosis. In: *Ecrits, A Selection*, o.c., 1977, p. 221.
117 Freud, *The Ego and the Id* (1923b). S.E. 19, pp. 31-32. The clinical value of this theory is demonstrated at its best by its opposite, that is, through a discussion of psychosis as determined by the foreclusion of the Name-of-the-father. Where this basic signifier is missing, the effects must be predictable based on the theory described in the text above. The predictable consequence of foreclusion is that the language system will no longer operate in the way it normally does with neurotics, i.e. along metonymical and metaphorical lines. This concerns the long since familiar language disorders in psy-

chosis, the differential-diagnostic criterion avant la lettre being determined already by Shakespeare (...it is not madness that I have utter'd: bring me to the test, and I the matter will re-word; which madness would gambol from.", Hamlet, act III, scene 4). A second consequence is that reality disappears, because it is not symbolically founded: the 'Weltuntergangserlebnis'. Thirdly, the delusion being an attempt at recovery, must always contain two elements: a renewed elaboration of language, as an attempt at giving it back its normal function of representation (Schreber's 'Grundsprache' and Wolfsson's writings) and a 'pousse-à-la-femme', as an effect of the unregulated lack in the Other, which the psychotic tries to fill in by himself. This is appropriately illustrated by Schreber's delusion about becoming the wife of God, that is: The Woman, i.e. becoming what lacks to the Other.

118 Usually, with hysteria, this is not the case: it is the representational authority which will be attacked, removed and replaced. The pervert and the psychotic structure will focus on the law itself, each of them in its peculiar structurally defined way.

119 Freud, S.E. 13,o.c., p. 74.

120 J.Lacan, R.S.I. *Ornicar?*, 1975, No. 5, p. 21.

121 Lacan, *Television. A Challenge to the Psychoanalytic Establishment* (1974). New York, W.W. Norton & Company, 1990, pp. 27-28 and p. 30.

THE ROCK OF CASTRATION

1 Van Der Sterren, The 'King Oedipus' of Sophocles. *International Journal of Psycho-Analysis*, 1952, 33, p. 347.

2 Lacan, *D'un discours qui ne serait pas du semblant*. Unpublished seminar 1970-1971, lesson of June 9, 1971

3 Freud, *On Narcissism: an Introduction* (1914c). S.E. 14, pp. 92-93.

4 - "Que nous la voyions ressurgie, à tout instant dans le discours du névrosé mais sous la forme
d'une crainte, d'un évitement, c'est justement en cela que la castration reste énigmatique."
- "Disons qu'à l'hystérique il faut le partenaire châtré."
- "C'est bien en effet sous la dicteé des hystériques que, non pas s'élabore, car jamais l'Oedipe n'a été par Freud véritablement élaboré, il est indiqué en quelque sorte à l'horizon, dans la fumée, si l'on peut dire, de ce qui s'élève comme sacrifice de l' hystérique." Lacan, *D'un discours qui ne serait pas du semblant*. Unpublished seminar 1970- 1971, lesson of June 16, 1971. Lacan's conception of Freud's oedipal theory is clearly expressed in the following statement:
"Est-ce que ce n'est pas en tant que le meurtre du père ici est le substitut de cette castration refusée, que l'Oedipe a pu venir s'imposer, si je puis dire, à la pensée de Freud dans la filière de ses abords de l'hystérique" (Ibid.).

5 Freud, *An Autobiographical Study* (1925d). S.E. 20, p. 37 and p. 39.

6 Freud, *Some Psychical Consequences of the Anatomical Distinction between the Sexes* (1925j). S.E. 19, pp. 248-258. Freud, *Female Sexuality* (1931b). S.E. 21, pp. 225-243. Freud, *Femininity*, XXIII. Lecture (1933a). S.E. 22, pp. 112-135.

7 Strachey, *Editor's note*. S.E. 19, pp. 243-247.

8 Jones, *Sigmund Freud, Life and Work*. London, The Hogarth Press, 1974, part III, pp. 281-285.

9 Ellenberger, *The Discovery of the Unconscious*. New York, Basic Books, 1970, pp. 218-223.

10 Mitchell, *Psychoanalysis and Feminism*. Harmondsworth, Penguin Books, 1975, p. 109 e.v.

11 Freud, *Some Psychical Consequences of the Anatomical Distinction between the Sexes* (1925j). S.E. 14, p. 251.

12 Freud, *Femininity* (1933a). S.E. 22, p. 118.

13 Freud, *Female Sexuality* (1931b). S.E. 21, p. 229. Freud, *Femininity* (1933a). S.E.22, pp. 126-130.

14   Freud, *Female Sexuality* (1931b). S.E. 21, p. 229.
15   Freud, *Femininity* (1933a). S.E. 22, p. 128.
16   Abraham, Manifestations of the Female Castration Complex (1920). In: *Selected Papers on Psycho-Analysis*. London, Hogarth Press, 1973, pp. 338-369. Horney, On the Genesis of the Castration Complex in Women. *International Journal of Psycho-Analysis*, V, 1924, pp. 50-56.
17   Deutsch and Jones quoted in: J. Mitchell, o.c, pp. 125-131.
18   Lacan, *Le Séminaire, Livre IV, La relation d'objet* (1956-1957). Paris, Seuil, 1994, pp. 69-73.
19   Freud, *Female Sexuality* (1931b). S.E. 21, p. 226 and p. 237.
20   Ibid, p. 235.
21   Ibid., p. 126. Freud, *Femininity* (1933a). S.E. 22, pp. 120-121.
22   Ibid. , p. 126.
23   Freud, *Inhibitions, Symptoms and Anxiety* (1926d). S.E. 20, p. 130.
24   Lacan, *Le Séminaire, Livre XVII, L'envers de la psychanalyse* (1969-1970). Paris, Seuil, 1991, p. 129.
25   Readers who are familiar with the post-Freudian developments will probably formulate the objection that Lacan is not very original with his theory of the mother as the first Other, that other analysts, both in the Freudian and the post-Freudian period, have drawn attention to her position. It can be found in Abraham, Rank, Ferenczi, Groddeck and Jung. The whole theory and practice of Winnicott and his pupils bathes in the light of the mother figure, in which the cure becomes a reparation, a correction of a failed maternal care. To answer this objection it is important to acknowledge the distance between Lacan's theory and practice of reparation. It is well-known that Freud always occupied the position of the father in the transference, that he explicitly refused the position of the mother. There is a structurally defined reason for this: while it may be true that the first love comes from the first object, the mother, we should not neglect the fact that this object is definitively lost, and that this loss is a necessary one, so that any reparation is senseless. For Lacan, castration always implies castration of the mother. The child discovers her lack and thereby her desire. Neurosis starts at the point where the child supposes it has to fulfil this desire, staying a captive of imaginary castration. The intervention of the symbolic father allows the step to symbolic castration. By way of conclusion, we can postulate that this is the interface between psychoanalysis and ethics: in the cure the analysand must be given the chance to symbolize the Law beyond the real father, at the point of difference between the father who represents the Law and the father who is himself subjected to it. The analytical cure will undoubtedly be confronted with the figure of the mother as point of cristallization of this loss, lack and want, but as a treatment, it does not intend to repair this lack, it rather aims to symbolize it.
26   Freud, *The Infantile Genital Organization* (1923e). S.E. 19, p. 145.
27   Freud, *Femininity* (193a). S.E. 22, p. 113 and p. 130.
28   Freud, *Female Sexuality* (1931b). S.E. 21, pp. 226-227.
29   Freud, *Femininity* (1933a). S.E. 22, pp. 120-121.
30   Freud, *Some Psychical Conseqences of the Anatomical Distinction between the Sexes* (1925j). S.E. 19, p. 251. Freud, *Female Sexuality* (1931b). S.E. 21, p. 225. Freud, *Femininity* (1933a). S.E. 22, pp. 119-120.
31   Freud, *Female Sxuality* (1931b). S.E. 21, p. 230.
32   Freud, *Femininity* (1933a). S.E. 22, p. 133.
33   Ibid., p. 134.
34   Que faites-vous là petite fille
     Avec ces fleurs fraîchement coupées
     Que faites-vous là jeune fille
     Avec ces fleurs ces fleurs séchées
     Que faites-vous là jolie femme

Avec ces fleurs qui se fanent
Que faites-vous là vieille femme
Avec ces fleurs qui meurent
J'attends le vainqueur.

Prévert, *Paroles*. Paris, Folio, Gallimard, 1972, p. 202.

35 Lacan, *Le Séminaire, Livre XX, Encore* (1972-1973). Paris, Seuil, 1975, pp. 73-82.
36 Freud, *Moses and Monotheism* (1939a). S.E. 23, pp. 1-137.
37 Ibid., p. 7.
38 Strachey, *Editor's Note*. S.E. 23, pp. 3-5.
39 Freud, *Moses and Monotheism* (1939a). S.E. 23, pp. 80-84 and pp. 130-132.
40 Ibid, p. 80.
41 It is very important to see that this understanding of matriarchy is completely wrong from a historical point of view; secondly, that it merely gives expression to the neurotic fear of the first big Other by projecting it back into supposedly historical realities. The individual neurotic does the same thing in his development, even if in a very equivocal way: once the division between mother and child has taken place, the subject will long for what he fears, namely, the original fusion with the first great Other, in which he did not have any existence of his own. It is only in regression that so-called "matriarchy" exists, it is this very regression that makes it exist, both on the ontogenetic and the phylogenetic level. Actual reality is different, so different that it is scarcely possible for us to grasp it. The reader can refer to the splendid book by E. Reed, *Woman's Evolution. From matriarchal clan to patriarchal family*, London, Pathfinder,1974.
42 Freud, *Moses and Monotheism* (1939a). S.E. 23, p. 82 and p. 132.
43 Freud, *Moses and Monotheism* (1939a). S.E. 23, p. 129 and p. 107.
44 Ibid., p. 13.
45 Freud, *Moses and Monotheism* (1939a). S.E. 23, p. 112. See also: S. Freud, *Female Sexuality* (1931b). S.E. 21, pp. 228-229.
46 Freud, *Moses and Monotheism* (1939a). S.E. 23, p. 118.
47 Ibid., p. 119.
48 Ibid., pp. 120-121.
49 Freud, *Moses and Monotheism* (1939a). S.E. 23, pp. 128-129.
50 Ibid., pp. 97-99 and p. 132.
51 Dostoevsky's construction of an imaginary father figure was not purely imaginary, given the real father who seems to have been a really traumatic character. Freud, *Dostoevsky and Parricide* (1928b). S.E. 21.
52 Freud, *Moses and Monotheism* (1939a). S.E. 23, pp. 97-98.
53 Ibid., pp.98-101.
54 Ibid., pp. 71-73,p. 126 and p. 129.
55 Ibid., p.43 and p.43, footnote 3.
56 Ibid., pp. 112-113.
57 Ibid., p.81.
58 Ibid., p.26, p.44, p.122.
59 Quackelbeen, The psychoanalytic view of the symptom. An approach from a reading of J. Lacan. *Rondzendbrief uit het Freudiaanse Veld*, II, 1982, nr. 1, p. 6.
60 S.Freud, *The Infantile Genital Organization* (1923e). S.E. 19, p.145. S.Freud, *Analysis of a phobia in a Five-Year-Old Boy* (1909b). S.E. 10, p.8, footnote 2, added in 1923.
61 S.Freud, *Analysis Terminable and Interminable* (1937c). S.E. 23, pp. 250-252.
62 Ibid., p.224.
63 Ibid., pp. 227-228.
64 Ibid., p. 222.
65 André, *La théorie de la castration*. Lecture at the "Psychoanalytische Perspectieven", Ghent, January 30, March 13 and 27, 1985.
66 S.Freud, *Analysis Terminable and Interminable* (1937c). S.E. 23, pp. 250-252.

67   C.Millot, La princesse Marie Bonaparte. *L'Ane, le magazine freudien*, mai-juin 1983, p.26.
68   S.Freud, *Analysis Terminable and Interminable* (1937c). S.E. 23, p.250.
69   Ibid., p. 237.
70   This is the title of a medieval poem, edited by L. Elaut, *De Vrouwen Heimelijkheid*. Dichtwerk uit de XIVde eeuw, in modern Nederlands gezet en ingeleid door Dr. Elaut, Gent, Story, 1974. It was J.Quackelbeen who gave us the text of this "didactic poem", in which the Freudian findings are confirmed: the "Heimelijkheid" means the female genitalia.
     This title cannot be adequately translated intlo English; it is the Dutch version of the German "das (un)heimliche"; we refer the reader to Freud and his semantic explanations in: *The Uncanny* (1919h). S.E. 17.
71   S.Freud, *The Uncanny* (1919h). S.E. 17, pp. 224-226.
72   Ibid., pp. 247-249.
73   Ibid., p. 231.
74   Freud, *The Psycho-Analytic View of Phylogenetic Disturbance of Vision* (1910i). S.E. 11.
75   Sophocles, *Oedipus the King*. With an English translation by F. Storr. London, Harvard Press, Loeb Classical Library, 1977, pp. 118-119, nr. 1270-1280.
76   André, *Que veut une femme?* Paris, Navarin, Bibliothèque des Analytica, 1986, pp.17-19.
77   Freud, *The Uncanny* (1919h). S.E. 17, p. 235-236.
78   Ibid., p. 244.
79   Ibid., p. 238.
80   Compare this to: "Freud dans son 'Au-delà' fait place au fait que le principe du plaisir à quoi il a donné en somme un sens nouveau d'en installer dans le circuit de la réalité, comme processus primaire, l'articulation signifiante de la répétition, vient à en prendre un plus nouveau encore de prêter au forçage de sa barrière traditionnelle de côté d'une jouissance, - dont l'être alors s'épingle du masochisme, voire s'ouvre sur la pulsion de mort". Lacan, De Nos antécédents. In: *Ecrits*, Paris, Seuil, 1966, p. 67.
81   S.Freud, *Medusa's Head* (1940c). S.E. 18, pp. 273-274; *The Uncanny* (1919h). S.E. 17, p. 235; *The Interpretation of Dreams* (1900a). S.E. 5, p. 357.
82   Wisdom, A methodological approach to the problem of hysteria. *International Journal of Psychoanalysis*, 1975, 42, p. 225.
83   S.Freud, *The Interpretation of Dreams* (1900a). S.E. 5, pp. 412-413, added in 1919, originally published in: International Zeitschrift Für Psychoanalyse, 1914, II, p. 384.
84   Freud, *Splitting of the Ego in the Process of Defence* (1940e). S.E. 23, pp. 275-276.
85   Ibid., p. 277.
86   Ibid., p. 278.
87   S.Freud, *An Outline of Psycho-Analysis* (1940a). S.E. 23, pp. 205-207.
88   S.Freud, *Female Sexuality* (1931b). S.E. 21, pp. 228-229.
89   And further: "Le père réel comme agent de la castration, fait le travail de l'Agence Maître.(...)Il faudrait qu'ils voient que c'est dans la position du père réel comme impossible - Freud l'articule - que cette position même imagine le père comme privateur".
90   Lacan, *Le Séminaire, Livre XVII, L'envers de la psychanalyse* (1969-1970). Paris, Seuil, 1991, pp. 144-147.
91   Lacan, subversion of the subject and dialectic of desire, in: *Ecrits. A Selection*. New York, W.W. Norton & Company Inc., 1977, p. 324.
92   'l'achose' is a Lacanian pun J. Lacan *D'un discours qui ne serait pas du semblant* Unpublished seminar (1970-1971) lesson of March 10, 1971
93   Ibid., lesson of March 10, 1971.
94   Ibid., lesson of February 10, 1971. *Vor dem Gesetz* the title of a parable by Kafka. Initially it formed part of the text of *The Trial*. The parable can be found in *Almanach Neue Dichtung: Vom Jungsten Tag* 1916 Leipzig:Kurt Wolff.

BIBLIOGRAPHY

Abbreviations

- The American Journal of Psychiatry / *Amer. J. Psychiatry*
- Archives of General Psychiatry / *Arch. Gen. Psychiat.*
- British Journal of Medical Psychology / *Brit. J. Med. Psychol.*
- Comprehensive Psychiatry / *Compreh. Psychiat.*
- Confrontations Psychiatriques / *Confr. Psychiat.*
- L'Evolution Psychiatrique / *Evol. Psychiat.*
- International Journal of Psychoanalytic Psychotherapy / *I.J.P.P.*
- The International Journal of Psycho-Analysis / *Int. J. Psycho-Anal.*
- Journal of the American Psychoanalytic Association / *J. Amer.Psa. Ass.*
- Lettres de l'Ecole Freudienne de Paris / *Lettres de l'Ecole*
- The New England Journal of Medicine / *New Eng. J. Med.*
- Ornicar? Bulletin Périodique du Champ Freudien de Paris / *Ornicar?*
- Psychiatric Communication / *Psychiat. Comm.*
- Psychoanalytische Perspektiven / *Psychoanal. Perspekt.*
- Revue Française de Psychanalyse / *R. F. Psa.*
- Rivista Sperimentale di Freniatria / *Riv. sper. Freniat.*

ABRAHAM, K., *Selected Papers on Psycho-Analysis*, London:Hogarth 1973.
ADAM, J., L'amour de l'hysterie. *Actes de l'Ecole de la Cause Freudienne* Oct. 1983, vol5, pp31-33
AJURIAGUERRA, J. de, Le problème de l'hysterie. *L'Encéphale*, 1951, 1 pp.50-87
AMSTRONG, L., *Krijgt pappie geen nachtzoen? Vrouwen over incest.* Vertaald door S. Bodnar, Baarn, Anthos, 1980, pp. 1-220
ANDRE, S., W. Fliess, 1858-1928 - l'analyste de Freud?, *Ornicar?*, Autumn 1984 No. 30, pp.155-165.
ANDRE, S., Twee homoseksuele vrouwen, één analyse. *Psychoanalytische Perspektiven*, 1984 No. 6, pp. 83-90
ANDRE, S., *Le psychanalyste, réponse a l'hysterie?* Voordracht te Dootnik, 16/10/1984.
ANDRE, S., De kastratie. Voordrachtenreeks: 30th Jan., 13th to 27th March, 1985, in het kader van de Psychoanalytische Perspektieven, Nederlandse rapportering en verwerking door L. Van de Vijver *Rondzendbrief uit het Freudiaanse Veld* , 1985, IV, nt. 3, pp17-30
ANDRE, S., *Que veut une femme?* Paris, Seuil-Navarin, 1986
ANZIEU, D., *L'auto-analyse de Freud et la découverte de la psychanalyse.* Tome 1 & 2 Paris, P.U.F. 1975, pp.VII-462 + 463-853
ASSOUN, P.-L, Un problème de femme. *Ornicar?* 1981, No. 22/23, pp. 266-268
AULAGNIER, P., Angoisse et identification. *Riv.sper.Freniat.*, 1965, No.89, pp13-30
BALINT, M., Early Developmental States of the Ego. Primary Object Love (1937). *Int. J. Psycho-Anal.*, 1949, No.30, pp265-273
BATAILLE, L., Fantasme et interprétation. *Ornicar?* 1982, No.25, pp.75-79
BETTELHEIM, B., *The Uses of Enchantment* London, Penguin1980, pp1-403.
BRAM, F., The Gift of Anna O. *Brit. J. Med. Psychol.*, 1965, No.38, pp.53-58
BROUARDEL, P., *Les Attentats aux Moeurs* Paris, Baillière, 1909, pp.1-226
CALLIGARIS, C., *Hypothèse sur le fantasme.* Paris, Seuil, 1983, pp.1-250
CAROLA, P., Propos sur un cas d'hystérie. *Ornicar?* Analytica, s.d. No. 15, pp.26-37
CARTER, A., The Prognosis of Certain Hysterical Symptom. *British Medical Journal*, 1949, No.1, pp.1076-1079
CARTER, R., *On the Pathology and Treatment of Hysteria.* London, Churchill, 1853, pp. VIII + 161
CENAC, M., L'hystérie en 1935 *Evol. Psych.* 1935, No. 4, pp.25-32

CHEMAMA, R., Quelques réflexions sur la névrose obsessionelle àpartir de "quatre discours". *Ornicar?* May1975, No.3 pp.71-83

CHEMAMA, R., A propos du discours de l'hysterique. *Lettres de l'Ecole,* 1977, No.21, pp.311-326

CHODOFF, P., A Re-examination of Some Aspects of Conversion Hysteria. *Amer. J. Psychiatry,*1953, No.17, pp.75-81

CHODOFF, P. & LYONS, H., Hysteria, the Hysterical Personality and "Hysterical" Conversion. *Amer. J. Psychiatry,* 1958, No.114, pp734-740

CHODOROW, N. *Waarom vrouwen moederen - Psychoanalyse en de maatschappelijke verschillen tussen vrouwen en mannen.* Amsterdam, Sara, 1980, pp.1-318

CLAES, J., *Psychologie, een dubbele geboorte - 1590-1850: bakens voor modern bewustzijn.* Kapellen, De Nederlandsche Boekhandel, 1982, pp.1-219

CLASTRES, M., La question du père chez l'hystérique. *Ornicar? Analytica* Vol. 32,s.d., pp.87-93

CLAVREUL, J., *L'ordre médical.* Paris, Seuil, 1978, pp.1-284

CODET, H., Le problème actuel de l'hystérie. *Evol. Psych.,* 1935, No. 2, pp.3-44.

DE SAUSSURE F., *Cours de linguistique générale* (Edition critique, préparée par Tullio de Mauro). Paris, Payot, 1976, pp. XVIII + 1-509

DESCARTES, R., *Discourse on Method and The Meditations* London, Penguin 1968

DEUTSCH, F., Apostille au "Fragment de l'analyse d'un cas d'hystérie" de Freud. *R.F.Psa.,* ParisMay 1973, Vol. XXXVII, No. 3, pp.405-414

DEVEREUX, G., *Ethnopsychanalyse complémentariste.* Paris, Flammarion, 1972, pp.1-282

DEVEREUX, G., *Baubo, la vulve mythique.* Paris, Jean-Cyrille Godefroy, 1983, pp.1-202.

DIAMANTIS, I., Recherches sur la fémininité. *Ornicar? Analytica,* s.d.,No.5, pp.25-34

DIATKINE, R.,L'abord pscyanalytique de l'hystérie. *Confr. Psychiat.* Paris, 1968, No. 1, pp.85-100

DIDI-HUBERMAN, G., *Invention de l'hysterie, Charcot et l'iconographie photographique de la Salpêtrière.* Paris, Macula, 1982

DINNERSTEIN, D., *The rocking of the Cradle and The Ruling of The World* London: The Women's Press 1987

DOR, J., *Bibliographie des travaux de Jacques Lacan.* Paris, Inter Editions, 1983, pp.1-207

DORAY, B., Le cas de Denise. *Ornicar? Analytica,* s.d., No.15, pp.38-52

DRESEN-COENDERS, L., *Het verbond tussen heks en duivel* Baarn, Ambo, 1983, pp.1-328

DSM-III, Diagnostic and Statistical Manual of Mental Illness

EASSER, B.,& LESSER. R., Hysterical personality: a re-evaluation. *Psychoanlytic Quarterly,* 1965, No. 34, pp.390-405

ELAUT, L., *Der Vrouwen Heimelijkheid* (In modern Nederlands gexet en ingeleid door Dr. L. Elaut). Gent, Story, 1974, pp.1-63

ELAUT, L., *Der Vrouwen Heimelijkheid, dichtwerk der XIVde eeuw.* Gent, Drukkerij C. Annoot-Braeckman, s.d., in de reeks Maetschappij der Vlaemsche Bibliophilen, 2de serie, No.3, pp.1-68

ELLENBERGER, H., *The Discovery of the Unconscious* NewYork, Basic Books, 1970, pp.1-932

ELLENBERGER, H., L'histoire d'Anna O. Etude critique avec documents nouveaux. *Evol. Psych.,* 1972, No.4, pp.693-717

ELLENBERGER, H., L'Histoire d'Emmy von N. *Evol.Psych.,*1977, XLII (III, 1), pp.519-540

EWENS, Th., Female Sexuality and the Role of the Phallus. *The Psychoanalytic Review* 1976, vol.63 No.4, pp.615-637

EY, H., Introduction to the present-day study of Hysteria. *Rev. Prat.,* 1964, No.14, pp.1417-1431

FAIRBAIRN, W. Observations on the Nature of Hysterical States. *Brit. J. Med. Psychol.,* 1954, No.27, pp105-125

FECHNER, G., Ueber das Lustprinzip des Handelns. *Zeitschrift für Philosophie und Philosophische Kritik,* 1848

FECHNER, G., *Einige Ideen zur Schöpfungs- und Entwicklungsgeschichte der Organismen.* Leipzig, Breitkopf und Härtel, 1873

FERENCZI, S., *Final Contributions to the Problems and Methods of Pscyho-Analysis* London, Hogarth 1994.

FILUMANO, M., Notes sur l'hystérie. *Lettres de l'Ecole,* 1977, No. 21, pp.341-346

FLIESS, R., Phylogenetic vs. Ontogenetic Experience. Notes on a Passage of Dialogue between 'Little Hans' and his Father. *Int.J.Psycho-Anal.,* 1956, No.37, pp.46-60

FOLLIN,S., CHAZAUD, J., & PILON, L., Cas cliniques de psychoses hystériques. *Evol. Psych.,* 1961, T. XXVI, II, pp. 257-286

FOUCAULT, M., "The Discourse on Language" Appendix to *The Archeology of knowledge* New York, Pantheon 1972

FOUCAULT, M., *Madness and Civilization: A History of Insanity in the Age of Reason* New York, Pantheon, 1965

FOUCAULT, M., *The History of Sexuality, Vol. I: An Introudction.* New York, Pantheon 1978.

FREEMAN, L., *The History of Anna O.* Paris, P.U.F. 1977, pp1-326.

FREUD, S., *Standard Edition* (S.E.) VosI-XXIV London:Hogarth. *Gesammelte Werke* (G.W.) London, Imago, 1952.

FREUD, S., (1886) , Ueber männliche Hysterie. *Wiener Medizinische Wochenschrift,* 23rd Oct., 1886, 36 (43), pp.1444-1446

FREUD, S., (1975 [1887-1902]), *Aus den Anfängen der Psychoanalyse. Briefe an W.Fliess, Abhandlungen und Notizen.* Frankfurt, Fisher, 1975 (korrigierter Nachdruck), pp.1-455

FREUD, S. & SALOME, L.A., *Briefwechsel.* Frankfurt, Fisher, 1980, pp.1-301

GACHNOCHI, G.,& PRAT, P., L'hystérique à l'hôpital psychiatrique. *Perspectives Psychiatriques,* 1973, V, No.44, pp.17-28

GORMAN, W., Body words. *The Psychoanalytic Review,* 1964-65, No. 51, pp.15-28

GORMAN, W., & HELLER, L., The psychological significance of words. *The Psychoanalytic Review,* 1964-65 No.51 pp.5-14

GREEN, A., Névrose obsessionnelle et hystérie, leurs relations chez Freud et depuis. *R.F.Psa.,* 1964, No.28, pp.679-716

GREEN, A., L'objet (a) de J. Lacan, sa logique et la théorie freudienne. *Cahiers pour Analyse,* 1966, No.3, pp.15-37

GREENACRE, P., Certain relationships between fetishism and body image. *The Psychoanalytic Study of the Child,* 1953, No.8

GRUNBERGER, B., Conflit oral et hystérie. *R.F.Psa.,* 1953, 17, No.3, pp.250-265

HAAG, M., & FELINE, A., Une stylistique quantitivedu langage oral des hystériques. *Confr.Psychiat.,* 1968, t. I, pp.119-129

HALEY, A., *De machtspolitiek van Jezus Christus.* Amsterdam, Aplha Boeken, 1972

HAMON, M.-Chr., Faire la mère *Ornicar?* 1982, No.25, pp.51-58

HEAD, M., An address on the diagnosis of Hysteria. *British Medical Journal,* 1922, No.1, pp.827-829

HESNARD, O., L'hystérie, névrose d'expression. *Evol. Pscyh.,* 1936, No.2 p17

HIRSCHMUELLER, A., Eine bisher unbekannte Krankengeschichte Sigmund Freuds Und Josef Breuers aus der Entstehungszeit der "Studiën über Hysterie". *Jahrbuch der Psychoanalyse. "Beiträge zur Theorie und Praxis",* 1978, Bd. X, pp.136-168

HOLLANDE, C., A propos de l'identification hystérique. *R.F.Psa.* Paris, 1973, Vol. XXXVII, No.3, pp.322-330

HOLLENDER, M., Perfectionism. *Compreh. Psychiat.,* 1965, No.6, pp.94-103

HOLLENDER, M., Conversion Hysteria: a post-Freudian reinterpretation of 19th Century Psychosocial Data. *Arch. Gen. Psychiat.,* 1972, vol.72, pp.311-314

HOMMEL, S., Une rencontre avec le réel. *Actes de l'Ecole de la Cause Freudienne,* 1982, volIII, pp.9-11, in *Ornicar?,* 1984, No.31, pp.138-143

HORNEY, K., On the Genesis of the Castration Complex in Women. *Int.J.Psycho-Anal.,* 1924, V, pp.50-65

HORNEY, K., *La psychologie de la femme*. Paris, Payot, 1971, pp.1-284

IRIGARAY, L., Approche d'un grammaire d'énonciation de l'hysterique et de l'obsession-nel. *Langages*, March 1967, No.5 pp.99-109

ISRAEL, L., La victime de l'hystérique. *Evol. Psych.*, 1967, No.32, pp517-546

ISRAEL, L., De hysterische uitdaging. *Psychoanal. Perspekt.*1984, No.6, pp.37-44

ISRAEL, L., *Hysterie, sekse en de geneesheer*. Leuven-Amersfoort, Acco, 1984, pp.1-293

ISRAEL, L., & GURFEIN, L., L'entourage de l'hystérique. *Confr. Psychiat.*, 1968, I, pp.147-174

ISRAEL, L., & GURFEIN, L., Le vieillissement de l'hystérique *Evol. Psych.* 1970, vol. XXXV (II), pp.365-376

JANET, P.M.F., *L'état mental des hystériques*. Paris Rueff, 1894

JOHNSTONE, Mc Clain, Features of orality in an hysterical character. *The Psychoanalytic Review*, 1963, NO. 50, pp.663-681

JONES, E., Early Development of Female Sexuality. *Int. J. Psycho-Anal.*, 1927, No.8, pp.459-472

JONES, E., The Phallic Phase. *Int.J.Psycho-Anal.*, 1933, No.14, pp1-33

JONES, E., *Sigmund Freud, Life and Work* (Vol.1, The young Freud, 1856-1900, pp.1-454; Vol.2 Years of Maturity, 1901-1919, pp.1-534; Vol.3, The last Phase, 1919-1939, pp.1-536). London, Hogarth, 1974.

JONCKHEERE, L., Het onbehagen in de universitaire kultuur. *Psychoanal. Perspekt.*,1985, No.7, pp.141-158

KALFON, D., Ma mère est une femme. *Ornicar?* 1982, No. 25, pp.63-69

KALTENBECK, F., Problèmes d'éthique et de technique dans la cure de l'hystérique. *Actes de l'Ecole de la Cause Freudienne*, Oct. 1983, vol.5, pp.59-64.

KERNBERG, O., Borderline Personality Organisation. *J. Amer.Psa.Ass.*, 1967, No. 15, pp.641-685.

KHAN, M., Grudge and the hysteric, *I.J.P.P.* 1975, vol. 4, pp.349-357.

KLEIN, M.,*The Psychoanalysis of Children* London, Virago Press, 1989.

KLEIN, M.I., Freud's seduction theory, its Implications for Fantasy and Memory in Psychoanalytic Theory. *Bulletin of the Meninger Clinic.*May 1981, vol. 45, No. 3, pp. 185-208.

KLOTZ, J.-P., Transfert et éthique de l'analyste. A propos d'un cas d'hystérie. *Actes de l'Ecole de la Cause Freudienne*, Oct. 1983, vol. 5, pp. 38-38

KNEBELMANN, S. & GENIN, M.-Fr. Dora ou la madone. *Lettres de l'Ecole*, 1977, No. 21, pp.336-341.

KNIGHT,C., *Blood Relations. Menstruation and the origins of culture*. New Haven, Yale University Press, 1991

KORTMANN, F., Hysterie, een stoornis in het uitdrukkingsvermogen. *Tijdschrift voor Psychiatrie*, 1982-83, No.24, pp.171-181

LACAN, J., *Ecrits* Paris, Seuil, 1966, 924 pp.

LACAN, J., *Ecrits - A Selection* London, Routledge 1977.

LACAN, J., (1938) La famille: le complex, facteur concret de la psychologie familiale. Les complexs familiaux en pathologie. In: *Encyclopédie Française*. Paris, Larousse, 1938, Tome 8, No.40, pp.3-16 in No. 42, pp1-8.

LACAN, J., (1951), Some reflections on the Ego, British Psychoanalytic Society, 2/5/1951. *Int. J. Psycho-Anal.*, 1953, No.34, pp. 11-17.

LACAN, J., (1953), Le mythe individuel du névrosé ou Poésie et Vérité dans la névrose. *Ornicar?*, 1979, No. 17-18, pp. 289-307.

LACAN, J., (1954) *The Seminar of Jacques Lacan, Book I Freud's Papers on Technique 1953-1954* edited by J.-A. Miller, translated with notes by J. Forrester, Cambridge, Cambridge University Press, 1988.

LACAN, J., (1955) *The Seminar of Jacques Lacan, Book II, The Ego in Freud's Theory and in the Technique of Psychoanalysis 1954-1955* edited by J.-A. Miller, translated by S. Tomaselli, with notes by J. Forrester, Cambridge, Cambridge University Press, 1988.

LACAN, J., & GRANOFF W., Fetishism: the Symbolic, the Imaginary and the Real. In: *Perversions: psychodynamics and therapy*. New York, Random House, 1956. 2nd Edition: S. Loran & M. Balint (eds.), London, Ortolan Press, 1965, pp.265-276.

LACAN, J., (1956), Cours à l'Université de Louvain, March 1956. Indexed in : *L'Excommunication*. Supplement to *Ornicar?*, 1977, No. 8, pp. 13.

LACAN, J., (1956) *The Seminar of Jacques Lacan, Book III, The Psychoses 1955-1956* edited by J.-A. Miller, translated with notes by R. Grigg. London, Routledge, 1993.

LACAN, J., (1956), Compte-rendu par J.B. Pontalis (agréé par Lacan) du Séminaire "La Relation d'objet et les structures freudiennes", Livre IV, 1956-57. *Bulletin de Psychologie*, Tome X, 1956-57, No. 7, pp. 426-430; Tome X, 1956-57, No. 10, pp. 602-605; Tome X, 1956-57, No. 12, pp. 742-743; Tome X, 1956-57, No. 14, 851-854; Tome XI, 1957-58, No. 1, pp.31-34.

LACAN, J., (1957), Compte-rendu par J.B. Pontalis (agréé par Lacan) du Séminaire "Les formations de l'inconscient", Livre V, 1957-1958, *Bulletin de Psychologie*, Tome XI, 1957-1958, No. 4-5, pp.293-296; Tome X11, 1958-59, No. 2-3, pp. 182-192; Tome XII, 1958-59, No. 4, pp.250-256

LACAN, J., (1959), Compte-rendu de J.B. Pontalis (agréé par Lacan) du Séminaire "Le désir et son interprétation", Livre VI, 1958-1959. *Bulletin de Psychologie* , Tome XIII, 1959-1960, No. 5, pp.263-272; Tome XIII, 1959-1960, No. 6, pp. 329-335.

LACAN, J., (1961), Maurice Merleau-Ponty. *Les Temps Modernes*, 1961, No. 184-185, pp.245-254.

LACAN, J., (1964) The Seminar of Jacques Lacan, Book XI *The Four Fundamental Concepts of Psycho-Analysis* 1964-1965 edited by J.-A. Miller, translated by A. Sheridan, London, Penguin, 1979.

LACAN, J., (1965) Hommage fait à Marguerite Duras, du ravissement de Lol V. Stein. *Cahiers Renaud-Barrault*, 1965, No.52, pp.7-15.

LACAN, J., (1966), Interview à R.T.B. 14/12/1966. *Quarto*, 1982, No. 7, pp.7-11.

LACAN, J., (1967), Proposition du 9 Octobre, 1967 sur le psychanalyste de l'Ecole. *Scilicet*, 1968, No. 1., pp.14-30.

LACAN, J., (1969), Premier Impromptu de Vincennes: le discours de l'Universitaire 3/12/1969. (première de quatre conférences devant avoir lieu dans le cadre du Séminaire 1969-70 et réunies sous le titre "Analyticon"). *Magazine Littéraire*, 1977, No. 121, pp.21-24.

LACAN, J., (1969), Teneur de l'entretien avec J. Lacan, Décembre 1969, Paru dans: *Jacques Lacan*, A. Rifflet-Lemaire, Bruxelles, P. Mardage, 1970, pp. 401-407. Deuxième édition, 1977, pp.365-370.

LACAN, J., (1970) Radiophonie, 5/10/19/26 juin 1970 - R.T.B. 7 juin 1970 - O.R.T.F. *Scilicet*, 1970, No. 2-3, pp.55-99.

LACAN, J., (1971) Intervention sur l'exposé de S. Leclaire: "L'objet *a* dans la cure". Congrès de l'Ecole Freudienne de Paris sur "La technique psychanalytique", Aix-en-Provence, 20-23/5/1971. *Lettres de l'Ecole Freudienne*, 1972, No. 9, pp.445-450.

LACAN, J., (1972), Intervention sur l'exposé de M. Safouan: "La fonction du père réel". Journées de l'Ecole Freudienne de Paris, 29-30/9/1972 et 1/10/1972. *Lettres de l'Ecole Freudienne*, 1972, No. 11, pp.140-141.

LACAN, J., (1972), Jacques Lacan à Louvain 13/10/1972, *Quarto*, 1981, No. 3, pp.5-20.

LACAN, J., (1972), Jacques Lacan à l'Ecole Belge de Psychanalyse. Séance extraordinaire de l'Ecole Belge de Psychanalyse 14/10/1972. *Quarto*, 1982, No. 5, pp. 4-23.

LACAN, J., (1973) Encore. Le Séminaire, Livre XX, 1972-1973, texte établi par J.-A. Miller. Paris, Seuil, 1975, pp.1-135.

LACAN, J., (1973), Introduction à l'édition allemande des *Ecrits*, Walter-Verlag 7/10/1973. *Scilicet*, 1975, No. 5, pp.4-42.

LACAN, J., (1973) Intervention dans la séance de travail sur: "Le Dictionnaire" présentée par Ch. Melman. Congrès de L'Ecole Freudienne de Paris, La Grande Motte 1-4/11/1973. *Lettres de l'Ecole Freudienne*, 1975, No.15, pp. 206/208/210.

LACAN, J., (1973), *Télévision*. Noël 1973, texte établi par J.-A. Miller. Paris, Seuil, 1973, pp.

1-73.

LACAN, J., (1975), Peut-être à Vincennes? Proposition de Lacan, Janvier 1975. *Ornicar?*, 1975, No. 1, pp. 3-5.

LACAN, J., (1976), Le sinthome. *Le Séminaire, Livre XXIII, 1975-1976. Ornicar?*, 1976, No. 6, pp. 3-11; 1976, No. 6, pp. 12-20; 1976, No. 7, pp. 3-9; 1976, No. 7, pp.10-17; 1976, No. 7, pp.17-18; 1976, No. 8, pp. 6-13; 1976, No. 8, pp. 14-20; 1977, No. 9, pp. 32-40; 1977, No. 10, pp. 5-12; 1977, No. 11, pp. 2-9.

LACAN, J., (1977), Propos sur l'hystérie, Bruxelles 26/2/1977. *Quarto*, 1981, No. 2, p.5-10.

LACAN, J., (1977), C'est à la lecture de Freud ... *Cahiers Cistre*, 1977, No. 3, pp. 7-17.

LACAN, J., (1991) *Le Séminaire Livre XVII L'envers de la psychanalyse* texte établi par J.-A. Miller, Paris, Seuil, 1991.

LACAN, J., (1991) *Le Séminaire Livre VIII, Le transfert (1960-61)*. Paris, Seuil, 1991.

LACAN, J., (1994) *Le Séminaire, Livre IV, La Relation d'objet 1956-1957* texte établi par J.-A. Miller Paris, Seuil, 1994.

LANGS, R., The Misalliance Dimension in Freud's Case Histories: 1. The case of Dora. *I.J.P.P.* 1976, vol.5, pp.301-317.

LAPLANCHE, J., (reporter), Panel on 'Hysteria today'. *Int. J. Psycho-Anal.*, 1974, No. 55, pp. 459-469.

LAPLANCHE, J., & PONTALIS, J.-B., Fantasme originaire, fantasmes des origines, origine du fantasme. *Les Temps Modernes*, 1964, No. 215, pp. 1833-1868.

LAPLANCHE, J., & PONTALIS, J.-B., The Language of Psychoanalysis. London, Hogarth, 1973.

LAZARE, A., The hysterical character in psychoanalytic theory. *Arch.Gen.Psychiat.*, 1971, No. 25, pp. 131-137.

LAZARE, A., KLERMAN, G.L. et al., Oral, obsessive, and hysterical personality patterns. *Arch.Gen.Psychiat.*, 1966, No. 14, pp. 624-630.

LAZARE, A., KLERMAN, G.L. et al., Oral, obsessive, and hysterical personality patterns: replication of factor analysis in an independent sample. *Journal of Psychiatric Research*, 1970, No. 7, pp. 275-290.

LE BOULANGE, Chr., Geniet(t) Hans. *Psychoanal. Perspekt.* 1985, No. 7, pp.66-76

LECLAIRE, S., L'objet *"a"* dans la cure. *Lettres de l'Ecole*, No. 9 (Congrès de l'E.F.P., Aix-en-Provence, Mai 1971), Déc. 1972, pp. 422-450.

LEMOINE, G., L'hystérie est-elle une structure nosographique? *Actes de l'Ecole de la Cause Freudienne*, oct. 1982, vol. II, pp. 13-19.

LEMPERIERE, T., La personnalité hystérique. *Confr.Psychiat.* 1968, t. I, pp. 53-66.

LERES, G., LAVAL, G. et al., Hysterie. *Lettres de l'Ecole*, 1973, No. 15, pp. 245-283. (Congrès de l'Ecole Freudienne de Paris, La Grande Motte, 1-4 nov. 1973).

LEVI-STRAUSS, Cl., *Les structures élémentaires de la parenté*. Paris, Mouton, 1949.

LEWIN, K.K., Dora Revisited. *The Psychoanalytic Review*, 1973, vol. 60, No. 4, pp. 519-532.

LEWIS, A., [Survival of hysteria] Survivance de l'hystérie, traduit par Mme. A. Vergneaud. *Evol.Psych.*, 1966, No. 31, pp. 159-165.

LIBBRECHT, K., *Hysterical psychosis, a historical survey*. London, Transaction Publishers, 1995.

LIPTON, B.D., The advantage of Freud's technique as shown in his analysis of the Rat Man. *Int.J.Psycho-Anal.*, 1977, No. 58, pp. 255-273.

LORRE, D., De ambivalentie tegenover de vader: een verkeerd gelegde teoretische knoop. *Psychoanal.Perspekt.*, 1984, No. 6, pp. 91-98.

LUBTCHANSKY, le point de vue économique dans l'hystérie. A partir de la notion de traumatisme dans l'oevre de Freud. *R.F.Psa.*, Paris, 1973, No. 3, pp. 373-405.

MAJOR, R., L'hystérie: rêve et révolution. *R.F.Psa.*, Paris, 1973, No. 3, pp. 303-312.

MALEVAL, J.-C. *Folies hystériques et psychoses dissociatives*. Paris, Payot, 1981, pp. 1-312.

MALEVAL, J.-L., Les illusions verbales hystériques. *Spirales, Journal de Culture Internationale*, oct. 1982, No. 19, pp.59-64.

MALEVAL, J.-L., & CHAMPANIER, J.-P. Pour une réhabilitation de la folie hystérique. *Annales Médico-psychologiques*, 1977, t. 2, No. 2, pp. 229-272.

MARMOR, J., Orality in the hysterical Personality. *J.Amer.Psa.Assoc.*, oct. 1953, vol.1, pp. 656-671.

MASSON, J., *The Assault on Truth - Freud and Child Sexual Abuse*. London, Fontana, 1992.

MEISSNER, W., Studies on Hysteria - Katharina. *The Psycho-analytic Quarterly*, 1979, XLVIII, No. 4, pp. 587-600.

MENARD, A., Interprétation, reconstruction et fantasme: à propos d'un cas clinique. *Actes de l'Ecole de la Cause Freudienne*, juni 1984, vol. 6, pp. 5-7.

MEYERSON, P., The hysteric's experience in psychoanalysis. *Int.J.Psycho-Anal.*, 1969, No. 50, pp. 373-384.

MICALE, M., *Approaching Hysteria. Disease and its Interpretations*. New York, Princeton, University Press, 1995.

MILLER, J.-A., De la fin de l'analyse dans la théorie de Lacan. *Quarto*, 1982, No. 7, pp.15-24.

MILLER, J.-A., Symptôme-Fantasme. *Actes de l'Ecole de la Cause Freudienne*, Oct. 1982, vol. III, pp. 12-19.

MILLER, J.-A., D'un autre Lacan, Intervention à la première rencontre internationale du champ freudien - Caracas, 1980. *Ornicar?*, printemps 1984, No. 28, pp. 48-58.

MILLER, J.-A., Les structures quadripartites dans l'enseignement de J. Lacan, R.U.G.., 8 March, 1985. *Psychoanal.Perspekt.*, 1986. 8, pp. 23-42. (vert.: L. Jonckheere).

MILLER, G., Le secret de Mesmer. *Ornicar?Analytica*, s.d., No. 5, pp. 46-59.

MILLOT, C., L'Irrésistable ascension de mother Mary. *Ornicar?*, 1979, No. 19, pp. 159-163.

MILLOT, C., Les jouissances de l'autre *Ornicar?*, 1981, No. 22/23, pp. 253-259.

MILLOT, C., L'hystérique et l'Autre. *Actes de l'Ecole de la Cause Freudienne* févr. 1982, vol. II, pp. 7-11.

MITCHELL, J., *Psychoanalysis and Feminism*. London, Pelican Books, 1975.

MOI, T., Representation> of Patriarchy: Sexuality and Epistemology in Freud's Dora. *Feminist Review*, Autumn 1981, pp. 60-74.

MOSS, C., e.a., An additional study in hysteria: the case of Alice M. *International Journal of Clinical and Experimental Hypnosis*, 1962, No. 10 (2), pp. 59-74.

NEU, J., Fantasy and memory: the aetiological role of thoughts according to Freud. *Int.J.Psycho-Anal.*, 1973, No. 54, pp. 383-398.

NYSSEN, R., Le problème de la constitution et du caractère hystérique. *Acta Neurol.Psychiat.Belg.*, 1948, No. 48, pp. 47-56.

PANKOW, G., L'image du corps dans la psychose hystérique. *R.F.Psa.*, Mai 1973, XXXVII, pp. 415-438.

Papyrus Ebers, le plus grand document médical égyptien, trad. B. Ebbel, Copenhagen, Levin & Muntesgaard, 1937.

PARCHEMINEY, G., Le problème de l'hystérie. *R.F.Psa.* 1935, I, pp. 12-35.

PARCHEMINEY, G., Critique de la notion d'hystérie de conversion. *Evol.Psych.*, 1949, I.

PERLEY, J. & GUZE, S., Hysteria: the stability and usefulness of clinical criteria. *New Eng.J.Med.*, 1962, No. 266, pp. 421-426.

PERRIER, F., Phobies et hystérie d'angoisse. *La Psychanalyse*, 1956, No. 2, pp. 165-195.

PERRIER, F., Psychanalyse de l'hypochondriaque. *Evol.Psych.*, 1959, III, pp. 413-433.

PERRIER, F., Structure hystérique et dialogue analytique. *Confr.Psychiat.*, Paris, Specia, 1968, No. 1, pp. 101-117.

PETO, A., Body image and archaic thinking. *Int.J.Psycho-Anal.*, 1959, No. 40, pp. 223-231.

PICHOT, P., Histoire des idées sur l'hystérie. *Confr.Psychiat.*, Paris, Specia, 1968, t. I, pp. 9-28.

PLATO, *The Symposium*. New York, Penguin Classics, 1951, pp. 1-122.

PLATTEAU, W., Een referentiekader voor de gavalsstudies van Freud. *Psychoanal. Perspekt.*, 1982, No. 2, pp. 11-183.

PORGE, E., Traverser le fantasme. *Delenda*, 1980, No. 4, pp. 54-57.

POUILLON, J., Doctor and patient: same and/or the other? (Ethnological remarks). *The Psychoanalytic Study of Society*, 1972, No. 5, pp. 9-32.

PURTELL, J. et al., Observations on clinical aspects of hysteria: quantitative study of 50 patients and 156 control subjects. *Journal of the American Medical Association*, 1951, No. 146, pp. 902-909.

QUACKELBEEN, J., Prolegomena voor een psychoanalytische kliniek. *Psychoanal. Perspekt.*, 1981, No. 1, pp. 5-10.

QUACKELBEEN, J., (ed.), Schreber-Dokumenten I. *Psychoanal.Perspekt.*, 1981, No. 1, pp. 1-164.

QUACKELBEEN, J., Pedagoog/psychoanalyst. Het pedagogisch discours als het omgekeerde van het analytisch discours. In: *Liber Amicorum Prof. Dr. J. Verbist, Pedagogische Perpectieven en Vluchtlijnen*, Gent, 1981, pp. 151-172.

QUACKELBEEN, J., De psychoanalytische visie op het symptoom. Een benadering vanuit een lektuur van J. Lacan. *Rondzendbrief uit het Freudiaanse Veld*, 1982, II, No. 1, pp.3-16.

QUACKELBEEN, J., Een problematisch herlezen van de gevalsstudies van Freud. *Psychoanal.perspekt.*, 1982, No. 2, pp. 5-9.

QUACKELBEEN, J., Dichters zijn reeds lang Lacanianen. *Rondzendbrief uit het Freudiaanse Veld*, 1983, III, No. 2, pp. 3-8.

QUACKELBEEN, J., Forclusion. *Psychoanal.perspekt.*, 1983, No. 3, p141.

QUACKELBEEN, J., D'autres textes publiés ou non, de D. Paul Schreber. *Psychoanal.perspekt.*, 1983, No. 3, pp. 6-34.

QUACKELBEEN, J., (ed.), II. Nieuwe teksten van Paul Schreber. *Psychoanal.perspekt.*, 1983, No. 3, pp.5-124.

QUACKELBEEN, J., Tussen het "geloofin De Man" en de "kultus van De Vrouw" - een afgrenzing tussen patologische hysterie en die van elk spreekwezen. *Psychoanal.perspekt.*, 1984, No. 6, pp. 123-138.

QUACKELBEEN, J., Hysterie: psychoanalyse tussen inzicht en hermeneutiek of daaraan voorbij? *Psychoanal.perspekt.*, 1984, No. 6, p. 162.

QUACKELBEEN, J., Naar een vernieuwde visie op de hysterie. *Psychoanal.perspekt.*, 1984, No. 6, pp.23-26.

QUACKELBEEN, J., *Zeven avonden met Jacques Lacan. Psychoanalytische commentaren bij "Télévision"*. Gent, Academia Press, 1991.

QUACKELBEEN, J., The psychoanalytic discourse theory of J. Lacan, Introduction and application. In: *Flanders Report East Europe, Seminar on the mentally handicapped in Flanders*, May 1992, pp. 93-105.

QUACKELBEEN, J., & VERHAEGHE P. Over alle diskoursopvattingen heen: een formalisatie. De preliminaire vraagstelling door Lacan, en zijn antwoord met de vier diskours. *Psychoanal.perspekt.*,1984, No. 6, pp. 59-82.

RACAMIER, P., Hystérie et théâtre. *Evol.Psych.*, 1952, pp. 258-291.

RANGELL, L., The nature of conversion. *J.Amer.Psa.Ass.*, 1959, VII, pp. 632-662.

REED. E., *Women's Evolution. From matriarchal clan to patriarchal family*. New York, Pathfinder, ninth reprinting. 1993.

REICH, W., *Character Analysis*. London, Vision Press, 1973, pp. X + 545.

REIK, T., Der Mut nicht zu verstehen. *Die Psychoanalytische Bewegung*, 1932, IV, pp.12-17.

RIESE, W.,Wandlungen in den Erscheinungsformen der Hysterie. *Die Medizinische Welt*, 1927, 1, No. 32, pp. 1160-1161.

ROBINS, E., & O'NEAL, P., Clinical features of hysteria in children, with a note on prognosis. A 2 to 17 year follow-up study of 41 patients. *New Child*, 1953, No. 10, pp.246-271.

ROGOW, A., Dora's brother. *International Review of Psycho-Analysis*, 1979, No. 6, pp. 239-259.

ROSEN, V., Introduction to a panel on language and psychoanalysis. *Int.J.Psycho-Anal.*, 1969, No. 50, pp. 113-116.

ROSOLATO, G., L'hystérie. Structures psychanalytiques. *Evol.Psych.* 1962, No. 27, pp.225-

259.
RUSSELMAN, G., *Van James Watt tot Sigmund Freud. De opkomst van het stuwmodel van de zelfexpressie.* Deventer, Van Loghum Slaterus, 1983, pp.1-413.
SACHS, O., Distinctions between fantasy and reality elements in memory and reconstructions. *Int.J..Psycho-Anal.*, 1967, vol. 48, pp. 416-423.
SAFOUAN, M., La fonction du père réel. *Lettres de l'Ecole*, sept. 1973, No. 11, pp. 123-144.
SAFOUAN, M., *La sexualité féminine dans la doctrine freudienne.* Paris, Seuil, 1976, pp. 1-157.
SAFOUAN, M., Traverser le fantasme. *Delenda*, 1980, No. 4 pp. 57-58.
SATOW, R., Where has all the hysteria gone? *The Psychoanalytic Review*, Winter 1979-80, vol. 66, No. 4, pp. 463-477.
SCHIFFER, I., Psychoanalytic observations on the mechanisms of conversion symptoms. *The Psychoanalytic Review*, 1964-65, No. 51, pp. 201-210.
SCHIMMEL, I., Rêve et transfert dans "Dora". *R.F.Psa.*, Paris, 1973, No.3, pp. 313-321.
SCHNEIDER, M., *De l'exorcisme à la psychanalyse. Le féminin expurgé.* Paris, Retz, 1979, pp. 1-190.
SCHNEIDER, P.-B., Contribution à l'étude de l'hystérie. In: *Proceedings of the Psychiatry and Neurology Congress of French Language* (63rd Session, Lausanne 13-18 Sept. 1965). Paris, Masson, 1965, pp. 127-245.
SCIACCHITANO, A., Dora et les signifiants. *Lettres de l'Ecole*, 1977, No. 21, pp.347-355.
SHOENBERG, P., The symptom as stigma or communication in hysteria. *I.J.P.P.*, 1975, vol. 4, pp. 507-516.
SIBONY, M., L'infini, la castration et la fonction paternelle. *Lettres de l'Ecole*, Sept. 1973, No. 11, pp. 114-122.
SIEGMAN, A., Emotionality, a hysterical character defense. *Psychoanalytic Quarterly*, 1954, NO. 23, pp. 339-359.
SILBER, A., Childhood seduction, parental pathology and hysterical symptomatology: the genesis of an altered state of consciousness. *Int.J.Psycho-Anal.* 1979, No. 60, pp. 109-116.
SILVESTRE, D., Chercher la femme. *Ornicar?* 1982, No. 25, pp. 57-62.
SILVESTRE, M., L'identification chez l'hystérique. *Actes de l'Ecole de la Cause Freudienne*, févr. 1982, vol. II, pp. 11-13.
SILVESTRE, M., L'aveu du fantasme. Voordracht op het congres van de "Ecole de la Cause Freudienne", Paris, 13-14 oktober 1984, publicatie in voorbereiding in de *Actes de l'Ecole de las Cause Freudienne.*
SLATER, E., Hysteria 311. *The Journal of Mental Science*, 1961, vol. 107, No. 448, pp. 359-381.
SLATER, E., Diagnosis of "Hysteria". *British Medical Journal*, 1965, No. 1, pp. 1395-1399.
SLATER, E., & GLITHERO, E., A follow-up of patients diagnosed as suffering from "hysteria". *Journal of Psychosomatic Research*, 1965, vol. 9, pp. 9-13.
SOLER, C., Abords du nom du père. *Quarto*, 1982, No. 8, pp. 56-65.
SOLER, C., Le corps dans l'enseignement de J. Lacan. *Quarto*, mai 1984, NO. 16, pp. 44-59.
SOLER, C., Transfert et interprétation dans la névrose. *Actes de l'Ecole de la Cause Freudienne*, Juin 1984, vol. 6, pp. 7-9.
SOPHOCLES, *Oedipus the king, Oedipus at Colonus, Antigone.* London, Harvard University Press, 1977, pp. 1-419.
STRACHEY, J., General Introduction to the Standard Edition of the Complete Psychological Works of S. Freud. Indexes, bibliographies, comments and editor's notes to several concepts and articles. *Standard Edition.* 1-24, London, The Hogarth Press, 1974.
STRAUSS, M.,Quatre tableaux cliniques. *Ornicar? Analytica*, s.d. No. 15, pp. 3-23.
SUGARMAN, A., The infantile personality: orality in the hysteric revisited. *Int.J.Psycho-Anal.* 1979, No. 60, pp. 501-513.
SUTTER, J.M., & SCOTTO, J.-C. & BLUMEN, G., Aspects cliniques des accidents hystériques. *Confr.Psychiatr.*, 1968, t 1, pp. 29-52.
THIBAUT, D.-M., La fin de la séance comme fantasme de l'hystérique. *Lettres de l'Ecole*, 24 juillet 1978, pp. 95-104.

280 *Does the Woman Exist?*

TRILLAT, E., Regards sur l'hystérie. *Evol.Psych.*, 1970, 19 (2), pp. 353-364.

VALABRAGA, J.-P., *Phantasme, mythe, corps et sens. Une théorie psychoanalytique de la connaissance.* Payot, paris, 1980, pp. 1-383.

VAN DER STERREN, A., The 'King Oedipus' of Sophocles. *Int.J.Psycho-Anal.*, 1952, ee, pp. 343-350.

VAN DER VENNET, L., Transfert bij Lacan. *Psychoanal.Perspekt.*, 1985, No. 7, pp. 119-128.

VAN DE VIJVER, L., Psychoanalyse van kinderen als geborte van de Andere. *Rondzendbrief uit het Freudiaanse Veld*, II, 1982, No. 2, pp. 17-26.

VAN HOORDE, H., De hysterische psychose, nosologische struikelsteen en eeherstel? *Psychoanal.Perspekt.*, 1984, No. 6, pp.45-58.

VEITH, I., *hysterica - the history of a Disease.* Chicago, University of Chicago Press, 1965, pp. 1-301.

VERHAEGHE, P., Psychotherapy, Psychoanalysis and Hysteria. *The Letter*, 1994, 2, pp.47-68.

VERHAEGHE, P., From impossibility to Inability: Lacan's theory on the four discourses. *The Letter*, 1995, 3, pp. 76-100.

VILLE, E., Analité et hystérie *R.F.Psa.*, Paris, 1973, Vol. XXXVII. Mp/ 3, [[/ 439-450.

VOGEL, P., Eine erst unbekannt geliebene Darstellung der Hysterie von S. Freud. *Psyche*, 1953, No. 7, pp.481-485.

WAJEMAN, G., La convulsion de Saint-Médard. *Ornicar?*, été 1978, No. 15, pp. 13-30.

WAJEMAN, G., La sorcière. *Ornicar?*, 1981, No. 22/23, pp. 260-265.

WAJEMAN, G., *Le Maître et l'Hystérique.* Paris, Navarin/Seuil, 1982, pp. 1-287.

WAJEMAN, G., La médicalisation de l'hystérie. *Ornicar? Analytica*, s.d. No. 1, pp.38-55.

WAJEMAN, G., Un bon petit diable. *Ornicar? Analytica*, s.d. No. 3, pp. 31-41.

WHITLOCK, F.A., The Aetiology of Hysteria. *Acta. Psychiatrica Scandinavia.* 1967, 43, pp. 144-162.

WINNICOTT, D.W., Transitional objects and transitional phenomena, a study of the first not-me possession. *Int.J.Psycho-Anal.*, 1953, XXXIV, pp. 89-97.

WINTER, J.-P., Sur l'hystérie masculine. *Le Discours Psychanalytique*, I, No. 1, Oct. 1981, pp. 6-9.

WINTER, J.-P., L'hystérie masculine (première partie). *Les Carnets de Psychanalyse*, 1983, No.4, pp.1-17.

WINTER, J.-P., L'hystérie masculine (seconde partie). *Les Carnets de Psychanalyse*, 1983, No.5, pp. 1-32.

WISDOM, J., A methodological approach to the problem of hysteria. *Int.J.Psycho-Anal.*, 1957, 42, pp. 224-237.

ZETZEL, E.R., The so-called good hysteric. *Int.J.Psycho-Anal.*, 1968, 49, pp. 256-260.

ZIEGLER, D. & PAUL, N., On the natural history of hysteria in women (follow-up study 20 years after hospitalization). *Diseases of the nervous system*, 1954, No. 15, pp. 301-306.

ZIEGLER, F. & IMBODEN, J. & MEYER, E., Contemporary conversion reactions: a clinical study. *Amer.J.Psychiatry*, 1960, No. 116, pp. 901-910.

ZLATINE, S., Réflexions sur la technique, employée par Freud dans Dora. *Lettres de l'Ecole*, Mai 1973, No. 10, pp. 175-193.

ZLATINE, S., La distance de la femme à la Madone. *Lettres de l'Ecole*, 1977, No. 21, pp. 327-335.

INDEX

Abreaction   10-12, 15, 18, 21, 24-25, 128, 142
Active-passive   210
Affect   10, 12-16, 21-22, 24, 27, 29, 35, 81, 128, 134, 196
Agency   37, 197, 238
Alienation   50, 110, 133, 174, 176, 182, 264
Ambivalence   195-196
Analysis   2, 28, 34-38, 46, 53, 55, 57, 59, 83, 113, 118, 121, 123, 131, 229-231, 245
Anna O.   22, 85, 129, 142, 217, 223
Anxiety   12, 27-29, 37, 151-152, 158, 173, 177, 180-184, 186, 188, 197, 206, 208, 212, 229, 232-233, 235-238, 244
Anxiety   154, 177, 182
Anxiety neurosis   13, 27
Anxiety hysteria   12, 27, 183, 174
Basic lack 56, 118, 165-166
Basic signifier   156, 158, 163
Bisexuality   46-47, 61
Body   9-13, 16-19, 22, 42-43, 45, 61, 124, 143-144, 213, 218, 236-237, 239, 243
Body image   42, 157
Borderline   92, 97, 143
Boundary   41, 45
Boundary representation   40-41, 45, 152
Case studies   7, 23, 60, 83, 131
Castration   2, 60, 107-108, 110, 112, 150, 152, 155, 157-158, 161-162, 164, 171, 175-176, 179-180, 190, 192, 197, 200, 203, 205-214, 219-221, 227-239, 241-244
Catharsis 24-25
Cathexis 14, 137-138
Causality 105, 245
Communication   10, 99-103
Condensation   15
Conflict   11, 13, 21, 25, 37, 45-46, 48-49, 136
Construction   28, 30, 34, 39, 41, 132, 134, 146, 150, 162, 166, 168, 171-172, 176, 185-186, 188-190, 194-195, 197-198, 221-223, 225, 239, 243
Conversion   1, 10-13, 18-19, 27, 34, 40, 42, 79, 83, 92, 124, 177, 236
Counter-representation   151-152
Countercathexis   151
Dead   63, 91, 109, 112, 195, 199-200, 206, 227
Death drive   137, 139

Defence   11, 13, 21, 25-26, 29, 33-34, 36, 38, 40-41, 45-46, 127, 147, 150, 153, 180, 196-197, 231, 233, 235, 237, 241, 243
Defensive   44
Defensive interpretation   237
Delusion   78, 267
Desire   8, 12, 14-16, 23, 25, 36, 50, 55-56, 58-59, 64-65, 80, 89-90, 99, 101, 103-105, 107-109, 111-114, 116-118, 121, 124-125, 128-129, 135, 140-142, 144-147, 149, 155, 159, 162-163, 171-175, 177, 179-182, 184-185, 187-189, 195-198, 206-209, 212-216, 219, 227-229, 237-239, 241-243, 245-246
Diagnosis7, 78-80, 83, 98
Discourse1-2, 5, 14, 29, 51, 59, 67, 69, 75, 87, 90-91, 93, 95-96, 98-104, 106-109, 112-115, 117, 121, 123, 128, 140, 153, 155, 178, 180, 185, 187, 198, 201-202, 205-206, 219, 239, 245-246
Disjunction of   102-103
Disjunction of impotence   102-104, 113, 117, 219
Displacement   12-16, 19, 145, 150, 208, 215, 231, 242, 244
Divided   16, 21, 50
Divided   104-105, 107, 109, 113, 117, 138, 140, 142, 144
Divided subject   21, 153, 160, 172, 174-175, 178, 182, 187, 206, 239, 239, 228, 245
Division of the Subject   2, 104, 107, 117, 144, 174, 238, 241
Dora   37, 43, 46, 55-65, 67, 83-84, 108, 111, 118, 123, 125, 129, 169, 216-217, 220, 223
Dostoyevsky   55, 225
Drive   28, 51, 88, 101, 135, 137-140, 145, 163, 226, 229-230, 238
Ecouteurism   118
Ego   10-13, 16, 21-22, 59-60, 72, 80, 86, 101, 108, 124, 133-136, 138, 200, 229, 231-232, 234-235, 237-238, 244
Ego psychology   72, 86, 92
Ego-ideal 60, 233
Emmy von N.   67, 85, 88, 129
Energy   11-16, 18, 33, 90, 137
Enjoyment   140, 142, 145, 149, 171, 173, 181, 183, 197-198, 200, 205-206, 211-213, 218-219, 228, 233-234, 237-239, 243-245
Entropy   108
Erogenous   38, 46

Erogenous zones   27, 35-36, 43-44, 52
Eros   137-142
Fading of the subject   176, 182
False connection   15, 22
Family romance   45, 87, 190-192, 194, 197, 199
Fantasy   21, 25-26, 29, 35, 37-38, 41-42, 44, 46, 48, 64, 107, 113, 115, 118, 121, 132, 134, 141-142, 144-146, 149, 158-166, 170-172, 174-179, 181-182, 188-191, 197-199, 214-215, 217, 219, 234, 241-242, 245
Father   2, 25, 28-29, 37-38, 45, 50, 56, 58-64, 68, 82, 90, 97-98, 107-108, 111-112, 121, 129, 141, 144, 148-150, 152-154, 158, 160-171, 173, 176-179, 182-186, 188-203, 205-209, 211-229, 235, 238-239, 241-244, 246
Female   46-48, 62-63, 82, 98, 111, 129, 141, 205, 207-209, 215, 220, 222, 233, 237-238, 243
Femininity   38-40, 43, 49-50, 64, 69, 149, 164, 209, 211, 214-215, 219, 230-231, 233, 235, 241
Foreplay 143
Forgetting   28, 34, 132-134
Frigidity 81, 92, 131
Fundamental fantasy   149, 159
Guarantor   199
Hallucination   42, 129, 145
Hydraulic   124, 128
Hypnoid 21
Hypnosis 22, 67, 70, 84, 125
Hypochondria   85
Hysteria 1-2, 7-8, 10-11, 13, 15-17, 21-22, 24-27, 29-30, 34-41, 43-45, 48, 50-51, 55-56, 62, 67-69, 71, 73, 77-91, 95, 97, 106, 109, 111, 114, 117, 121, 123-124, 129, 132, 140-142, 146, 149-150, 152, 154, 157-159, 161, 165-167, 170-173, 175-177, 182, 188-190, 195, 202-203, 206, 214-222, 228, 236, 241-243, 245, 249-250, 254-256, 258, 260-264, 267, 269, 276
Hysteric 2, 8, 10, 18, 24, 26, 29, 33, 41-46, 48, 56, 58, 60-62, 64, 67-69, 77, 80-81, 83-85, 89-93, 95, 97-99, 101, 103, 105-107, 109-118, 123, 129, 131, 135, 142, 144, 146, 148; 206, 210, 214-221, 223, 228-231, 233, 241-246, 249, 252, 254-256, 259-260, 262, 265-266, 274, 276
Hysterical   1-2, 7, 9-10, 16-19, 23-26, 29, 33-35, 38, 41-44, 47-48, 51-52, 55-56, 61-62, 64, 67-68, 78-81, 84, 86-88, 90, 108-111, 114-115, 121, 123-126, 128, 130-131, 141-142, 144-145, 149-150, 158-161, 165-

168, 171-173, 175-176, 179, 187-189, 198-199, 202
Hysterical attack   1, 25, 84, 91
Identification   30, 37-38, 45, 60-61, 86, 109, 125, 141, 144, 153, 210, 216-217, 234, 264, 271, 273
Identity 45, 47, 61-62, 64, 87, 90, 99, 105, 109, 133, 141-143, 160, 166-167, 169, 171-172, 176-177, 206, 230, 242, 260
Imaginary   2, 13, 19, 26, 28-29, 33, 35, 37, 39, 41-47, 49, 51, 53, 59-60, 62-63, 81, 98, 107, 118, 144, 190, 200, 202, 206, 213-214, 219, 221, 230-231, 234, 239, 242, 244, 252, 258, 262, 275
Impossibility   10, 100, 102-104, 108-110, 113-115, 139-141, 203, 219-220, 262
Incest prohibition   205, 223-224, 243
Inertia   127, 137
Infantile sexuality   25, 35-36, 49, 51, 125
Interpretation   1, 36, 38, 41, 44, 100, 115, 118, 121, 125, 129, 131, 145, 157, 162, 165, 171-172, 178-179, 182, 189, 198, 205, 212, 219, 221, 228, 233, 236-237, 239, 251-253, 256-258, 260, 265, 269
Investment   10-12, 14, 138
Jouissance   29, 50, 92, 95, 99, 104-106, 108, 111-112, 114-115, 117, 135, 140, 239, 269
Kernel   29, 234
Knowledge   1, 7, 9, 37-38, 44, 46, 55, 57-58, 60, 62, 64, 67-69, 80, 86-87, 89, 91-92, 105-108, 110-114, 116-118, 121, 123-124, 126-129, 159-160, 163-164, 168, 172, 178, 180, 186-188, 191, 193-195, 198-199, 202, 225, 241, 245, 262, 273
Lack   2, 39-44, 48, 52, 61-65, 89-90, 102, 105, 108, 110-112, 144, 146, 150-153, 155, 158, 160, 163-164, 166, 171-175, 180-183, 187, 198, 201-203, 206, 211-215, 217, 219-220, 227-230, 232-233, 235, 239, 242, 244-247
Libido   12-14, 27, 30, 46
Little Hans   223-224, 263, 266, 273
Male   17, 38, 46, 88, 128, 184, 196, 213-214, 217, 223, 229, 259
Masculinity complex   209, 216, 229
Master   5, 9, 55-57, 59-60, 62, 67-71, 87, 89-92, 95, 98, 101-102, 104, 106-118, 121, 123, 129, 145-146, 163, 171, 178, 185, 187-188, 198-199, 202, 214, 217, 219, 221, 239, 241, 245, 260
Master signifier   158

Matriarchy 207, 222-223, 225-227, 269

Meaning 7, 26, 34, 39-40, 65, 99, 112, 136, 202, 223, 232, 239, 245, 250, 260-261

Metonymy 16, 244-245

Mirror 60, 144

Model 14, 34, 121, 128, 232, 242

Monde du semblant113

Moral 85, 121

Mother 28, 49-50, 58-59, 61-63, 84, 121, 132, 141-143, 146-148, 205-223, 227-228, 232-235, 237, 243-244, 247, 261, 264-265, 268-269

Myth 97, 99, 137, 140-142, 202, 205-207, 218, 221-222, 224-225, 243, 266

Name-of-the-fathe 183

Name-of-the-Father50, 150, 157, 175, 182-183, 187, 200-202, 227

Narcissism 43, 101

Negative therapeutic 134

Negative therapeutic reaction 149

Neurasthenia 12

Neurosis 2, 12, 33, 36, 38-39, 47-48, 50, 52, 79, 87, 124-125, 131, 133-135, 140, 145, 230, 239, 241, 253, 258-259, 268

Nirvana principle 127, 138-139

Non-divided subject 181, 183

Nosography 7, 78

Object 18, 27, 58, 64, 77, 80, 102, 105, 107-113, 116-118, 123, 142-145, 153, 159-160, 166, 171-176, 178, 180-185, 188, 194, 197, 205-208, 210-214, 216, 218, 220, 226, 228, 233, 239, 244-245, 257, 259-260, 262, 268

Object *a* 16, 50, 105-106, 110, 113, 141, 145-146

Oedipus complex 27, 50, 60-61, 97, 107, 125, 147, 197, 200, 203, 205, 207-208, 210, 215, 218, 220-221, 228-229, 234, 238, 243

Omnipotence 210, 212, 226, 232-234

Other 23, 29, 39, 50, 65, 87, 89-90, 99, 104-105, 108, 133, 141-148, 206, 212-215, 218-220, 227-229, 234-239, 243-245, 264-265, 267-269

Pansexualism 43

Paradigm 91-92, 96-97, 162, 177

Paranoia 176, 190, 193, 210, 257-258

Passive 34, 38-40, 46, 48-49, 52, 65, 67, 102, 121, 142, 156, 181, 208, 210-213, 219, 231, 233, 244, 266

Passivity 38-39, 49-50, 52, 209-211, 213, 217-219, 231, 241

Penis 154, 156-157, 165, 179-180, 182, 208-209, 211-212, 216-217, 219, 228-230, 232-233, 235-238

Penis envy 2, 203, 206, 208-209, 211-212, 214, 216, 228-229, 244, 259

Phallic 43-44, 48, 52-53, 128, 140, 142, 145, 206, 208-211, 213, 216, 219, 228, 233-235, 237, 239, 244-246

Phallocracy 88, 210

Phallus 19, 43, 46, 50, 60, 72, 143, 206, 212, 219, 227, 235, 244-246, 260

Phenomena 34, 42, 89, 136, 143-144, 252, 257

Phobia 11-12, 27, 154-155, 177, 180, 182-186, 194, 258-259, 264, 269

Phobic 199

Pleasure principle 12, 35, 103-105, 126-127, 131, 135-140, 145, 149, 175, 177, 181, 234-235, 237, 241-242, 257

Primal father 107, 112, 144, 185, 187, 189-190, 192, 194-196, 198-200, 205-206, 214, 221-222, 225, 227, 243-244, 263

Primal scene 23, 28, 34, 242, 250

Primary 41, 45, 48, 52, 102, 144

Primary fixation 40, 49

Primary object love 271

Primary repression 38, 40, 149-156, 159, 181, 183, 202-203, 215, 230, 242, 263

Principle 14, 126-128, 223-224, 231

Principle of constancy 12, 127, 135, 138, 177, 241

Privation 143, 239

Proton pseudos 24

Psychology 9, 17, 21, 71-72, 96-97, 127, 249-250, 253, 255, 257

Psychophysics 9

Psychosis17, 33, 59, 79-80, 92, 142, 144-145, 250, 253-255, 259, 261-262, 265-267, 276

Reaction 33-34, 39-40, 61, 64, 72, 79, 110, 129, 134, 210, 233, 237, 244, 246, 258, 260

Reality principle 126, 128-129, 136, 139

Relationship 2, 11-12, 16-17, 22, 26, 28, 30, 34, 36, 43-45, 50-51, 58, 61, 63-64, 67, 83, 87, 89-90, 99-101, 103-109, 113, 117, 123, 135, 137, 140-141, 205, 210-213, 215, 218-220, 226-228, 232, 242-243, 245-247, 259, 266, 273

Remembering 125, 132, 134, 256-257

Repetition compulsion 133-137, 140, 146, 234, 242

Representation 10-11, 13, 22-23, 28, 34, 41-42, 45, 124, 129, 137, 220, 241, 249, 251, 265, 267

Repression   13, 19, 22, 25-27, 29-30, 33-41, 43-53, 55, 63, 85, 88, 102, 124-125, 128, 131-134, 136, 144, 209, 215, 225, 230-231, 241-242, 249, 251, 258
Resistance   13, 15, 22, 26, 28, 33, 35-38, 56, 59, 62, 67, 70, 118, 121, 125, 131, 133-136, 145, 208, 242, 262
Retention 21
Secondary repression   230
Self-analysis   17, 26, 67
Separation   50, 105, 213, 264
Sexual   12, 24-25, 28-29, 34, 38, 40, 42, 44-49, 52, 56, 58, 60-64, 81, 85, 87-91, 103, 112, 125, 138, 141-143, 203, 207, 209, 213, 215-217, 219, 228-230, 239, 242-243, 251-252, 259-261, 266
Signification   16, 28, 137, 205, 210, 237, 244, 258
Signifier   1, 19, 28, 39-41, 43, 45-47, 49-53, 61-64, 90-91, 100, 102-105, 107-109, 112-114, 116-117, 121, 124, 132, 137, 141-142, 145, 205-206, 211-214, 218-219, 227, 230, 234-239, 243-247, 249, 258, 262, 266
Splitting   11, 33, 233, 235-239, 241, 244, 269
Structure 1, 16, 18, 26, 34, 40-42, 44, 59, 98, 100-102, 104, 106-107, 112, 115, 118, 123, 145-146, 210, 213, 221-222, 227, 243-244, 246, 256, 259-260, 262-263, 266-267, 276
Subject   1, 3, 16, 21-22, 27-28, 50, 64, 78, 80, 89, 98-99, 102, 104-114, 117, 121, 133-134, 138, 140-142, 144-146, 148, 205-206, 209, 212-214, 216, 218-220, 222, 226-228, 230, 233, 235-239, 241-242, 244-246, 258-259, 261-263, 266, 269
Subjectivity   80, 87, 109, 114, 117
Subversion   250, 263, 269
Suggestion   8, 22, 84, 249
Super-ego151, 200, 208, 220, 238, 246
Symbolic 2, 13, 26, 28-29, 39, 41-45, 47-48, 50, 55, 57, 59-63, 65, 90, 107, 110, 141, 144, 206, 211-214, 219, 222-224, 227-228, 230, 237-239, 242, 244-245, 252-253, 258, 261-262, 268, 275
Symptoms   1, 7-8, 18-19, 22-24, 30, 34, 42, 48, 51, 55, 58-59, 62, 64, 67, 78-79, 81, 83-84, 88-89, 91-92, 97, 124-125, 128-129, 133-134, 142, 151, 160, 162, 164-165, 172, 178, 215, 228-229, 237, 257-259, 268
Talking cure   23, 85
Thanatos 137-138, 140-141
Therapy   87, 89-90, 124-125, 128, 142, 165, 198, 255-257, 264, 266, 271, 275

Transference   22, 59, 61, 67-68, 80, 87, 113, 117, 125, 133-136, 143, 145, 241, 245, 263, 268
Transitional   143, 222, 257
Trauma   8-11, 15, 21-22, 24-29, 33-35, 37-40, 44, 56, 62, 89-90, 121, 124, 132, 137, 140, 211, 219, 226, 237, 242, 250
Treatment2, 8, 16, 21, 23, 34-35, 72, 83, 85-87, 121, 128-129, 131, 134, 136, 145-146, 209, 229, 232, 236, 242-245, 249-250, 259-260, 262, 266, 268, 271
Truth   3, 27, 57, 101-103, 107-108, 110-111, 113, 115-117, 224-225, 231, 237, 262
Uncanny 136, 232-234, 256-257, 269
Unconscious   1-2, 9, 14-17, 21-23, 26-27, 29-30, 41, 44, 55-57, 61, 67, 80, 87, 99, 104-105, 113, 117-118, 132, 134, 141, 145, 221, 225, 228, 243, 249, 255-256, 258-259, 262-263, 267, 272
Uterus   17, 19, 43
Wolf Man135

Zones   28, 36, 44, 52, 157